Current Debates in Peace and Conflict Studies

Houston Wood

Hawai'i Pacific University

New York   Oxford

OXFORD UNIVERSITY PRESS

Oxford University Press is a department of the University of Oxford. It furthers the University's objective of excellence in research, scholarship, and education by publishing worldwide. Oxford is a registered trade mark of Oxford University Press in the UK and certain other countries.

Published in the United States of America by Oxford University Press

198 Madison Avenue, New York, NY 10016, United States of America.

For titles covered by Section 112 of the US Higher Education Opportunity Act, please visit www.oup.com/us/he for the latest information about pricing and alternate formats.

Library of Congress Cataloging-in-Publication Data

Names: Wood, Houston, 1944– author.
Title: Current debates in peace and conflict studies / Houston Wood, Hawai'i Pacific University.
Description: First edition. | New York : Oxford University Press, 2017.
Identifiers: LCCN 2017025176 | ISBN 9780190299781 (paperback)
Subjects: LCSH: Peace—Study and teaching. | Conflict management—Study and teaching. | BISAC: POLITICAL SCIENCE / Peace.
Classification: LCC JZ5538 .W66 2017 | DDC 303.6/6071—dc23
LC record available at https://lccn.loc.gov/2017025176

9 8 7 6 5 4 3 2 1

Printed by Webcom Inc., Canada

Brief Contents

This book is dedicated to my many encouraging and actively peace-promoting colleagues in the Peace and Justice Studies Association (PJSA). PJSA merges activism, education, and research, modelling one way to refashion higher education to serve the common good.

Contents

This anthology is intended to introduce readers to peace and conflict studies. It focuses on contemporary controversies and so does not attempt to survey all topics associated with the field. The book can be read by itself or in tandem with books that do try to review the entire peace and conflict studies field. For example, much more context for the contemporary debates this book explores is found in the editor's own *Invitation to Peace Studies* (2016). And readers interested in a more historically oriented anthology can consult David P. Barash's *Approaches to Peace* (4th ed., 2018), which collects pioneering and classical peace studies texts.

Key Pedagogical Features

- Most selections published in the last decade
- Selections from a broad range of academic and journalistic sources
- Introductions that guide readers to each of the seven parts
- Further introductions that assist readers' understanding of each of the 14 sections
- Notes describing the credentials of every author
- Sets of discussion questions for each of the 14 sections

Acknowledgments

Mahalo plenty again to Susan, my editor-wife now for 20 years and four books.

I consulted hundreds of texts to pare the list down to the 52 selections included here. The final choices would not have been nearly as representative or interesting without advice from dozens of people who offered suggestions. I am especially grateful for the help provided by Randall Amster, Janet Gray, Leo Guardado, Heidi Huse, Danielle Fulmer, Jesse James, Tony Jenkins, and Roger Mac Ginty.

I also thank the many scholars and instructors who reviewed the manuscript of *Current Debates in Peace and Conflict Studies*: Deina Abdelkader (University of Massachusetts), Clement E. Adibe (DePaul University, Chicago), Alexandra Nicewicz Carroll (The George Washington University), Richard W. Coughlin (Florida Gulf Coast University), Denise DeGarmo (Southern Illinois University Edwardsville) Shodhin Geiman (Valparaiso University), Jeannie Grussendorf (Georgia State University), Nahla Yassine-Hamdan (Wayne State University), Tom H. Hastings (Portland State University), Marike Janzen (University of Kansas), George A. Lopez (University of Notre Dame and Grinnell College), James M. Scott (Texas Christian University), James Woelfel (University of Kansas), Ozum Yesiltas (St. Norbert College), and Stephen Zunes (University of San Francisco).

Peace and conflict studies is a loosely connected, international network of people and organizations committed to promoting peace. This network arose in part as a response to the destruction and death caused by World War II. In the 1950s, it became clear that the world's strongest nations were preparing to wage even more horrific wars, including nuclear conflagrations that could quickly kill more millions than had died in World War II. Pioneers in peace and conflict studies joined together in a mutual cry of protest against these catastrophic plans to insist that humans seek peaceful ways to resolve their disagreements.

By the 1970s, peace studies researchers had learned enough to be able to authoritatively proclaim that, whereas human conflict is inevitable, violence and war are not. And now, over a half century since its beginning, peace and conflict studies has assembled an impressive body of knowledge about how best to steer conflicts toward nonviolent resolutions. Thousands of books and articles, organizations, curricula, and training programs exist to spread this important knowledge. The breadth and quality of this work is impressive and represents a formal field of research unlike any previously known in human history.

Some people believe humans today face unprecedentedly dangerous challenges. If so, we should be comforted to know humans also now possess an unprecedentedly rich array of effective alternatives to violence.

Peace and conflict studies is one relatively small node in a much larger global peace network (Wood, 2014; 2016). This vast network includes hundreds of thousands of peace-promoting organizations and millions of committed individuals working to increase local, regional, and global levels of peace. Although it is but a single node within the global peace network, peace and conflict studies plays a vital role as it seeks to map, research, and strengthen the much larger web within which it is but a part.

Peace and conflict studies is built on three major pillars. One pillar focuses on *research* to learn more about the causes of violence and the best methods for building peace. This research takes place in multiple academic fields, including biology, history, philosophy, psychology, public health, and all the social sciences. A second pillar within peace and conflict studies emphasizes *practical actions* aimed at peacemaking, peacekeeping, and peacebuilding. A third element promotes *peace education* and outreach, disseminating peace and conflict studies' discoveries and skills to people of all ages across the world.

Much of the core knowledge established by researchers in peace and conflict studies is accepted without dispute. It has been well established, for example, that nonviolent resolutions of conflict are almost always possible. Research has also found that conflicts follow patterns and exhibit phases; responses to conflicts must thus be built on recognition of these phases. There is little debate as well over the belief that individuals, groups, nations, and the international community would be much more peaceful if governments supported peace research with even one-tenth as much money as they now support research into improving methods of harm. Peace educators have also found effective pedagogies for increasing peace in schools and among school-age populations.

And yet, despite the many agreements, peace and conflict studies is simultaneously chock-full of controversies and debates, the emphasis of this book. Some of these disagreements are fundamental—such as, for example, the continuing disagreements over what is the best way to understand the very meaning of peace (see part 1) or about whether a person should first seek an inner peace before trying to bring peace to others (see part 7). Some other debates center around how gender should be treated in thinking about peace, conflict, and violence (see part 3); which of the many forms of nonviolent action is most likely to succeed (see part 4); and what effects climate change will have on future conflicts (see part 6). Debates also rage about what conclusions can be drawn about current trends in war (see part 2); about the role of religion in promoting peace, conflict, and violence (see part 4); and about whether peace requires that victims forgive perpetrators of violence against them (see part 5).

Negative and Positive Peace

As should be clear, although it draws from research in many academic disciplines, peace and conflict studies is a different type of discipline because it seeks knowledge not as an end in itself but rather as a guide for policies and actions. *Peace research is a form of peace search*. Peace and conflict studies is thus often compared to medical science, as both openly admit to their biases—medical science to a bias for health rather than disease and peace and conflict studies to a bias for peace rather than violence. David P. Barash (2014, 3) even suggests peace and conflict studies offers people a kind of "planetary medicine."

A conceptual distinction between negative and positive peace, first articulated by Jane Addams (1907), grounds how most people in peace and conflict studies understand peace. In his selection following in part 1, David Cortright defines *negative peace* as the absence of war and *positive peace* as the presence of justice.

Some writers go further and define negative peace as the absence of all physical harms that a person, group, or nation inflicts on others. Definitions of positive peace are often extended to include the presence of life-enhancing economic, political, and social traditions supported by stable social structures. In conditions of positive peace, people live fairly and cooperatively with one another.

This distinction between negative and positive peace looms in the background of many of the debates found in this book. Some authors argue that establishing negative peace should be the principle goal of peace and conflict studies. Other authors argue that the main focus of peace and conflict studies should be building a sustainable positive peace.

A Guide to the Selections

This book presents supporters of contending views writing in their own voices about currently controversial topics. Taken together, the selections may seem to suggest that peace and conflict studies is a quarrelsome and unsettled field. In fact, however, these and other controversies do not weaken but instead invigorate and enliven the field. As mentioned, conflicts between humans are inevitable; they are not in themselves either good or bad. Conflict over the issues that peace and conflict studies addresses have generally been beneficial to the field by encouraging both deeper thinking and more carefully designed research projects.

I hope the selections in this book will encourage readers to learn more and to become active contributors to the lively debates that animate peace and conflict studies. Some of the debates discussed here are likely to describe issues about which you already have strong views. In such cases, please try to maintain an open mind as you read opposing arguments. You may find that learning more about "the other side" simply confirms what you already believe. However, if you read without prejudice, you may discover that your earlier opinion was based on misconceptions. In many cases, I suspect you will find that most sides to these debates make some valid claims. The best position on many of these issues may be to search for new ways of thinking that merge perspectives to create new, better approaches to old conceptual conflicts.

The selections are drawn from a variety of sources, most published in the last ten years. The selections include some articles written by specialists that were first published in peer-reviewed journals. Some other selections are drawn from chapters in books written by experts. Magazine and newspaper articles are also included; some of these are authored by experts, and some are by journalists who specialize in reporting on peace and conflict related topics. There are, in addition, some selections from reports prepared by peace and research organizations and also selections from web-based magazines and blogs. Notes for each selection describe both the credentials of each author and the place of original publication. In aggregate, the selections showcase the richness and diversity of authors currently engaged with the most contentious topics in peace and conflict studies.

About one third of the selections are authored by women. This is noteworthy, as it represents a significantly higher proportion of female authors than ever before included in a general anthology focused on peace and conflict. Nonetheless, clearly the number of women selected for this volume still falls short of the proportion of females in the general population. As some of the research presented in parts 1 and 3 reveal, including women in peace research, policymaking, and projects is an especially effective way to decrease levels of violence. Soon, I hope, research, articles, and books by women in the field of peace and conflict studies will be at least as common as those by men.

The book is divided into seven parts that, when read sequentially, offer one way to understand how the main controversies in peace and conflict studies are connected. However, each part can also be read independently; and each alternative sequencing of the seven parts will yield alternative perspectives. The seven parts each contain two sections; and these fourteen sections, too, may usefully be read in the sequence offered here or in many alternative orders.

Discussion questions are provided at the end of each of the fourteen sections. These are intended to provoke thought and can serve as conversation starters in the classroom, as homework assignments, and as essay prompts.

REFERENCES

Addams, Jane. *Newer Ideals of Peace*. New York: Macmillan & Co., Ltd., 1907.

Barash, David P. *Approaches to Peace*. 3rd ed. New York: Oxford University Press, 2014.

Wood, Houston. "The Global Peace Network." *Peace Review* 26, no. 2 (April 3, 2014): 258–64.

Wood, Houston. *Invitation to Peace Studies*. New York: Oxford University Press, 2016.

CONCEPTS AND CAUSES

As the first section in part 1 makes clear, although peace and conflict studies seeks to promote peace, peace promoters often disagree about what "peace" really means. Deciding how to define peace is important because definitions often become guides for choosing policies and actions. These choices are commonly shaped as well by ideas about what causes people to be violent or to encourage violence in others. The second section of part 1 reviews these debates about the causes of violence.

Disputes about the meaning of peace and about the causes of violence intertwine. Controversies about the meaning of peace in section 1 foreground the light and positive side of peace studies, whereas debates about the causes of violence in section 2 emphasize the dark and negative side (Nagler 2004, 47). Promoting peace requires understanding both the light and the dark, both peace and violence, and their connections with each other.

REFERENCES

Nagler, Michael N. *Is There No Other Way?: The Search for a Nonviolent Future*. Makawao, HI: Inner Ocean, 2004.

Debates about the Meanings of Peace

The first selection is taken from the last book published by the late sociologist Elise Boulding, one of the pioneering founders of peace and conflict studies. Boulding maintains that histories of Western civilization have systematically overlooked the peaceful activities that make up everyday life. Attention instead has been lavished on glorifications of conquests, empires, war, and violence. Boulding argues that people need to embrace more accurate representations of the past. A full picture, she says, reveals that there are now and have always been extensive, effective "living peace cultures." These cultures deserve celebration and nourishing.

In a second selection, historian David Cortright explores some of most common concepts that peace and conflict analysts use in their attempts to understand peace, conflict, and violence. Many of these concepts play important roles in later debates presented in this book, including the concepts of negative and positive peace, discussed in the Introduction to this book. Cortright also claims that peace, however defined, should not be thought to signal the end of conflict. "Conflict is intrinsic to human relationships," Cortright maintains. Peace is not stasis, not a quiet end point, but rather better understood to be a dynamic process, always containing some tension.

In a third selection, historian Catia C. Confortini argues that most of the major concepts of peace studies are profoundly flawed because they ignore the importance of girls and women. Much as Boulding points to the systematic exclusion from history of ordinary people, Confortini maintains that the female half of the population is often overlooked in the approaches that peace researchers use in thinking about conflict, peace, and violence. Confortini puts particular emphasis on the need to reformulate three core concepts: negative and positive peace and structural violence. (More debates about the utility of a gender perspective can be found in part 3.)

Social scientists often attempt to resolve debates about the meaning of concepts by creating *operational definitions*. This leads to identifying otherwise ambiguous terms with specific measurable indicators. The final selection describes the Institute for Economics and Peace operational definition for peace, which the Institute uses to produce an annual Global Peace Index (GPI). The Institute operationally defines peace as a score based on twenty-three indicators; and it creates separate scores for 162 countries, which together include over ninety-nine percent of the world's population. These yearly reports provide a way to track trends and to signal which countries and which regions are becoming more or less peaceful each year.

The twenty-three indicators used by the Institute for Economics and Peace primarily measure levels of direct physical violence and so the Institute's GPI rankings mostly offer a snapshot of levels of negative peace. In an effort to understand trends in indirect violence, the Institute has also begun measuring a second set of indicators to produce a Positive Peace Index. Their latest ranking of countries on this Positive Peace Index can be found online.

History at Sword's Point?

The War-Nurtured Identity of Western Civilization

BY ELISE BOULDING

Sociologist Elise Boulding was an early promoter of peace and conflict studies as an academic field. Boulding's emphases on holistic perspectives, the family, gender, and peace cultures have become increasingly influential. From *Cultures of Peace: The Hidden Side of History*. Syracuse, NY: Syracuse University Press, 2000. Used by permission.

History is generally thought of as the story of the rise and fall of empires, a chronicle of reigns, wars, battles, and military and political revolutions; in short, the history of power—who tames whom, who controls whom. The story of the ingestion of weaker societies by stronger ones and of rivalries among the strong is the story of humankind, says macrohistorian William McNeill.[1] In his version of history, every empire eventually reaches a limit-boundary region beyond which it has no control. When that point is reached, its people can either sit down and write poetry, opting out of history, or fight and push on.

Arnold Toynbee notes a countervailing fashion of a more complex storytelling, one that involves interspersing records of military activity with accounts of art, religion, and technology.[2] However, he points out that very few historians attempt to record that complex interplay of human activities in the various domains of life-work and play, art and architecture, intellectual inquiry and spiritual search. Why? At least part of the answer lies in the records intentionally left for posterity, in the rulers' habits of erecting monuments that glorify achievements in battle. The great inventions of writing, the developments from pictographs and hieroglyphics through cuneiform to actual alphabets, while

developed by priestly classes for the keeping of economic and administrative records, is better known for its use to record the triumphs of priest-kings and their gods in this world and the next. Voices from the past—Mesopotamian, Egyptian, Greco-Roman, Hindu, Chinese, and Mayan civilizations and others—have each left ample monuments and records attesting to their conquests.

The very identity of Western civilization at the end of the twentieth century is intimately bound up with its Greco-Roman heritage: the destruction of Troy in 1193 B.C.E.; the Battle of Marathon, when the Greeks defeated the Persians; the Battle of Thermopylae, when the Persians defeated the Spartans; the three decades of Peloponnesian Wars between Athens and Sparta; and the century of Punic Wars, ending with the destruction of Carthage and the triumph of Rome in 46 B.C.E. In the West we think of this as *our* history. The great cultural achievements of Greco-Roman civilization ("our past") are seen as the fruits of military power. Simone Weil, in her haunting study *The Iliad: or The Poem of Force*, shows how the sword, in the West, has derived much of its power from the culture of that famous work of Homer.[3] Less noticed are the ecological fruits of military power—the destruction of the once luxuriant forests of the Mediterranean for timber for battleships and war chariots, leaving the stripped and parched earth we see today on the northern and southern shores of that great sea. Moving on to the Common Era, *our* history records the rise and decline of the Holy Roman Empire and centuries of war in Europe, including two centuries of crusades to reclaim the Holy Land and the holding at bay of a spreading Islam that threatened the very heart of Europe as the Turks reached the gates of Vienna. This history is seen as holding the seeds of the greatness of the West. Even the Vikings, ruthless pirates of the far North who plundered Europe for over two centuries, are part of our glory. William, the Norman Conqueror, was victorious in 1066 at the Battle of Hastings. This victory is taken as a major milestone in British history.

That heritage received a different input from a fortunately sheltered community of European monks and scholars. This community maintained peaceful contact with their more advanced colleague-scholars who were generating Islamic science and technology in Andalusia during the very centuries when Christian and Muslim soldiers fought for control of the Mediterranean. That knowledge transmission from Islam to Christianity, however, set the stage for a new series of conquests—the conquest of nature, the conquest of the world's seas, and the colonizing of the world's continents by Europeans.

Seen through the eyes of the colonized, the 1400s began a five-century process of forcible imposition, based on superior military force, of European values and culture on the many cultures, lifeways, and civilizations of the Asia-Pacific, Africa, and the Americas. This imposition was accompanied by a process of systematically mining the resources and the labor power of the colonized. From the perspective of the colonizers, these centuries nurtured the unprecedented flowering of Western science, technology, and culture. They furthered what was considered an evolutionary process resulting in a new universal civilization with values, material culture, and lifeways surely destined to supersede all other cultures and civilizations. A necessary part of this civilizing process was the development of military and political technologies to destroy competing or resisting societies in the name of social progress.

One drawback to the tremendous success of advanced military technologies, however, is that they have made present-day wars increasingly gruesome. In response, some societies retreat to the reliving of ancient, more glorious wars. Histories of famous battles become best-sellers.[4] In the United States, groups of patriots annually reenact famous battles of the Revolutionary War and, in the South, of the Civil War.

However, changes have been taking place in the attitude to war as a central mechanism in human history, as a more sophisticated civil society and a culture of transnationalism have evolved in the nineteenth and twentieth centuries, both in the One-Third World of Euro-North America and the Two-Thirds World of other continents. Among historians, Toynbee has in this century been a widely-noted member of an innovative group of scholars who have broadened the agendas of macrohistory. He writes: "I hate war, and at the same time I am fascinated by the study of it, and give a great deal of attention to it. At the same time, too, I am reluctant to admit that the use of force has had decisive effects on the course of human history."[5] Toynbee, in fact, goes to great lengths to maximize the effect of what he calls spiritual factors. This, however, hardly affects the centrality of war in public consciousness. Rather, it spiritualizes it. The missing element in social awareness of the nature of the human experience through history is an image of the dailiness of life—of the common round from dawn to dawn that sustains human existence. The fact that most human activity revolves around raising and feeding families, organizing the work of production, solving problems and meeting human needs, interspersed with times of feasting and celebration of human creativity in poetry, song, dance, and art, rarely shows through in history books.

Yet a closer inspection of social records, the bias toward reporting wars notwithstanding, reveals a much richer tapestry of human activities. Samuel Kramer was a pioneer recorder of the quality of everyday life in ancient times, using documents from early Sumer.[6] He gives vivid evidence of what went on in families, schools, and public life, and of debates over morality and the nature and purpose of human existence. At the macrohistorical level, the remarkable historical undertaking of Bernhard Crun's *Timetables of History* is a brave beginning for a fuller account of the range of human doings over time.[7] *Timetables* tabulates events year by year from 501 B.C.E. (and by half-centuries before that starting at 4000 B.C.E.). The column entries for the year-by-year record include (a) History, Politics; (b) Literature, Theater; (c) Religion, Philosophy, Learning; (d) Visual Arts; (e) Music; (f) Science, Technology, Growth; and (g) Daily Life. The (a) column, listing the battles and kingdoms won and lost, is the fullest, but other columns get fuller over time, recording peaceful human activities in the civil society.

The importance of war is, of course, not to be downplayed. In fact, it is the recurring distortions war inflicts on everyday life that help perpetuate the systemic reproduction of war, fighting in generation after generation. Current research on violence in contemporary societies suggests that high levels of aggression in the civil society are associated with recent participation of that society in war. The socialization for aggression involved in the preparation for and fighting of wars has subsequent effects on civilian behavior. In short, wars produce socialization for aggression as well as socialization for aggression producing war.[8] This free-floating aggression affects the language and behavioral responses in political life, in social movements (including peace movements!), in sports, in the visual and performing arts; and it affects the content and style of social reporting by the media. Characterized as a rise in the level of incivility and meanness in public life, it is being widely commented on in contemporary U.S. circles concerned with this development in their own society.

If we add to this postwar syndrome of learned behavioral violence the abundant imagery about war in the historical record, civilian society has to deal with a heavy burden of war-consciousness in "peacetime."

Societies Can Change

Although a strong commitment to peaceable ways may, in one sense, be thought of as representing minority, almost dissenting beliefs—the warrior theme being both spiritually and politically more accessible—belief in nonviolence nevertheless has great staying power and never completely disappears. In times of rapid social change, it is an especially important resource because of its emphasis on peaceful problem solving, cooperative human relations, and sharing. And cultures do change. UNESCO's *Peace Anthology*, through the proclamations of "peace kings" and "peace emperors" and quotations by wise public leaders from ancient times onwards, gives a vivid picture of dramatic shifts from the warrior stance to that of the peacemaker. One well-known example can be found in the behavior of Emperor Ashoka of India, who, after great conquests of nearby peoples in the third century B.C.E., repented of his war making and issued the Rock Edicts, calling on all neighboring kingdoms as well as his own people to live in peace and joy with one another. He made his own empire safe for all travelers, with special protected resting places on every highway.

Another interesting example of culture change drawing on hidden resources is found in the history of an early European warrior society turned peaceful: the Vikings. The transformation of the Northmen, the "scourge of Europe," into the architects of the most peaceful region in Europe, Scandinavia, and the designers of strategies and institutions to replace war is an intriguing story.

The skills of negotiation developed in the pre-Viking institution of the *thing*, the gatherings of landholders to make decisions by consensus, were centuries later seen to be more useful in interaction with other peoples than the conqueror's approach. Similarly, negotiated trade turned out to be more productive than simple pillaging. Settlement replaced conquest in Britain. The Vikings left their warrior gods and adopted some of the gentler teachings of Christianity, meanwhile learning to listen to the soil as well as to the sea and increasingly becoming farmers. This new awareness also led to the eventual abandonment of the conquest of Russia. In much more recent times, the choice of a peaceful separation of Norway from Sweden in 1905, even though both sides had been armed for war, was a notable example of a new style of diplomatic initiatives that has been important in the evolution of the League of Nations and its successor, the United Nations, in this century.[9]

Peace movements and images of alternative societies with alternative approaches to conflict are not new phenomena on the historical scene. They go back to antiquity. However, the latter part of the nineteenth century brought a new wave of awareness of the alternatives to war and violence. It is ironic that the greatest breakthroughs by scholars and diplomats in institutions for peaceful settlement of disputes came side by side with counter breakthroughs in military technology.

The Hague Peace Conference that ushered in the twentieth century was intended to begin the construction of diplomatic structures and processes that would render war obsolete as means of settling disputes among states. In 1910, William James wrote his famous essay "The Moral Equivalent of War," proposing to replace the old morality of military honor with a new morality of civic honor and civic responsibility by instituting conscription for socially useful service instead of war.[10] The establishment of the League of Nations after the setback of World War I, and of the United Nations after the setback of World War II, each in turn demonstrated the seriousness of the social and political intentions of deeply thoughtful internationalists on several continents and the difficulties of realizing them. In 1926, Quincy Wright broke new leadership paths for American internationalist thought when he began the Study of War Project at the University of Chicago. The project's purpose was to initiate a multidimensional understanding of war and to pursue serious professional research on how war could be abolished. *The Study of War*, first published in 1942, was a major conceptual breakthrough in questioning the inevitability of war in human history.[11]

During the same period, Sorokin analyzed dynamics of historical change in culture systems from the fifth century B.C.E. through the 1920s and the relationship between culture types (ideational/idealistic or sensate/materialistic) and the frequency of warfare over time.[12] From the macrohistorical perspective, was warfare dying out or increasing? The news was, *neither*. Sorokin found only random fluctuations over the centuries. Sometimes war was associated with cultural flowering, other times with cultural decline.

Sometimes it flourished during ideational/idealistic periods, sometimes during sensate/materialistic periods. There was only one clear trend: war was becoming more lethal over time. The very fact of random fluctuations gave hope to those who sought to create alternatives to war. Again the message was: war itself was not inevitable!

During the 1930s, 1940s, and 1950s a small group of interdisciplinary minded scholars and activists were working to lay the foundations of a new social science discipline that would focus on alternative methods of conflict resolution between states. Since the "war to end all wars" (World War I) had failed in its mission, they had to struggle against the continuing persistence of the idea that wars were inevitable and beyond human control.

Historians Reconsider the Sword

By the early 1960s the international situation looked very bleak. A group of American historians, disturbed by the Cold War-fueled arms race and signals of rising levels of intra- and interstate violence, such as the assassination of President Kennedy and the early rumblings of the coming war in Indochina, became keenly aware of how little effort had been made in their field to study the causes and processes of peace. Accordingly, they formed the Council on Peace Research in History to encourage, support and coordinate peace research in history, These American historians at the same time also were active in the larger peace research movement within the social sciences that became the International Peace Research Association. By the early 1970s they were working closely with their European counterparts, who eventually formed the European Working Group on Peace Research in History and have, in the decades since, made remarkable contributions to the documentation of peace movements and peace processes in history. The members of these new networks of historians first drawn largely from North America and

Europe, now include diplomatic historians, analysts of military policy, chroniclers of movements for peace and social justice, and teachers, students, peace activists, and concerned citizens from each world region.[13] Their task has been not only to change the image of human history as the record of war, by documenting the far more ubiquitous activities of everyday problem solving and conflict resolution at every level—from local communities to interstate relations—but also to demonstrate how often such behavior created effective alternatives to military action.

At the same time, UNESCO encouraged the establishment of bilateral committees of historians from European countries that had been at war to agree on textbook versions of the history of the relations between the countries that would not keep old animosities alive. UNESCO also commissioned several world history projects that emphasized the positive contributions of each civilization to humankind.[14]

While a number of scholars continue to hold to the conviction that war is both genetically programmed in the human species and essential to its survival fitness, a consensus is growing that war is, as Margaret Mead put it, "a social invention, not a biological necessity,"[15] and an increasingly dysfunctional invention at that. UNESCO's Culture of Peace Program provides many examples of peace processes as social inventions in conflict prevention. Macrohistorical studies of the effectiveness of military preparedness and of war fighting as an instrument of the state to achieve peace and security for its people show little relationship between military preparedness and security. Naroll and his coauthors' careful and methodologically brilliant analysis of deterrence in nine civilizations for periods ranging from four to twenty-five centuries shows that military preparedness does not deter enemies but may, rather, incite them.[16] Studies of the arms races that preceded World War I and World War II and continued through the Cold War dramatically emphasize that each increase in arms levels by one state will be matched by its opponent, thus ensuring that arms races increase the insecurity of each party and frequently end in war.[17] Recent analyses of the Cold War, considered by many strategists and international relations specialists to be a masterly example of the effectiveness of deterrence (because the United States "won" it solely by a superior level of military preparedness), are now suggesting different conclusions. New evidence indicates that the expensive deterrence policy may, in fact, have prolonged the Cold War by slowing down Soviet-initiated resolution processes that finally succeeded in spite of, and not because of, United States deterrence strategy.[18]

Warfare has traditionally put soldiers at risk—civilians rarely so. Today civilian casualties far outnumber military casualties. This pattern began to be true in World War I with the use of chemical and bacteriological warfare. During World War II the saturation bombing of European cities and the tragic nuclear bombing of Hiroshima and Nagasaki brought about a dramatic increase in civilian deaths. Today landmines primarily target civilians, perhaps children most of all, in the rural hinterlands of warfare areas—in Africa, Asia, Central America, and Europe as well. Such developments dangerously lower the social threshold for what is considered morally acceptable strategy in conflict situations.

The economic analyses of war that have come out of the peace research movement clarify the enormous cost of military preparedness to economic and social well-being.[19] While these costs are most damaging in the Two-Thirds World, they also drag down industrial economies, providing fewer jobs per dollar invested than civilian production and contributing to an increasing maldistribution of income. The environmental destruction involved—first in military preparedness on military reservations within the preparing state and then in the target states once weapons are unleashed—is enormous. And finally, World Health Organization reports on rising rates of mental illness around the world in current decades, the fruit of high levels of intrastate and interstate violence, remove from military supremacy the last vestiges of its credibility as symbol of a nation's true greatness.

In spite of the many delegitimating forces at work, the deeply held belief that war is a basic, inevitable, and divinely ordained process in human history will not easily be changed. In fact, change will come about only with a much wider recognition of the actual peace processes at work in every society and a wider awareness of the success stories of conflicts resolved and wars avoided. An important part of this change will be the increasing awareness of the peace cultures that have reproduced themselves side by side with the war cultures right inside the same society, over time, as in the examples given of the two cultures within each religious tradition.

Sometimes the peace culture has been a hidden culture, kept alive in the cracks of a violent society. At other times the peace culture has predominated, and violence has receded to a minimum. Given how destructive war has become in this century, we are lucky that we have living peace cultures to look to and to build on in this transition era for the human race. They can help us move away from global destruction and toward a world alive with a great diversity of peaceable lifeways.

NOTES

1. William McNeill, *The Rise of the West: A History of the Human Community* (Chicago: University of Chicago Press, 1963).

2. Arnold Toynbee, *Reconsiderations,* vol. 12 of A *Study of History* (New York: Oxford University Press, 1964).

3. Simone Weil, *The Iliad: or The Poem of Force* (Wallingford, Pa.: Pendle Hill, 1956).

4. For example, note E. S. Creasy, *Fifteen Decisive Battles of the World: From Marathon to Waterloo* (New York: Dorset, 1987).

5. Toynbee, *Reconsiderations,* 609.

6. Samuel N. Kramer, *History Begins at Sumer* (New York: Doubleday Anchor, 1959).

7. Bernard Grun, *The Timetables of History: A Horizontal Linkage of People and Events* (New York: Simon & Schuster, 1975).

8. These points are developed in Carol R. Ember and Melvin Ember, "War, Socialization and Interpersonal Violence: A Cross-Cultural Study," *Journal of Conflict Resolution* 38, no. 4 (1994): 620–46.

9. H. Mouritzen, "The Nordic Model of a Foreign Policy Instrument: Its Rise and Fall," *Journal of Peace Research* 3, no. 1 (1995): 9–21. G. Steinsland and P. M. Sörenson, *Menneske Og Makter i Vikingenes Verden* (Oslo: Umvcrsitetsforlagct, 1991). Note: My vastly oversimplified account here of a very complex history does not even touch on the special qualities of local democracy in Scandinavia once slavery was abolished, on renewed acknowledgment of an older tradition of strong roles for women, and on the fostering of community education programs that led to high levels of literacy at the local level.

10. William James, "The Moral Equivalent of War," in *War: Studies from Psychology, Sociology and Anthropology,* ed. Leon Bramson and George Goethals (New York: Basic Books, 1968), 21–31.

11. Quincy Wright, *A Study of War,* 2d ed. (Chicago: University of Chicago Press, 1983).

12. Pitirim Sorokin, *Social and Cultural Dynamics* (Boston: Porter Sargent, 1957).

13. These developments are documented in the following books: Charles Chatfield and Peter van den Dungen, *Peace Movements and Political Cultures* (Knoxville: University of Tennessee Press, 1988). Ralph Summy and M. Saunders, "Why Peace History?" *Peace and Change* 20, no. 1 (1995) [Special Issue: Peace History Forum]: 7–38.

14. The UNESCO-sponsored *History of Mankind,* published by Harper & Row, is in six volumes, the last of which, by Caroline Wax, K. M. Panikkar, and J. M. Romain, under the tile *The Twentieth Century,* appeared in 1966.

15. Margaret Mead, "Warfare Is Only an Invention—Not a Biological Necessity," in *War: Studies from Psychology, Sociology and Anthropology*, ed. Bramson and Goethals. 269–74.

16. Raoul Naroll, Vern Bullough, and Frada Naroll, *Military Deterrence in History* (Albany: SUNY Press, 1971).

17. The classic study in this field is Lewis F. Richardson, *Statistics of Deadly Quarrels* (Pittsburgh and Chicago: Boxwood, 1960).

18. These issues are discussed in the following publications: R. L. Garthoff, *The Great Transition: American-Soviet Relations and the End of the Cold War* (Washington, D.C.: Brookings Institution, 1994), R. N. Lebow and J. G. Stein, *We All Lost the Cold War* (Princeton: Princeton University Press, 1994).

19. Major authors here include: Kenneth Boulding, *The Economics of Peace* (New York: Prentice-Hall, 1945). Lloyd Dumas, *Overburdened Economy* (Berkeley: University of California Press, 1986). Ann Markusen and J. Yudken, *Dismantling the Cold War Economy* (New York: Basic Books, Harper Collins, 1992). Seymour Melman, *The Demilitarized Society: Disarmament and Conversion* (Montreal: Harvest House, 1988).

What Is Peace?

BY DAVID CORTRIGHT

David Cortright is the author of 17 books and serves as the Director of Policy Studies at the Kroc Institute for International Peace Studies at the University of Notre Dame. Selections from *Peace: A History of Movements and Ideas*. Cambridge: Cambridge University Press, 2008. Used by permission.

Jesus said that peacemakers are to be blessed as children of God, but in the real world they are often dismissed as utopian dreamers or worse, quaking defeatists who live in denial of reality. Jane Addams was one of the most admired persons in the United States in the years before World War I, but when she opposed US entry into the war she was ridiculed and reviled.[1] Those who advocated peace during the 1930s were accused of helping Hitler and aiding appeasement. Disarmament activists during the cold war were sometimes considered dupes of the Soviet Union. Throughout history the cause of peace has been on trial, standing like a forlorn defendant before the court of established opinion, misunderstood and maligned on all sides. Peace is "naked, poor, and mangled," wrote Shakespeare.[2] To be called a pacifist is almost an insult, to be labeled cowardly or selfish, unwilling to fight for what is right. It is easy to arouse people to war, said Hermann Goering at the Nuremberg trials. "All you have to do is tell them they are being attacked and denounce the pacifists for lack of patriotism. . . ."[3]

This is a response to the charges against pacifism. It is an attempt to set the record straight by exploring the history of movements and ideas for peace—an opportunity for the cause of peace to have its day in court. This is not an apologia for or paean to pacifism, however—far from it. I am often critical of peace advocacy, especially absolute pacifism, and I try to present both the strengths and weaknesses of the various movements and theories for peace that have emerged over the centuries. I write as one who has been engaged with these issues for decades. I strive for rigorous scholarly standards and objective analysis, but I am hardly neutral in this debate. Questions of war and peace intruded into my life when I was drafted for the Vietnam War, and they have remained with me ever since. I spoke out against that war as an active duty soldier, was the director of the National Committee for a Sane

Nuclear Policy (SANE) during the disarmament campaigns of the 1980s, and helped to found the Win Without War coalition to oppose the US invasion and occupation of Iraq. I have written about nuclear disarmament, economic sanctions, and nonviolent social change and have taught peace studies courses. I know only too well the many limitations of movements for peace and the inadequacy of theories on the causes and prevention of war. It is precisely because of my engagement with these issues that I feel qualified to offer this witness for the defense, to present the case of peace, and to examine its practices and principles.

Defining Terms

At the outset we face definitional challenges and the need to differentiate among different terms and concepts. What exactly do we mean by peace? The term is highly emotive, historian Michael Howard wrote, and is often abused as a tool of political propaganda.[4] When peace is defined narrowly it can imply passivity and the acceptance of injustice.[5] During the cold war the word had subversive implications and was often associated with communism. Moscow sponsored ersatz "peace councils," which gave the word a negative connotation. Hesitancy about the meaning of peace existed long before the cold war. In the years before World War I Andrew Carnegie lavishly funded programs to prevent war and advance international cooperation, but he was uncomfortable with the word peace and wanted to leave it out of the title of the international endowment he left as his legacy.[6]

Peace is more than the absence of war. It is also "the maintenance of an orderly and just society," wrote Howard—orderly in being protected against the violence or extortion of aggressors, and just in being defended against exploitation and abuse by the more powerful.[7] Many writers distinguish between negative peace, which is simply the absence of war, and positive peace, which is the presence of justice. "Peace can be slavery or it can be freedom; subjugation or liberation," wrote Norman Cousins. Genuine peace means progress toward a freer and more just world.[8] Johan Galtung developed the concept of "structural violence" to describe situations of negative peace that have

violent and unjust consequences.[9] Violence in Galtung's expansive definition is any condition that prevents a human being from achieving her or his full potential. Leonardo Boff, the Brazilian priest and theologian, employed the term "originating violence," which he defined as an oppressive social condition that preserves the interests of the elite over the needs of dispossessed and marginalized populations.[10] Originating or structural violence can include impoverishment, deprivation, humiliation, political repression, a lack of human rights, and the denial of self-determination. Positive peace means transcending the conditions that limit human potential and assuring opportunities for self-realization.

Gandhi spoke of nonviolence rather than peace and emphasized the necessity of overcoming injustice. Gandhi's meaning was deftly summarized by Jonathan Schell: "Violence is a method by which the ruthless few can subdue the passive many. Nonviolence is a means by which the active many can overcome the ruthless few." Yet the word nonviolence is "highly imperfect," wrote Schell. It is a word of "negative construction," as if the most important thing that can be said about nonviolence is that it is *not* something else. It is a negation of the negative force of violence, a double negative which in mathematics would yield a positive result. Yet English has no positive word for it. Schell attempted to resolve this dilemma by defining nonviolence as "cooperative power"— collective action based on mutual consent, in contrast to coercive power, which compels action through the threat or use of force.[11]

Peace does not mean the absence of conflict, argued peace researcher and former Australian ambassador John W. Burton. Conflict is intrinsic in human relationships, although it does not have to be and usually is not violent. The challenge for peace practitioners is to find ways in which communities can resolve differences without physical violence. In this context peace is understood as a dynamic process not an absolute end point. The goal of peacemakers is to develop more effective ways of resolving disputes without violent conflict, to identify and transform the conditions that cause war.

NOTES

1. Victoria Bissell Brown, "Addams, Jane," February 2000. Available online at American National Biography Online, www.anb.org/articles/15/15-00004.html (accessed November 22, 2006).

2. *The Life of King Henry V,* act V, scene ii, line 34.

3. G. M. Gilbert, *Nuremberg Diary* (New York: Farrar, Straus and Co., 1947), 279.

4. Michael Howard, "Problems of a Disarmed World," in *Studies in War and Peace* (New York: Viking Press, 1971), 225.

5. David P. Barash, *Introduction to Peace Studies* (Belmont, CA: Wadsworth Publishing, 1991), 6.

6. Charles Chatfield, *The American Peace Movement: Ideals and Activism* (New York: Twayne Publishers, 1992), 23.

7. Howard, "Problems of a Disarmed World," 226.

8. Norman Cousins, *Modern Man Is Obsolete* (New York: Viking Press, 1946), 45–6.

9. Johan Galtung, "Violence, Peace, and Peace Research," *Journal of Peace Research* 6, no. 3 (1969): 167—97.

10. Leonardo Boff, "Active Nonviolence: The Political and Moral Power of the Poor," in *Relentless Persistence: Nonviolent Action in Latin America,* ed. Philip McManus and Gerald Schlabach (Philadelphia, PA: New Society Publishers, 1991), vii.

11. Jonathan Schell, *The Unconquerable World: Power, Nonviolence, and the Will of the People* (New York: Metropolitan Books, 2003), 144, 227, 351.

Galtung, Violence, and Gender: The Case for a Peace Studies/Feminism Alliance

BY CATIA C. CONFORTINI

Catia C. Confortini is a peace activist and historian whose work includes *Intelligent Compassion: Feminist Critical Methodology in the Women's International League for Peace and Freedom* (Oxford University Press, 2012). She is a past US representative to the Women's International League for Peace and Freedom International Board and teaches in the Peace and Justice Studies program at Wellesley College. Footnotes have been omitted from this selection. Selections from "Galtung, Violence, and Gender: The Case for a Peace Studies/Feminism Alliance." *Peace & Change* 31, no. 3 (July 1, 2006): 333–67. Used by permission.

Drawing from a nineteenth- and early twentieth-century feminist tradition, some feminists in the 1970s and 1980s proposed that women were, by nature, upbringing, and/or by virtue of being mothers and caretakers, morally superior to and more peaceful than men. This association of women with pacifism disconcerted many other feminists. In particular, Jean Bethke Elshtain argued that claims of women's natural or cultural superiority in matters of peace and war only serve to reproduce, if inverted, a world based on gendered dichotomies and power hierarchies.

Echoing Elshtain's concerns, Christine Sylvester was critical of the assumptions about women's homogeneity that radical/standpoint feminists implied when generalizing about women's peacefulness. In agreement, Ann Tickner observed that

The association of femininity with peace lends support to an idealized masculinity that depends on constructing women as passive victims in need of protection. It also contributes to the claim that women are naïve in matters relating to international politics. An enriched, less militarized notion of citizenship cannot be built on such a weak foundation.

These feminists found such association disempowering for both women and peace. While I agree that there are "dangers in merging feminist and peace projects," I believe that feminism and peace studies have much in common and should not disregard the contributions they can each make to the other's field.

. . .

The first step toward incorporating gender studies into peace theories is to analyze what is missed by not confronting feminist contributions to a theory on violence. I take Johan Galtung's widely accepted theory of violence as a point of departure, as his conception is one on which much of peace studies research (including feminist peace research) is based.

Johan Galtung formulated a theory of violence based on the recognition that direct, personal violence (from bar brawls to international wars) is only one of three shapes which violence assumes. The other two categories of violence, namely structural (or indirect) and cultural violence are present in society in more subtle, but not less damaging ways. For instance, Galtung acknowledges that poverty (structural violence) or media glorification of violence (cultural violence) are also forms of violence. Furthermore, Galtung conceives of peace as both negative (absence of direct violence) and positive (presence of social justice). Only the elimination of violence at all levels can lead to true peace (negative as well as positive). Understanding how violence originates and operates at all levels, and how and why violence is used as a method of conflict resolution is, therefore, necessary to develop a theory of peace.

The problem is that Galtung fails to explore the role of gender in the social construction of violence, with the consequence that his prescriptions for nonviolent methods can at best be temporary piecemeal solutions to a persistent, deeply ingrained attitude to accept violence as "natural." They cannot effectively transform society's inclination to violence. Feminists in International Relations and in other social sciences argue that gender as a social construct organizes social life in hierarchical, mutually exclusive categories, which are in a relationship of sub/super ordination to one

another. This not only means that violence can at times be valued over nonviolence as a way of ending conflicts (as the current war against Iraq has amply showed), but also that the construction (justification?) of this superior status of violence owes much to gender relations. In this paper, I will explore how feminist theories on violence can shed light on the concept and legitimization of violence, in ways important to, yet currently underestimated by, much of the peace studies literature.

I identify four possible interrelated but distinct contributions of feminist thought to Galtung's theory of violence. First, I argue that Galtung's theory would benefit from an understanding of gender as a social construct that embodies power relations, rather than as a synonym for sex. Second, this feminist understanding allows us to see how several categories that shape and permit us to make sense of our social life are deeply gendered and involved in the production and reproduction of violence at all levels. Third, many feminists see language as constitutive of our social relations and they have successfully shown that language both reflects and reproduces existing gender relations. Furthermore, some feminists have shown that gendered language actualizes possibilities and impossibilities, so that certain social worlds only become imaginable (thus pursuable) through some rather than other forms of verbal communication. Violence or peace can be constituted through language. Finally, recent feminist work on masculinities has presented evidence that violence is deeply implicated in the construction and reproduction of gender relations, and in particular in the construction and reproduction of hegemonic masculinity.

. . .

Galtung and Feminist Thought on Violence

The relationships Galtung sees between direct, structural, and cultural violence need to be revisited in light of feminist contributions. Violence needs to be seen as a *process* rather than as a system or structure. Talking of violence as a structure, or a system, hints at a static and monolithic entity. Conceptualizing violence as a process allows us both to understand the complexities and contestations behind violence as a social practice and to envision possibilities of change.

Gender Understood as a Social Construct

Following common understandings, Galtung sees gender as a fault line that separates people into two distinct categories: men and women. Gender for Galtung is a property of individual people and a space where (direct) violence happens. Seen in this way, gender becomes relevant to an analysis of violence insofar as violent men use violence against feeble women or men and/or insofar as there exists a structure that allows for or precipitates men's violence. However, feminists have long argued that gender is only marginally related to biological sex. It is instead a social construct, "socially learned behavior and expectations that distinguish between masculinity and femininity." Gender can be seen as an analytic category, which helps to organize the way people think about the world. People thus come to see social reality as a set of mutually exclusive dichotomous categories, in relationship of super/subordination one to the other.

Essential in contemporary feminist thought about gender is the concept of power. Feminist theories in the social sciences have especially derived theoretical understandings of social phenomena from power as understood by French philosopher Michel Foucault, who viewed power as a pervasive regulatory system for social control, in which all individuals and social institutions participate....

Failing to understand gender as an analytical category, which has much to do with power in social relations, has profound consequences for Galtung's thought, as it makes him unable to recognize the vast implications gender has for violence and peace as social practices. In the first place, Galtung fails to seriously problematize the equation man : woman = war : peace. Whether by biology or socialization, Galtung concludes that men tend to be more violent and women tend to be more peaceful. With gender understood as sex, Galtung identifies the male sex with aggressiveness and violence and locates the source of violence in male sexuality and socialization. He hypothesizes that male sexuality and violence are neurological neighbors, thus they might be mutually triggered.

It has now been amply demonstrated that genetic and hormonal explanations of aggression and violence are scientifically unsound and have repeatedly failed their own tests of scientific validity and verifiability. Moreover, the supposed biological links between male sexuality and aggression have also been proven weak. Joshua Goldstein surveys scientific findings in this area, and concludes that most men do not find combat sexy/sexual in any way and that testosterone levels are not a cause of aggression. In addition, maternal behaviors in women (as in the animal world) vastly vary and they include maternal aggression as well as nurturing.

. . .

More compelling, from a "scientific" point of view, are explanations of the sex/violence nexus that are based on socialization. Galtung's assertion that boys are socialized into aggression finds empirical support across cultures, where sex segregation is marked by boys' rougher group play. However, these data are by no means clear on the direction of such supposed causation: is aggression caused by socialization into sex roles or are gender identities produced by different socialization practices? Although within a very different framework, far from the positivist idea of causation, most feminists would be closer to a position that supports the latter statement. I will discuss this further in the following sections.

The Problem of Gendered Categories

Robert Connell stated that gender "means practice organized in terms of, or in relation to, the reproductive division of people into male and female." As previously mentioned, then, feminists see gender as a way of organizing the world into sets of distinct, mutually exclusive, categories. These categories are in a relationship of super/subordination one to the other and they both reflect and reproduce the gender order. According to Sandra Harding, gender symbolism is the process through which gender metaphors are assigned to various perceived dichotomies, so that when people think in terms of dichotomies, they also associate each of them with either femininity or masculinity. The categories that are associated with femininity are valued less than the ones associated with masculinity. Activity versus passivity, rationality versus emotion, and strength versus weakness are some of these dualisms and so are war/violence versus peace. The first of each pair of terms is usually associated with masculinity and is assigned a higher value than the second term. Many feminists would argue that reversing the hierarchy implied in each pair would not constitute a solution to existing social inequalities, as each pair would still hide, reproduce, and naturalize unequal social relations of power.

Therefore, when social scientists think in terms of dichotomies, they reproduce gender relations of power in their own theory, thus legitimizing relationships of dominance and subordination at all levels. Galtung is not immune to this, as he frames the concept of violence in dichotomous terms, in opposition to the concept of peace. He relies on a binary opposition, when he defines peace as the absence of violence or violence as the opposite of peace. Although in his view peace and nonviolence are superior to violence, he ends up reproducing theoretically a distinction based on unequal power relations. This is not to say that violence and peace are or should be equally valued. However, a feminist analysis would complicate the relationship between the two terms; look at how violence and peace are not monolithic mutually exclusive categories, and how islands of violence can exist within seas of peace or vice versa. For example, feminist scholars in international relations have observed that when IR [international relations] scholars talk about peace, they ignore the wars going on inside the home, in the form of domestic violence. This is due to the fact that nonfeminist IR reproduces the gendered opposition between public and private sphere; it establishes its boundaries at the edge of the public sphere, therefore ignoring the feminized domestic life. This has led the discipline to overlook issues such as rape in wartime, battering in intimate relationships, and other forms of violence against women as they relate to the world of international affairs. However, feminists claim that, far from being strictly domestic or private matters, instances of violence against women are often related to international relations in unsuspected ways.

. . .

Violence as a method for social control is also seen in rape, which, rather than being an individual's aberration, is "deeply embedded in power inequalities and ideologies of male supremacy." In the case of sex work, attempts at "saving" prostitutes are, themselves, viewed by prostitutes as another form of control, violence, and colonization. Feminist analysis posits a mutually reinforcing relation between the different kinds of violence and all interact to maintain social relations of power. The gender order makes violence possible and, as I will later show in further detail, violence acts as a constitutive element of the gender order. One of the vehicles through which this relationship is worked out is gendered language, a mechanism through which violence is legitimated in society.

The Relation between Gendered Language and Violence

Feminists contend that gender relations are embedded in the legitimation of violence. One of the channels through which legitimation occurs is language. Galtung recognizes the role that language plays in breeding a culture of violence. In *Peace by Peaceful Means*, he sees language as one element of cultural violence, which serves to legitimize all other types of violence. So, in Galtung's view the language of sex serves to legitimize the biologically and socially derived association between (hetero) sexual acts and violence. Violence becomes sexy as it is associated with copulation. A look at feminist works on the gendering of language again offers a more sophisticated and more troubling view of the role of language in the reproduction of violence. In particular, Galtung doesn't talk about the mechanisms through which violence discourse gets abstracted, and which not only serve to justify violence as domination (and sex as domination), but also to limit our choices for political options. . . .

Most importantly, learning to understand and use technostrategic language is a process through which the mind becomes militarized, even when the intent is to outsmart or get the better of nuclear strategists at their own game.

This highly gendered discourse is also a curtain behind which political decisions are made, and it is used to legitimize such decisions. Debunking its rationality myth and exposing its highly gendered nature and dependence on denigration of the feminine, fear of death, homoeroticism, heterosexism, and the enjoyment of belonging to a privileged community, is an important way to challenge the power of such discourse and the destructive possibilities it creates.

In summary, feminist analysis is important to underscore the ways in which language both legitimizes and creates certain realities, rather than others. Because it allows us to see the processes through which language is constitutive as well as reflective of reality, gender analysis also permits us to imagine ways in which alternative realities can be created. This is especially relevant when thinking about the language that creates and recreates violence as a real possibility in people's lives, whether it is war or battering of intimate partners.

Gender and Violence Are Mutually Constituted

Galtung relies on biological sex to understand the process by which violence becomes acceptable and accepted in society. Feminists talk about masculinities and femininities. Masculinity and femininity are not biologically determined categories. They are, instead, socially constituted ideal types to which "real" men and women must conform.

Drawing on Robert Connell's influential work on *Gender and Power*, many feminists see the gender order as constituted by and dependent on a power hierarchy of masculinities and femininities, at the top of which stands the ideal of hegemonic masculinity. This, in turn, "is always constructed in relation to various subordinated masculinities as well as in relation to women." For most contemporary feminist social scientists, violence is a socially learned expression of this specific kind of masculinity (i.e., hegemonic masculinity). Furthermore, violence is seen as implicated in the construction of hegemonic masculinity. Since gender is a practice, produced and reproduced through social relations, violence can be seen as a method for the reproduction of the "gender order."

. . .

Official sources would obviously deny that violence is endemic to the military as an institution. A theory consistent with Johan Galtung's definition of violence could claim that the military inherently possesses a culture of violence that legitimates

violence against women. However, feminists would go further than that and contend that the building of a violent culture and behavior depends on the building of a hatred and subjugation of the feminine. Thus, violence is involved in the construction of masculinity through the shaping of the male body and the domination of women, the female body, and all that is associated with the feminine. "The threat of feminization is a tool with which male conformity to a hegemonic ideal is policed," and strategies of feminization are used in the formation of "hierarchies of masculinities," thus in the subordination of groups of men by other men.

. . .

This discussion about violence and masculinities reveals that more than constituting the cultural environment that makes violence acceptable and legitimate, as Galtung claims, gender relations are implicated in the very creation of violence. Violence is both made possible by the existence of power/gender relations, and power/gender relations rely on violence for their reproduction. Violence and gender are involved in a relationship of mutual constitution.

A Peace Studies/Feminism Alliance? Conclusion

Many scholars have problematized the relationship between women and peace. Christine Sylvester, Jean Elshtain, J. Ann Tickner, and Berenice Carroll, among others, have correctly pointed out that the association of women with peace is disempowering and harmful for both women and peace. It is also disempowering for men who are peacemakers, because somehow, according to this view, they have to accept the idea that they are emasculated males.

Gender lenses allow us to see how the three components of the violence triangle posited by Galtung (direct, structural, and cultural violence) are related to each other, and contribute to the preservation of violence in society. The different levels of violence cannot be viewed in isolation from each other, and they cannot be viewed as independent from the social construction of hegemonic identities, be it hegemonic masculinities or hegemonic races.

In opposition to IR theorists of various shapes, Christine Sylvester asserted that security is an ever-contested, ever-moving process, a site of struggles, partial achievements, and incoherences. Against a universalizing, timeless, either-or approach to international security, Sylvester suggested that security "is always partial . . . both elusive and mundane." I propose that, similarly, violence can be seen as a process that involves different, at times contradictory, practices, at different but coexisting and interdependent levels. Violence is not a static entity: it involves constant change and adaptation to society's new requirements. Violence is aided, sustained, and reproduced through institutions, practices, and discourses. It is in a relationship of mutual constitution to institutions, practices, and discourses. It is not a static system, thus it also embodies change and the elements of its own dismantling as a practice or process. Violence as a process is embedded in language and in all social institutions. It is constituted by and constitutive of gender relations of power. It depends on gendered dichotomies for its existence. The different levels at which violence manifests itself might well be exemplified by Galtung's violence triangle, but they cannot be divorced from gender.

EXECUTIVE SUMMARY

BY THE INSTITUTE FOR ECONOMICS AND PEACE

The Institute for Economics and Peace is an Australian-based organization that has been producing a global peace index since 2007. The Institute sponsors research aimed at calculating the impact of improved peacefulness on global markets, costs, structures, and profits. Selections from "Global Peace Index 2015."[1] Used by permission of the Institute for Economics and Peace.

This is the ninth edition [2015] of the Global Peace Index (GPI), which ranks the nations of the world according to their level of peacefulness. The index is composed of 23 qualitative and quantitative indicators from highly respected sources and ranks 162 independent states, covering 99.6 per cent of the world's population. The index gauges global peace using three broad themes: *the level of safety and security in society,* the extent of *domestic and international conflict* and the degree of *militarisation.*

In addition to presenting the findings from the 2015 GPI and its eight-year trend analysis, this year's report provides an updated methodology to account for the economic impact of violence on the global economy. The report also contains a new analysis on Positive Peace and describes its relationship to development and other significant and positive societal outcomes. A detailed thematic analysis of the three aforementioned domains of the GPI is also included.

Last year [2014] the global GPI score remained stable. However, while the average level of global peacefulness was stable, a number of indicators and countries did deteriorate while others improved. Four out of the nine geographical regions experienced an improvement in peace: Europe, North America, sub-Saharan Africa and Central America and the Caribbean. The other five regions became less peaceful. The most substantial changes in the Index occurred in the Middle East and North Africa (MENA) where several countries suffered from an upsurge in violence related to sectarian strife and civil conflicts, resulting in the region being ranked as the least peaceful in the world.

The *societal safety and security domain* improved slightly last year, driven by falls in the *homicide rate* and the *likelihood of violent demonstrations.* The improvements in homicide rates mainly reflected data updates in some high homicide countries. This improvement was counterbalanced by deteriorations in the *ongoing conflict* and *militarisation*

1 http://economicsandpeace.org/wp-content/uploads/2015/06/Global-Peace-Index-Report-2015_0.pdf, accessed May 23, 2017.

domains, owing to increases in *deaths from internal conflict,* non-payment of UN peacekeeping dues, and a continuing deterioration in the *impact of terrorism* indicator.

Iceland is the most peaceful country, with the ten highest ranking nations in the GPI all being stable democracies. Nordic and Alpine countries are particularly well represented. Asia-Pacific is also represented at the top, with New Zealand ranked 4th, Japan at 8th and Australia at 9th.

MENA now ranks as the most violent region, overtaking South Asia from last year's GPI. Yet again, Europe maintained its position as the most peaceful region in the world, supported by a lack of domestic and external conflicts. It was also the region that experienced the largest improvement in its score compared with 2014, continuing its eight-year trend of improving peacefulness.

This year [2015] Guinea-Bissau had the largest improvement in peace, resulting in a rise of 24 places in the rankings to 120th. The next four largest improvements occurred in Cote d'Ivoire, Egypt, Tajikistan and Benin. A common theme among the largest improvers was a fall in the level of organised conflict, which occurred in all of the four aforementioned African nations.

Cancelling out its strong improvement in the 2014 edition of the GPI, Libya experienced the largest deterioration this year. Its score deteriorated substantially and consequently it fell 13 places down to 149th to become the 14th least peaceful country. Unsurprisingly the second biggest decline was recorded for the Ukraine, due to the conflict between Russian separatists and the Ukrainian government as well as the instability caused by Russia's annexation of Crimea. Other countries that substantially deteriorated were Djibouti and Niger which fell 42 and 28 places, respectively.

Over the past eight years the average country score deteriorated 2.4 percent, highlighting that on average the world has become slightly less peaceful. However, this decrease in peacefulness has not been evenly spread, with 86 counties deteriorating while 76 improved. MENA has suffered the largest decline of any region in the world, deteriorating 11 per cent over the past eight years.

The eight-year downward trend in peacefulness has been driven predominately by the deterioration in indicators of internal peacefulness. Of the five key indicators which deteriorated by more than five per cent, four are internal and one external:

> *refugees and IDPs* [internally displaced persons] *as a percentage of the population, deaths from internal conflict,* the *impact of terrorism,* the *likelihood of violent demonstrations* and *perceptions of criminality.*

The deterioration in the indicators measuring the number of *refugees and IDPs* and the *impact of terrorism* is most concerning. The latest UNHCR [United Nations High Commissioner for Refugees] estimates indicate that more than 50 million people are now either refugees or internally displaced because of conflict and violence, which is the highest number since the end of the Second World War. A third of people displaced by conflict inside their own countries in 2014 are in Iraq and Syria alone.

Terrorism has grown steadily over the last decade, a trend that shows no sign of abating. Deaths caused by terrorism increased by 61 per cent in 2013, which resulted in almost 18,000 people being killed in terrorist attacks. Of those deaths, 82 per cent occurred in just five countries: Iraq, Afghanistan, Pakistan, Nigeria and Syria. The threat of terrorism has also affected many of the world's most peaceful countries, with terrorist attacks occurring in France, Denmark and Australia in the last year.

On the positive side, several indicators of external peacefulness actually improved over the last eight years. *Relations with neighbouring countries* has grown stronger, particularly in South America, *financial contributions to UN peacekeeping* funding has improved and the number and intensity of external conflicts has fallen as many countries wound down their military involvement in Iraq and Afghanistan.

It is important to note that peace is becoming more unevenly distributed. While Europe continued its long-term trend of improvement, the Middle East continued its recent trend of deterioration, further increasing the distance between the most and least peaceful regions and countries. In Europe and in many other developed countries, homicide rates and other forms of interpersonal violence continue to drop and are at historic lows.

In 2008, there were only three countries that had a score worse than 3 out of 5: Somalia, Iraq and Sudan. However, by 2015 this increased to nine countries: Syria, Iraq, Afghanistan, South Sudan, Central African Republic, Somalia, Sudan, Democratic Republic of the Congo and Pakistan, highlighting the further deterioration amongst the least peaceful countries in the world.

The economic impact of violence on the global economy in 2014 was substantial and is estimated at US$14.3 trillion or 13.4 per cent of world GDP [Gross Domestic Product]. This is equivalent to the combined economies of Brazil, Canada, France, Germany, Spain and the United Kingdom. Since 2008, the total economic impact on global GDP has increased by 15.3 per cent, from US$12.4 trillion to US$14.3 trillion.

Large increases in costs are due to the increases in deaths from internal conflict, increases for IDP and refugee support, and GDP losses from conflict, with the latter accounting for 38 per cent of the increase since 2008. The major expenditure categories are military spending at 43 per cent, homicide and violent crime at 27 per cent and internal security officers, including police, at 18 per cent. While the cost of UN peacekeeping has more than doubled since 2008, it still only accounts for less than 0.17 per cent of violence containment expenditure.

The report outlines **new findings on Positive Peace,** highlighting its impact on peace, development and other important societal goals. In societies where Positive Peace is stronger, developmental goals are more likely to be achieved. These societies are more resilient when faced with crisis and have fewer grievances. They are more likely to achieve non-violent positive outcomes when faced with resistance movements and are more likely to adapt and make concessions to reconcile grievances. Additionally, Positive Peace is also statistically associated with many other outcomes considered desirable: stronger business environments, better performance on well-being measures, gender equality and better performance on ecological measures.

The report also includes a thematic analysis of the three domains of the GPI:

Ongoing domestic and international conflicts:

This section comments on the six major MENA conflicts occurring in Syria, Iraq, Yemen, Libya, Israel and Lebanon. It identifies many of the drivers of these conflicts, which include challenges to government legitimacy, deepening sectarian divides, the destabilising presence of ISIL [Islamic State in Iraq and the Levant] and the cross-cutting proxy conflict between Saudi Arabia and Iran.

Societal safety and security:

This section analyses the effects of urbanisation on violence, and finds that peace generally increases with higher levels of urbanisation. This is a by-product of higher levels of development. However, countries that have weak rule of law, high levels of intergroup grievances and high levels of inequality are more likely to experience deteriorations in peace as urbanisation increases.

Militarisation:

Since 1990, there has been a slow and steady decrease in measures of global militarisation, with large changes in militarisation occurring rarely and usually associated with larger, globally driven geopolitical and economic shifts. Surprisingly, very few major socio-economic measures are associated with militarisation; however, the research did find that countries with weak Positive Peace factors are more likely to use the military for internal suppression.

VIOLENCE COSTS 13.4% OF WORLD GDP

RANK	COUNTRY	SCORE
1	Iceland	1.148
2	Denmark	1.150
3	Austria	1.198
4	New Zealand	1.221
5	Switzerland	1.275
6	Finland	1.277
7	Canada	1.287
8	Japan	1.322
9	Australia	1.329
10	Czech Republic	1.341
11	Portugal	1.344
12	Ireland	1.354
13	Sweden	1.360
14	Belgium	1.368
15	Slovenia	1.378
16	Germany	1.379
17	Norway	1.393
18	Bhutan	1.416
19	Poland	1.430
20	Netherlands	1.432
21	Spain	1.451
22	Hungary	1.463
23	Slovakia	1.478
24	Singapore	1.490
25	Mauritius	1.503
26	Romania	1.542
27	Croatia	1.550
28	Malaysia	1.561
29	Chile	1.563
30	Qatar	1.568
31	Botswana	1.597
32	Bulgaria	1.607
33	Kuwait	1.626
34	Costa Rica	1.654
35	Taiwan	1.657
36	Italy	1.669
37	Lithuania	1.674
38	Estonia	1.677
39	United Kingdom	1.685

THE STATE OF PEACE

- Very high
- High
- Medium
- Low
- Very low
- Not included

2015 GLOBAL PEACE INDEX

A SNAPSHOT OF THE GLOBAL STATE OF PEACE

RANK	COUNTRY	SCORE
80	Mozambique	1.976
81	Equatorial Guinea	1.987
82	Cuba	1.988
83	Burkina Faso	1.994
84	Bangladesh	1.997
84	Ecuador	1.997
86	Morocco	2.002
87	Kazakhstan	2.008
88	Angola	2.020
89	Paraguay	2.023
90	Bolivia	2.025
91	Armenia	2.028
92	Guyana	2.029
92	Peru	2.029
94	United States	2.038
95	Saudi Arabia	2.042
96	Papua New Guinea	2.064
97	Trinidad and Tobago	2.070
98	Haiti	2.074
99	Gambia	2.086
100	Dominican Republic	2.089
101	Swaziland	2.102
102	Djibouti	2.113
103	Brazil	2.122
104	Algeria	2.131
105	Cote d'Ivoire	2.133
106	Turkmenistan	2.138
107	Bahrain	2.142
108	Tajikistan	2.152
109	Jamaica	2.153
110	Belarus	2.173
111	Cambodia	2.179
111	Uganda	2.179
113	Uzbekistan	2.187
114	Sri Lanka	2.188
115	Congo	2.196
116	Honduras	2.210
117	Guinea	2.214
118	Guatemala	2.215
119	Ethiopia	2.234
120	Guinea-Bissau	2.235
121	Kyrgyzstan	2.249
122	Mauritania	2.262
123	El Salvador	2.263

40	Latvia	1.695	49	United Arab Emirates	1.805	60	Argentina	1.865	70 Moldova 1.942
41	Laos	1.700	51	Malawi	1.814	61	Greece	1.878	71 Jordan 1.944
42	South Korea	1.701	52	Albania	1.821	62	Nepal	1.882	71 Togo 1.944
43	Mongolia	1.706	53	Bosnia & Herzegovina	1.839	63	Lesotho	1.891	71 Macedonia 1.944
44	Uruguay	1.721	54	Ghana	1.840	64	Panama	1.903	74 Nicaragua 1.947
45	France	1.742	55	Zambia	1.846	64	Tanzania	1.903	74 Oman 1.947
46	Indonesia	1.768	56	Vietnam	1.848	66	Gabon	1.904	76 Tunisia 1.952
46	Serbia	1.768	57	Montenegro	1.854	67	Madagascar	1.911	77 Benin 1.958
48	Namibia	1.784	58	Timor-Leste	1.860	68	Cyprus	1.924	78 Liberia 1.963
49	Senegal	1.805	59	Sierra Leone	1.864	69	Kosovo	1.938	79 Georgia 1.973

124	China	2.267	135	Turkey	2.363	146	Colombia	2.720	
125	Zimbabwe	2.294	136	South Africa	2.376	147	Yemen	2.751	
126	Thailand	2.303	137	Egypt	2.382	148	Israel	2.781	
127	Eritrea	2.309	138	Iran	2.409	149	Libya	2.819	156 Sudan 3.295
128	Mali	2.310	139	Rwanda	2.420	150	Ukraine	2.845	157 Somalia 3.307
129	Niger	2.320	140	Chad	2.429	151	Nigeria	2.910	158 Central African Republic 3.332
130	Burundi	2.323	141	Philippines	2.462	152	Russia	2.954	159 South Sudan 3.383
130	Myanmar	2.323	142	Venezuela	2.493	153	North Korea	2.977	160 Afghanistan 3.427
132	Azerbaijan	2.325	143	India	2.504	154	Pakistan	3.049	161 Iraq 3.444
133	Kenya	2.342	144	Mexico	2.530	155	Democratic Republic of the Congo	3.085	162 Syria 3.645
134	Cameroon	2.349	145	Lebanon	2.623				

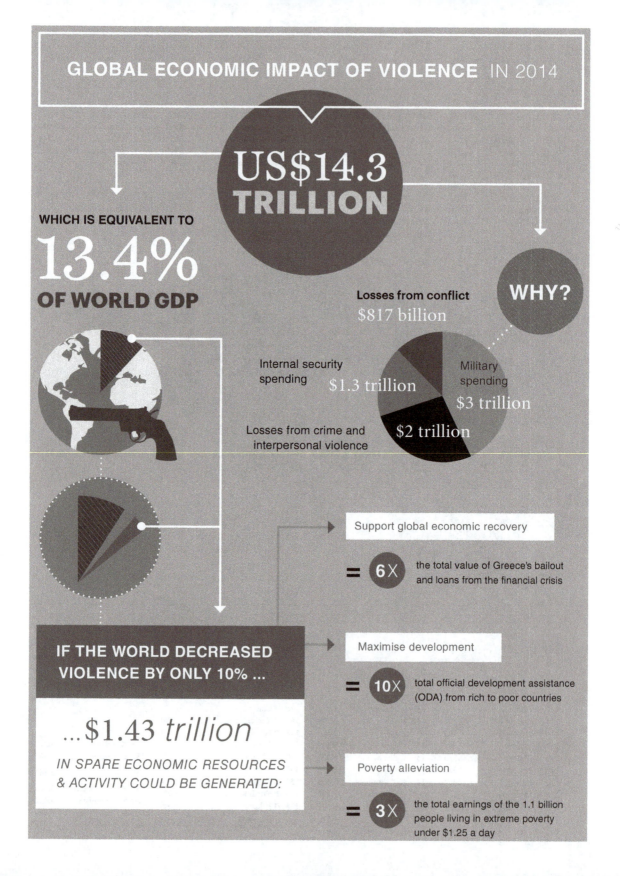

GLOBAL ECONOMIC IMPACT OF VIOLENCE IN 2014

US$14.3 TRILLION

WHICH IS EQUIVALENT TO

13.4%
OF WORLD GDP

WHY?

Losses from conflict
$817 billion

Internal security
spending $1.3 trillion

Military
spending
$3 trillion

$2 trillion

Losses from crime and
interpersonal violence

Support global economic recovery

= 6X   the total value of Greece's bailout
and loans from the financial crisis

**IF THE WORLD DECREASED
VIOLENCE BY ONLY 10% ...**

Maximise development

= 10X   total official development assistance
(ODA) from rich to poor countries

...$1.43 *trillion*

*IN SPARE ECONOMIC RESOURCES
& ACTIVITY COULD BE GENERATED:*

Poverty alleviation

= 3X   the total earnings of the 1.1 billion
people living in extreme poverty
under $1.25 a day

DISCUSSION QUESTIONS

1. Explain why histories of "who tames whom, who controls whom," as Elise Boulding writes, have for so long been much more common than histories focused on how people lead their everyday lives.

2. Describe some of what Boulding calls the "cultures of peace" that can be found in a society or community with which you are personally familiar.

3. Using David Cortright's definitions, explain how peace and conflict studies as a research and action program changes depending on whether it adopts (a) negative peace, (b) positive peace, or (c) structural violence as its major focus.

4. Evaluate the accuracy of Catia C. Confortini's claim that gender relations and violence "are involved in a relationship of mutual constitution."

5. Review the principle ways that Confortini maintains peace studies would be improved if it formed an alliance with feminism.

6. Establish your own criteria to guide an assessment of both the strengths and weaknesses of the Global Peace Index. Indicate whether in general you judge it to be a valid measure of peace.

7. Use Boulding's perspective to evaluate the usefulness of the Global Peace Index. Use Confortini's perspective to complete a second evaluation.

Debates about the Origins of Violence

Why do humans sometimes choose to harm other humans? This is one of the oldest and most fundamental questions within peace and conflict studies. Many believe that humans are violent because they are now, and have always been, fundamentally flawed. Humans carry dark and evil genes within them, it is claimed, making them into "killer apes," prone to violence. Hopes for substantial human progress or a wider global peace is therefore bound to lead to disappointments. Just such a pessimism was foundational in the Greek, Roman, and Christian traditions that gave rise to the modern era.

David P. Barash, a prominent evolutionary psychologist, summarizes multiple examples of this pessimistic view of human nature in the first selection following. Barash acknowledges the ubiquity of this view, even among some biological and social scientists. However, Barash argues, the pessimists err in failing to distinguish between interpersonal violence and collective violence. Interpersonal, face-to-face, and small group violence is "deeply entrenched in human nature," Barash maintains; but collective violence—war—is a learned and culture-based activity, "no more 'natural' than a bridal shower or the assembly line used to construct a stealth bomber." People have clearly shown they have a capacity to wage war, but they have just as clearly shown that waging war is not a biological necessity. Barash advises researchers use different conceptual strategies when thinking about interpersonal violence and about war.

Although he denies biological predispositions cause wars, Barash does maintain that human biology causes community- and family-based interpersonal violence. A second selection, by Robert Burrowes, instead argues that neither war nor interpersonal violence are necessary. Burrowes maintains that almost all violence at all levels is caused by what he calls the "invisible violence" inflicted on children by their caregivers. Burrowes's perspective is but one of many that identify the origins of violence in individual, psychological causes. Such emphases on psychological accounts are especially prominent in the United States, where explanations of social phenomenon are often centered more in individualistic than in situational and structural causes.

A final selection by Frances Moore Lappé illustrates how situational and structural explanations of violence are constructed. While Burrowes bases his explanations on how well needs are met in childhood, Lappé focuses on how well society meets the needs of adults. She argues that contemporary social structures are increasingly failing to meet the human needs to belong, to feel respected, and to be included. Martin Luther King called this a failure to provide a sense of "membership" and of a "right to exist." Lappé argues these structural failures lead to suicide, murder, terrorism, and war. Lappé concludes that social policies promoting inclusive "communities of trust" are needed to reduce all forms of violence.

Do Human Beings Have an Instinct for Waging War?

BY DAVID P. BARASH

David P. Barash is a psychologist at the University of Washington who has written and edited over two dozen books, including *Approaches to Peace*, an anthology of canonical peace studies texts. Selections from "Do Human Beings Have an Instinct for Waging War?" *Aeon*, September 19, 2013. This article was originally published by Aeon Media (http://www.aeon.co, twitter: @aeonmag). Used by permission.

There is something peculiarly—even paradoxically—appealing about taking a dim view of human nature, a view that has become unquestioned dogma among many evolutionary biologists. It is a tendency that began some time ago. When the Australian-born anthropologist Raymond Dart discovered the first australopithecine fossil in 1924, he went on to describe these early hominids as:

> Confirmed killers: carnivorous creatures that seized living quarries by violence, battered them to death, tore apart their broken bodies, dismembered them limb from limb, slaking their ravenous thirst with the hot blood of the victims and greedily devouring living writhing flesh.

This lurid perspective has deep antecedents, notably in certain branches of Christian doctrine. According to the zealous 16th century French theologian John Calvin:

> The mind of man has been so completely estranged from God's righteousness that it conceives, desires, and undertakes, only that which is impious, perverted, foul, impure and infamous. The human heart is so steeped in the poison of sin, that it can breathe out nothing but a loathsome stench.

It's bad enough for the religious believer to be convinced of humanity's irrevocable sinfulness, punishable in the afterlife. But I'm even more

concerned when those who speak for science and reason promote a theory of human nature that threatens to become a self-fulfilling prophecy. For example, in his influential book *African Genesis* (1961) the American playwright Robert Ardrey described humans as "Cain's children":

> Man is a predator whose natural instinct is to kill with a weapon. It is war and the instinct for territory that has led to the great accomplishments of Western Man. Dreams may have inspired our love of freedom, but only war and weapons have made it ours.

The drumbeat that argues for war as a defining feature of the human condition has, if anything, increased in recent decades, spreading beyond the evolutionary and anthropological worlds. Here is how the English philosopher Simon Critchley began his review of John Gray's *The Silence of Animals* (2013) in the *Los Angeles Review of Books*: "Human beings do not just make killer apps. We are killer apes. We are nasty, aggressive, violent, rapacious hominids."

Then there is the American anthropologist Napoleon Chagnon, who devoted decades to studying the Yanomami people of the Venezuelan/Brazilian Amazon. His best-selling book *The Fierce People* (1968) has been especially influential in enshrining an image of tribal humanity as living in a state of "chronic warfare."

Chagnon has been the subject of intense criticism but, to my mind, there is simply no question about the empirical validity and theoretical value of his research. In a field (call it evolutionary psychology or, as I prefer, human sociobiology) that has often been criticised for a relative absence of hard data, his findings, however politically distasteful, have been welcome indeed. Among these, one of the most convincing has been Chagnon's demonstration that, among the Yanomami, not only is inter-village "warfare" frequent and lethal, but that Yanomami men who have killed other men experience significantly higher reproductive success—evolutionary fitness—than do non-killers. His data, although disputed by other specialists, appear altogether reliable and robust.

So I admire the man, and his work, but I have a growing sense of discomfort about the way that Chagnon's Yanomami research has been interpreted and the inferences that have been drawn from it.

I fear that many of my colleagues have failed, as previously have I, to distinguish between the relatively straightforward evolutionary roots of human violence and the more complex, multifaceted and politically fraught question of human war. To be blunt, violence is almost certainly deeply entrenched in human nature; warfare, not so much. A fascination with the remarkably clear correlation between Yanomami violence and male fitness has blinded us to the full range of human non-violence, causing us to ignore and undervalue realms of peacemaking in favour of a focus on exciting and attention-grabbing patterns of war-making.

As an evolutionary scientist, I have been enthusiastic about identifying the adaptive significance— the evolutionary imprint—of apparently universal human traits. For a long time, it seemed that Chagnon's finding of the reproductive success of Yanomami men who were killers was one of the most robust pieces of evidence for this. Now I am not so sure, and this is my *mea culpa*.

There has also been a tendency among evolutionary thinkers to fix upon certain human groups as uniquely revelatory, not simply because the research about them is robust, but also because their stories are both riveting and consistent with our pre-existing expectations. They are just plain fun to talk about, especially for men.

Remember, too, the journalists' edict: "If it bleeds, it leads." You are unlikely to see a newspaper headline announcing that "France and Germany Did Not Go To War," whereas a single lethal episode, anywhere in the world, is readily pounced upon as news. Language conventions speak volumes, too. It is said that the Bedouin have nearly 100 different words for camels, distinguishing between those that are calm, energetic, aggressive, smooth-gaited, or rough, etc. Although we carefully identify a multitude of *wars*—the Hundred Years War, the Thirty Years War, the American Civil War, the Vietnam War, and so forth—we don't have a plural form for *peace*.

It makes evolutionary sense that human beings pay special attention to episodes of violence, whether interpersonal or international: they are matters of life and death, after all. But when serious scientists do the same and, what is more, when they base "normative" conclusions about the human species on what is simply a consequence of their selective attention, we all have a problem.

The most serious problem with Chagnon's influence on our understanding of human nature is one familiar to many branches of science: generalising from one data set—however intensive—to a wider universe of phenomena. Academic psychologists, for example, are still reeling from a 2010 study by the University of British Columbia which found that the majority of psychological research derives from college students who are "Western, Educated, Industrialised, Rich, and Democratic"—in short, WEIRD. Similarly, the Yanomami are only one of a large number of very different, tribal human societies. Given the immense diversity of human cultural traditions, *any* single group of *Homo sapiens* must be considered profoundly unrepresentative of the species as a whole.

Just as the Yanomami can legitimately be cited as notably violence-prone—at both the individual and group level—many other comparable tribal peoples do not engage in anything remotely resembling warfare. These include the Batek of Malaysia, the Hadza of Tanzania, the Martu of Australia, a half-dozen or more indigenous South Indian forager societies, and numerous others, each of whom are no less human than those regularly trotted out to "prove" our inherent war-proneness.

In the Dark Ages of biology, taxonomists used to identify a "type species" thought to represent each genus, but the idea no longer has any currency in biology. The great evolutionary biologist Ernst Mayr effectively demonstrated that statistical and population thinking trumps the idea of a Platonic concept of "types," independent of the actual diversity of living things, not least *Homo sapiens*. Yet anthropologists (and biologists, who should know better) seem to have fallen into the trap of seizing upon a few human societies, and generalising them as representative of *Homo sapiens* as a whole. Regrettably, this tendency to identify "type societies" has been especially acute when it comes to establishing the supposed prevalence of human warfare.

In his justly admired book *The Better Angels of our Nature* (2011), the evolutionary psychologist Steven Pinker made a powerful case that human violence—interpersonal as well as warring—has diminished substantially in recent times. But in his eagerness to emphasise the ameliorating effects of historically recent social norms, Pinker exaggerated our pre-existing "natural" level of war-proneness, claiming that "chronic raiding and feuding characterised life in a state of nature." The truth is otherwise. As recent studies by the anthropologist Douglas Fry and others have shown, the overwhelmingly predominant way of life for most of our evolutionary history—in fact, pretty much the *only* one prior to the Neolithic revolution—was that of nomadic hunter-gatherers. And although such people engage in their share of interpersonal violence, warfare in the sense of group-based lethal violence directed at other groups is almost non-existent, having emerged only with early agricultural surpluses and the elaboration of larger-scale, tribal organisation, complete with a warrior ethos and proto-military leadership.

Other well-regarded scientists have been similarly misled. Thus, in *The Social Conquest of Earth* (2012), the biologist Edward O. Wilson calls warfare "humanity's hereditary curse." I applaud both Pinker's and Wilson's distaste for war, but I wish they had thought more deeply and consulted the cross-cultural and archaeological evidence more

carefully before jumping on the "war has always been with us" bandwagon.

Human history demonstrates how recent warfare is in our own evolutionary story. But what about our closest ape relatives? As with human societies, we have no living ancestors among the apes. We doubtless share a *common ancestor* with today's chimpanzees, bonobos, gorillas, orang-utans and gibbons, but the social behaviour of the latter three are all dramatically different from that of modern human beings, while that of chimpanzees and bonobos are almost exactly opposed to one another: chimpanzees are known to engage in violent, group-level encounters, complete with search-and-destroy missions that conjure images of human skirmishing and outright warfare. Bonobos, on the other hand—genetically, no more distant from *Homo sapiens*—do nothing of the sort, and are renowned for making love, not war.

When it comes to human aggression, violence and war, there simply is no unitary direction impelled by evolution. On the one hand, we are capable of despicable acts of horrific violence; on the other, we evince remarkable compassion and self-abnegation. Our selfish genes can generate a wide array of nasty, destructive and unpleasant actions; and yet, these same selfish genes can incline us toward altruistic acts of extraordinary selflessness. It is at least possible that our remarkably rapid brain evolution has been driven by the pay-off derived by successful warlike competition with other primitive human and humanoid groups. But it is equally possible that it was driven by the pay-off associated with co-operation, co-ordination and mutual care-taking.

Indeed, it is easy to develop models whereby animals and people who are adroit at these tasks—along with genes that predispose in such directions—will be favoured by natural selection over alternative individuals and alleles that are comparatively more bellicose. Moreover, even as warfare is new to the human experience and therefore liable to be culturally induced rather than biologically based, behavioural systems of restraint are old, shared by numerous animal species, and therefore likely to be deep-seated in our nature. After all, even in a war-ridden world, actual wars are much rarer than are examples of non-violent conflict resolution; the latter happens every day, among nations no less than between individuals.

I have never argued that human beings are biologically equipotential, capable of doing or becoming anything they wish, independent of their evolutionary bequest—and I don't intend to now. We could never be as altruistic as worker honeybees, or as solitary as deep-sea angler fish. There are no human societies in which all members are expected to have sex a dozen times each day, or not at all. But there is a limit to our genetically influenced proclivities—and this, please note, is written by an evolutionary biologist who has been accused of hypothesising genes for just about everything.

A useful distinction in this regard is between evolved *adaptations* and *capacities*. Language is almost certainly an *adaptation*, something that all normal human beings can do, although the details vary with circumstance. By contrast, reading and writing are *capacities*, derivative traits that are unlikely to have been directly selected for, but have developed through cultural processes. Similarly, walking and probably running are adaptations; doing cartwheels or handstands are capacities. In my view, interpersonal violence is a human adaptation, not unlike sexual activity, parental care, communication and so forth. It is something we see in every human society. Meanwhile, war—being historically recent, as well as erratic in worldwide distribution and variation in detail—is almost certainly a capacity. And capacities are neither universal nor mandatory.

Let me be clear. Violence is widespread and, sadly, deeply human, just as the adaptation for violence under certain circumstances is similarly ingrained in many other species. But war is something else. It is a capacity, and involves group-oriented lethal violence. Thus it deserves to be distinguished from rivalry, anger, "crimes of passion" or revenge, or other forms of homicide. To engage an absurdly positive simile: violence is like marriage, in the sense that some sort of process whereby adults solemnise their relationship appears to be a cross-cultural universal, and is a likely candidate for being an adaptive part of human nature. War, on the other hand, is

like arranging a wedding with a bridal shower or bachelor party, and laying on a hotel ballroom, an orchestra, a four-course meal and dancing. It is safe to assume that neither employing a photographer, serving a multi-tiered wedding cake, enlisting bridesmaids nor tying baby shoes to the bumper of the newly-weds' car spring from the human genome, although people are capable of doing all these things. By the same token, plain, old interpersonal violence is a real, albeit regrettable, part of human nature. War is even more regrettable, but is no more "natural" than a bridal shower or the assembly line used to construct a stealth bomber.

The psychologist B. F. Skinner wrote that "no theory changes what it is a theory about; man remains what he has always been." True enough for most phenomena: the solar system is as it was when Ptolemaic thinking held sway; nor did this change after Copernicus, Kepler and Galileo came up with a more accurate descriptive theory. And gravity was gravity before and after Newton.

But theories of human nature are rather different. When I write or lecture about the social behaviour and reproductive strategies of different marmot species, no sociopolitical implications are involved. But when I write or lecture about violence, aggression and/or war-making in humans, it makes a huge difference whether I describe the pacific Lepcha of the Himalayas or the fierce Yanomami.

It's not that any particular theory changes human nature itself. Rather, our expectations and thus our behaviour changes, and with very serious consequences. If we are convinced, for example, that Thomas Hobbes was correct and people are naturally inclined to be nasty and brutish, this has implications for our politics, including our sense of national budgetary priorities—how much to invest in, say, education and health care versus the police and the military—which in turn is liable to become a self-fulfilling prophecy. How many arms races and cycles of international distrust have been fed by a pre-existing view that the other side is aggressive, potentially violent and irremediably warlike, which in turn leads to policies and actions that further confirm such assumptions?

Especially when they speak to matters of war and peace, theories about the fundamental nature of human beings are more insidious and influential than other evolutionary research, such as whether modern humans carry Neanderthal genes, or the potency of gene *versus* individual *versus* group selection, and so forth. It's not that I believe in a postmodern world in which language and ideology construct reality. Rather, I recognise that these particular ideas have real effects on crucial topics such as national levels of defence spending and whether or not to go to war.

I am not arguing that scientific perspectives should be evaluated by their ideological, political, and social implications. Unlike matters of ideology, theology, or ethics, science must be assessed only by the degree to which its fruits are, or are not, falsified, the confidence with which we can agree on their usefulness, and the extent to which they generate further testable ideas. But we must also remain alert when science risks being misused for ideological purposes, not to mention the subtle extent to which researchers can unintentionally bias their findings, simply by their choice of research subjects—as when one or a few human societies are taken as indicative of our entire species. Worse yet is when the danger goes beyond being misled on the "merely scientific" to embracing consequences for social and political policy.

The human mind is drawn toward simple either/or statements—God versus the devil, cowboys versus Indians, you're either with us or you're with the terrorists—but reality is more nuanced and complex. This applies particularly to the seemingly simple question of whether human beings are "naturally" or "instinctively" aggressive or violent. In the past, popular treatments of human beings as "killer apes" have clearly been misguided in their single-mindedness; ditto for others purporting to demonstrate that we are uniformly co-operative and peaceful. Our human nature is neither Rousseauian nor Hobbesian; instead, both a devil and an angel perch on our shoulders, gesturing toward evolutionary predilections in both directions.

At this point, readers looking to evolution for guidance can be forgiven if they feel confused, even frustrated by the fact that our biological heritage is so ambiguous, or ambivalent. It is certainly worthwhile interrogating the evolutionary background to our predilections, but the answers will lead us back to Jean-Paul Sartre's formulation that human beings are "condemned to be free." Advocates for peace might be relieved that we are not biologically obliged to war, or be distraught that we are not unilaterally predisposed to peace, but we are all stuck with an obligation (if not necessarily a predisposition) to assess our uniquely human situation as honestly as we can.

When dealing with matters of war-proneness versus peaceful capabilities, it would be far better, not only for scientific accuracy but also for social consequence, if we took seriously this pronouncement by one of the premier authorities on human nature, Theodore Geisel (aka Dr. Seuss): "You have brains in your head. You have feet in your shoes. You can steer yourself any direction you choose."

Why Are Humans Being Violent?

BY ROBERT J. BURROWES

Robert J. Burrowes has been a nonviolent activist since 1981 and has published multiple articles exploring the origins of violence. He is also the author of *The Strategy of Nonviolent Defense: A Gandhian Approach* (1996). From *On Line Opinion*, August 8, 2012.[1] Used by permission.

The [2012] shootings in Colorado (not to mention the ongoing wars and other violence occurring around the world) again raise the perennial question "Why are human beings violent?" Are we genetically programmed to be violent? Is violence socially learned? Or are some individuals just "psychotic"?

Perhaps the most important question is this: Can we do anything to end human violence?

Because of the death of my two uncles in World War II, I have been researching the question "Why are human beings violent?" since 1966, including spending 14 years living in seclusion from 1996 to 2010 with Anita McKone, undertaking a deep psychological examination of our own minds.

. . .

In essence, human beings are violent because of the "invisible" and "utterly invisible" violence that we adults unconsciously inflict on children. And this is in addition to the "visible" violence that we inflict on them consciously.

So what is "invisible" violence? It is the "little things" we do everyday [sic], partly because we are just "too busy." For example, when we do not allow time to listen to, and value, a child's thoughts and feelings, the child learns to not listen to itSelf [sic] thus destroying its internal communication system. When we do not let a child say what it wants (or ignore it when it does), the child develops communication and behavioral dysfunctionalities as it keeps trying to meet its own needs (which, as a basic survival strategy, it is genetically programmed to do).

When we blame, condemn, insult, mock, embarrass, shame, humiliate, taunt, goad, guilt-trip, deceive, lie to, bribe, blackmail, moralize with and/or judge a child, we both undermine its sense of Self-worth and teach it to blame, condemn, insult, mock, embarrass, shame, humiliate, taunt, goad, guilt-trip, deceive, lie, bribe, blackmail, moralize and/or judge.

The fundamental outcome of being bombarded throughout its childhood by this "invisible" violence is that the child is utterly overwhelmed by feelings of fear, pain, anger and sadness (among many others). However, parents and other adults also actively interfere with the expression of these feelings and the behavioral responses that are naturally generated by them and it is this "utterly invisible" violence that explains why the dysfunctional behavioral outcomes actually occur.

For example, by ignoring a child when it expresses its feelings, by comforting, reassuring or distracting a child when it expresses its feelings, by laughing at or ridiculing its feelings, by terrorizing a child into not expressing its feelings (e.g. by screaming at it when it cries or gets angry), and/or by violently controlling a behavior that is generated by its feelings (e.g. by hitting it, restraining it or locking it into a room), the child has no choice but to unconsciously suppress its awareness of these feelings.

However, once a child has been terrorized into suppressing its awareness of its feelings (rather than being allowed to have its feelings and to act on them) the child has also unconsciously suppressed its awareness of the reality that caused these feelings. This has many outcomes that are disastrous for the individual, for society and for nature because the individual will now easily suppress its awareness of the feelings that would tell it how to act most functionally in any given circumstance and it will progressively acquire a phenomenal variety of dysfunctional behaviors, including some that are violent towards itself, others and/or the Earth.

From the above, it should also now be apparent that punishment should never be used. "Punishment," of course, is one of the words we use to obscure our awareness of the fact that we are using violence. Violence, even when we label it

1 http://www.onlineopinion.com.au/view.asp?article=13961, accessed May 23, 2017

"punishment," scares children and adults alike and cannot elicit a functional behavioural response. If someone behaves dysfunctionally, they need to be listened to, deeply, so that they can start to become consciously aware of the feelings (which will always include fear and, often, terror) that drove the dysfunctional behaviour in the first place. They then need to feel and express these feelings (including any anger) in a safe way. Only then will behavioural change in the direction of functionality be possible.

"But these adult behaviors you have described don't seem that bad. Can the outcome be as disastrous as you claim?" you might ask. The problem is that there are hundreds of these "ordinary," everyday behaviors—many of them perpetrated in school—that destroy the Selfhood of the child. It is "death by a thousand cuts" and most children simply do not survive as Self-aware individuals. And why do we do this? We do it so that each child will fit into our model of "the perfect citizen": that is, obedient and hardworking student, reliable and pliant employee/soldier, and submissive law-abiding citizen.

The tragic reality of human life is that few people value the awesome power of the individual Self with an integrated mind (that is, a mind in which memory, thoughts, feelings, sensing, conscience and other functions work together in an integrated way) because this individual will be decisive in choosing life-enhancing behavioral options (including those at variance with social laws and norms) and will fearlessly resist all efforts to control it or coerce it with violence.

So how do we end up with people like Adolf Hitler, Idi Amin, Pol Pot and all those other perpetrators of violence, including political leaders who conduct wars and those who perpetrate their violence in our homes and on our streets? We create them.

And can we do anything to end human violence? Yes we can. Each one of us.

Here is the formula, briefly stated:

If you want a child who is nonviolent, truthful, compassionate, considerate, patient, thoughtful, respectful, generous, loving of itself and others, trustworthy, honest, dignified, determined, courageous and powerful, then the child must be treated with—and experience—nonviolence, truth, compassion, consideration, patience, thoughtfulness, respect, generosity, love, trust, honesty, dignity, determination, courage and power.

And if you need an incentive, ask yourself this: Do you think it is possible to successfully tackle the many manifestations of violence—war, terrorism, street violence, the ongoing climate catastrophe, the ongoing exploitation of Africa, Asia and Central/South America . . . —without addressing its fundamental cause?

It's a big task. But we have a world to save. Literally.

"Could Our Deepest Fears Hold the Key to Ending Violence?"

BY FRANCES MOORE LAPPÉ

Frances Moore Lappé is the author of 18 books including the global best seller *Diet for a Small Planet*. Lappé is also the cofounder of three national organizations that explore the roots of hunger, poverty, and environmental crises. From *Yes! Magazine*, April 18, 2013. Used by permission.

In his book *Violence*, psychologist James Gilligan asked a Massachusetts prison inmate, "What do you want so badly that you would sacrifice everything in order to get it?"

The inmate declared, "Pride. Dignity. Self-esteem . . . And I'll kill every motherfucker in that cell block if I have to in order to get it."

Or, as another inmate said, "I've got to have my self-respect, and I've declared war on the whole world till I get it."

Pride, dignity, respect, agency—a sense that we matter—these are feelings largely shaped interpersonally. We depend upon the social fabric to get them. But for many, these things are in tatters.

Fewer and fewer of us feel a sense of belonging, and we're more and more preoccupied with the desperate scramble for belongings.

We see fear's face everywhere, whether in a Congress debating assault weapons or in schools introducing lock-down drills. French philosopher Patrick Viveret has called fear the "emotional plague of our planet."

For most species fear is key to survival. Sensing danger, a healthy animal experiences instantaneous physical changes that enable it to escape; then, once the threat has passed, the impala literally shakes off its fear and runs back to join its group.

But could it be that for human animals fear itself has become a danger? To explore the possibility, a place to start is asking what humans fear most.

It is the loss of standing with others, the fear of being cast out by the tribe. Rather than being hyper-individualists, *Homo sapiens* are profoundly social creatures—the most social of all species. This sense of standing is inseparable from trust. To thrive, we need to trust that we count in the eyes of others and will, therefore, be treated with respect. In a word, our fear is loss of dignity.

Almost equal is our fear of powerlessness. Human beings need to feel that we make a difference. Social psychologist Erich Fromm argued in *The Heart of Man* that what characterizes man is that "he is driven to make his imprint on the world." And later he dismissed Descartes' axiom about a human essence centered in thought, declaring instead: "I am, because I effect."

When these essential needs for connection and agency are unmet, we go nuts. We try to get respect by whatever means possible. If peaceful means seem closed off, violence it is.

Inequality has soared to historic levels. In 2010, the top 1 percent garnered 93 percent of all income gains. And in countries and states, "high levels of trust are linked to low levels of inequality," report British scholars Richard Wilkinson and Kate Pickett in *The Spirit Level*.

Trapped in a giant game of musical chairs, we run faster and faster to edge out the guy ahead. With economic rules that increasingly concentrate wealth, we know we could be the next one kicked out, no matter how quick our pace. So we take on debt, juggle three jobs, cheat in school—whatever it takes to stay "in."

And our children are most sensitive to this fear of exclusion. Those who've felt bullied, unable to fit in, misunderstood, without a voice in those most social of places—schools—are more likely to become psychotic and violent, including against themselves.

In a culture of fear of disconnection, those at the bottom feel most dismissed and discounted. Adam Smith, the supposed (but misunderstood) champion of the market more than two centuries ago grasped the devastating power of exclusion: Poverty, he wrote in his *Theory of Moral Sentiments*, "places . . . [a person] out of the sight of mankind . . . [T]o feel that we are taken no notice of, necessarily damps the most agreeable hope . . . of human nature."

In this vein, joblessness isn't just about money. It's about loss of "membership." Martin Luther King once said that "in our society it is murder, psychologically, to deprive a man of a job or an income. You are in substance saying to that man he has no right to exist."

And that is exactly how many feel: A rise of 1 percent in joblessness in the United States is accompanied by an increase of roughly 1 percent in the suicide rate.

In our world of increasing inequalities, suicide now claims more lives than homicide and war combined. Americans own more than four in ten of the world's privately held guns, and two-thirds of U.S. gun deaths are suicides.

And when people feel "dissed," violence toward the powerless increases, too: The *Washington Post* reports that each 1 percent increase in unemployment is "associated with at least a 0.50 per 1,000 increase in confirmed child maltreatment reports one year later." Since the recession [that] began in 2007, the number of U.S. children killed by maltreatment has risen by about 20 percent to more than five children each day. Thus, our culture of fear gets passed down from one generation to another.

So, what can we do to break free from the spiral of fear and worsening violence?

Maybe we begin here: recognizing that our crisis is not that we humans are too individualistic or too selfish. It's that we've lost touch with how deeply social we really are. Easing the fear at the root of so much pain and violence that generates more fear—from suicide to child abuse to school massacres—comes as we embrace the obvious: We are creatures who, in order to thrive individually, depend on inclusive communities in which all can thrive.

Freedom starts there. We build it by standing up for rules on which inclusive, trusting community depends: fair rules, for example, that keep wealth circulating and strictly out of public decision-making, and rules that ensure decent jobs for all.

This pathway out of a violence-soaked culture is no foreign "ism." It is what's proven essential to our species' thriving—communities of trust without which we destroy not just others, but ourselves as well.

DISCUSSION QUESTIONS

1. Summarize David P. Barash's argument about the biological bases of violence by emphasizing his distinction between evolutionary adaptations and cultural capacities. Explain why you do, or do not, accept his central claim about the biological roots of violence.

2. Explain why both Barash and your own personal perspective on peace, violence, and war may have (as Barash writes) "real effects on crucial topics" in contemporary societies.

3. Use examples from your own childhood or from the childhoods of people you know to explain how what Robert Burrowes calls the "invisible violence" of adults impacts children.

4. Using Burrowes's article as an example, describe the main strengths and weaknesses of relying on individual, psychological perspectives to explain the causes of violence.

5. Describe some current conditions in your own society that discourage the flourishing of what Frances Moore Lappé calls healthy "communities of trust."

6. Synthesize two or more of the three perspectives presented in this section to create your own perspective on the main causes of peace, violence, and war.

PART 2

WAR AND SECURITY

Peace and conflict studies emerged as a new area of research in the 1960s largely in reaction to the horrors of WWII, the Korean War, and the threat of worldwide nuclear war produced by the Cold War. Even though many other topics have become common in recent decades, war continues to be a major focus of the field. Section 1 presents some of the current debates about the significance of war in the contemporary world. Some researchers argue, for example, that we are living in the most war-free era known to humans in the last 5,000 to 10,000 years. Section 2 shifts to another set of debates associated with even broader questions about peace, conflict, and violence. In this section, analysts dispute whether war and other forms of coercion help make people safe. Researchers disagree about the relative benefits and deficits produced by war, violence, and coercion.

Debates about War

It is a common belief that we are today living in especially violent times. However, in selection 1, Steven Pinker argues that this belief is incorrect. In fact, Pinker maintains, since 1945 we have been living in a period we should call "the long peace." Developed countries have entered an unprecedented era in which wars between them have been mostly eliminated, even as a strategic option.

A second selection by David Swanson vigorously rebuts Pinker's conclusions. Swanson focuses particularly on Pinker's claims about the decreasing frequency of war and of war fatalities. "Wars appear to be a constant, enduring, and growing presence," Swanson contends, and we are seeing bloodier wars than ever before.

In a third and final selection, historian Andrew J. Bacevich argues that most people in the United States have dangerously inaccurate views about war. Bacevich maintains that American wars in what he calls the "Short Twentieth Century" between 1914 and 1989 helped build a false belief that wars are morally justifiable and economically beneficial. However, Bacevich says adopting a broader view of history reveals "a different lesson." This lesson teaches that war devastates, impoverishes, and coarsens its participants even as many leaders repeatedly declare that war helps their nation remain powerful and prosperous.

The Long Peace: Some Numbers

BY STEVEN PINKER

Steven Pinker is a professor of psychology at Harvard and the author of several acclaimed books about psycholinguistics and cognitive science, including *The Blank Slate* (2002), and *The Stuff of Thought* (2007). Due to space limitations, footnotes have been omitted from this selection. "The Long Peace: Some Numbers," from THE BETTER ANGELS OF OUR NATURE: WHY VIOLENCE HAS DECLINED by Steven Pinker, copyright© 2011 by Steven Pinker. Used by permission of Viking Books, an imprint of Penguin Publishing Group, a division of Penguin Random House LLC.

. . . Now we are ready for the most interesting statistic since 1945: zero. Zero is the number that applies to an astonishing collection of categories of war during the two-thirds of a century that has elapsed since the end of the deadliest war of all time. I'll begin with the most momentous.

- Zero is the number of times that nuclear weapons have been used in conflict. Five great powers possess them, and all of them have waged wars. Yet no nuclear device has been set off in anger. It's not just that the great powers avoided the mutual suicide of an all-out nuclear war. They also avoided using the smaller, "tactical" nuclear weapons, many of them comparable to conventional explosives, on the battlefield or in the bombing of enemy facilities. And the United States refrained from using its nuclear arsenal in the late 1940s when it held a nuclear monopoly and did not have to worry about mutually assured destruction. I've been quantifying violence . . . using proportions. If one were to calculate the amount of destruction that nations have actually perpetrated as a proportion of how much they *could* perpetrate, given the destructive capacity available to them, the postwar decades would be many orders of magnitudes more peaceable than any time in history.

  None of this was a foregone conclusion. Until the sudden end of the Cold War, many experts (including Albert Einstein, C. P. Snow, Herman Kahn, Carl Sagan, and Jonathan Schell) wrote that thermonuclear doomsday was likely, if not inevitable. The eminent international studies scholar Hans Morgenthau, for example, wrote in 1979, "The world is moving ineluctably towards a third world war—a strategic nuclear war. I do not believe that anything can be done to prevent it." The *Bulletin of the Atomic Scientists,* according to its Web site, aims to "inform the public and influence policy through in-depth analyses, op-eds, and reports on nuclear weapons." Since 1947 it has published the famous Doomsday Clock, a measure of "how close humanity is to catastrophic destruction—the figurative midnight." The clock was unveiled with its minute hand pointing at 7 minutes to midnight, and over the next sixty years it was moved back and forth a number of times

between 2 minutes to midnight (in 1953) and 17 minutes to midnight (in 1991). In 2007 the *Bulletin* apparently decided that a clock with a minute hand that moved two minutes in sixty years was due for an adjustment. But rather than tuning the mechanism, they redefined midnight. Doomsday now consists of "damage to ecosystems, flooding, destructive storms, increased drought, and polar ice melt." This is a kind of progress.

- Zero is the number of times that the two Cold War superpowers fought each other on the battlefield. To be sure, they occasionally fought each other's smaller allies and stoked proxy wars among their client states. But when either the United States or the Soviet Union sent troops to a contested region (Berlin, Hungary, Vietnam, Czechoslovakia, Afghanistan), the other stayed out of its way. The distinction matters a great deal because as we have seen, one big war can kill vastly more people than many small wars. In the past, when an enemy of a great power invaded a neutral country, the great power would express its displeasure on the battlefield. In 1979, when the Soviet Union invaded Afghanistan, the United States expressed its displeasure by withdrawing its team from the Moscow Summer Olympics. The Cold War, to everyone's surprise, ended without a shot in the late 1980s shortly after Mikhail Gorbachev ascended to power. It was followed by the peaceful tear-down of the Berlin Wall and then by the mostly peaceful collapse of the Soviet Union.

- Zero is the number of times that any of the great powers have fought each other since 1953 (or perhaps even 1945, since many political scientists don't admit China to the club of great powers until after the Korean War). The war-free interval since 1953 handily breaks the previous two records from the 19th century of 38 and 44 years. In fact, as of May 15,1984, the major powers of the world had remained at peace with one another for the longest stretch of time since the Roman

Empire. Not since the 2nd century B.C.E., when Teutonic tribes challenged the Romans, has a comparable interval passed without an army crossing the Rhine.

- Zero is the number of interstate wars that have been fought between countries in Western Europe since the end of World War II. It is also the number of interstate wars that have been fought in Europe as a whole since 1956, when the Soviet Union briefly invaded Hungary. Keep in mind that up until that point European states had started around two new armed conflicts *a year* since 1400.

- Zero is the number of interstate wars that have been fought since 1945 between major developed countries (the forty-four with the highest per capita income) anywhere in the world (again, with the exception of the 1956 Hungarian invasion). Today we take it for granted that war is something that happens in smaller, poorer, and more backward countries. But the two world wars, together with the many hyphenated European wars from centuries past (Franco-Prussian, Austro-Prussian, Russo-Swedish, British-Spanish, Anglo-Dutch) remind us that this was not always the way things worked.

- Zero is the number of developed countries that have expanded their territory since the late 1940s by conquering another country. No more Poland getting wiped off the map, or Britain adding India to its empire, or Austria helping itself to the odd Balkan nation. Zero is also the number of times that any country has conquered even *parts* of some other country since 1975, and it is not far from the number of permanent conquests since 1948.... In fact the process of great power aggrandizement went into reverse. In what has been called "the greatest transfer of power in world history," European countries surrendered vast swaths of territory as they closed down their empires and granted independence to colonies, sometimes peacefully, sometimes because they had lost the will to prevail in colonial wars.... Two entire categories of war—the imperial war to acquire colonies, and the colonial war to keep them—no longer exist.

- Zero is the number of internationally recognized states since World War II that have gone out of existence through conquest. (South Vietnam may be the exception, depending on whether its unification with North Vietnam in 1975 is counted as a conquest or as the end of an internationalized civil war.) During the first half of the 20th century, by comparison, twenty-two states were occupied or absorbed, at a time when the world had far fewer states to begin with. Though scores of nations have gained independence since 1945, and several have broken apart, most of the lines on a world map of 1950 are still present on a world map in 2010. This too is an extraordinary development in a world in which rulers used to treat imperial expansion as part of their job description.

———

The point of this chapter is that these zeroes—the Long Peace—are a result of one of those psychological retunings that take place now and again over the course of history and cause violence to decline. In this case it is a change within the mainstream of the developed world (and increasingly, the rest of the world) in the shared cognitive categorization of war. For most of human history, influential people who craved power, prestige, or vengeance could count on their political network to ratify those cravings and to turn off their sympathies for the victims of an effort to satisfy them. They believed, in other words, in the legitimacy of war. Though the psychological components of war have not gone away—dominance, vengeance, callousness, tribalism, groupthink, self-deception—since the late 1940s they have been disaggregated in Europe and other developed countries in a way that has driven down the frequency of war.

Some people downplay these stunning developments by pointing out that wars still take place in the developing world, so perhaps violence has only been displaced, not reduced.... For now it's worth noting that the objection makes little sense.

There is no Law of Conservation of Violence, no hydraulic system in which a compression of violence in one part of the world forces it to bulge out somewhere else. Tribal, civil, private, slave-raiding, imperial, and colonial wars have inflamed the territories of the developing world for millennia. A world in which war continues in some of the poorer countries is still better than a world in which it takes place in both the rich *and* the poor countries, especially given the incalculably greater damage that rich, powerful countries can wreak.

A long peace, to be sure, is not a perpetual peace. No one with a statistical appreciation of history could possibly say that a war between great powers, developed countries, or European states will never happen again. But probabilities can change over spans of time that matter to us. The house odds on the iron dice can decline; the power-law line can sink or tilt. And in much of the world, that appears to have happened.

The same statistical consciousness, though, alerts us to alternative possibilities. Perhaps the odds haven't changed at all, and we're overinterpreting a random run of peaceful years in the same way that we are liable to overinterpret a random cluster of wars or atrocities. Perhaps the pressure for war has been building and the system will blow at any moment.

But probably not. The statistics of deadly quarrels show that war is not a pendulum, a pressure cooker, or a hurtling mass, but a memoryless game of dice, perhaps one with changing odds. And the history of many nations affirms that a peace among them can last indefinitely. As Mueller puts it, if war fever were cyclical, "one would expect the Swiss, Danes, Swedes, Dutch, and Spaniards to be positively *roaring* for a fight by now." Nor are Canadians and Americans losing sleep about an overdue invasion across the world's longest undefended border.

What about the possibility of a run of good luck? Also unlikely. The postwar years are by far the longest period of peace among great powers since they came into being five hundred years ago. The stretch of peace among European states is also the longest in its bellicose history. Just about any statistical test can confirm that the zeroes and near zeroes of the Long Peace are extremely improbable, given the rates of war in the preceding centuries. Taking the frequency of wars between great powers from 1495 to 1945 as a baseline, the chance that there would be a sixty-five-year stretch with only a single great power war (the marginal case of the Korean War) is one in a thousand. Even if we take 1815 as our starting point, which biases the test against us by letting the peaceful post-Napoleonic 19th century dominate the base rate, we find that the probability that the postwar era would have at most four Wars involving a great power is less than 0.004, and the probability that it would have at most one war between European states (the Soviet invasion of Hungary in 1956) is 0.0008.

The calculation of probabilities, to be sure, critically depends on how one defines the events. Odds are very different when you estimate them in full knowledge of what happened (a post hoc comparison, also known as "data snooping") and when you lay down your prediction beforehand (a planned or a priori comparison). Recall that the chance that two people in a room of fifty-seven will share a birthday is ninety-nine out of a hundred. In that case we are specifying the exact day only after we identify the pair of people. The chance that someone will share *my* birthday is less than one in seven; in that case we specify the day beforehand. A stock scammer can exploit the distinction by sending out newsletters with every possible prediction about the trajectory of the market. Several months later the fraction of recipients that got the lucky matching run will think he is a genius. A skeptic of the Long Peace could claim that anyone making a big deal of a long run of nonwars at the end of that very run is just as guilty of data snooping.

But in fact there is a paper trail of scholars who, more than two decades ago, noticed that the war-free years were piling up and attributed it to a new mindset that they expected to last. Today we can say that their a priori predictions have been confirmed. The story can be told in titles and dates: Werner Levi's *The Coming End of War* (1981), John Gaddis's "The Long Peace: Elements of Stability in the Postwar International System" (1986), Kalevi Holsti's "The Horsemen of the Apocalypse: At the Gate, Detoured; or Retreating?" (1986), Evan Luard's *The Blunted Sword: The Erosion of Military Power in Modern World Politics* (1988), John Mueller's *Retreat from Doomsday: The Obsolescence, of Major War* (1989), Francis Fukuyama's "The End of History?" (1989), James Lee Ray's "The Abolition of Slavery and the End of International War" (1989), and Carl Kaysen's "Is War Obsolete?" (1990). In 1988 the political scientist Robert Jervis captured the phenomenon they were all noticing:

> The most striking characteristic of the postwar period is just that—it can be called "postwar" because the major powers have not fought each other since 1945. Such a lengthy period of peace among the most powerful states is unprecedented.

These scholars were confident that they were not being fooled by a lucky run but were putting their finger on an underlying shift that supported predictions about the future. In early 1990, Kaysen added a last-minute postscript to his review of Mueller's 1989 book in which he wrote:

> It is clear that a profound transformation of the international structure in Europe—and the whole world—is underway. In the past, such changes have regularly been consummated by war. The argument presented in this essay supports the prediction that this time the changes can take place without war (although not necessarily without domestic violence in the states concerned). So far—mid-January—so good. The author and his readers will be eagerly and anxiously testing the prediction each day.

Precocious assessments of the obsolescence of interstate war are especially poignant when they come from military historians. These are the scholars who have spent their lives immersed in the annals of warfare and should be most jaded about the possibility that this time it's different.

In his magnum opus *A History of Warfare,* John Keegan (the military historian who is so habitually called "distinguished" that one could be forgiven for thinking it is part of his name) wrote in 1993:

> War, it seems to me, after a lifetime of reading about the subject, mingling with men of war, visiting the sites of war and observing its effects, may well be ceasing to commend itself to human beings as a desirable or productive, let alone rational, means of reconciling their discontents.

The equally distinguished Michael Howard had already written, in 1991:

> [It has become] quite possible that war in the sense of major, organized armed conflict between highly developed societies may not recur, and that a stable framework for international order will become firmly established.

And the no-less-distinguished Evan Luard, our guide to six centuries of war, had written still earlier, in 1986:

> Most startling of all has been the change that has come about in Europe, where there has been a virtual cessation of international warfare.... Given the scale and frequency of war during the preceding centuries in Europe, this is a change of spectacular proportions: perhaps the single most striking discontinuity that the history of warfare has anywhere provided.

More than two decades later, none of them would have a reason to change his assessment. In his 2006 book *War in Human Civilization,* a military history that is more sweeping than its predecessors and salted with the Hobbesian realism of evolutionary psychology, Azar Gat wrote:

> Among affluent liberal democracies.... a true *state* of peace appears to have developed, based on genuine mutual confidence that war between them is practically eliminated even as an option. Nothing like this had ever existed in history.

Counting Dollars

BY DAVID SWANSON

David Swanson has written several books, including *War Is a Lie* (2010) and *When the World Outlawed War* (2011). He hosts the weekly syndicated radio show Talk Nation Radio. A selection coauthored by Swanson appears in part 7 of this book. Selections from *War No More: The Case for Abolition*. Charlottesville, VA: David Swanson, 2013. Used by permission.

When Americans hear "the cost of war" they often think of two things: dollars and U.S. soldiers' lives. During the G.W.O.T. (global war on terror/terra) Americans have not been asked to sacrifice, to cut back, to pay more taxes, or to contribute to the cause. In fact, they've had their taxes reduced, especially if they have large incomes or are among the population of "corporate persons." (Wealth concentration is a common result of wars, and these wars are no exception.) U.S. people have not been drafted for military or other duty, except through the poverty draft and the deceptions of the military recruiters. But this lack of sacrifice hasn't meant no financial cost. Below is a menu of past wars and price tags in 2011 dollars. The trend seems to be moving mostly in the wrong direction.

- War of 1812 — $1.6 billion
- Revolutionary War — $2.4 billion
- Mexican War — $2.4 billion
- Spanish-American War — $9 billion
- Civil War — $79.7 billion
- Persian Gulf — $102 billion
- World War I — $334 billion
- Korea — $341 billion
- Afghanistan — $600 billion
- Vietnam — $738 billion
- Iraq — $810 billion
- Total post-9/11 — $1.4 trillion
- World War II — $4.1 trillion

Joseph Stiglitz and Linda Bilmes in 2008 calculated the true total cost of OIL (the Iraq War) as three to five trillion (higher now that the war went on for years longer than they expected). That figure includes impacts on oil prices, future care of veterans, and—notably—lost opportunities.

Who Says War Is Vanishing?

Most influentially, the argument that war is going away has been made by Steven Pinker in his book *The Better Angels of Our Nature: Why Violence Has Declined*. But it is an argument that can be found in various forms in the work of numerous Western academics.

War, as we have seen, is not actually going away. One way to suggest that it is involves conflating war with other varieties of violence. The death penalty seems to be going away. Spanking and whipping children seems to be going away in some cultures. And so on. These are trends that should help convince people of the case I [have] made . . . : War can be ended. But these trends say nothing about war actually being ended.

The fictional account of war going away treats Western civilization and capitalism as forces for peace. This is done, in large part, by treating Western wars on poor nations as the fault of those poor nations. The U.S. war in Vietnam was the fault of the Vietnamese who weren't enlightened enough to surrender as they should have. The U.S. war in Iraq ended with Bush's declaration of "mission accomplished!" after which the war was a "civil war" and the fault of the backward Iraqis and their lack of Western capitalism. And so on.

Missing from this account is the relentless push for more wars in the U.S., Israeli, and other governments. U.S. media outlets routinely discuss "the next war" as if there simply must be one. Missing is the development of NATO into a global aggressive force. Missing is the danger created by the proliferation of nuclear technology. Missing is the trend toward greater corruption of elections and governance, and the growing—not shrinking—profits of the military industrial complex. Missing is the expansion of U.S. bases and troops into more nations; as well as U.S. provocations toward China, North Korea, Russia, and Iran; increases in military spending by China and many other nations; and misconceptions about past wars including the recent war in Libya and proposals for wider war in Syria.

Wars, in the view of Pinker and other believers in war's vanishing, originate in poor and Muslim nations. Pinker indicates no awareness that wealthy nations fund and arm dictators in poor countries, or that they sometimes "intervene" by dropping that support and dropping bombs along with it. Also likely countries to make war are those with ideologies, Pinker tells us. (As everyone knows, the United States has no ideology.) "The three deadliest postwar conflicts," Pinker writes, "were fueled by Chinese, Korean, and Vietnamese communist regimes that had a fanatical dedication to outlasting their opponents." Pinker goes on to blame the high death rate in Vietnam on the willingness of the Vietnamese to die in large numbers rather than surrender, as he thinks they should have.

The U.S. war on Iraq ended, in Pinker's view, when President George W. Bush declared "mission accomplished," since which point it was a civil war, and therefore the causes of that civil war can be analyzed in terms of the shortcomings of Iraqi society. "[I]t is so hard," Pinker complains, "to impose liberal democracy on countries in the developing world that have not outgrown their superstitions, warlords, and feuding tribes." Indeed it may be, but where is the evidence that the United States government has been attempting it? Or the evidence that the United States has such democracy itself? Or that the United States has the right to impose its desires on another nation?

Early in the book, Pinker presents a pair of charts aimed at showing that, proportionate to population, wars have killed more prehistoric and hunter-gatherer people than people in modern states. None of the prehistoric tribes listed go back earlier than 14,000 B.C.E., meaning that the vast majority of human existence is left out. And these charts list individual tribes and states, not pairs or groups of them that fought in wars. The absence of war through most of human history is left out of the equation, dubious statistics are cited for earlier wars, those statistics are compared to the global population rather than the population of the tribes involved, and—significantly—the deaths counted from recent U.S. wars are only U.S. deaths. And

they're measured against the population of the United States, not the nation attacked. At other times, Pinker measures war deaths against the population of the globe, a measure that doesn't really tell us anything about the level of devastation in the areas where the wars are fought. He also omits indirect or delayed deaths. So the U.S. soldiers killed in Vietnam get counted, but those killed more slowly by Agent Orange or PTSD do not get counted. Of course spears and arrows used in ancient wars did not have the same delayed effects as Agent Orange. U.S. soldiers killed in Afghanistan get counted by Pinker, but the greater number who die a bit later from injuries or suicide do not.

Pinker acknowledges the danger of nuclear proliferation only in a very glass-half-full kind of way:

> If one were to calculate the amount of destruction that nations have actually perpetrated as a proportion of how much they could perpetrate, given the destructive capacity available to them, the postwar [meaning post-World War II] decades would be many orders of magnitudes more peaceable than any time in history [italics added].

So, we're more peaceful because we've built more deadly weapons!

And civilization's progress is good because it progresses.

And yet, after all the fancy footwork calculating our path to peace, we look up and see bloodier wars than ever before, and machinery in place to wage more of them—machinery accepted as unquestionable or literally unnoticed.

Our Wars Aren't Bad Like Your Wars

Pinker isn't alone. Jared Diamond's latest book, *The World Until Yesterday: What We Can Learn from Traditional Societies*, suggests that tribal people live with constant war. His math is as fuzzy as Pinker's. Diamond calculates the deaths from war in Okinawa in 1945, not as a percentage of Okinawans, but as a percentage of all the combatant nations' populations, including the population of the United States, where the war was not fought at all. With this statistic, Diamond claims to prove that World War II was less deadly than violence in an "uncivilized" tribe.

Daniel Jonah Goldhagen's *Worse Than War: Genocide, Eliminationism, and the Ongoing Assault on Humanity* argues that genocide is distinct from war and worse than war. By this means, he redefines portions of wars, such as the U.S. firebombing of Japan or the Nazi holocaust, as not war at all. The portions of wars that are left in the category of war are then justified. For Goldhagen, the war on Iraq was not mass-murder because it was just. The 9/11 attacks were genocide, despite their smaller scale, because unjust. When Saddam Hussein killed Iraqis it was mass murder, but when the United States killed Iraqis it was justified. (Goldhagen doesn't comment on U.S. assistance to Hussein in killing Iraqis.)

Goldhagen argues that ending war should be a lower priority than ending mass murder. But without his Western blinders, war looks like a type of mass murder. War is, in fact, the most acceptable, respectable, and widest spread form of mass-murder around. Making war unacceptable would be a huge step in the direction of making all killing unacceptable. Keeping war in place as a "legitimate" foreign policy tool guarantees that mass murder will continue. And redefining much of what war consists of as non-war fails dramatically at making the case that war is going away.

"There Is Evil in the World"

A common response to arguments for abolishing war is. "No. No. No. You need to understand that there is evil in the world. The world is a dangerous place. There are bad people in the world." And so forth. The act of pointing out this obvious piece of information suggests a very deep acceptance of war as the only possible response to a troubled world, and a complete conviction that war is not itself something evil. Opponents of war do not, of course, believe there is nothing evil in the world. They just place war in that category, if not at the very top of it.

It is the unthinking acceptance of war that keeps war going. Campaigning for president, Hillary Clinton said that if Iran were to launch a nuclear attack against Israel, she would "totally obliterate" Iran. She meant this threat as deterrence, she said. (See video at WarIsACrime.org/Hillary.) At

the time, the Iranian government said, and U.S. intelligence agencies said, that Iran had no nuclear weapons and no nuclear weapons program. Iran had nuclear energy, pushed on it decades earlier by the United States. Of course, Iran's theoretical obliteration of Israel would be just as evil as a U.S. obliteration of Iran. But the United States really does have the capability to launch nuclear weapons at Iran and has repeatedly threatened to do so, with both the Bush and Obama White Houses showing great affection for the phrase "All Options are on the table." They shouldn't be. Such threats should not be made. Talk of obliterating nations should be left behind us. That sort of talk makes it much more difficult to make peace, to truly engage with another nation, to move relations forward to the point where no nation imagines that another is going to develop a horrible weapon and use it.

The MIC

Authors who view war as ending, and as a third-world phenomenon, tend to miss some of the major contributing factors to war, including those encompassed by the phrase "military industrial complex." These factors include the skill of propagandists, the open bribery and corruption of our politics, and the perversion and impoverishment of our educational and entertainment and civic engagement systems that lead so many people in the United States to support and so many others to tolerate a permanent state of war in search of enemies and profits despite decades-long demonstrations that the war machine makes us less safe, drains our economy, strips away our rights, degrades our environment, distributes our income ever upward, debases our morality, and bestows on the wealthiest nation on earth miserably low rankings in life-expectancy, liberty, and the ability to pursue, happiness.

None of these factors are insurmountable, but we won't surmount them if we imagine the path to peace is to impose our superior will on backward foreigners by means of cluster bombs and napalm meant to prevent primitive atrocities.

The military industrial complex is a war-generating engine. It can be dismantled or transformed, but it is not going to stop generating wars on its own without a big push. And it is not going to stop just because we come to the realization that we would really, really like it to stop. Work is going to be required.

A couple of years ago, National Public Radio interviewed a weapons executive. Asked what he would do if the hugely profitable occupation of Afghanistan were to end, he replied that he hoped there could be an occupation of Libya. He was clearly joking. And he didn't get his wish—yet. But jokes don't come from nowhere. Had he joked about molesting children or practicing racism his comments would not have aired. Joking about a new war is accepted in our culture as an appropriate joke. In contrast, mocking war as backward and undesirable is just not done, and might be deemed incomprehensible, not to mention unfunny. We have a long way to go.

The Revisionist Imperative: Rethinking Twentieth Century Wars

ANDREW J. BACEVICH

Andrew J. Bacevich retired from the US Army with the rank of Colonel and subsequently became a professor of International Relations and History at Boston University. He is the author of several books, including *Washington Rules: America's Path to Permanent War* (2010) and *Breach of Trust: How Americans Failed Their Soldiers and Their Country* (2013). Due to space limitations, footnotes have been omitted from this selection. Selections from "The Revisionist Imperative: Rethinking Twentieth Century Wars." *Journal of Military History* 76, no. 2 (April 2012): 333–42. Used by permission.

Not long before his untimely death the historian Tony Judt observed that "For many American commentators and policymakers the message of the twentieth century is that war works." Judt might have gone even further. Well beyond the circle of experts and insiders, many ordinary Americans even today at least tacitly share that view.

This reading of the twentieth century has had profound implications for U.S. policy in the twenty-first century. With the possible exception of Israel, the United States today is the only advanced democracy in which belief in war's efficacy continues to enjoy widespread acceptance. Others—the citizens of Great Britain and France, of Germany and Japan—took from the twentieth century a different lesson: War devastates. It impoverishes. It coarsens. Even when seemingly necessary or justified, it entails brutality, barbarism, and the killing of innocents. To choose war is to leap into the dark, entrusting the nation's fate to forces beyond human control.

Americans persist in believing otherwise. That belief manifests itself in a number of ways, not least in a pronounced willingness to invest in, maintain, and employ military power. (The belief that war works has not made soldiering per se a popular vocation; Americans prefer war as a spectator sport rather than as a participatory one.)

Why do Americans cling to a belief in war that other advanced nations have long since abandoned? The simple answer is that for a time, war *did* work or seemed to anyway—at least for the United States, even if not for others. After all, the vast conflagration we remember not altogether appropriately as "World War II" vaulted the United States to the very summit of global power. The onset of that conflict found Americans still struggling to cope with a decade-long economic crisis. Recall that the unemployment rate in 1939 was several percentage points above the highest point it has reached during our own Great Recession.

Notwithstanding the palliative effects of Franklin Roosevelt's New Deal, the long-term viability of liberal democratic capitalism during the 1930s remained an open question. Other ideological claimants, on the far left and far right, were advancing a strong case that they defined the future.

By 1945, when the conflict ended, almost all of that had changed. At home, war restored economic prosperity and set the stage for a decades-long boom. At least as important, the war reinvigorated confidence in American institutions. The challenges of war management had prodded Washington to get its act together. Prodigious feats of production in places like Cleveland, Detroit, and Pittsburgh had enabled the United States to raise vast air, sea, and land forces, which it then employed on a global scale with considerable effectiveness.

The American way of war implied a remarkable knack for doing big things in a big way, sweeping aside whatever obstacles might stand in the way. The bumptious wartime motto of the army corps of engineers testified to this approach: "The difficult we do at once; the impossible takes a little longer." This wasn't empty bluster: the Manhattan Project, culminating in the development of the atomic bomb, testified to American technical prowess, but also implied broader claims of superiority. The United States was once again a country that did things—really big things—that no other country could do.

Meanwhile, with the gross domestic product doubling in barely half a decade, the American way of life once again signified levels of material abundance that made its citizens the envy of the world. Thanks in considerable part to war, in other words, the United States had become an economic, technological, political, military, and cultural juggernaut without peer.

/ . . .

. . . For history to serve more than an ornamental function, it must speak to the present. The version of past formed by World War II and perpetuated since—the version persuading Americans that war works—has increasingly little to say. Yet even as the utility of that account dissipates, its grip on the American collective consciousness persists. The times, therefore, are ripe for revisionism. Replacing the canonical account of the twentieth century with something more germane to actually existing circumstances prevailing in the twenty-first century has become an imperative.

And that requires rethinking the role of war in contemporary history. In any such revisionist project, military historians should play a prominent part. . . .

. . . To illustrate the possibilities of revisionist inquiry, let me advance the following broad proposition for your consideration: for citizens of the twenty-first century, the twentieth century actually has two quite different stories to tell. The first story is familiar, although imperfectly understood. The second is little known, with large implications that have gone almost entirely ignored.

Enshrined today as a story of freedom besieged, but ultimately triumphant, the familiar story began back in 1914 and continued until its (apparently) definitive conclusion in 1989. Call this the Short Twentieth Century.

The less familiar alternative recounts a story in which freedom as such has figured only intermittently. It has centered on the question of who will dominate the region that we today call the Greater Middle East. Also kicking into high gear in 1914, this story continues to unfold in the present day, with no end in sight. Call this the story of the Long Twentieth Century.

The Short Twentieth Century, geographically centered on Eurasia, pitted great powers against one another. Although alignments shifted depending on circumstance, the roster of major players remained fairly constant. That roster consisted of Great Britain, France, Germany, Russia, and Japan, with the United States biding its time before eventually picking up most of the marbles.

From time to time, the Long Twentieth Century has also pitted great powers against one another. Yet that struggle has always had a second element. It has been a contest between outsiders and insiders. Western intruders with large ambitions, preeminently Great Britain until succeeded by the United States, pursued their dreams of empire or hegemony, typically cloaked in professions of "benevolent assimilation," uplift, or the pursuit of world peace. The beneficiaries of imperial ministrations—from Arabs in North Africa to Moros in the southern Philippines along with sundry groups in between—seldom proved grateful and frequently resisted.

The Short Twentieth Century had a moral and ideological aspect. If not especially evident at first, this became clearer over time.

Viewed in retrospect, President Woodrow Wilson's effort to portray the cataclysm of 1914–1918 as a struggle of democracy versus militarism appears more than a little strained. The problem is not that Germany was innocent of the charge of militarism. It is, rather, that Western theories of democracy in those days left more than a little to be desired. After all, those who labored under the yoke of British, French, and American rule across large swathes of Africa, Asia, and the Middle East enjoyed precious little freedom.

Yet the advent of the Third German Reich produced a moral clarity hitherto more theoretical than real. The war against Nazi Germany was indubitably a war on behalf of liberal democracy against vile, murderous totalitarianism. Of course, sustaining that construct is easier if you survey the events of World War II with one eye covered.

The central event of the Short Twentieth Century loses some of its moral luster once you acknowledge the following:

- First, concern for the fate of European Jewry exercised no discernible influence on allied conduct of the war, allied forces failing to make any serious attempt to avert, halt, or even retard the Final Solution;
- Second, in both Europe and the Pacific, allied strategic bombing campaigns killed noncombatants indiscriminately on a scale dwarfing, say, the atrocity of 9/11;
- Third, the price of liberating western Europe included the enslavement of eastern Europeans, a direct consequence of allocating to Uncle Joe Stalin's Red Army primary responsibility for defeating the Wehrmacht;
- Fourth, at war's end, the victors sanctioned campaigns of ethnic cleansing on a scale not seen before or since, while offering employment to scientists, engineers, and intelligence operatives who had loyally served the Third Reich;
- Fifth, on the American home front, the war fought for freedom and democracy left intact a well-entrenched system of de facto apartheid, racial equality not numbering among Franklin Roosevelt's Four Freedoms.

None of these disturbing facts, it need hardly be said, made any significant impact on the way World War II became enshrined in American memory. I do not recall encountering any of them while watching *Victory at Sea*.

Yet these facts matter. They remind us that if the Short American Century was *sometimes* about values, it was *always* about politics and power. The allies who joined together to defeat the Axis (a righteous cause) did not hesitate to employ means that were anything but righteous. In pursuit of that righteous cause, they simultaneously connived and jockeyed against one another for relative advantage on matters related to oil, territory, markets, and the preservation of imperial privilege.

Whether out of conscience or expediency, the onset of the postwar era soon enough prompted Americans to rethink some (but not all) of the morally dubious practices that made it necessary to sanitize the narrative of World War II.

So after 1945, liberal democracies, the United States now in the vanguard, turned on the leftwing totalitarianism that had played such a crucial role in the fight against rightwing totalitarianism. No longer a valued ally, Stalin became the new Hitler. At home meanwhile, the United States also began to amend the pronounced defects in its own approach to democratic practice. However haltingly, for example, the modern civil rights movement commenced. Both of these facilitated efforts by Cold Warriors to infuse the anti-communist crusade, successor to the anti-Axis crusade, with an ennobling moral clarity. The ensuing struggle between an American-led West and a Soviet-led East, in their view, deserved to be seen as an extension of World War II.

As with World War II, therefore, so too with the Cold War: American leaders insistently framed the contest in ideological rather than in geopolitical terms. The Free World ostensibly asked nothing more than that freedom itself should survive. This served to camouflage the real stakes: rival powers, previous wars having reduced their ranks to two, were vying for primacy in Eurasia, that long contest now reaching its penultimate chapter.

This framing device had important implications when the era of bipolarity came to its abrupt and surprising end. I don't know about you, but recalling the events that unfolded between 1978 when John Paul II became pope and 1989 when the Berlin Wall came down still makes me dizzy.

Right before our very eyes, history had seemingly handed down a conclusive verdict. The search for alternatives to liberal democratic capitalism had failed. That failure was definitive. The Short Twentieth Century was kaput. Born 1914. Died 1989. Finis.

During what turned out to be a very abbreviated post–Cold War era, American politicians and commentators vied with one another to devise a suitably grandiose conception of what the passing of the Short Twentieth Century signified.

Whatever the specifics, the results were sure to be very good and very long lasting. As the "sole superpower," America now stood in solitary splendor, recognized by all as the "indispensable nation," able to discern even as it simultaneously embodied "the right side of history."

My text encloses those phrases in quotes. But during the 1990s, ostensibly serious people issuing such pronouncements did not intend to be ironic. They were merely reciting what had become the conventional wisdom. As well they might. Expanding on or embroidering such themes got your books on bestseller lists, your columns in all the best newspapers, and your smiling face on the Sunday talk shows.

My favorite artifact of this era remains the *New York Times Magazine* dated 28 March 1999. The cover story excerpted *The Lexus and the Olive Tree*, Tom Friedman's just-released celebration of globalization-as-Americanization. The cover itself purported to illustrate "What the World Needs Now." Alongside a photograph of a clenched fist adorned with the Stars and Stripes in brilliant red, white, and blue appeared this text: "For globalism to work, America can't be afraid to act like the almighty superpower that it is."

This was the *New York Times*, mind you, not the *Weekly Standard* or the editorial pages of the *Wall Street Journal*.

More or less overlooked amidst all this triumphalism was the fact that the other twentieth century—the one in which promoting freedom had never figured as a priority—continued without interruption. In Egypt, Saudi Arabia, the West Bank, Iraq, Iran, and Afghanistan, the collapse of communism did not qualify as a cosmic event. In such places, the competition to dominate Eurasia had been a sideshow, not the main event. So the *annus mirabilis* of 1989 notwithstanding, the Long Twentieth Century continued apace, drawing the almighty superpower ever more deeply into what was fast becoming one helluva mess.

For those with a taste for irony try this one: 1991 was the year in which the U.S.S.R. finally gave up the ghost; it was also the year of the First Persian Gulf War. One headache went away; another was about to become a migraine.

In making the case for war against Iraq, George H. W. Bush depicted Saddam Hussein as a Hitler-like menace—neither the first nor the last time the infamous Führer would play a walk-on role in climes far removed from Germany. Indeed, Adolf Hitler has enjoyed an impressive second career as a sort of stunt-double for Middle Eastern villains. Recall that back in 1956, to justify the reckless Anglo-French-Israeli assault on Egypt, Prime Minister Anthony Eden had fingered Colonel Nasser as another Hitler. Not long ago, Lindsey Graham, the reflexively hawkish Republican senator from South Carolina, likened Libya's Muammar Gaddafi to the Nazi leader. More recently still, the journalist Max Boot, who has made a career out of promoting war, has discovered Hitler's spirit lurking in present-day Iran.

However absurd such comparisons, the Nazi dictator's periodic guest appearances make an important point. They illustrate the persistent Western disinclination to see the struggle for the Greater Middle East on its own terms. Instead, to explain developments there, Western leaders import clichés or stock figures ripped from the more familiar and, from their perspective, more reassuring Short Twentieth Century. In doing so, they confuse themselves and us.

Alas, the elder Bush's effort to eliminate his Hitler came up short. Celebrated in its day as a great victory, Operation Desert Storm turned out to be anything but that. The First Persian Gulf

War deserves to be remembered chiefly as a source of wildly inflated and pernicious illusions. More than any other event, this brief conflict persuaded Washington, now freed of constraints imposed by the Cold War, that the application of U.S. military power held the key to reordering the Greater Middle East in ways likely to serve American interests. Here, it seemed, was evidence that war still worked and worked handsomely indeed.

Flexing U.S. military muscle on the battlefields of Europe and the Pacific had once made America stronger and the world a better place. Why not count on American power to achieve similar results in the Persian Gulf and Central Asia? Why not take the means that had seemingly brought the Short Twentieth Century to such a happy conclusion and apply them to the problems of the Greater Middle East?

Throughout the 1990s, neoconservatives and other jingoists vigorously promoted this view. After 9/11, George W. Bush made it his own. So in explaining what had happened on 11 September 2001 and what needed to happen next, President Bush appropriated precepts from the Short Twentieth Century. It was going to be World War II and the Cold War all over again.

"We have seen their kind before," the president said of the terrorists who had assaulted America. The occasion was an address before a joint session of Congress barely more than a week after the attack on the World Trade Center. "They're the heirs of all the murderous ideologies of the 20th century," he continued.

> By sacrificing human life to serve their radical visions, by abandoning every value except the will to power, they follow in the path of fascism, Nazism and totalitarianism. And they will follow that path all the way to where it ends in history's unmarked grave of discarded lies.

Lest there be any doubt of where Bush was situating himself historically, he made a point of warmly welcoming the British prime minister to the proceedings. "America has no truer friend than Great Britain," the president declared, adding that "once again, we are joined together in a great cause." The implications were clear: the partnership of Tony and George revived the tradition of Winston and Franklin and of Maggie and Ron. Good once again stood firm against evil.

. . .

Even so, many gullible (or cynical) observers endorsed President Bush's interpretation. September 2001 became December 1941 all over again. Once again World War II—unwelcome or inconvenient details excluded, as always—was pressed into service as "a moral memory palace." As the bellicose authors of a great agitprop classic published in 2004 put it, "There is no middle way for Americans: it is victory or holocaust." And so a new crusade—preposterously dubbed World War IV in some quarters—commenced.

Since then, more than a decade has elapsed. Although President Bush is gone, the war he declared continues. Once commonly referred to as the Global War on Terror (World War IV never really caught on), today we hardly know what to call the enterprise.

Bush's attempt to graft the putative rationale for war during the Short Twentieth Century onto the new wars in the Greater Middle East didn't take. His Freedom Agenda withered and died. Even so, with Bush's successor closing down some fronts, ratcheting up others, and opening up new ones in places like Pakistan, Yemen, and Libya, the conflict itself persists. It's become the Long War—a collection of nominally related "overseas contingency operations," defined chiefly by their duration. Once begun, campaigns continue indefinitely.

What then of the American conviction, drawn from the remembered experience of the Short Twentieth Century, that "war works"? What evidence exists to suggest that this proposition retains any validity? Others may differ, but I see little to indicate that our affinity for war is making the country more powerful or more prosperous. If anything, a plethora of socio-economic indicators suggest that the reverse is true.

Whatever the United States is experiencing today, it's not a reprise of World War II. Newsmagazines may enthuse over today's Iraq and Afghanistan veterans as our "New Greatest Generation," but they overlook a rather large distinction. In contrast to the opportunities that awaited the previous "Greatest Generation" when its members came home, the wars fought by today's veterans point toward a bleaker rather than a brighter future.

History—the version that privileges the Short Twentieth Century above all other possibilities—makes it difficult to grasp the quandary in which we find ourselves as a consequence of our penchant for using force. After all, that account instructs us that "war works" or at least ought to if we simply try hard enough.

Yet it's just possible that a more expansive and less self-congratulatory accounting of the recent past—one that treats the Long Twentieth Century with the respect it deserves—could potentially provide a way out. To put it another way, we need to kick down the doors of the moral memory palace. We need to let in some fresh air.

I am not thereby suggesting that the canonical lessons of the Short Twentieth Century have lost all relevance. Far from it. Yet it's past time to restock our storehouse of policy-relevant parables. This means according to the Sykes–Picot agreement and the Hussein–McMahon correspondence, FDR's tête-à-tête with King Ibn Saud and the killing of Count Bernadotte by Zionist assassins, the Anglo-American conspiracy to depose Mohammed Mossadegh and the bizarre Suez crisis, the Iran-Contra affair and, yes, Operation Iraqi Freedom, pedagogical weight equal to that habitually accorded to Munich, Pearl Harbor, and Auschwitz.

We could do with just a bit less of the Churchill who stood defiantly alone against Hitler. We might permit a bit more of the Churchill who, seeking ways after World War I to police the Middle East on the cheap, pushed for "experimental work on gas bombs, especially mustard gas" as a way to "inflict punishment on recalcitrant natives."

Implicit in the standard American account of the Short Twentieth Century is the conviction that history is purposeful, with the vigorous deployment of U.S. power the best way to hasten history's arrival at its intended destination. A sober appreciation of the surprises, miscalculations, and disappointments permeating the Long Twentieth Century, beginning with Great Britain's cavalier decision to dismember the Ottoman Empire and running all the way to George W. Bush's ill-fated attempt to transform the Greater Middle East, should temper any such expectations. What the Long Twentieth Century teaches above all is humility.

. . .

William Faulkner famously said of the past that "It's not dead. It's not even past." As a general proposition, there's something to be said for that view. Not in this case, however. The past that Americans know is worse than dead; it's become a cause of self-inflicted wounds. As historians, we need to do better. The means to do so are readily at hand.

DISCUSSION QUESTIONS

1. Analyze which of the zeros in the seven "collection of categories of war" that Pinker describes most strongly and which least supports his claim we are living in a period of long peace.

2. Evaluate how well David Swanson refutes Pinker's claim that the dangers of war are decreasing.

3. Summarize the conclusions that Andrew J. Bacevich says can be drawn from the United States' wars in the Long Twentieth Century and show how he claims that these correct the false conclusions commonly drawn from the United States' wars in the Short Twentieth Century.

4. Explain which of the three selections in this section you believe offers the most accurate perspective on contemporary trends in war; next, explain which of the three selections you believe to be the least accurate.

5. Adopt one of the three perspectives on contemporary trends in war presented in this section and use it to construct some principles that could be used to guide a major nation's public and foreign policies.

Debates about Security
and Effects of War

In the final selection of section 1, Andrew J. Bacevich argues that the United States' many wars over the last 100 years have failed to make the country safer. Debates about claims like Bacevich's often prove inconclusive, in part because there is disagreement about what "safety" means. For many, safety is associated with a strong, active military that is able when called on to project lethal force across the world. The United States' and many other nations' foreign policies rely on just such an approach to safety through force projection. These policies identify safety with national security, with the preservation of nation-state borders and current governments, rather than with human security and with assuring the human rights of individuals, communities, and groups within nation-states.

In the first selection following, Ian Morris explains why he believes global projections of lethal military force are necessary for nations that aspire to be both rich and safe. Morris focuses on the militarized understanding of national security that encouraged the United States to use its resources to kill or to support others in killing people in well over two dozen countries since the end of WWII. Today, the United States simultaneously maintains over one million people in its active-duty military, possesses the world's largest air force and stockpile of nuclear weapons, and deploys the world's largest navy to patrol international waters along the coasts of all continents. In addition, the United States currently maintains about 800 military bases in over 60 countries beyond its own borders. All other nations combined maintain about 30 such overseas bases.

In the second selection, Martin Longman disputes Morris's support for foreign policies that emulate the British, Roman, and other earlier empires. Longman proposes that it is not aggressive military action but rather healthy, functioning central governments that are more likely to create riches and safety today.

Tom Engelhardt offers additional arguments against Morris's positive view of war in a third selection. Engelhardt maintains that the United States' "military-first approach to the world" has been an "unparalleled failure." Engelhardt details five separate lessons from the last half century of American wars, which, he contends, demonstrate that war does not foster either safety or peace.

A final selection, Christopher Holshek's "People Power," calls for foreign policies that shift from an emphasis on national security to ones that promote human security. *National security* approaches encourage wars that at best attack troublesome symptoms, Holshek contends, while *human security* policies can build sustainable peace systems that treat social diseases. He asserts that government programs, budgets, and operations should promote human rights for people in every region of the world. People feel and actually are safer, Holshek argues, when their leaders wage few or no wars while focusing instead on protecting human rights.

The selections in section 2 focus primarily on the United States, but the arguments each writer makes apply to other contemporary nation-states as well.

In the Long Run, Wars Make Us Safer and Richer

BY IAN MORRIS

Ian Morris, a professor of classics at Stanford University, is the author of *War! What is it Good For? Conflict and the Progress of Civilization from Primates to Robots* (2014). From *The Washington Post*, April 25, 2014 © 2014 The Washington Post. All rights reserved. Used by permission and protected by the Copyright Laws of the United States. The printing, copying, redistribution, or retransmission of this Content without express written permission is prohibited.

Norman Angell, the Paris editor of Britain's Daily Mail, was a man who expected to be listened to. Yet even he was astonished by the success of his book "The Great Illusion," in which he announced that war had put itself out of business. "The day for progress by force has passed," he explained. From now on, "it will be progress by ideas or not at all."

He wrote these words in 1910. One politician after another lined up to praise the book. Four years later, the same men started World War I. By 1918, they had killed 15 million people; by 1945, the death toll from two world wars had passed 100 million and a nuclear arms race had begun. In 1983, U.S. war games suggested that an all-out battle with the Soviet Union would kill a billion people—at the time, one human in five—in the first few weeks. And today, a century after the beginning of the Great War, civil war is raging in Syria, tanks are massing on Ukraine's borders and a fight against terrorism seems to have no end.

So yes, war is hell—but have you considered the alternatives? When looking upon the long run of history, it becomes clear that through 10,000 years of conflict, humanity has created larger, more organized societies that have greatly reduced the risk that their members will die violently. These better organized societies also have created the conditions for higher living standards and economic growth. War has not only made us safer, but richer, too.

Thinkers have long grappled with the relationships among peace, war and strength. Thomas Hobbes wrote his case for strong government, "Leviathan," as the English Civil War raged around him in the 1640s. German sociologist Norbert Elias's two-volume treatise, "The Civilizing Process," published on the eve of World War II, argued that Europe had become a more peaceful place in the five centuries leading to his own day. The difference is that now we have the evidence to prove their case.

Take the long view. The world of the Stone Age, for instance, was a rough place; 10,000 years ago, if someone used force to settle an argument, he or she faced few constraints. Killing was normally on a small scale, in homicides, vendettas and raids, but because populations were tiny, the steady drip of low-level killing took an appalling toll. By many estimates, 10 to 20 percent of all Stone Age humans died at the hands of other people.

This puts the past 100 years in perspective. Since 1914, we have endured world wars, genocides and government-sponsored famines, not to mention civil strife, riots and murders. Altogether, we have killed a staggering 100 million to 200 million of our own kind. But over the century, about 10 billion lives were lived—which means that just 1 to 2 percent of the world's population died violently. Those lucky enough to be born in the 20th century were on average 10 times less likely to come to a grisly end than those born in the Stone Age. And since 2000, the United Nations tells us, the risk of violent death has fallen even further, to 0.7 percent.

As this process unfolded, humanity prospered. Ten thousand years ago, when the planet's population was 6 million or so, people lived about 30 years on average and supported themselves on the equivalent income of about $2 per day. Now, more than 7 billion people are on Earth, living more than twice as long (an average of 67 years), and with an average income of $25 per day.

This happened because about 10,000 years ago, the winners of wars began incorporating the losers into larger societies. The victors found that the only way to make these larger societies work was by developing stronger governments; and one of the first things these governments had to do, if they wanted to stay in power, was suppress violence among their subjects.

The men who ran these governments were no saints. They cracked down on killing not out of the goodness of their hearts but because well-behaved subjects were easier to govern and tax than angry, murderous ones. The unintended consequence, though, was that they kick-started the process through which rates of violent death plummeted between the Stone Age and the 20th century.

This process was brutal. Whether it was the Romans in Britain or the British in India, pacification could be just as bloody as the savagery it stamped out. Yet despite the Hitlers, Stalins and Maos, over 10,000 years, war made states, and states made peace.

War may well be the worst way imaginable to create larger, more peaceful societies, but the depressing fact is that it is pretty much the only way. If only the Roman Empire could have been created without killing millions of Gauls and Greeks, if the United States could have been built without killing millions of Native Americans, if these and countless conflicts could have been resolved by discussion instead of force. But this did not happen. People almost never give up their freedoms—including, at times, the right to kill and impoverish one another—unless forced to do so; and virtually the only force strong enough to bring this about has been defeat in war or fear that such a defeat is imminent.

The civilizing process also was uneven. Violence spiked up and down. For 1,000 years—beginning before Attila the Hun in the A.D. 400s and ending after Genghis Khan in the 1200s—mounted invaders from the steppes actually threw the process of pacification into reverse everywhere from China to Europe, with war breaking down larger, safer societies into smaller, more dangerous ones. Only in the 1600s did big, settled states find an answer to the nomads, in the shape of guns that delivered enough firepower to stop horsemen in their tracks. Combining these guns with new, oceangoing ships, Europeans exported unprecedented amounts of violence around the world. The consequences were terrible; and yet they created the largest societies yet seen, driving rates of violent death lower than ever before.

By the 18th century, vast European empires straddled the oceans, and Scottish philosopher Adam Smith saw that something new was happening. For millennia, conquest, plunder and taxes had made rulers rich, but now, Smith realized, markets were so big that a new path to the wealth of nations was opening. Taking it, however, was complicated. Markets would work best if governments got out of them, leaving people to truck and barter; but markets would only work at all if governments got into them, enforcing their rules and keeping trade free. The solution, Smith implied, was not a Leviathan but a kind of super-Leviathan that would police global trade.

After Napoleon's defeat in 1815, this was precisely what the world got. Britain was the only industrialized economy on Earth, and it projected power as far away as India and China. Because its wealth came from exporting goods and services, it used its financial and naval muscle to deter rivals from threatening the international order. Wars did not end—the United States and China endured civil strife, European armies marched deep into Africa and India—but overall, for 99 years, the planet grew more peaceful and prosperous under Britain's eye.

However, the Pax Britannica rested on a paradox. To sell its goods and services, Britain needed other countries to be rich enough to buy them. That meant that, like it or not, Britain had to encourage other nations to industrialize and accumulate wealth. The economic triumph of the 19th-century British world system, however, was simultaneously a strategic disaster. Thanks in significant part to British capital and expertise, the United States and Germany had turned into industrial giants by the 1870s, and doubts began growing about Britain's ability to police the global order. The more successful the globocop was at doing its job, the more difficult that job became.

By the 1910s, some of the politicians who had so admired Angell's "Great Illusion" had concluded that war was no longer the worst of their options. The violence they unleashed bankrupted Britain and threw the world into chaos. Not until 1989 did the wars and almost wars finally end, when the Soviet collapse left the United States as a much more powerful policeman than Britain had ever been.

Like its predecessor, the United States oversaw a huge expansion of trade, intimidated other countries into not making wars that would disturb the world order, and drove rates of violent death even lower. But again like Britain, America made its money by helping trading partners become richer,

above all China, which, since 2000, has looked increasingly like a potential rival. The cycle that Britain experienced may be in store for the United States as well, unless Washington embraces its role as the only possible globocop in an increasingly unstable world—a world with far deadlier weapons than Britain could have imagined a century ago.

American attitudes toward government are therefore not just some Beltway debate; they matter to everyone on Earth. "Government," Ronald Reagan assured Americans in his first inaugural address, "is not the solution to our problem; government is the problem." Reagan's great fear—that bloated government would stifle individual freedom—shows just how far the continuing debates over the merits of big and small government have taken us from the horrors that worried Hobbes. "The 10 most dangerous words in the English language," Reagan said on another occasion, "are 'Hi, I'm from the government, and I'm here to help.'" As Hobbes could have told him, in reality the 10 scariest words are, "There is no government and I'm here to kill you."

To people in virtually any age before our own, the only argument that mattered was between extremely small government and no government at all. Extremely small government meant there was at least some law and order; no government meant that there was not.

I suspect even Reagan would have agreed. "One legislator accused me of having a 19th-century attitude on law and order," Reagan said when he was governor of California. "That is a totally false charge. I have an 18th-century attitude. That is when the Founding Fathers made it clear that the safety of law-abiding citizens should be one of the government's primary concerns."

Orwellian Piece by Ian Morris

MARTIN LONGMAN

Martin Longman is the web editor for the *Washington Monthly* and a former political consultant for Democracy for America. He is a frequent guest blogger at *Political Animal*. From *Washington Monthly*. April 27, 2014. © 2014 Washington Monthly Publishing, LLC. Used by permission.

Ian Morris, a professor of Classics at Stanford, argues in the *Washington Post* that, in the long run, wars make us safer and richer. Perhaps it is just too difficult to make such a counterintuitive argument within the limited space of an opinion column, but his piece is one big mess.

The essence of his point is that modern people are much less likely to die violent deaths (at the hands of other humans) than stone-age people were, and that the reason for this is because we have formed large societies. In order to form large societies, we needed a long series of subjugations where the vanquished were not killed but brought into the conquerors' system. To accomplish this, governments were formed with the primary job of pacifying their subjects through a variety of means, including law enforcement. Therefore, war and coercion are not the evils that they may seem to be at first consideration. He might have added religion to the mix here, but he didn't.

One might ask why he wrote this column in the first place. Does he think we aren't fighting enough wars? To get some idea of his motivation, you have to read to near the end, where he appears to compare the United States to the British Empire and suggest that we need to have the stomach to be the global sons of bitches the whole world needs us to be.

. . .

Why is this piece such a mess?

First, retracing the history of societal formation and noting that war and coercion were indispensable tools in those formations doesn't obviously tell us anything about whether or not we can improve people's safety or make them richer by using war and coercion today.

Even in his piece, Prof. Morris notes that war may not make societies bigger and stronger, even in the long term.

> For 1,000 years—beginning before Attila the Hun in the A.D. 400s and ending after Genghis Khan in the 1200s—mounted invaders from the steppes actually threw the process of pacification into reverse everywhere from China to Europe, with war breaking down larger, safer societies into smaller, more dangerous ones.

In fact, he begins his piece by referencing a retrospectively naive book written in 1910 that predicted that war had become obsolete. But he doesn't explain how World War One made people safer or richer.

I think we can see in places like Congo, Syria, Sudan, Libya, and Iraq that the absence of sufficient force can make people less safe and much poorer. Perhaps the people in those countries would benefit if someone came along who was strong enough to subjugate all the warring factions and make them live peacefully together. But, of course, these theoretical strongmen would have to kill and threaten to kill a lot of people in order to accomplish their goals. And that would definitely *not* make people safer or richer in the short term.

To some degree, Prof. Morris seems to be arguing in favor of larger societies that use bigger governmental organizations because these bring more people together and protects them better than smaller societies with less coercive capability. He could have made an argument in favor of the nation-state as an innovation that brought more peace than war. But he chose to argue that war is, in itself, even in this day and age, a positive good. War is Peace, in other words.

And America needs to bring the peace.

Post-9/11 US Foreign Policy: A Record of Unparalleled Failure

BY TOM ENGELHARDT

Tom Engelhardt, cofounder of the American Empire Project, runs the Nation Institute's TomDispatch.com. His latest book, coauthored with Nick Turse, is *Terminator Planet: The First History of Drone Warfare, 2001-2050* (2012). From TomDispatch.com, June 10, 2014. Used by permission.

The United States has been at war—major boots-on-the-ground conflicts and minor interventions, firefights, air strikes, drone assassination campaigns, occupations, special ops raids, proxy conflicts, and covert actions—nearly nonstop since the Vietnam War began. That's more than half a century of experience with war, American-style, and yet few in our world bother to draw the obvious conclusions.

Given the historical record, those conclusions should be staring us in the face. They are, however, the words that can't be said in a country committed to a military-first approach to the world, a continual build-up of its forces, an emphasis on pioneering work in the development and deployment of the latest destructive technology, and a repetitious cycling through styles of war from full-scale invasions and occupations to counterinsurgency, proxy wars, and back again.

So here are five straightforward lessons—none acceptable in what passes for discussion and debate in this country—that could be drawn from that last half century of every kind of American warfare:

. . .

1. ***American-style war doesn't work***. Just ask yourself: Are there fewer terrorists or more in our world . . . after the 9/11 attacks? Are al-Qaeda-like groups more or less common? Are they more or less well organized? Do they have more or less members? The answers to those questions are obvious: more, more, more, and more. In fact, according to a new RAND report, between 2010 and 2013 alone, jihadist groups grew by 58%, their fighters doubled, and their attacks nearly tripled.

On September 12, 2001, al-Qaeda was a relatively small organization with a few camps in arguably the most feudal and backward country on the planet, and tiny numbers of adherents scattered elsewhere around the world. Today, al-Qaeda-style outfits and jihadist groups control significant parts of Syria, Iraq, Pakistan, and even Yemen, and are thriving and spreading in parts of Africa as well.

Or try questions like these: Is Iraq a peaceful, liberated state allied with and under Washington's aegis, with "enduring camps" filled with U.S. troops on its territory? Or is it a riven, embattled, dilapidated country whose government is close to Iran and some of whose Sunni-dominated areas are under the control of a group that is more extreme than al-Qaeda? Is Afghanistan a peaceful, thriving, liberated land under the American aegis, or are Americans still fighting there . . . against the Taliban, an impossible-to-defeat minority movement it once destroyed and then, because it couldn't stop fighting the "war on terror," helped revive? Is Washington now supporting a weak, corrupt central government in a country that once again is planting record opium crops?

But let's not belabor the point. Who, except a few neocons still plunking for the glories of "the surge" in Iraq, would claim military victory for this country, even of a limited sort, anywhere at any time in this century?

2. ***American-style wars don't solve problems***. In these years, you could argue that not a single U.S. military campaign or militarized act ordered by Washington solved a single problem anywhere. In fact, it's possible that just about every military move Washington has made only increased the

burden of problems on this planet. To make the case, you don't even have to focus on the obvious like, for example, the way a special operations and drone campaign in Yemen has actually al-Qaeda-ized some of that country's rural areas. Take instead a rare Washington "success": the killing of Osama bin Laden in a special ops raid in Abbottabad, Pakistan. (And leave aside the way even that act was over-militarized: an unarmed Bin Laden was shot down in his Pakistani lair largely, it's plausible to assume, because officials in Washington feared what once would have been the American way—putting him on trial in a U.S. civilian court for his crimes.) We now know that, in the hunt for bin Laden, the CIA launched a fake hepatitis B vaccination project. Though it proved of no use, once revealed it made local jihadists so nervous about medical health teams that they began killing groups of polio vaccination workers, an urge that has since spread to Boko Haram-controlled areas of Nigeria. In this way, according to Columbia University public health expert Leslie Roberts, "the distrust sowed by the sham campaign in Pakistan could conceivably postpone polio eradication for 20 years, leading to 100,000 more cases that might otherwise not have occurred." The CIA has since promised not to do it again, but too late—and who at this point would believe the Agency anyway? This was, to say the least, an unanticipated consequence of the search for bin Laden, but blowback everywhere, invariably unexpected, has been a hallmark of American campaigns of all sorts.

Similarly, the NSA's surveillance regime, another form of global intervention by Washington, has—experts are convinced—done little or nothing to protect Americans from terror attacks. It has, however, done a great deal to damage the interests of America's tech corporations and to increase suspicion and anger over Washington's policies even

among allies. And by the way, congratulations are due on one of the latest military moves of the Obama administration, the sending of U.S. military teams and drones into Nigeria and neighboring countries to help rescue those girls kidnapped by the extremist group Boko Haram. The rescue was a remarkable success . . . oops, *didn't happen* (and we don't even know yet what the blowback will be).

3. *American-style war is a destabilizing force.* Just look at the effects of American war in the twenty-first century. It's clear, for instance, that the U.S. invasion of Iraq in 2003 unleashed a brutal, bloody, Sunni-Shiite civil war across the region (as well as the Arab Spring, one might argue). One result of that invasion and the subsequent occupation, as well as of the wars and civil wars that followed: the deaths of hundreds of thousands of Iraqis, Syrians, and Lebanese, while major areas of Syria and some parts of Iraq have fallen into the hands of armed supporters of al-Qaeda or, in one major case, a group that didn't find that organization extreme enough. A significant part of the oil heartlands of the planet is, that is, being destabilized.

Meanwhile, the U.S. war in Afghanistan and the CIA's drone assassination campaign in the tribal borderlands of neighboring Pakistan have destabilized that country, which now has its own fierce Taliban movement. The 2011 U.S. intervention in Libya initially seemed like a triumph, as had the invasions of Iraq and Afghanistan before it. Libyan autocrat Muammar Gaddafi was overthrown and the rebels swept into power. Like Afghanistan and Iraq, however, Libya is now a basket case, riven by competing militias and ambitious generals, largely ungovernable, and an open wound for the region. Arms from Gaddafi's looted arsenals have made their way into the hands of Islamist rebels and jihadist extremists from the Sinai Peninsula to Mali, from Northern Africa to northern Nigeria, where Boko Haram is entrenched. It is even possible, as Nick Turse has done, to trace the growing U.S. military presence in Africa to the destabilization of parts of that continent.

4. *The U.S. military can't win its wars.* This is so obvious (though seldom said) that it hardly has to be explained. The U.S. military has not won a serious engagement since World War II: the results of wars in Korea, Vietnam, Afghanistan, and Iraq ranged from stalemate to defeat and disaster. With the exception of a couple of campaigns against essentially no one (in Grenada and Panama), nothing, including the "Global War on Terror," would qualify as a success on its own terms, no less anyone else's. This was true, strategically speaking, despite the fact that, in all these wars, the U.S. controlled the air space, the seas (where relevant), and just about any field of battle where the enemy might be met. Its firepower was overwhelming and its ability to lose in small-scale combat just about nil.

It would be folly to imagine that this record represents the historical norm. It doesn't. It might be more relevant to suggest that the sorts of imperial wars and wars of pacification the U.S. has fought in recent times, often against poorly armed, minimally trained, minority insurgencies (or terror outfits), are simply unwinnable. They seem to generate their own resistance. Their brutalities and even their "victories" simply act as recruitment posters for the enemy.

5. *The U.S. military is not "the finest fighting force the world has ever known" or "the greatest force for human liberation the world has ever known," or any of the similar over-the-top descriptions that U.S. presidents are now regularly obligated to use.* If you want the explanation for why this is so, see points one through four above. A military whose way of war doesn't work, doesn't solve problems, destabilizes whatever it touches, and never wins simply can't be the greatest in history, no matter the firepower it musters. If you really need further proof of this, think about the crisis and scandals linked to the Veterans Administration [VA]. They are visibly the fruit of a military mired in frustration, despair, and defeat, not a triumphant one holding high history's banner of victory.

Is there a record like it? More than half a century of American-style war by the most powerful and potentially destructive military on the planet adds up to worse than nothing. If any other institution in American life had a comparable scorecard, it would be shunned like the plague. In reality, the VA has a far better record of success when it comes to the treatment of those broken by our wars than the military does of winning them, and yet its head administrator was forced to resign amid scandal and a media firestorm.

People Power: The United States Has the Blueprint for a Smarter Way to Make Peace

BY CHRISTOPHER HOLSHEK

Christopher Holshek is a Senior Fellow with the Alliance for Peacebuilding and a Veterans for Smart Power Leadership Council member of the U.S. Global Leadership Coalition. Holshek is a retired U.S. Army Civil Affairs officer. From *Foreign Policy*, July 10, 2010. Used by permission.

A little more than a decade ago, as an Army civil affairs officer in a part of Iraq that is now in the hands of Sunni extremists, I questioned my commander's use of conventional tactics in a "battlespace" that was clearly more psychological than physical. "The Iraqi people were the prize in this fight, not the playing field," wrote Tom Ricks, recounting the incident in his book *Fiasco*. As he told my story, Ricks was conveying one of the major lessons of the wars in Iraq and Afghanistan—one that might explain why many Iraqis now prefer the militants of the Islamic State of Iraq and al-Sham (ISIS), which is now calling itself just the Islamic State, over Iraqi forces trained by the same U.S. Army to be warriors far more than public servants. The lesson is remembering that the most important element of Clausewitz's "remarkable trinity"—the people, not the government or the army—is the ultimate determinant of war and peace.

Many responsible for U.S. foreign and national security policy prefer to shelve this critical insight: namely, that the ultimate source of security is with the people. But reality keeps getting in their way—and will continue to as long as they do not fully understand this.

Vietnam began to expose the inefficacies of the industrial-era American way of war—the application of overwhelming force and technology known as the "strategy of annihilation." This wholesale, materialistic approach peaked during World War II and the Cold War, but its limitations—and decline—were sketched in Southeast Asia and later by the "Blackhawk Down" incident in Somalia and then in the Balkans, where the U.S. military reluctantly participated in NATO peace support operations. The clear need for a more people-centric understanding of conflict, security, and ultimately peace has been mounting for decades, but faces the inertia of a military-industrial complex that finds it difficult at best to process this paradigm.

In recent years, one major challenge after another— Libya, Egypt, Syria, Somalia, Burma, Mali, the Central African Republic, Ukraine, Nigeria, and now Iraq again—has demonstrated what former Defense Secretary Robert Gates outlined in a major defense policy speech in 2007: that "military success is not sufficient to win." Instead, fostering economic development, institution building, and the rule of law; promoting internal reconciliation and good governance; providing basic services to the people; and other "non-kinetics" have become the better, less costly, and less risk-laden tools of choice.

As President Barack Obama finally framed it . . . in his [2014] commencement speech at West Point, "to say that we have an interest in pursuing peace and freedom beyond our borders is not to say that every problem has a military solution. . . . Just because we have the best hammer does not mean that every problem is a nail."

Nor should every foreign policy challenge be viewed through a national security prism. "Foreign assistance is not an afterthought, something nice to do apart from our national defense, apart from our national security," he said at his commencement speech at West Point. It is, in fact, the primary means to create the peace and stability that we've often sought, unsuccessfully, through military action.

Making good on that potential, though, requires more than understanding that "the future of war is about winning people, not territory," or "leaving behind an outmoded view of nation-on-nation warfare," wrote Eliza Griswold, paraphrasing Brig. Gen. James B. Linder who commands U.S. Special Operations in Africa, in the *New York Times Magazine*. It requires changing how American power is projected in the world, empowering people more than governments, and pursuing peace and justice with the same fervor as engaging enemies. This emerging civil-military enterprise, however, is not just about power to the people. It's about finding and leveraging the power in the people.

***

Twenty years ago, the United Nations Development Program's Human Development Report introduced a dialectic to the conventional national security paradigm: "human security." Human security is about the security of the tribe, the community, and, above all, the individual. Put simply, it is a democratization of the concept of security.

Human security has emerged as the alter ego of national security mainly because, as Obama has pointed out, "technology and globalization has put power once reserved for states in the hands of individuals." Unlike national security's fixation with threats, human security's concern is with the "drivers of conflict"—the difference between treating symptoms and curing the disease, or preventing its outbreak in the first place. One is primarily tactical; the other is more strategic.

Despite the already long life of human security as an idea and the United States' professed interest in it, the country's strategic capabilities to wage war still far outweigh those to make peace. Defense budgets are dropping, but so are those for diplomacy and development—where the most relevant equities to foster human security reside. As I . . . [have written], the diplomatic corps is underfunded, overstretched, and set up to fail. One-third of ambassadorial posts remain vacant, and country teams are so thinly staffed they cannot execute national security programs, let alone venture beyond their fortress embassies to pursue commercial interests that lead to jobs at home or to fulfill Obama's promise at West Point to "form alliances not just with governments, but also with ordinary people."

Efforts by the United States to help countries bolster their own security are typically driven by an obsession with terrorism and "bad guys"—not the human security concerns of resident populations. This habit of being distracted from the bigger picture by personalities and groups—from Osama bin Laden to Joseph Kony to Abu Bakr al-Baghdadi—often does little to create lasting security. "Train-and-equip" efforts that teach client military forces how to shoot, move, and communicate often exacerbate the internal instabilities of weak and fragile states well catalogued in the Fragile States Index and Global Peace Index. While "there is some reason to believe that counterterrorism assistance can work in the absence of governance reform," James Traub wrote for Foreign Policy . . ., "the gains are very modest, and very tenuous."

There are further complications to this approach. "The host country has to have the political will to fight terrorism, not just the desire to build up an elite force that could be used for regime protection," J. Peter Pham, director of the Africa Center of the Atlantic Council, told the *New York Times*. "And the military has to be viewed well or at least neutrally by a country's population."

For any security force to be effective, it needs to protect the people more than the state, as just seen in Iraq. After all, people have to want what you are offering. In Syria, for example, there is no definitive evidence that suggests a majority of Syrians wants to see President Bashar al-Assad replaced by an opposition faction, especially one associated with jihadists. Popular support for the opposition may have shrunk to as low as 10 percent of the Syrian public, according to NATO estimates. And yet, the Obama administration has asked Congress to fund a $500 million train-and-equip mission to help "vetted elements" of the Syrian armed opposition "defend the Syrian people, stabilize areas under opposition control, facilitate the provision of essential services, counter terrorist threats, and promote conditions for a negotiated settlement."

But it should not be about us—it should be about them. In order to engender sustainable peace, what they want and need should come before what we want and need, at least in the short term, and that means focusing on human not national security.

Seen this way, it becomes clear that security sector assistance is really a development challenge, which is why such programs should be led and managed by the U.S. Agency for International Development, not the Defense Department.

Addressing the real drivers of conflict that bad guys look to exploit in the first place is the key. Instead of "building partnership capacity" to deal with threats like terrorism, "training must involve not just soldiers but police officers, judges, and prosecutors, with a strong emphasis on the rule of law and human rights," admonished the *New York Times* editorial board about the proposed $5-billion Counterterrorism Partnership Fund [CPF], "so cracking down on extremists does not end up radicalizing more people or empowering authoritarian leaders." The concern is valid: The ratio of security assistance dollars devoted to building relationships and institutions versus train-and-equip has held steadfastly at around 1:9. It looks like it will remain so under the CPF.

Much of it will be spent in Africa, where human security approaches are most relevant. Boko Haram's abduction of young girls . . . was facilitated by poor governance and weak civil society institutions; socioeconomic shortfalls, especially with respect to youth and women; and illicit activities such as transnational drug and human trafficking. The bad behavior of Nigeria's military, and its poor relationship to the country's citizens, poses an even greater threat to local citizens than terrorism. As Amnesty International's Kolawole Olaniyan said in an op-ed in *Vanguard*, "corruption seems to be present and potentially widespread in law enforcement and security services, eroding the citizenry's trust in the rule of law, and contributing to a sense of lawlessness that encourages violence and abuse."

Instead, the U.S. has been sending soldiers and special operators to teach counterparts in Nigeria and other client countries battle skills in what the U.S. sees as the next front to combating terrorism—often in an overwhelmingly enemy-centric way not because people like Linder see it as such, but because, as he told the New York Times Magazine, "I see Kony because Congress tells me to." The focus of attention, in other words, is still more on the guys with the guns, not the conditions that allow them to use them.

***

. . . "There is nothing so terrible as activity without insight," Goethe once said. Today, "smart power" must involve strategic insight applied operationally—specifically, approaches that put foreign assistance out in front of security assistance, bring together public and private sectors, and demonstrate democratic values. This power must be premised on the (admittedly slow and painful) withdrawal process from an addiction with enemies and "send in the troops" reflex response to more of a "military as the last resort" default.

Goethe also said, "Thinking is easy, acting is difficult, and to put one's thoughts into action is the most difficult thing in the world." It will take a while longer for America to make the transition to a greater balance between national and human security approaches in its engagement with the world. There is no paradigm shift, after all, until it reflects in programs, budgets, and operations—not just in speeches and policy papers.

The "battlespace" has changed, but because human security is really about democratic governance, America has the right model for how to succeed in that space. Now it just has to use it.

DISCUSSION QUESTIONS

1. Evaluate the strongest and then the weakest evidence that Ian Morris offers to support his claim that wars make nation-states possible and nation-states then, in turn, make peace possible.
2. Develop arguments to support, or to refute, Martin Longman's suggestion that governments and not wars are mostly responsible for peace in the modern world.

3. Explain which of Tom Engelhardt's five "lessons" is the most credible; also explain which of the five is the least credible.

4. Compose a brief letter to an influential lawmaker either supporting or repudiating Engelhardt's claim that the United States' experience with war over the last half a century has been an "unparalleled failure."

5. Describe the policy implications that flow from Christopher Holshek's claim that emphasizing human security requires "finding and leveraging the power in the people."

6. Adopt a national security perspective as a lens with which to analyze weaknesses in human security approaches to foreign and domestic policymaking. Or, alternatively, adopt a human security perspective as a lens with which to analyze weaknesses in national security approaches.

PART 3

GENDER

In most places for many centuries, women have been systematically excluded from decision-making about war and peace. In most places, as well, for many centuries women have been assaulted and murdered by male family and community members at extraordinarily higher rates than women have assaulted and murdered men. It is only in the past century or so that a vocal minority of people in many parts of the world has begun to voice the radical thought that humans might be capable of treating women as equal to men. Although ascendant in many parts of the global north, the idea that women should exercise equal rights with men is still rejected by the majority of Earth's peoples.

Although there is currently no country in the world where men and women live equally free of gender- and sex-based violence, improvements in the status and safety of girls, women, and sex-based minorities are underway. The selections in part 3 debate the broad consequences of these changes. Some of the writers maintain, for example, that seeking equality and safety for women is likely the best and perhaps the only way to secure peace for men as well.

Debates about a Gender Perspective

In part 1, section 1, Catia C. Confortini argues that several fundamental peace studies concepts ignore the experiences of girls and women. Cynthia Enloe's selection below offers a related argument. Enloe contends that most discussions of international conflicts assume that men act while women are merely acted on. She points out, for example, that analysts generally ignore the many ways in which societies depend on the paid and unpaid work of women. Enloe maintains a gender perspective is necessary to produce more accurate analyses and also to assure that effective methods can be found to solve most contemporary world problems.

In a second selection, Cynthia Cockburn offers support for the idea that "war is masculinity by other means." War and many other forms of violence, Cockburn maintains, are a manifestation of male dominance and cannot be stopped until patriarchies are eliminated. Peace promotion requires transformed societies where women are as safe from the violence of men as men are safe today from the violence of women.

Where Are the Men?

BY CYNTHIA ENLOE

Cynthia Enloe, a professor of political science at Clark University, is the author of nine books and a leading figure in international studies. Selections from *Bananas, Beaches and Bases: Making Feminist Sense of International Politics*, 2nd Ed. Berkeley, CA: University of California Press, 2014. Used by permission.

Most of the time we scarcely notice that many governments still look like men's clubs, with the occasional woman allowed in the door. We see a photo of members of Russia's cabinet, Wall Street's inner circle, the Chinese Politburo, or Europe's central bankers, and it is easy to miss the fact that all the people in these photographs are men. One of the most useful functions that the British prime minister Margaret Thatcher served during the 1980s was to break through our gender numbness. Thatcher herself was not an advocate for women, but when she stood at a 1987 meeting in Venice alongside France's Mitterrand, Japan's Nakasone, the United States' Reagan, and the other heads of government, we suddenly noticed that everyone else was male. Twenty-five years later, Angela Merkel, the German chancellor, provided a similar gender-consciousness-raising function when she stood for a photograph with the other heads of government in the Group of Eight, the world's economic powers. One woman in a photo makes it harder for us to ignore that the men are *men*.

Once we start looking at men as men, we are more likely to become curious about masculinities—what it means to be manly—and about the contests over diverse, unequally ranked sorts of masculinity.

It is widely asserted today that we live in a "dangerous world." It was commonly stated during the four decades of the Cold War, when the threats posed by nuclear weapons were used by both the United States and the Soviet Union to raise the stakes of international rivalries. The notion that we live in a dangerous world gained new saliency after the attacks on New York's towering World Trade Center in September 2001. Since 2001, countless American politicians have based their calls for rolling back citizens' privacy rights, curtailing due process legal protections, giving surveillance agencies free rein, equipping local police forces with heavier weaponry, casting new immigrants as potential threats, launching weaponized drones, and turning a blind eye toward the antidemocratic actions of U.S. international allies by justifying each move as a contributor to the "war on terror."

Among its many questionable consequences, the absorption of the idea that we live in a dangerous world serves to reinforce the primacy of particular forms of masculinity while subordinating most women and femininity itself. Men living in a dangerous world are commonly imagined to be the natural protectors. Women living in a dangerous world allegedly are those who need protection. Those relegated to the category of the protected are commonly thought to be safe "at home" and, thus, incapable of realistically assessing the dangers "out there."

Notions of masculinity are not identical across generations or across cultural boundaries. That is why one needs to explore the workings and rankings of masculinities in particular places at particular times—and then track them over generations.[1] Comparison may reveal striking similarities but also expose significant differences.

A masculinized rivalry is one in which diverse masculinities are unequally ranked and contested: there is a contest over which expression of manliness is deemed most "modern," which most "rational," which the "toughest," which the "softest," which the "weaker." In such rivalries, women are marginalized unless (withstanding ridicule as "unfeminine") they can convincingly cloak themselves in a particular masculinized style of speech and action. Thus a common British assessment of Britain's first and only woman prime minister: "Margaret Thatcher was the toughest man in the room."

While political contests over masculinity marginalize all but a very few women, such contests always put femininity into play. In a patriarchal society—a society whose relationships and inequalities are shaped by the privileging of particular masculinities and by women's subordination to and dependence on men—anything that is feminized can be disparaged. Consequently, rival men are prone to try to tar each other with the allegedly damning brush of femininity. The intent is to rob the opposing man of his purchase on such allegedly manly attributes as strength, courage, and rationality.[2] This masculinized wielding of femininity happens not only on the playground and in local elections but also in international nuclear politics.[3]

Furthermore, this femininity-wielding masculinized contest between men shapes not only the international politics of war and national security but also the international politics of domestic servants, sex workers, wives, women factory workers, and women plantation workers. This contest determines what is considered mere "women's work" and thus unfit for any manly man. What presumptions about a manly man's access to any woman's sexuality fuels sexual harassment of women on and off the job?

In conventional commentaries, men who wield influence in international politics are analyzed in terms of their national, ethnic, and racial identities; their positions in organizations; their class origins; their paid work; and sometimes their sexual preferences. Rarely, though, are men analyzed as *men*, people who have been taught, since childhood, how to be manly, how not to be a "girl," how to size up the trustworthiness or competence of other men by assessing their manliness. If international commentators do find masculinity interesting, it is typically when they try to make sense of "great men"—Napoleon Bonaparte, Abraham Lincoln, Mao Zedong, Nelson Mandela—not when they seek to understand the actions of male factory owners, male midlevel officials, male banana workers, or male tourists. It is a lack of feminist curiosity that makes comfortably invisible such men's efforts to be seen by other men as masculine in doing their jobs, exercising influence, nurturing alliances, or seeking relief from stress. In so doing, such a lack of feminist curiosity also makes dangerously invisible these men's attempts (sometimes thwarted) to use diverse women in their daily pursuits of precarious masculine status.

Beyond the Global Victim

Some men and women active in campaigns to influence their country's foreign policy—on the right, as well as the left—have called on women to become more educated about international issues, to learn more about "what's going on in the world." Women are told, "You have to take more interest in international affairs because it affects how you live." The gist of the argument is that women need to devote precious time and energy to learning about events outside their own country because, as women, they are the *objects* of those events. For instance, a woman working for a software company in Ireland is told she should learn more about the European Union [EU] because what the EU commissioners decide in Brussels is going to help determine her wages and maybe even the hazards she faces on the job. An American woman similarly will be encouraged to learn about the ongoing fighting in Syria because political contests in the Middle East will affect her children's chances of a safe future.

There are two things striking about this conventional line of argument. First, those who are trying to persuade women to "become informed" are not inviting women to reinterpret international politics by drawing on their own experiences as women. If the explanations of how the EU and Middle East politics work do not already include any concepts of femininity, masculinity, or patriarchy, they are unlikely to do so after more women start listening to the recognized gender-incurious international experts. Because these persuaders are not curious about what paying close attention to women's complex experiences could contribute to an understanding of international politics, many women, especially those whose energies are already stretched to the limit, may be understandably wary of spending precious time reading about fighting in Syria or decisions made in Brussels.

When the common women-need-to-learn-more-about-foreign-affairs approach is articulated by gender-incurious activists (women or men), women are usually portrayed as the objects, even victims, of the international political system. Women should learn about capitalist globalization, or the Middle East's Arab Spring, or the workings of the United Nations, or climate change because each has an impact on them. In this worldview, women are forever being acted *upon*. They are the victims of garment factory disasters; they are the targets of sexual assaults in wartime; they are the trafficked, the low paid, the objectified. Rarely are women seen as the explainers or the reshapers of the world. Rarely are they made visible as *thinkers* and *actors*.

If women are asked to join an international campaign—for peace, for refugees, against war, for religious evangelism, against hunger—but are not allowed to define the problem and its causes, it looks to many locally engaged women like abstract do-gooding with minimal connection to the battles they are waging for a decent life in their households and in their own communities.

A lot of books about international politics leave their readers with a sense that "it's all so complex, decided by people who don't know or care that I exist." The spread of capitalist economics, even in countries whose officials call themselves socialists, can feel as inevitable as the tides (which, we are learning, are actually not inevitable). Governments' capacities to wound people, to destroy environments and dreams, are constantly expanding through their uses of science and bureaucracy. International relationships fostered by these governments and their allies use our labor and our imaginations, but it seems beyond our reach to alter them. These relationships seem to have created a world that can turn tacos and sushi into bland fast foods, destroy rain forests, melt arctic ice, globalize pornography, and socialize men from dozens of cultures into a common new culture of high-risk banking. One closes most books on "international security" or "international political economy" with a sigh. They purport to explain how it works, but they offer knowledge that makes one feel as though it is more rewarding to concentrate on problems closer to home.

Most important, many of these analyses of international affairs leave one with the impression that "home" has little to do with international politics. When home is imagined to be a feminized place—a place where womanly women and feminine girls should feel most comfortable, and where manly men and real boys should stop in now and then for refueling—then this consequence of many mainstream explanations can send the roots of masculinized international politics down even more deeply.

There is an alternative incentive for delving into international politics. That is, seeing oneself in it, not just being acted upon by it. To do this, however, requires remapping the boundaries of the "international" and the "political": it requires seeing how one's own family dynamics, consumer behaviors, travel choices, relationships with others, and ways of thinking about the world actually help shape that world. We are not just acted upon; we are actors. Though, even recognizing that one is not part of any elite, acknowledging oneself as an international actor can be unnerving. One discovers that one is often complicit in creating the very world that one finds so dismaying.

The world is something that has been—and is being—made every day. And ideas about and practices of both femininity and masculinity, combined with attempts to control women, are central to that world-making. So are challenges to those conventions and resistance to those attempts. It is not always easy to see those attempts and, thus,

to resist them. Policy makers may find it more "manly" (even if some of the policy makers themselves now are women) to think of themselves as dealing in guns and money, rather than in notions of femininity, marriage, and sexuality. So they—and most of their critics as well—try to hide and deny their reliance on women as feminized workers, as respectable and loyal wives, as "civilizing influences," as sex objects, as obedient daughters, as unpaid farmers, as coffee-serving campaigners, and as spending consumers and tourists. If we can expose their dependence on feminizing women, we can show that this world is also dependent on artificial notions of masculinity.

As a result, this seemingly overwhelming world system may begin to look more fragile and open to radical change than we have been led to imagine.

Thus this . . . is only a beginning. [I] draw on the theoretical and organizational work of women in Britain in the 1890s, Algeria in the 1950s, the Philippines in the 1980s, Chile in the 1990s, and Egypt in the beginning of the twenty-first century. Most of the conclusions here are tentative. What readers themselves write in the margins of these pages as they test the descriptions and explanations against their own experiences of the internationalized politics of femininity and masculinity will be at least as valuable in creating a different world as what appears here in deceptively solid print.

Male officials who make foreign policy might prefer to think of themselves as dealing with high finance or military strategy, but in reality they have self-consciously designed immigration, tourism, labor, foreign service, cultural, and military-base policies in order to divide and control women. They rarely admit it, but they have acted as though their government's or organization's place in world affairs has hinged on how women behaved.

Uncovering these efforts has exposed men *as men*. International politics have relied not only on the manipulation of femininity's multiple meanings but also on the manipulation of ideas about masculinities. Ideas about adventure, modernity, civilization, progress, expertise, rationality, stability, growth, risk, trust, and security have been legitimized by certain kinds of masculinized values, systems, and behavior. That is one of the reasons that each of these ideas has become so potent.

Frequently, male government officials and company executives seek to control women in order to optimize their influence over other men: men as husbands, voters, migrant workers, soldiers, diplomats, intelligence operatives, plantation and factory managers, editors, and bankers. Thus, understanding the international workings of masculinity is important to making feminist sense of international politics. Men's sense of their own manhood has derived from their perceptions both of other men's masculinity and of the femininities of women of different races and social classes. Thus a caveat: one cannot make adequate sense of the international politics of masculinity by avoiding paying close attention to women and femininity. Ideas about masculinities—the full array of masculinities—have been crafted out of ideas about, myths about, and uncertainties about femininities and about actual women. To conduct a reliable investigation of masculinity, one must take women seriously.

Climate change, capitalist globalization, the new arms race, and widening gaps between rich and poor—it is tempting to plunge into the discussion of any of these contemporary issues without bothering to ask, "Where are the women?" In fact, the more urgent the issue—"New York will soon be under water!" "China's military build up is going to set off a world war!"—the more reasonable it seems to *not* ask "Where are the women?" In patriarchal hands, "urgency" is the enemy of feminist investigation.

. . . [I] suggest, however, that these urgent issues demand a gendered analysis precisely because they are urgent, because they call for the fullest, most realistic understandings. As feminist environmental researchers and activists already are revealing, the causes of climate change, for example, and not just its effects, can be realistically tracked only if one exposes the workings of ideas about manliness and femininity and the relations between women and men, each fostered by the deliberate uses of political power. So too can the causes of the new arms race, exploitive globalization, and the widening gaps between rich and poor.

NOTES

1. There is a growing body of provocative studies that track the evolutions of, and contests between, masculinities within particular countries, many of them conducted by gender-curious ethnographers. See, for instance, John Osburg, *Anxious Wealth: Money and Morality among China's New Rich* (Stanford, CA: Stanford University Press, 2013); Robin Le Blanc, *The Art of the Gut: Manhood, Power, and Ethics in Japanese Politics* (Berkeley: University of California Press, 2010); Daniel Conway, *Masculinities, Militarisation and the End Conscription Campaign: War Resistance in Apartheid South Africa* (Manchester: Manchester University Press, 2012). Among the innovative cross-national studies of diverse masculinities, their interactions, and their political implications are: Marysia Zalewski and Jane Parpart, eds., *The "Man" Question in International Relations* (Boulder, CO: Westview Press, 1998); Jane Parpart and Marysia Zalewski, eds., *Rethinking the Man Question: Sex, Gender and Violence in International Relations* (London: Zed Books, 2008); Paul Kirby and Marsh Henry, eds., "Rethinking Masculinity and Practices of Violence in Conflict Settings," special issue, *International Feminist Journal of Politics* 14, no. 4 (2012); Paul Higate, ed., *Military Masculinities: Identity and the Sate* (Westport, CT: Praeger, 2003); Paul Amar, "Middle East Masculinity Studies," *Journal of Middle East Women's Studies* 7, no. 3 (Fall 2011): 36–71; Terrell Carver, "Being a Man," *Government and Opposition* 41, no. 3 (2006): 477–95.

2. Sandra Harding, a pioneering theorist in the feminist studies of science, has written extensively on how rational thinking has been presumed to be a hallmark of masculinity. See, for instance, Sandra Harding, *The Science Question in Feminism* (Ithaca, NY: Cornell University Press, 1986); Sandra Harding, *Sciences from Below: Feminisms, Postcolonialities and Modernities* (Durham, NC: Duke University Press, 2008).

3. Carol Cohn, "Sex and Death in the Rational World of Defense Intellectuals," *Signs* 12, no. 4 (1987): 687–718; Carol Cohn with Felicity Hill and Sara Ruddick, *The Relevance* *of Gender in Eliminating Weapons of Mass Destruction* (Stockholm: Weapons of Mass Destruction Commission, 2005).

Gender, Violence and War: What Feminism Says to War Studies

BY CYNTHIA COCKBURN

Cynthia Cockburn has written and coauthored over a dozen books, and has worked in both the international feminist antimilitarist networks Women in Black against War and in the Women's International League for Peace and Freedom. Selections from *From Where We Stand: War, Women's Activism and Feminist Analysis*. London: New York: Zed Books, 2007. Used by permission.

When feminists make reference to gender, to masculinities, to patriarchy when talking about war, we're often taken to task for "not looking at the big picture." The big picture: states and sovereignty, national rivalries, global capitalism. Cynthia Enloe has been one among us brave enough to say "But suppose this is the big picture?" (Enloe 2005).... I want to argue that gender relations are indeed a significant part of the big picture of militarism and war. This is not to say they are the whole story—far from it. But gender relations are right in there alongside class relations and ethno-national relations, intersecting with them, complicating them, sometimes even prevailing over them, in the origins, development and perpetuation of war. So here I adopt a feminist standpoint derived from the various kinds of anti-war activism described in some detail in earlier chapters. Standing among the activists, how does war look? Why does war persist? Why, despite all humankind has learned in five thousand years, despite all our social and moral resources, do we step towards the horror time after time? Why is war still thinkable?

. . .

Patriarchy as system, structure and institutions is in continual cyclical interaction with (shaping and shaped by) gender relations as process and praxis. For men as a social group to retain supremacy over women, as they have done extraordinarily well for at least five thousand years, it's necessary not only for women and femininity to be constituted in the way Anna G. Jónasdóttir [1994] describes but for men and masculinity to acquire a shape that is adequate to power. Michel Foucault (1981) has helped us see that power is not just "held," it's exercised relationally in many interpersonal interactions. This relational quality of power is more evident in the case of sex/gender relations than in those of any other power structure. The ruling class has, and indeed is defined by, material wealth and the means to put it to use to create yet more. In this resides its power. The ruling ethno-national group has its institutionalized cultural supremacy. In a breathtaking metaphor, Arnold Toynbee described the penetrating "beam of light" the ascendant minority of a dominant civilization radiates beyond its frontiers across those lands it dominates, with nothing to restrict its range "but the inherent limitation of its own carrying-power" (Toynbee 1972: 234). We might prefer not to see Coca-Cola, Nike trainers, Hollywood and Google in such glorious terms, but propelled by economic interests though they may be, they are manifestations of cultural dominance. Like Christian religion and the valorization of whiteness, they travel with a powerful agency from Western into adjacent ethno-national spaces.

By contrast with the ruling economic class and ascendant "peoples," the ruling sex, as such, has rather few and pitiful resources. Men don't have a larger or more complex brain than women, nor greater manual dexterity. They do have a 20–25 per cent advantage in musculature and a little more height, a sex-specific hormonal energy and a penis. But the latter is a notoriously unreliable resource. To achieve supremacy for men as a social group, it must be culturally transformed into the phallus. The consolidation of the phallus, the symbolic power that extends physical power (like that beam of light) into the social domain, is achieved through the social and cultural process of masculinization. Masculinity must be produced in appropriate forms and activated in social institutions such as economic enterprises and political structures where patriarchy (men as men) can share some of the wealth and authority deriving from the systems of class and racial supremacy. The church and the military are two institutions where, assisted on the one hand by ideology and on the other by hardware, patriarchy has sustained the ascendency of men with striking success.

The cultural process of masculinization not only produces men as different from women, it produces men as different from each other. In certain modes it gives the individual man a good chance not only of dominating women individually and collectively but acceding to some of the resources of the ruling class and, if he is a member of it, the ability to deploy to his own and his descendants' advantage the authority of the ruling ethno-national group. Another version of masculinity fits men well for male dominance in proletarian cultures and contexts but positively unfits them for class rule and can sometimes pit them against ruling-class men and their institutions of law and order. The heterosexual competition for women also sets individual men against each other. So we see, as R. W. Connell (1995) has pointed out, that the effective reproduction of male supremacy, the continual production of men in multiple and hierarchical yet functional masculine forms, is nothing if not riven with tensions and contradictions. Some men are continually vulnerable to humiliation or subversion by others. Some of the contradictions in patriarchal

masculinism arise in the context of militarism and war, so that our oppositional movements can, in theory, look to exploit them. This occurs rarely, but when it does it hinges on the perception that not only is patriarchy strengthened by militarism, militarism needs patriarchy. Subverting patriarchal relations, therefore, can be an antimilitarist strategy, as we've seen some gay conscientious objectors discovering for themselves.

Let's take as examples two locations among many others where we can see masculinity in play in the maintenance of a war stance. First is the grooming of properly masculine national cultures disposed to war; second, the cultural grooming of actual men for war-fighting.

The notion of "honour" is something that links men and patriarchy in the family with men and patriarchy in the nation and state. In South-East Turkey, a heavily militarized region, I found women struggling to support each other against the practice of putting to death women whose behaviour is seen as betraying patriarchal honour. I simultaneously learned that across the nearby hillside facing the national frontier are written in massive letters the words "The Border is Honour." This isn't just a quaint archaism from a country well known for its manly/militarist construction of the nation (Altinay 2004); the USA too knows that the making of men and nations goes hand-in-hand. If you neglect manhood you imperil the nation, and a national defeat is a disaster for manhood. As already mentioned, a flush of interesting studies of masculinity has appeared recently. I will single out some where the focus is on US political and popular culture. Suzanne Clark, for instance, set out to understand the invisibility of women writers, and indeed of the work of any category of men or women expressing subversion or hybridity, during the forty years of the Cold War. What she reveals in US national policy of that era is "a male gendering elevated above all questions of marked gender," a "hypermasculine national mythology that joined manhood, realism and the frontier ethic" (Clark 2000: 3, 5).

Robert Dean is another who has taken a gender lens to observe the US establishment during the

Cold War period, looking in close-up at the small fraternity of policy-makers who took the decision to intervene in Vietnam. "How," he asks himself, "did highly educated men, who prided themselves on their hard-headed pragmatism lead the United States into a prolonged, futile, and destructive war in Vietnam and Southeast Asia?" His answer is that foreign policy in this period was profoundly shaped by a masculinist conception of the national interest. "The notion of a brotherhood, of privilege, power, 'service,' and 'sacrifice,'" he says, "was central to the identity narrative of Kennedy's foreign policy elite." It demanded a relentless defence of boundaries and an utter rejection of appeasement (Dean 2001: 1, 13). Carol Cohn . . . went out of her way to obtain a position in an institution where she could for a while participate in the world of defence intellectuals, mainly men, who "spend their days matter-of-factly discussing nuclear weapons, nuclear strategy, and nuclear war." She traces the way masculine bonding between them generates a bland, even humorous and "sexy," techno-strategic language to describe mass death. It results in an "astounding chasm between image and reality." She shows, like Dean, the acute sensitivity of this fraternity to the potentially demasculinizing effect of toying with notions such as suffering, peace or even negotiation (Cohn 1990: 33).

. . .

Military Needs: Enough Aggression, Not Too Much

If these careful studies are to be believed, then, masculinity plays a significant part in the US national social policies at home that underpin "full spectrum dominance" abroad. It no doubt plays a part in the policy thinking of other nation states too (see, for instance, Joanna Liddle and Sachiko Nakajima, 2000, on the manipulation of gender relations in Japanese post-war foreign policy). Masculinity also plays an important part in the more practical matter of producing and managing effective armed forces.

There are two apparently conflicting views of masculinity in relation to war-fighting. One view is that men are often excited by soldiering and war because it satisfies and legitimates aggressive impulses they already feel. This view is supported by accounts that show many quite ordinary men to have found pleasure, even ecstasy, in bloodletting. Examples include Joanna Bourke's contemporary study of veterans' recollections of their emotions during battlefield killing (Bourke 1999) and Barbara Ehrenreich's historical review of the exultant feelings war evokes in those who fight (Ehrenreich 1997).

The contrary view is that most men are not naturally aggressive—the intense training to which they must be subjected to turn them into effective soldiers would otherwise be superfluous. The facts are probably more complicated than either view suggests. Either way, chiefs of staff and battlefield commanders have a serious human resource management problem, for neither non-aggressive nor over-aggressive men are what they want in their armed services.

How is a functional army to be created out of hundreds of thousands of individual men, shaped heretofore in a variety of cultures, none of which can be assumed to be exactly appropriate to the tasks they are going to be expected to perform in war? Masculinity takes many forms in the civilian world in which fresh young recruits to the military have grown to adulthood. There are different variants in different social classes and ethnic groups, and teenage boys in particular inhabit a range of subcultures—of music, IT, different kinds of sport, the drugs scene, criminality. The system itself, on the other hand, has clear needs and expectations of military men. Each one must be willing at some future moment to kill and to die, but to do so only in a disciplined and approved manner.

Historians and analysts of war routinely make the point that war is not just aggression. A characteristic formulation is that of Colin Creighton and Martin Shaw in their introduction to *The Sociology of War and Peace*: "Aggression is not force, force is not violence, violence is not killing, killing is not war" (Creighton and Shaw 1987: 3). In one sense, this often-repeated dictum is clearly correct; war is an institution, not fisticuffs. State policy-makers and military planners seldom make war in anger. War is calculated. On the other hand, coming to war as a feminist it is not so easy to set aside "ordinary" aggression/force/violence as "not war," since women are saying loud and clear that they experience coercion by men in similar forms in war and peace. We see in newspaper and TV accounts and in human rights reports that the gentlemen's agreement concerning the violence acceptable in war is continually broken. Peacekeepers (like the Canadians in Somalia in 1993) beat up and murder local men in the sheer excitement of the hunt. Invading troops (such as the US unit in Iraq's Abu Ghraib prison in 2003) subject male victims to humiliating torture, indulging sadistic fantasies and destroying masculine self-respect in the enemy. In the wars I've described . . . there is evidence that women have been raped with penises, fists and miscellaneous weapons, their breasts cut off, their foetuses sliced out. They have been impaled. Is the rationality of institutionalized war enough to explain these things?

I suggest that to understand war and its perpetuation through long historical periods we need to break the academic taboo on noticing and analysing the aggression/force/violence that does occur in military preparation and war. We can learn something useful by digging below the cool policy-making surface of war and bringing to view some of the uncomfortable cultural realities of training and fighting. Individual and collective emotions and responses do play a part in war-fighting. Some of them are violent, and some of these are positively cultivated. War as institution is made up of, refreshed by and adaptively reproduced by violence as banal practice, in the everyday life of boot camp and battlefield. Masculinity in its various cultural forms is an important content of that cycle: masculinity shapes war and war shapes masculinity. John Home made a study of masculinity in war and politics over the hundred years from 1850. What he learned from a close look at two world wars led him to adapt Clauswitz's dictum "war is a continuation of policy by other means" so as to say "war is masculinity by other means" (Home 2004: 31).

To understand war, then, we need to explore, as Home put it, "the dense associative life of men" (ibid.: 27). It's through hard cultural work, the shaping and manipulation of that sociality, that military managers create their armies. And they meet many challenges as they do so. One is the governance of testosterone. While individual men in their lived lives are not necessarily more aggressive than individual women, both social and physical factors tend to produce them as such. The presence of the Y-chromosome in the unborn child prompts a surge of male hormones a quarter of the way through pregnancy, again soon after birth and once more at puberty. Without these occurrences male genitalia do not develop—they literally produce men. At the same time, the level of testosterone in any one body at any one moment, and the level of the excitement and aggression associated with its presence, can be stimulated or diminished by social conditions, occurring by chance or intentionally manipulated (Jones 2002).

In certain widespread and influential male subcultures, the masculinity fostered and rewarded is aggressive and violent. We see this in computer games, in certain forms of music, in popular film, in a fascination with knives, in the gun lobby, and in sport. The mindset they produce is a valuable resource for the military, but it calls for cautious handling. . . .

. . .

A factor war-managers have to take into account is that violence is widely experienced by men as erotic. The work of Lisa Price is important for helping us see the connection between masculine violence in peace and war. Sexuality itself, she stresses, is gendered, a relationship of power in which men dominate women. What's more, "[t]he socially-organized and organizing practices of gender and sexuality [are such that] violence is experienced as sex, and, too often, sex is experienced as violence." Women are constituted as socially sanctioned targets against whom men learn it's appropriate to direct violence. Men's violence against women is different from their violence against other men because it's an expression of male supremacist ideology that endows men with "a sense of entitlement," a right of access to women's bodies. Women may be battered and subdued by men in the absence of an erotic motivation, or the assault may be erotically charged, as in rape. In both cases the act is aggression and is about domination (Price 2005).

The expressions of male violence against women in war suggest a deep misogyny among militarized men, a hatred of women and the feminine. Only this can account for this kind of sexualized violence in which penises, fists and weapons are interchangeable and the purpose of assault is not only the woman's physical destruction but her social annihilation—"dishonouring," insemination with the aggressor's seed, infection by HIV/AIDS. Misogyny, of course, is not only hatred, but fear. This was compellingly demonstrated by Klaus Theweleit in his analysis of certain novels written in the 1920s by men of the proto-fascist Freikorps, men who refused demilitarization after the First World War and in their volunteer bands contributed to the defeat of communism and rise of fascism in Germany. In a unique move he approaches these warrior males from the point of view not of their attitudes to war but their attitudes to women, women's bodies and sexuality. He shows that the masculine identity of the officers was shaped by their dread of women and that this dread was linked to an acute racism and anti-communism. (Again we see the intersectionality of gender, race and class.) In the novels authored by Freikorps men, when women are not entirely absent they appear in one of two modes: good and pure (as wife or mother); or evil and terrifying (active women, especially communist women, who not only may but must be destroyed). Masculinity has to dam and hold back the threatening flood, the bloody mass, of the active feminine. Theweleit doesn't suggest all men are like these fascists. But they are, he says, the tip of the iceberg, and "it's what lies beneath the surface that really makes the water cold" (Theweleit 1987: 171). Two decades on, he would feel chilled anew by the knowledge that Islamic extremist Mohammed Atta, anticipating his suicide in the attacks of 11 September 2001, specified in his will that no woman should be

allowed to touch his corpse or approach his grave (Ehrenreich 2003: 79).

It has been suggested, though, that misogyny alone is not enough to explain male violence against women. In a careful study of sexual killers, Deborah Cameron and Elizabeth Frazer point out that while sexualized murder is a crime they find to be committed only by men (women occasionally kill in jealousy or rage but the killing is not eroticized), the victims and objects of desire are not only women but also homosexual men. Of course homosexual men may be killed for their despised femininity. But these authors find a different link. It lies in the socialization of men to aspire to transcendence, "the struggle to free oneself, by a conscious act of will, from the material constraints which normally determine human destiny" (Cameron and Frazer 1987: 168–9). Transgressive sexual acts, a source of both pleasure and power to men, can be redefined as transcendence, the distinctive project of the masculine and the proof of masculinity. And though these men may act alone, they don't act in isolation; though they are extremists, they belong to their gender. As Simone de Beauvoir understood, in-loveness, devotion, these woman things, are immanence in which men fear drowning. This fear is the impulse to male bonding and to men's "civilizational" projects. "It is the existence of other men that tears each man out of his immanence and enables him to fulfil the truth of his being, to complete himself through transcendence, through escape towards some objective," if necessary by destroying "her" (de Beauvoir 1972: 171).

REFERENCES

Altinay, Ayse Gul (2004) *The Myth of the Military-Nation: Militarism, Gender, and Education in Turkey*, New York and London: Palgrave Macmillan.

Bourke, Joanna (1999) *An Intimate History of Killing: Face-to-face Killing in Twentieth Century Warfare*, London: Granta Books.

Cameron, Deborah and Elizabeth Frazer (1987) *The Lust to Kill*, Cambridge: Polity Press.

Clark, Suzanne (2000) *Cold Warriors: Manliness on Trial in the Rhetoric of the West*, Carbondale and Edwardsville: Southern Illinois University Press.

Cohn, Carol (1990) "'Clean Bombs' and Clean Language," in Elshtain, Jean Bethke and Sheila Tobias (eds.), *Women, Militarism and War: Essays in History, Politics and Social Theory*, Lanham, MD: Rowman and Littlefield.

Connell, R. W. (1995) *Masculinities*, Cambridge: Polity Press.

Creighton, Colin and Martin Shaw (eds.) (1987) *The Sociology of War and Peace*, London: Macmillan.

Dean, Robert D. (2001) *Imperial Brotherhood: Gender and the Making of Cold War Foreign Policy*, Amherst: University of Massachusetts Press.

De Beauvoir, Simone (1972) *The Second Sex*, Harmondsworth: Penguin Books.

Ehrenreich, Barbara (1997) *Blood Rites: The Origins and History of the Passions of War*, London: Virago.

— (2003) "Veiled Threat," in Joseph, Ammu and Kalpana Sharma (eds.), *Terror Counter-Terror: Women Speak Out*, London and New York: Zed Books.

Enloe, Cynthia (2005) "What if Patriarchy is 'The Big Picture'? An Afterword," in Mazurana, Dyan, Angela Raven-Roberts and Jane Parpart (eds.),

Gender, Conflict and Peacekeeping, Lanham, MD, Boulder, CO, New York, Toronto and Oxford: Rowman and Littlefield, pp. 280–4.

Foucault, Michel (1981) *The History of Sexuality, Volume 1, an Introduction*, Harmondsworth[, England]: Pelican.

Home, John (2004) "Masculinity in Politics and War in the Age of Nation-states and World Wars, 1850-1950," in Dudink, Stefan, Karen Hagemann and John Tosh (eds.), *Masculinities in Politics and War: Gender in Modern History*, Manchester and New York: Manchester University Press, pp. 22–40.

Jónasdóttir, Anna G. (1994) *Why Women are Oppressed*, Philadelphia: Temple University Press.

Jones, Steve (2002) *Y: The Descent of Man*, London: Abacus.

Liddle, Joanna and Sachiko Nakajima (2000) *Rising Suns, Rising Daughters: Gender, Class and Power in Japan*, London and New York: Zed Books.

Price, Lisa S. (2005) *Feminist Frameworks: Building Theory on Violence against Women*, Halifax, Canada: Fernwood Publishing.

Theweleit, Klaus (1987) *Male Fantasies*, Cambridge: Polity Press.

Toynbee, Arnold (1972) *A Study of History*, Oxford and London: Oxford University Press and Thames and Hudson.

DISCUSSION QUESTIONS

1. Explain what Cynthia Enloe means when she claims that the idea that "we live in a dangerous world" typically serves to reinforce the preeminence of males over females.
2. Summarize and evaluate the reasons why, as Enloe maintains, the wider adoption of a gender analysis would help men as much as women.
3. Offer evidence to support, or to contradict, Cynthia Cockburn's claim that cultures of masculinity shape wars and that wars shape cultures of masculinity.
4. Evaluate the accuracy of Cockburn's assertion that men sexualize their assaults and murders much more often than women do.

5. Explain why so many more female than male analysts adopt a gender perspective in their work in the fields of conflict, security, and peace studies.

6. Many well-respected analysts have been calling for an increased use of a gender perspective for over 30 years. Describe what you believe are the main reasons that applications of a gender perspective still remain relatively rare in peace studies and the social sciences.

Debates about Gender-
and Sex-based Violence

As discussed in the second section of part 2, many analysts believe that military force and violence are necessary to create peace. A related perspective is presented in the first selection below as Gayle S. Trotter argues that arming women with loaded weapons is the best way to increase their safety. In testimony before the United States Senate, Trotter contended that in violent situations, guns are "the great equalizer," as guns enable women to counter their male attacker's usual size and strength advantages.

Public Heath Watch offers a rebuttal to Trotter's position in a second selection below. Public Heath Watch points out that women are much more often attacked by current or former intimate partners than by mere acquaintances or strangers. The presence of guns in these situations is more likely to increase than to decrease the eruption of violence. According to Public Health Watch, a greater presence of guns, "arming women," as Trotter advises, would increase rates of assaults, coercion, and suicide.

A third selection moves beyond specific disagreements about the effect of gun possession to a very broad claim about the importance of increasing levels of female safety and well-being. Valerie M. Hudson asserts that eliminating violence against women and increasing gender equality are necessary to increase security for all people in all types of societies. Hudson uses information from the world's largest database on the status of women to contend that "the best predictor of a state's peacefulness is how well its women are treated." Hudson can be understood as providing empirical support for some of the theoretical claims made by Cynthia Cockburn in section 1 of this part 3. Hudson's analysis of the health of nation-states also offers an alternative to the conclusions drawn by the Global Peace Index presented in part 1.

A final selection by George Lakey includes specific suggestions for how greater justice for women and sexual minorities might be won. Lakey warns against the prominent contemporary tendency to rely mostly on insider, within-the-system, non-confrontational approaches. Change requires directly and openly facing up to the uncomfortable reality that championing the rights of women and sexual minorities challenges some fundamental values at the core of contemporary societies. Lakey maintains that history shows that emotionally unpleasant confrontations—although not violence—are necessary to change long-existing discriminatory patterns. In Lakey's view, building a more equitable world of gender relations requires disobedience, defiance, and nonviolent direct action, as well as some of the less confrontational work people commonly find so much easier to do.

"What Should America Do About Gun Violence?"

BY GAYLE S. TROTTER

January 30, 2013. Gayle S. Trotter is a lawyer and senior fellow at the Independent Woman's Forum in Washington, DC. From United States Senate Judiciary, online.[1] January 30, 2013.

Chairman Leahy, Ranking Member Grassley, and Members of the Committee, thank you for inviting me to appear before you today. We have seen unspeakable tragedy and now hear calls to action. This Committee has asked what America should do about gun violence.

Asking that question will undoubtedly invite impassioned debate in an area where reasonable and well-intentioned people can disagree on specific approaches. We all want a safer society. We differ on how to make our society safer and on whether some proposals, however appealing they may be, will actually increase public safety. And that is a key element of this debate. We need more than political philosophies to guide our discussion: We should consider the effectiveness of proposed changes.

This Committee should ask the same question about proposed gun regulations: What works? We should decline to accept any call to action that will fail to make Americans safer and, in particular, harm women the most.

I would like to begin with the compelling story of Sarah McKinley. Home alone with her baby, she called 911 when two violent intruders began to break down her front door. The men wanted to force their way into her home so they could steal the prescription medication of her deceased husband, who had recently died of cancer. Before the police could arrive, while Ms. McKinley was on the line with the 911 operator, these violent intruders broke down her door. One of the men brandished a foot-long hunting knife. As the intruders forced their way into her home, Ms. McKinley fired her weapon, fatally wounding one of the violent attackers and causing the other to flee the scene. Later, Ms. McKinley reflected on the incident: "It was either going to be him or my son," she said. "And it wasn't going to be my son."

Guns make women safer. Most violent offenders actually do not use firearms, which makes guns the great equalizer. In fact, over 90 percent of violent crimes occur without a firearm. Over the most recent decade, from 2001 to 2010, "about 6 percent . . . to 9 percent of all violent victimizations were committed with firearms," according to a federal study. Violent criminals rarely use a gun to threaten or attack women. Attackers use their size and physical strength, preying on women who are at a severe disadvantage.

Guns reverse that balance of power in a violent confrontation. Armed with a gun, a woman can even have the advantage over a violent attacker. How do guns give women the advantage? An armed woman does not need superior strength or the proximity of a hand-to-hand struggle. She can protect her children, elderly relatives, herself or others who are vulnerable to an assailant. Using a firearm with a magazine holding more than 10 rounds of ammunition, a woman would have a fighting chance even against multiple attackers. . . .

Concealed-carry laws reverse that balance of power even before a violent confrontation occurs. In this way, armed women indirectly benefit those

---

1   http://www.iwf.org/media/2790433/Gayle_Trotter_ Testimony_Gun_Violence, accessed May 24, 2017

who choose not to carry. For a would-be criminal, concealed-carry laws dramatically increase the cost of committing a crime, paying safety dividends to those who do not carry. All women in these jurisdictions reap the benefits of concealed-carry laws because potential assailants face a much higher risk when they attempt to threaten or harm a potential victim. As a result, in jurisdictions with concealed-carry laws, women are less likely to be raped, maimed or murdered than they are in states with stricter gun ownership laws.

Research has shown that states with nondiscretionary concealed handgun laws have 25 percent fewer rapes than states that restrict or forbid women from carrying concealed handguns. The most thorough analysis of concealed-carry laws and crime rates indicates that "there are large drops in overall violent crime, murder, rape, and aggravated assault that begin right after the right-to-carry laws have gone into effect" and that "in all those crime categories, the crime rates consistently stay much lower than they were before the law." Among the ten states that adopted concealed-carry laws over a fifteen-year span, there were 0.89 shooting deaths and injuries per 100,000 people, representing less than half the rate of 2.09 per 100,000 experienced in states without these laws.

Armed security works. Brave men and women stand guard over Capitol Hill, including the building where we are now. Snipers stand guard on the White House roof. Politicians and other high-profile individuals, including prominent gun-control advocates, have admitted to having gun permits either currently or in the past.

Armed guards often serve in the employ of those who themselves advocate for more restrictions on gun rights. Political figures seek to restrict gun rights, and Hollywood celebrities somberly urge Americans to "demand a plan" to reduce gun violence despite their own roles in graphically depicting lethal violence on the screen. In both cases, however, many of these political figures and celebrities already have their own plan: They rely on guns to safeguard their own personal safety. For example, armed guards protected a suburban newspaper in New York after the newspaper published the names and residential addresses of gun permit holders, and the newspaper's own reporter already used a gun for his protection. After publishing the story, the editors disclosed that their reporter owns a Smith & Wesson .357 Magnum and has "a residence permit in New York City."

While armed security works, gun bans do not. Anti-gun legislation keeps guns away from the sane and the law-abiding—but it does not keep guns out of the hands of criminals. Nearly all mass shootings have occurred in "gun-free" zones. Law-abiding citizens do not bring firearms to gun-free zones, so psychotic killers know they can inflict more harm in these unprotected environments. These laws make easy targets of the sane and the law-abiding. Gun-control advocates cheer the creation of legally mandated gun-free zones, touting increased safety while actually making citizens in those locations more vulnerable to the next horrible monster in search of soft targets. A moment's reflection confirms that statutory provisions and bold signs do not create a gun-free environment. No sober-minded person would advocate that approach when protecting banks, airports, rock concerts and government buildings. Instead, these publicly designated areas have the effect of creating high-visibility soft targets—conspicuous environments where madmen can wreak havoc.

We need sensible enforcement of the gun laws that are already on the books. Currently, we have more than 20,000 under-enforced or selectively enforced gun laws. Gun regulation affects only the guns of the law-abiding. Criminals will not be bound by such gestures, especially as we continually fail to prosecute serious gun violations or provide meaningful and consistent penalties for violent felonies using firearms.

Recently, a talk show host inadvertently exposed the absurdity of gun regulation in the District of Columbia when he displayed a 30-round magazine on national television, thereby embroiling himself in a police investigation. Ultimately, the Attorney General of the District of Columbia decided not to prosecute the matter. "Despite the clarity of the violation of this important law," he concluded, "a prosecution would not promote public safety." Why is it permissible to possess magazines to persuade people that guns are dangerous, but not for a woman to possess one to defend herself against gang rape? Overbroad anti-gun regulations unduly increase prosecutorial discretion and result in selective enforcement of the law. Equal justice under law should not depend on whether a prosecutor has a political or ideological motivation to seek enforcement. Nor should justice depend on whether a prosecutor has the good sense to decline enforcement of a knowing violation that does nothing more than unwittingly demonstrate the law's absurdity and overbreadth.

In lieu of empty, self-defeating gestures, we should address gun violence by doing what works. By safeguarding our Second Amendment rights, we preserve meaningful protection for women. Our nation made significant progress in that regard when, in recent memory, the United States Supreme Court held that the Second Amendment protects an individual's right to possess a firearm for traditionally lawful purposes, such as self-defense within the home.

For those who believe in safeguarding the civil liberties enshrined in our Bill of Rights, you would think this was an unremarkable conclusion. The constitutional text expressly guarantees the right "to keep and bear Arms," and that right is specifically enumerated—not implied—and guaranteed to "the people." In other words, unlike many of the individual rights that the Supreme Court has recognized—some would say invented—you can actually find the right to bear arms in the literal text of the Second Amendment. Moreover, the Constitution guarantees a "right of the people" only two other times, both of which clearly describe individual rights: The First Amendment protects the "right of the people" to assemble and to petition the government, and the Fourth Amendment protects the "right of the people" against "unreasonable searches and seizures."

Even so, dissenting liberals decried "the Court's announcement of a new constitutional right to own and use firearms for private purposes." Ironically, this claim originated from those who agree with the judicial philosophy that has discovered new fundamental individual rights hiding within "penumbras" that are "formed by emanations" from "specific guarantees in the Bill of Rights." Adherents to this view maintain that the Bill of Rights generates "penumbral emanations" that create assorted individual rights. However, they simultaneously claim that enforcing an individual right expressly written in the black letter of the constitutional text is the "announcement of a new constitutional right." On the one hand, shadowy secretions reveal the hidden meaning of rights secretly embedded in the Constitution and awaiting judicial divination. On the other hand, they view a specifically enumerated guarantee in the Bill of Rights as "a new constitutional right."

Moreover, the dissenting justices claimed that a local law could ban private possession of any form of operable firearm because "the adjacent states do permit the use of handguns for target practice, and those states are only a brief subway ride away." They called this a "minimal burden" on the Second Amendment right to bear arms, as if a law-abiding citizen who is facing down an attacker might somehow have the ability to coax him onto the subway and take a brief ride to the adjoining jurisdiction's nearest target range. Adherents of this judicial philosophy—which purports to allow the restriction of individual liberties as long as "a brief subway ride" would transport an aggrieved citizen to another jurisdiction where the penumbral emanations flow freely—would assuredly provide more robust protection for rights of their own judicial invention.

These are two dramatically different views of our Bill of Rights. One approach has repeatedly created new rights found nowhere in the Constitution while unflinchingly limiting the Second Amendment's "right of the people to keep and bear Arms" to protect only the right to have a gun in the army, as peculiar as that would be. The other approach, which has twice prevailed in the Supreme Court, takes seriously the people's enumerated rights—the ones actually written in the Constitution—and respects the Second Amendment.

In lieu of empty gestures, we should address gun violence based on what works. Guns make women safer. The Supreme Court has recognized that lawful self-defense is a central component of the Second Amendment's guarantee of the right to keep and bear arms. For women, the ability to arm ourselves for our protection is even more consequential than for men because guns are the great equalizer in a violent confrontation. As a result, we preserve meaningful protection for women by safeguarding our Second Amendment rights. Every woman deserves a fighting chance.

Thank you. It has been a pleasure to be here with you this morning to discuss these issues of such paramount importance to the safety of our citizens. I welcome any questions you may have.

The Gun Violence Threat That No One Is Talking About—And Why Women Should Be Concerned

BY PUBLIC HEALTH WATCH

October 5, 2015. Public Health Watch was a science-grounded blog aimed at "keeping an eye on the public health impact of modern politics." The blog has been discontinued and its posts are no longer online. From *Public Health Watch,* online. October 5, 2015. Used by permission.

Women's health issues are in the news a lot lately, and for good reason: across the nation, conservative lawmakers are targeting women's reproductive rights and access to basic health care services like contraceptive counseling and family planning. Attacks on women's health and rights have been particularly aggressive [lately] . . ., with Congressional Republicans nearly shutting down the government in an effort to defund Planned Parenthood.

But there's another issue facing women that doesn't get nearly as much attention, even though it's a major public health problem affecting women in the U.S. disproportionately more than women in other high-income countries. It sends almost 75,000 people to emergency rooms each year with life-threatening conditions. It's something that kills over 31,000 Americans each year, many during the prime of their life. And it's completely preventable.

What am I talking about?

Gun violence.

We all know that gun violence is a major problem in America, but the debate over gun safety rarely mentions the implications for women. When women *are* included in the discussion, we're usually being told by pro-gun advocates that we need guns to protect ourselves from scary intruders and home invasions. Take political commentator and attorney Gayle Trotter, for instance, who argued last year that not only do women need guns, but that we need *AR-15 semi-automatic weapons* to fend off attackers in our home:

An assault weapon in the hands of a young woman defending her babies in her home becomes a defense weapon. And the peace of mind that women has as she's facing three, four, five violent attackers, intruders in her home, with her children screaming in the background, the peace of mind that she has knowing that she has a scary looking gun gives her more courage when she's fighting hardened, violent criminals.

That was Trotter's testimony during last year's Senate Judiciary Committee hearing on gun violence. Trotter didn't provide any statistics on the frequency with which women successfully fight off "three, four, five violent attackers," but the data we *do* have show that this scenario is highly unlikely, if not entirely implausible.

Women and Guns: What the Research Shows

While men are most likely to be killed in the street or other public places, women are most likely to be murdered at home. Acquaintances pose the greatest risk for men, while women are overwhelmingly more likely to be killed by a current or former intimate partner.

Three women a day are murdered in the U.S., the vast majority of whom are killed by men who they once thought loved them, and who might argue that they still do. Of all female homicide victims each year, *eleven times as many* are murdered by someone they know—usually a current or former partner—than by a stranger. The number of females shot and killed by their spouse or intimate partner is more than *four times* higher than the total number murdered by strangers using *all weapons combined*.

As I've written about previously, guns often play a terrifying role in the lives of domestic violence victims. Guns kill more victims of domestic violence than all other weapons combined, and when a convicted abuser has access to a gun in the home, their victim is *eight times more likely* to be killed in a domestic dispute. According to researcher Dr. Susan Sorenson, "access to a gun is a potent predictor of a fatal assault" among victims of domestic violence.

Importantly, Dr. Sorenson points out that firearms are used for nonfatal forms of intimate partner violence, as well. "This observation is important because most intimate partner violence is ongoing, nonfatal abuse," writes Dr. Sorenson.

In cases where women are abused but not murdered by intimate partners in households with guns, firearms are frequently used to coerce behavior, such as sex, or to instill terror. And research shows that firearm ownership is more common in abusive homes than in the general population. In one study of residents of battered women's shelters, more than one third of the victims reported that there was a firearm in the home, whereas only about one sixth of women in the general population report that there is a firearm in the home.

Frighteningly, in *more than two thirds* of the abusive households that contained a firearm, the abusive partner used the gun(s) against the woman—usually threatening to shoot/kill her (71.4%). "In other words, when there was a gun in the home where battering had occurred, it commonly was used against the woman," the researchers conclude.

Moreover, the researchers also found that victims of domestic violence rarely used weapons to defend themselves against an abusive partner.

"Battered women were substantially less likely to use a weapon against an intimate partner than to have it used against them," the researchers said. For guns, specifically, the findings are even worse: a gun in the home is *more than 10 times more likely* to be used by an abuser to threaten, intimidate, or injure a victim than it is to be used by the victim in self-defense. In fact, in the few instances in which women did use weapons in self-defense, guns were among the least-used weapons: only about 2% of women who ever used a weapon in self-defense

used a gun, compared to approximately 80% who used their hands or fists, 30% who used a door or a wall, 15% who used a kitchen knife, and 25% who used other household items (note: numbers do not add up to 100% because some women used multiple types of weapons in self-defense).

Guns also greatly increase the risk of repeat abuse for victimized women. According to a 2014 study published in the journal *Violence Against Women*, abused women are up to 83 percent more likely to experience repeat abuse by their male partners if a gun is used in the initial abuse incident.

These findings overwhelmingly show that guns are an ineffective—and often dangerous—means of self-defense. And given that most incidents of violence against women, including rape, assault and murder, are perpetrated at the hands of an intimate partner, these studies undermine the claims of pro-gun advocates who say that guns make women safer in the face of violence. Not only do guns *not* protect women in violent situations, but they actually escalate the violence and increase their chances of being killed....

Involving Women in the Push For Smarter Gun Laws

Women have a special role to play in moving policy and culture when it comes to the detrimental impact of gun violence on women and society as a whole. In recent polling it has become clear that women view gun violence differently than men do and are nearly unanimous in wanting a multi-faceted response. Women are significantly less likely than men to say that having a gun in the home makes them feel safer, and support for gun safety laws like universal background checks is substantially higher among women.

And although we are rarely included in the political debate over gun violence prevention, more and more women are recognizing the importance of making our voices heard.

Former Rep. Gabby Giffords (D-AZ), who was shot during a 2011 campaign event in Tucson, Arizona, is among several female leaders involved in the push for safer gun laws. Last year, Giffords urged the Senate Judiciary Committee to hold a hearing on preventing gun violence against women as the first step towards passing new gun legislation.

"[M]any of those who perpetrate violence against women are still allowed easy access to firearms," Giffords wrote in an open letter to the Judiciary Committee. "On behalf of more than 500,000 members of Americans for Responsible Solutions, I strongly urge you to hold a hearing in the Senate Judiciary Committee to discuss ways to prevent gun violence against women."

Feminists are increasingly discussing the gendered politics of gun violence and bringing attention to the devastating toll that gun violence takes on women. And in towns and cities across the country, women are banding together to reach out directly to other women, educating them about the dangers of firearms and the risk they pose for women. *Ladies Involved in Putting a Stop to Inner-City Killing* (LIPSTICK) is a Boston-based group devoted to "reducing the willingness of women and girls to engage in high-risk behaviors involving guns." One of the main goals of the group is to prevent women from being used to buy, hide or hold guns for those who can't legally own them.

Unfortunately, women are often used in the illegal trafficking of guns, and many of these women are completely unaware of the role they are playing in the illegal sale and trade of firearms. Through education and advocacy, LIPSTICK involves women in stopping the flow of guns to criminals and reducing gun violence in communities across the country. . . .

Women have enormous potential to change the policies and politics that can reduce gun violence. In the wake of a string of tragic events including . . . [a] deadly mass shooting at an Oregon community college, and the daily gun violence we face in our communities, women are in a new moment for action on this issue—which is much broader than just guns, but gets to other deep-rooted societal issues we must tackle. By working on this issue together, we can also help build cohesion and strength among women leaders and activists, ultimately making the country a better, and safer, place to be a woman.

What Sex Means for World Peace

BY VALERIE M. HUDSON

Valerie M. Hudson is coauthor of the influential book, *Sex and World Peace* (2012), as well as sole author of several other books. She currently teaches political science at Texas A&M University. From *Foreign Policy*, April 24, 2012.[2] Used by permission.

In the academic field of security studies, realpolitik dominates. Those who adhere to this worldview are committed to accepting empirical evidence when it is placed before their eyes, to see the world as it "really" is and not as it ideally should be. As Walter Lippmann wrote, "We must not substitute for the world as it is an imaginary world."

Well, here is some robust empirical evidence that we cannot ignore: Using the largest extant database on the status of women in the world today, which I created with three colleagues, we found that there is a strong and highly significant link between state security and women's security. In fact, the very best predictor of a state's

peacefulness is not its level of wealth, its level of democracy, or its ethno-religious identity; the best predictor of a state's peacefulness is how well its women are treated. What's more, democracies with higher levels of violence against women are as insecure and unstable as nondemocracies.

Our findings, detailed in our . . . book . . ., *Sex and World Peace*, echo those of other scholars, who have found that the larger the gender gap between the treatment of men and women in a society, the more likely a country is to be involved in intra- and interstate conflict, to be the first to resort to force in such conflicts, and to resort to higher levels of violence. On issues of national health, economic growth, corruption, and social welfare, the best predictors are also those that reflect the situation of women. What happens to women

2 http://foreignpolicy.com/2012/04/24/what-sex-means-for-world-peace/, accessed on May 24, 2017.

affects the security, stability, prosperity, bellicosity, corruption, health, regime type, and (yes) the power of the state. The days when one could claim that the situation of women had nothing to do with matters of national or international security are, frankly, over. The empirical results to the contrary are just too numerous and too robust to ignore.

But as we look around at the world, the situation of women is anything but secure. Our database rates countries based on several categories of women's security from 0 (best) to 4 (worst). The scores were assigned based on a thorough search of the more than 130,000 data points in the WomanStats Database, with two independent evaluators having to reach a consensus on each country's score. On our scale measuring the physical security of women, no country in the world received a 0. Not one. The world average is 3.04, attesting to the widespread and persistent violence perpetrated against women worldwide, even among the most developed and freest countries. The United States, for instance, scores a 2 on this scale, due to the relative prevalence of domestic violence and rape.

It's ironic that authors such as Steven Pinker who claim that the world is becoming much more peaceful have not recognized that violence against women in many countries is, if anything, becoming more prevalent, not less so, and dwarfs the violence produced through war and armed conflict. To say a country is at peace when its women are subject to femicide—or to ignore violence against women while claiming, as Pinker does, that the world is now more secure—is simply oxymoronic.

Gender-based violence is unfortunately ingrained in many cultures, so much so that it can take place not only during a woman's life but also before she is even born. On our scale measuring son preference and sex ratio, the world average is 2.41, indicating a generalized preference for sons over daughters globally. And in 18 countries, from Armenia to Vietnam, childhood sex ratios are significantly abnormal in favor of boys. The United Nations Population Fund suggests that, as of 2005, more than 163 million women were missing from Asia's population, whether through sex-selective abortion, infanticide, or other means. Demographer Dudley Poston of Texas A&M University has calculated that China will face a deficit of more than 50 million young adult women by the end of the decade [in 2010]. Think of the ways this imbalance will affect China's state stability and security—and in turn its rise to world power—in this century.

Other global indicators are equally disheartening. In family law, women are disadvantaged in areas such as marriage, divorce, and inheritance. This inequity in turn serves as a foundation for violence against women, while also undercutting their ability to fend for themselves and their children. My colleagues and I found that the world's average score for inequity in family law is 2.06, indicating that most countries have laws that discriminate to a greater or lesser degree against women. And some of the countries in the Arab Spring, including populous Egypt, are actually poised to regress on this scale. Maternal mortality, meanwhile, clocks in globally at 2.45, a truly lamentable comment on state priorities and the value of female life.

Lastly, the inclusion of women's voices in decision-making bodies, as captured by the level of female participation in governments, measures an abysmal world average of 2.74. This is no surprise, given that the level of participation of women in government is less than 20 percent. But it's also true that some of the worst countries when it comes to the representation of women in national government include democracies such as Japan (13.4 percent in the Diet) and South Korea (14.7 percent), not to mention Hungary (8.8 percent). The United States is below average, with only 17 percent female participation in Congress. Ironically, when the United States invaded Afghanistan and Iraq, it urged that these countries have a minimum of 25 percent female participation, and now both countries score higher than their invader on this indicator: Afghanistan's parliament is nearly 28 percent female, and Iraq's is just over 25 percent. In that one respect, the United States has done better by Afghan and Iraqi women than by its own.

The evidence of violence against women is clear. So what does it mean for world peace? Consider the effects of sex-selective abortion and polygyny: Both help create an underclass of young adult men with no stake in society because they will never become heads of households, the marker for manhood in their cultures. It's unsurprising that we see a rise in violent crime, theft, and smuggling, whereby these young men seek to become contenders in the marriage market. But the prevalence of these volatile young males may also contribute to greater success in terrorist recruiting, or even state interest in wars of attrition that will attenuate the ranks of these men. For instance, the sole surviving terrorist from the 2008 Mumbai attacks testified that he was persuaded by his own father to participate in order to raise money for the dower that he and his siblings needed in order to marry.

We also know through experimental studies that post-conflict agreements that are negotiated without women break down faster than those that do include women, and that all-male groups take riskier, more aggressive, and less empathetic decisions than mixed groups—two phenomena that may lead to higher levels of interstate conflict.

On an even deeper level, the template for living with other human beings who are different from us is forged within every society by the character of male–female relations. In countries where males rule the home through violence, male-dominant hierarchies rule the state through violence. This was most poignantly expressed by male Iranian dissidents who, during the ill-fated 2009 Green Revolution, explained their decision to wear headscarves as a sign of protest against the regime—and an act of solidarity with the women long oppressed by it. As one supporter of the protests explained it, "We Iranian men are late doing this. . . . If we did this when *rusari* [the headscarf] was forced on those among our sisters who did not wish to wear it 30 years ago, we would have perhaps not been here today." This is a profound statement: Men who see women as beings to be subjugated will themselves continue to be subjugated. Men who see women as equal and valued partners are the only men who have a true chance to win their freedom and enjoy peace.

In a promising sign, U.S. Secretary of State Hillary Clinton has declared women's issues a central focus of American foreign policy, explaining in 2010 that "women's equality is not just a moral issue; it's not just a humanitarian issue; it is not just a fairness issue. It is a security issue," which, she added, is "in the vital interest of the United States." But given the overwhelming evidence that improving the security of women improves the security and stability of states, it is amazing that some still balk, suggesting that third parties are helpless before ingrained cultural practices. The most pressing example . . . is Afghanistan, where senior U.S. officials [who were] looking toward the United States' 2014 departure state baldly, "Gender issues are going to have to take a back seat to other priorities." We cannot but assume that the situation of Afghan women will only get worse when U.S. troops leave—Afghan women themselves tell us it will be. And how does that square with Clinton's view?

The United States is not impotent to assist Afghanistan's women, even as it leaves that benighted land. It can at least attempt to ensure a softer landing for them. . . . Before the United States leaves, it could set up an asylum policy for Afghan women facing the threat of femicide, or a scholarship program to send the best and brightest female Afghan students to American universities. It could ensure that women are well represented in the peace *jirga* talks with the Taliban. It could encourage the pursuit of International Criminal Court indictments against top Taliban leaders who have ordered femicides. It could complete funding for a Radio Free Women of Afghanistan station and establish mosque-based female education. The United States could insist to the Afghan government that women's shelters not be taken over by the government. And it could continue to condition aid to Afghanistan on specific and measurable improvements for women there. Hopefully, U.S. Ambassador Ryan Crocker and others will actively investigate these possibilities.

The evidence is clear: The primary challenge facing the 21st century is to eliminate violence against women and remove barriers to developing their strength, creativity, and voices. A bird with one broken wing, or a species with one wounded sex, will never soar. We know that. Humans have experienced it for millennia—and paid for it with rivers of blood and mountains of needless suffering. The countries of the world must try a different path, one that we have every empirical reason to believe will lead to greater well-being, prosperity, and security for the entire international system. Sex and world peace, then, with no question mark.

Lessons from the LGBT Equality Movement

BY GEORGE LAKEY

George Lakey has written five books and taught at several colleges. He has also led 1,500 workshops and participated in activist projects on five continents. From *Waging Nonviolence*, April 2, 2013. Used by permission.

As the U.S. Supreme Court wrestles with the question of whether to grant marriage equality, many people have been talking about the rapid progress of homosexual rights. My own feelings are different. In the time since I came out publicly in 1974 I've usually felt the progress has been maddeningly slow. The gay side of me has been impatient.

On the other hand, the student of social change in me can see the other point of view: Given deeply structured heterosexism and its link to patriarchal oppression, policies toward LGBT people are indeed changing fast.

That being the case, let's consider what can we learn from this struggle for equality that could help activist strategizing for other causes.

A movement's context, of course, matters hugely. Not everything depends on strategy. Various social forces in the United States have offered gays some wiggle room in the last half century compared with, say, the stunning obstacles set before the labor movement.

Still, when we consider the uncertain progress of the peace movement since the 1960s and the environmental movement since the 1970s—even though the reasons for backing both have become ever more compelling—we might look to gay equality as a clearly successful movement for possible strategic lessons. Four fundamental characteristics stand out for me.

Uncompromising Conflict

All successful movements make strategic compromises to gain some wins and make enough forward motion to keep morale high. They expect that their short-term compromises will yield space to tackle bigger issues later. The LGBT movement is no exception; I was part of visionary gay liberation's early days, and accepting short-term, winnable goals hasn't been easy for me.

Nevertheless, a core declaration remained present, whatever the strategic choices: "We're queer, we're here, and you'll have to get over it."

"You'll have to get over it." What has been uncompromising about the LGBT struggle has been the requirement that people let go of a fundamental attitude they inherited that had become part of their identity and dictated their politics. If that approach were taken toward those who resist the peace movement, it would require insisting at every turn on getting over our dependence on violence when threatened. For those who fight for eco-justice, it requires an insistence on getting over our individual dependence on more stuff rather than on quality of life. For middle class people who are caught in the class war, it requires getting over the default loyalty to the 1 percent.

LGBT activists have designed strategic campaigns around many concrete, forward-moving policy changes—but behind those small steps is a collision over fundamental beliefs, like that male-is-better-than-female and light-is-superior-to-dark: We're colliding with a basic attitude, and you are going to have to get over it!

The intensity of this confrontation may be easy for straights to miss if they're just looking at photos of happy same-sex couples cutting a wedding cake. But when you talk to the individuals involved, you hear stories of intense confrontation: the parent or admired uncle who turned their back, the people at work who didn't invite them into the inner circle, the grown-ups at church who visibly worried when they talked with their children.

Social change for sexual minorities is moving rapidly, so older LGBT people have more of these stories of confrontation than younger people. But gay teenagers still kill themselves more frequently than straights. Confrontation with an age-old attitude still makes for trouble.

Because homophobia comes up even when LGBT people demand something modest like equality at work, edginess is built in. Other movements might ask themselves: While we design campaigns for specific goals, how do we also build in an edgy confrontation with an underlying attitude that fuels ongoing resistance?

Turning a Problem into an Opportunity

Movements are often at their most brilliant when they turn a liability into an asset. Jawaharlal Nehru, India's first prime minister, argued for armed struggle for independence from Britain as a young man, borrowing from the American colonists' example. His friend Mohandas Gandhi reportedly asked him where he would get sufficient weapons to go up against the world's mightiest empire. Gandhi then challenged him to turn the liability into a strength: Unarmed revolution would force the British out.

A culture of gay oppression allows many of us to hide in plain sight and pass as straight. That reality has kept many people alive in tight spots, but it is also onerous in all kinds of ways—especially with respect to building a movement. The strategic turnaround has been to use coming out as one of our most powerful tactics.

Even politicians notorious for opposing progress have announced themselves as gay allies because a daughter or son has come out to them; after that, ideology is no longer enough to lock away their hearts. Our enemies, once they know we're in their families or workplaces or bowling leagues, realize sooner or later that we're still here and that they might as well get over it. *WNV* [*Waging Nonviolence*] contributor Eileen Flanagan has written about how this dynamic works.

The use of our feared identity as leverage for change raises a question for other groups: What do we on a surface level consider as an obstacle that might become a strength with the right kind of twist? I remember, for example, former Oregon Republican senator Mark Hatfield being quite open about his pacifism while serving on a committee that determined the size of military budgets; his colleagues knew he would be formidable to deal with and, despite the hawkishness that dominated his party, they would have to get over it.

Strategic and Tactical Breadth

The LGBT movement stands out when it comes to sheer variety of tactics. Gays famously go beyond some activists' stock repertoire of rallies and marches. Gene Sharp, in his list of 198 methods of nonviolent action, includes social disobedience: "disobedience of social customs or the rules, regulations, or practices" of social institutions. For decades LGBT folks have been staging collective kiss-ins or simply acting as couples publicly, holding hands or canoodling; we've been holding forbidden marriages and living as couples openly together.

That's the defiant side of the two-sided coin that Sharp writes about: "establishing new social patterns." That one—method #174 if you're counting—has a distinguished history: Abolitionist Quaker Lucretia Mott was reprimanded in the 1830s by Philadelphia's mayor for doing what was called "walk-alongs": white people chatting amiably on the street while strolling with African Americans. LGBT people have found countless ways of pushing the heterosexist cultural envelope, leaving it to the enforcers of homophobia to try to get the envelope back into conformity with straight society.

The LGBT movement has played the insider/outsider game, too; talented people have been lobbying, issuing reports, organizing within political parties, writing legislation and seeking legal redress. As in other movements, there's often tension between the advocates who choose to work inside structures and those who work outside, but for the most part the insiders have not become hegemonic. That contrasts with the health care reform movement of 2008, in which the insiders tried to suck the air out of the room for anyone who wanted to broaden the movement with a grassroots insurgency fueled by radical energy. In the health care reform case, the insiders' boring hegemony invited the Tea Party to manifest the drama and provide the edginess that successful movements need.

For LGBT people, the tension sometimes showed up in the annual Pride parades, in which drag and erotic expression could see the light of day right next to Parents and Friends of Lesbians and Gays. These parades, alongside impressively organized national boycotts and statewide fights against anti-gay referenda, show a movement full of diversity and life, humor and art.

Learning from the Civil Rights Movement

It's still an open question: How much are white activists willing to learn from black activists? U.S. environmentalists in the 1970s learned enough to win their biggest single victory to date—stopping the nuclear power industry's dream of building hundreds more nuclear reactors—only to retreat to a more tepid, insider style. The largely white antiwar movement learned enough to be a major factor in forcing the United States out of Vietnam, but since then has largely preferred unstrategic "witness" activity to the solid nonviolent direct action campaigns of the civil rights movement.

In 1965—before the Stonewall riot in New York that is given credit for inaugurating the U.S. LGBT movement—there was a sit-in campaign at a Philadelphia lunch counter that discriminated against gays. The action was shortly followed by picketing a national shrine, Independence Hall. Nonviolent confrontations with the homophobic mass media included "zaps," in which gays burst into studios where live broadcasts were going on in order to make statements before being dragged away. Nonviolent disruption, usually framed by campaigns, was typical of the movement. One of the clearest examples was the direct action for changes in responding to the HIV crisis, led by ACT UP [AIDS Coalition to Unleash Power].

Maybe the life-and-death character of gay oppression made whites within the LGBT movement more open to learning from the civil rights movement. They had in common the requirement of facing harsh violence when they stood up for themselves. Movements coming from a more privileged base, like middle-class environmentalists—or even those in the labor movement who are white working-class—may have believed that making change would be easier for them and that they wouldn't need the nonviolent lessons of survival that were battle-tested in Alabama and Mississippi.

What's clear to me, looking back from 2013, is that it pays to face up to the conflicts of fundamental values that underlie our movements' confrontations with the 1 percent, to transform our weaknesses into strengths, and to develop a breadth of strategy and tactics from direct action to lobbying. The fight for gay equality has made sure to learn from the most recent movement in the United States that had overcome great odds; now, even as the equality movement continues, other movements may benefit by learning from it.

DISCUSSION QUESTIONS

1. Evaluate the main arguments that Gayle S. Trotter offers to support her claim that possessing guns makes women safer.

2. Describe the strongest threads of evidence that Public Health Watch presents to refute the claim that possessing guns makes women safer.

3. Explain why you agree, or disagree, with Public Health Watch's assertion that "deep-rooted societal" problems rather than rates of gun availability should be addressed to make women safer.

4. Summarize and evaluate the main evidence that Valerie M. Hudson presents to support her argument that creating greater well-being, prosperity, and security for women is the best way to create greater levels of world peace.

5. Examine the practical political and social implications of Hudson's idea that "a species with one wounded sex will never soar."

6. Review the benefits to social activists in following George Lakey's advice to encourage defiant and disobedient confrontations. Also review the negative effects such confrontations might produce.

7. Describe what you believe is the most likely future for trends in rates of gender-based violence and gender equity both in your own nation-state and for nation-states in general across the world.

RELIGION
AND TERRORISM

Part 4 presents several debates associated with religion and terrorism. These two topics are grouped together here as they often are in the popular mind. In fact, however, history shows that terrorism is not necessarily or even most often associated with religion. Terrorism properly understood is a political tactic, an act or acts aimed at frightening people. This tactic is available to religious and secular people alike. Terrorism is often used by governments to frighten their own citizens and by political groups to frighten governments. Eliminating any one religion or even all religions would not end the use of the tactic of terrorism by governments or by others desperate to alter the political status quo.

Debates about Religion

Earlier sections explored some possible causes of violence and war, including human nature, national security worries, masculine values, and patriarchy. This section focuses on religion, another force that many people believe encourages violence and war. Psychologist James W. Jones, in the first selection, describes how people with "sacred beliefs" sometimes sacrifice their security and even their lives to serve an imagined higher purpose. Religious beliefs, Jones maintains, can encourage radical acts of violence that non-religious people would never choose.

A second selection, by Sean McElwee, disputes the belief that religion is a prominent cause of violence and war. McElwee argues that biased secular analysts blame sacred believers for atrocities without first undertaking the hard work of understanding how diverse religious traditions really are. Religions reflect a deep-seated need of humans to understand the worlds they live in, McElwee maintains, and many secular systems of thought reflect the same need in non-religious terms. McElwee advises analysts to seek the causes of violence and war not in religious beliefs but in histories of colonization and imperialism, and in present-day social structures and schemes of exploitation.

A final selection calls into question the very idea of trying to separate religious from nonreligious beliefs. William T. Cavanaugh argues that there are no fundamental, cross-cultural differences between religious and non-religious people. Cavanaugh maintains that the search for so-called religious causes of violence and war reflects a biased perspective that serves "a particular need for consumers in the West." The enemies of western powers are often dismissed as deluded religious fanatics, Cavanagh claims, while westerners depict themselves as rational, patriotic citizens.

Sacred Terror: How Religion Makes Terrorism Worse

BY JAMES W. JONES

James W. Jones teaches religion at Rutgers University. His research focuses on connections between religion, terrorism, and violence and include the book *Blood That Cries Out From the Earth: The Psychology of Religious Terrorism* (2012). From *Psychology Today*, June 26, 2010. Used by permission.

Abu Bakr Ba'asyir, alleged leader of Jamaah Islamiyah in Indonesia, the group responsible for several bombings including the Bali nightclub said, "The aim of jihad is to look for blessing from Allah."

The Rev. Paul Hill, who shot and killed a physician and a body guard in front of a women's health clinic in the United States, wrote from prison "I continued to lift up my heart to the Lord, thankful for success. I had not failed in my errand and He had not failed me. The Lord had done great things through me. . . . Soon I was alone in a large, one man cell and could direct all my praise and thanks to the Lord. I repeatedly sang a song . . . 'Our God is an Awesome God': He is . . . [I] never cease[d] rejoicing in the Lord for all He had done."

After the Madrid train bombing, the perpetrators issued a statement in which they said, "We choose death as a path to life while you chose life that is a path to death."

All these examples, and there are many, many more, indicate that religiously motivated terrorists experience their violent commitments as a form of spiritual striving: they act in the name of the divine, their goals reflect an ultimate purpose and a concern with ethics, they seek to experience a divine reality in their actions; by giving themselves to a greater cause, they transcend the self and seek an integration with a greater reality. As much as those outside their movements may regard them as evil and criminal, in their eyes through violence and killing they are seeking the highest moral and spiritual goods—the sacred community, the purification of the human race, the kingdom of justice and righteousness, immortality, and union with God.

What does this have to do with psychology? A series of studies on the psychological impact of considering an activity as sacred, found that those who denote a facet of life as sacred place a higher priority on that aspect of life, invest more energy in it, and derive more meaning from it than happens with things not denoted as sacred. Denoting something as sacred appears to have significant emotional and behavioral consequences, maybe even if that something is the jihad or ending abortion and turning America into a Biblical theocracy, or restoring the boundaries of Biblical Israel, or purifying the Hindu homeland, or converting the Tamils to Buddhism.

Studies also find that sacred values and ultimate concerns take precedence over more finite concerns.

The leader of Jamaah Islamiyah in Indonesia said, "Jihad is more important than making the hajj. . . . There is no better deed than jihad. None. The highest deed in Islam is jihad. If we commit to jihad, we can neglect other deeds."

The Rev. Paul Hill told his followers, "we must use all the means necessary . . . this duty comes directly from God and cannot be removed by any human government. . . . It is virtually impossible to overstate the importance of maintaining the eternal and immutable principles of the Moral Law. . . ."

A young Somali man who was part of a cohort who left the United States to join El Shabaab in Somalia, at least one of whom died in a suicide bombing, said of his colleagues, "if it was just nationalism, they could give money. But religion convinced them to sacrifice their whole life."

For the religiously motivated terrorist, acts of violence in the name of God become "ultimate concerns," that is they take precedence over any more mundane commitments. As ultimate, sacred concerns, these acts take on an over-powering, transcendental necessity for the believer. In the eyes of their proponents such "acts of terror" become a spiritual necessity. Love of and duty to family must not stand in the way of duty to God or to the sacred land. No secondary commitments must be allowed to interfere with commitment to Jihad, to the "unborn," to Greater Israel, to Hindutva. Thus sacred terror is non-negotiable terror. It is no wonder that research finds that counterterrorism interventions that threaten or seek to bargain with religiously motivated terrorists only evoke greater scorn and rage: asking someone to trade their ultimate values for financial gain or greater political power is universally understood as the voice of the devil. A crucial point to remember in formulating any counter-terrorism policy.

My point is not that sacred terror, or any religious behavior, is only motivated by sacred strivings and goals. Of course not. My point is rather that this research suggests that when a goal or striving or movement takes on the patina of the sacred, that changes it in significant ways. There is much research being done now on how people are recruited into terrorist movements through naturally occurring groups: neighborhood and family connections, sports teams, [I]nternet chat rooms. But once the cause gets sanctified, once it moves from the family gathering or the soccer league or the online discussion into the realm of sacred values and ultimate concerns it changes. Even if terrorists are recruited primarily through natural groups, once their cause gets sanctified, it is transformed.

Likewise with the classic motivations for terrorist action like politics, ethnicity and nationalism. Once the nation, the land, the race takes on an ultimate status, it is no longer simple politics or group pride. Actions done in the name of the nation, the land, the race become absolute, ultimate, sanctified as the examples of the Hindu Nationalist Party (the BJP), or the Settler Movement in Israel or the Aryan Nations or the Nazis all show. They are not just politics cloaked in religious dress, they have entered the realm of ultimate concerns.

The research on the psychology of sacred values, spiritual strivings, and sanctification underscores some of the crucial ways that contemporary religious terrorism differs from previous ethno-nationalistic and politically revolutionary terrorism. It is not simply the same old terrorism with a different motivation or rhetoric. We must recognize that in the case of jihadis, Christian Identity Soldiers, Hindu nationalists and Israeli settlers seeking the ethno-religious purification of their country, apocalyptic Christians awaiting the rapture and hungering for Armageddon, Sri Lankan and South Asian Buddhists seeking to forcefully convert or suppress their non-Buddhist minorities, evoking and invoking the sacred transforms these movements in potentially dangerous ways.

Stop Blaming Religion for Violence

BY SEAN MCELWEE

Sean McElwee is a research associate at Demos and a frequent contributor to *Salon*. From *Huffington Post*, December 10, 2013. Used by permission.

Religion has once again become the "opiate of the people." But this time, instead of seducing the proletariat into accepting its position in a capitalist society, it lulls atheists into believing that abolishing religion would bring about utopia.

It is rather disturbing trend in a country whose greatest reformer was a Reverend—Dick Gregory has said, "Ten thousand years from now, the only reason a history book will mention the United States is to note where Martin Luther King Jr. was born"—to believe that religion is the root of all evil. And yet this is what the "New Atheism" (an anti-theist movement led originally by Sam Harris, Richard Dawkins, Daniel Dennett and the late—and great—Christopher Hitchens) movement asserts.

The "New Atheist" argument gives religion far, far too much credit for its ability to mold institutions and shape politics, committing the classic logical error of post hoc ergo propter hoc—mistaking a cause for its effect.

During the first Gulf War, Christopher Hitchens famously schooled Charlton Heston, asking him to name the countries surrounding Iraq, the place he was so eager to invade. A flummoxed Heston sputtered, naming a few random Middle Eastern countries (including, rather humorously, the island nation of Cyprus).

But then Hitchens decided that, in fact, bombing children was no longer so abhorrent, because these wars were no longer neocolonial wars dictated by economics and geopolitics but rather a final Armageddon between the forces of rationality and the forces of religion. The fact that the force of rationality and civilization was led by a cabal of religious extremists was of no concern for Hitchens. To co-opt Steven Weinberg, "Good men will naturally oppose bad wars and bad will naturally support them. To make a good man support a bad war, for that, you need an irrational fear of religion."

Somehow the man who denounced Kissinger's war crimes now supported Bush's—both wars, of course, supported by the scantest of logic. The man who so eloquently chronicled the corruption of the Clinton administration became the shill of his successor.

Ruber Cornwell wrote of Hitchens in *The Independent*,

> At that point [during the Gulf War], Hitchens, still the left-wing radical, opposed the conflict against Saddam Hussein. By contrast, George W Bush's 2003 invasion of Iraq couldn't come soon enough for him. The great catalyst for change was, of course, 9/11. Appalled by what he saw as the left's self-flagellation over the terrorist attacks, and the argument that America had brought the disaster on itself, Hitchens became arguably the most eloquent advocate in Washington of the need to overthrow Saddam Hussein. He quit The Nation, made friends with the likes of Paul Wolfowitz and, in foreign policy at least, was indistinguishable from the neocons. . . . The fact that the terrorist

attacks were carried out by Islamic extremists also sealed—if sealing were needed—Hitchens' belief that religion, and the "absolute certainty" of its followers was nothing but trouble.

For something so dreadfully asinine to be written about a man as well-traveled and well-read would be almost obscene if it were not true. But after 9/11, Hitchens stopped seeing the world in terms of geopolitics but rather saw it, like the Neocons in the Bush administration, as a war between the good Christian West and the evil Muslim Middle East.

Religion has a tendency to reflect political and economic realities. Hitchens, in fact, has made ample use of this Marxist analysis, questioning religious experts whether it was Constantine or the truth of Christ's words that were largely responsible for its breakneck spread. Constantine was, and his proclivities shaped the church. The doctrine of the Trinity was not decided exclusively by decades of intense debate; the whimsy of Constantine and political maneuvering between Arius and Athanasius had a significant influence on the outcome.

But if Hitchens is right, as he is, then why not take the observation to its logical conclusion? Is not the best explanation for the Thirty Years' War more likely political than religious? Might it be better to see jihad as a response to Western colonialism and the upending of Islamic society, rather than the product of religious extremism? The goal of the "New Atheists" is to eliminate centuries of history that Europeans are happy to erase, and render the current conflict as one of reason versus faith rather than what it is, exploiter and exploited.

Bernard Lewis writes,

> For vast numbers of Middle Easterners, Western-style economic methods brought poverty, Western-style political institutions brought tyranny, even Western-style warfare brought defeat. It is hardly surprising that so many were willing to listen to voices telling them that the old Islamic ways were best and that their only salvation was to throw aside the pagan innovations of the reformers and return to the True Path that God had prescribed for his people.

I have to wonder if Hitchens, Dawkins and Harris truly believe that eliminating religion will also make the Islamic world forget about centuries of colonization and deprivation. Without religion, will everyone living in Pakistan shrug off drone strikes and get on with their lives? If religion motivated 9/11, what motivated Bill Clinton to bomb the Al-Shifa pharmaceutical factory and leave millions of Sudanese people without access to medicine?

Liberals who once believed that the key to understanding hate and violence is deprivation now have embraced the idea that religion is the culprit. Religion is both a personal search for truth as well as a communal attempt to discern where we fit in the order of things. It can also motivate acts of social justice and injustice, but broad popular movements of the sort generally indicate a manipulation of religion, rather than studied reflections on religious doctrine. Shall we blame Jesus, who advocated "turning the other cheek," for Scott Philip Roeder, or more plausibly his schizophrenia?

Of course, I'm entirely aware of the problems in modern American Christianity. I have written an essay excoriating what I see as the false Christianity. But any critique of religion that can be made from the outside (by atheists) can be made more persuasively from within religion. For instance, it would hardly be the theologian's job to point out that, according to *The Economist*, "Too many of the findings that fill the academic ether are the result of shoddy experiments or poor analysis. A rule of thumb among biotechnology venture-capitalists is that half of published research cannot be replicated." I'm sure scientists are well aware of the problem and working to rectify it. Similarly, within the church there are modernizers and reformers working to quash the Church's excesses, no Hitchens, Dawkins or Harris needed. Terry Eagleton writes,

> Card-carrying rationalists like Dawkins, who is the nearest thing to a professional atheist we have had since Bertrand Russell, are in one sense the least well-equipped to understand what they castigate, since they don't believe there is anything there to be understood, or at least anything

worth understanding. This is why they invariably come up with vulgar caricatures of religious faith that would make a first-year theology student wince. The more they detest religion, the more ill-informed their criticisms of it tend to be. If they were asked to pass judgment on phenomenology or the geopolitics of South Asia, they would no doubt bone up on the question as assiduously as they could. When it comes to theology, however, any shoddy old travesty will pass muster.

The impulse to destroy religion will ultimately fail. Religion is little different from Continental philosophy or literature (which may explain the hatred of Lacan and Derrida among Analytic philosophers). It is an attempt to explain the deprivations of being human and what it means to live a good life. Banish Christ and Muhammad and you may end up with religions surrounding the works of Zizek and Sloterdijk (there is already a[n] *International Journal of Zizek Studies* [italics added], maybe soon a seminary?). Humans will always try to find meaning and purpose in their lives, and science will never be able to tell them what it is. This, ultimately is the meaning of religion, and "secular religions" like philosophy and literature are little different in this sense than theology. Certainly German philosophy was distorted by madmen just as Christianity has been in the past, but atheists fool themselves if they try to differentiate the two.

As a poorly-practicing Christian who reads enough science to be functional at dinner parties, I would like to suggest a truce—one originally proposed by the Catholic church and promoted by the eminent Stephen J. Gould. Science, the study of the natural world, and religion, the inquiry into the meaning of life (or metaphysics, more broadly) constitute non-overlapping magisteria. Neither can invalidate the theories of the other, if such theories are properly within their realm. Any theologian or scientist who steps out of their realm to speculate upon the other is free to do so, but must do so with an adequate understanding of the other's realm.

Religion (either secular or theological) does not poison all of society and science should not be feared, but rather embraced. Both can bring humanity to new heights of empathy, imagination and progress. To quote the greatest American reformer, "Science investigates; religion interprets. Science gives man knowledge, which is power; religion gives man wisdom, which is control. Science deals mainly with facts; religion deals mainly with values. The two are not rivals."

"New Atheists" believe that religion threatens progress and breeds conflict and that were

religion eliminated, we would begin to solve the world's problems. But abolishing religion is not only unfeasible, it would ultimately leave us no closer to truth, love or peace. Rather, we need to embrace the deep philosophical and spiritual questions that arise from our shared existence and work toward a world without deprivation. That will require empathy and multiculturalism, not demagoguery.

Selections from *The Myth of Religious Violence*

BY WILLIAM T. CAVANAUGH

William T. Cavanaugh is a researcher at the Center for World Catholicism and Intercultural Theology at DePaul University in Chicago. Selections from THE MYTH OF RELIGIOUS VIOLENCE: SECULAR IDEOLOGY AND THE ROOTS OF MODERN CONFLICT by William T. Cavanaugh (2009) pp. 3–8, 14. By permission of Oxford University Press USA.

The idea that religion has a tendency to promote violence is part of the conventional wisdom of Western societies, and it underlies many of our institutions and policies, from limits on the public role of churches to efforts to promote liberal democracy in the Middle East. What I call the "myth of religious violence" is the idea that religion is a transhistorical and transcultural feature of human life, essentially distinct from "secular" features such as politics and economics, which has a peculiarly dangerous inclination to promote violence. Religion must therefore be tamed by restricting its access to public power. The secular nation-state then appears as natural, corresponding to a universal and timeless truth about the inherent dangers of religion.

... I challenge this piece of conventional wisdom, not simply by arguing that ideologies and institutions labeled "secular" can be just as violent as those labeled "religious," but by examining how the twin categories of religious and secular are constructed in the first place. A growing body of scholarly work explores how the category "religion" has been invented in the modern West and in colonial contexts according to specific configurations of political power.... I draw on

this scholarship to examine how timeless and transcultural categories of religion and the secular are used in arguments that religion causes violence. I argue that there is no transhistorical and transcultural essence of religion and that essentialist attempts to separate religious violence from secular violence are incoherent.

What counts as religious or secular in any given context is a function of different configurations of power. The question then becomes why such essentialist constructions are so common. I argue that, in what are called "Western" societies, the attempt to create a transhistorical and transcultural concept of religion that is essentially prone to violence is one of the foundational legitimating myths of the liberal nation-state. The myth of religious violence helps to construct and marginalize a religious Other, prone to fanaticism, to contrast with the rational, peace-making, secular subject. This myth can be and is used in domestic politics to legitimate the marginalization of certain types of practices and groups labeled religious, while underwriting the nation-state's monopoly on its citizens' willingness to sacrifice and kill. In foreign policy, the myth of religious violence serves to cast nonsecular social orders, especially Muslim societies, in the role of villain. *They* have not yet learned to remove the dangerous influence of religion from political life. *Their* violence is therefore irrational and fanatical. *Our* violence, being secular, is rational, peace making, and sometimes regrettably necessary to contain their violence. We find ourselves obliged to bomb them into liberal democracy.

Especially since September 11, 2001, there has been a proliferation of scholarly books by historians, sociologists, political scientists, religious studies professors, and others exploring the peculiarly violence-prone nature of religion. At the same time, there is a significant group of scholars who have been exploring the ideological uses of the construction of the term "religion" in Western modernity. On the one hand, we have a group of scholars who are convinced that religion as such has an inherent tendency to promote violence. On the other hand, we have a group of scholars who question whether there is any "religion as such," except as a constructed ideological category whose changing history must be carefully scrutinized.

There is much more at stake here than academics haggling over definitions. Once we begin to ask what the religion-and-violence arguments mean by "religion," we find that their explanatory power is hobbled by a number of indefensible assumptions about what does and does not count as religion. Certain types of practices and institutions are condemned, while others—nationalism, for example—are ignored. Why? My hypothesis is that religion and violence arguments serve a particular need for their consumers in the West. These arguments are part of a broader Enlightenment narrative that has invented a dichotomy between the religious and the secular and constructed the former as an irrational and dangerous impulse that must give way in public to rational, secular forms of power. In the West, revulsion toward killing and dying in the name of one's religion is one of the principal means by which we become convinced that killing and dying in the name of the nation-state is laudable and proper. The myth of religious violence also provides secular social orders with a stock character, the religious fanatic, to serve as enemy. Carl Schmitt

may be right—descriptively, not normatively—to point out that the friend-enemy distinction is essential to the creation of the political in the modern state.[1] Schmitt worried that a merely procedural liberalism would deprive the political of the friend-enemy antagonism, which would break out instead in religious, cultural, and economic arenas. Contemporary liberalism has found its definitive enemy in the Muslim who refuses to distinguish between religion and politics. The danger is that, in establishing an Other who is essentially irrational, fanatical, and violent, we legitimate coercive measures against that Other.

I have no doubt that ideologies and practices of all kinds—including, for example, Islam and Christianity—can and do promote violence under certain conditions. What I challenge as incoherent is the argument that there is something called religion—a genus of which Christianity, Islam, Hinduism, and so on are species—which is necessarily more inclined toward violence than are ideologies and institutions that are identified as secular. Unlike other books on religion and violence, I do not argue that religion either does or does not promote violence, but rather I analyze the political conditions under which the very category of religion is constructed.

This . . . then, is not a defense of religion against the charge of violence.[2] People who identify themselves as religious sometimes argue that the real motivation behind so-called religious violence is in fact economic and political, not religious. Others argue that people who do violence are, by definition, not religious. The Crusader is not really a Christian, for example, because he does not really understand the meaning of Christianity. I do not think that either of these arguments works. In the first place, it is impossible to separate religious from economic and political motives in such a way that religious motives are innocent of violence. How could one, for example, separate religion from politics in Islam, when most Muslims themselves make no such separation? . . . [T]he very separation of religion from politics is an invention of the modern West. In the second place, it may be the case that the Crusader has misappropriated the true message of Christ, but one cannot therefore excuse Christianity of all responsibility. Christianity is not simply a set of doctrines immune to historical circumstance, but a lived historical experience embodied and shaped by the empirically observable actions of Christians. I have no intention of excusing Christianity or Islam or any other set of ideas and practices from careful analysis. Given certain conditions, Christianity and Islam can and do contribute to violence. War in the Middle East, for example, can be justified not merely on behalf of oil and freedom, but on the basis of a millenarian reading of parts of the Christian scriptures. Christian churches are indeed complicit in legitimating wars carried out by national armies.

But what is implied in the conventional wisdom is that there is an essential difference between religions such as Christianity, Islam, Hinduism, and Judaism, on the one hand, and secular ideologies and institutions such as nationalism, Marxism, capitalism, and liberalism, on the other, and that the former are essentially more prone to violence—more absolutist, divisive, and irrational—than the latter. It is this claim that I find both unsustainable and dangerous. It is unsustainable because ideologies and institutions labeled secular can be just as absolutist, divisive, and irrational as those labeled religious. It is dangerous because it helps to marginalize, and even legitimate violence against, those forms of life that are labeled religious. What gets labeled religious and what does not is therefore of crucial importance. The myth of religious violence tries to establish as timeless, universal, and natural a very contingent set of categories—religious and secular—that are in fact constructions of the modern West. Those who do not accept these categories as timeless, universal, and natural are subject to coercion.

I use the term "myth" to describe this claim, not merely to indicate that it is false, but to give a sense of the power of the claim in Western societies. A story takes on the status of myth when it becomes unquestioned. It becomes very difficult to think outside the paradigm that the myth establishes and reflects because myth and reality become mutually reinforcing. Society is structured to conform to the apparent truths that the myth reveals,

and what is taken as real increasingly takes on the color of the myth. The more that some are marginalized as Other, the more Other they become. At the same time, the myth itself becomes more unquestioned the more social reality is made to conform to it. Society is structured in such a way as to make the categories through which the myth operates seem given and inevitable.

All of this makes the refutation of a myth particularly difficult. Linda Zerilli's comments about what she calls "a mythology" apply here:

> A mythology cannot be defeated in the sense that one wins over one's opponent through the rigor of logic or the force of evidence; a mythology cannot be defeated through arguments that would reveal it as groundless belief. . . . A mythology is utterly groundless, hence stable. What characterizes a mythology is not so much its crude or naïve character—mythologies can be extremely complex and sophisticated—but, rather, its capacity to elude our practices of verification and refutation.[3]

. . . The only way I can hope to refute the myth is to do a genealogy of these contingent shifts and to show that the problem that the myth of religious violence claims to identify and solve—the problem of violence in society—is in fact exacerbated by the forms of power that the myth authorizes. The myth of religious violence can only be undone by showing that it lacks the resources to solve the very problem that it identifies.

The definition of "violence" that I will assume . . . is therefore the same one that theorists of the supposed link between religion and violence appear to use, although only one of the figures I examine . . . offers an explicit definition of violence. "Violence" in their writings generally means injurious or lethal harm and is almost always discussed in the context of physical violence, such as war and terrorism.[4] I will assume the same general definition when discussing violence.

When I write of the myth of religious violence as a "Western" concept and discuss how it functions in the "West," I do not mean to imply that I think that such a monolithic geographical reality exists as such. The West is a construct, a contested project, not a simple description of a monolithic entity. The West is an ideal created by those who would read the world in terms of a binary relation between the "West and the rest," in Samuel Huntington's phrase.[5] The point of my argument is, of course, to question that binary.

When I use the terms "religion," "religious," and "secular," I recognize that they should often be surrounded by scare quotes. I have nevertheless tried to keep the use of scare quotes to a minimum to avoid cluttering the text.

Because of the pervasive nature of the myth of religious violence, I have tried to be as thorough as possible in showing the structure of the myth, providing a genealogy of it, and showing for what purposes it is used. Some readers may wonder if it is really necessary to examine nine different academic versions of the myth . . . or to cite more than forty different instances . . . where Protestant-Catholic opposition in the "wars of religion" did not apply. I have tried to be thorough and detailed to show how pervasive the myth is and to dispel any objections that I am picking out just a few idiosyncratic figures. I have also found it necessary to be thorough precisely because such a pervasive myth will not fall easily. The more a myth eludes our ordinary practices of verification and refutation, the more sustained must be the attempt to unmask it. It is not simply that the myth is pervasive, but that the very categories under which the discussion takes place—especially the categories of religious-secular and religion-politics—are so firmly established as to appear natural. Only a thorough genealogy can show that their construction is anything but inevitable. . . .

I do not wish either to deny the virtues of liberalism nor to excuse the vices of other kinds of social orders. I think that the separation of church and state is generally a good thing. On the other side, there is no question that certain forms of Muslim beliefs and practices do promote violence. Such forms should be examined and criticized. It is unhelpful, however, to undertake that criticism through the lens of a groundless religious-secular dichotomy that causes us to turn a blind eye to secular forms of imperialism and violence. Insofar as the myth of religious violence creates the villains against which

a liberal social order defines itself, the myth is little different from previous forms of Western imperialism that claimed the inferiority of non-Western Others and subjected them to Western power in the hopes of making them more like "us."

I do not have an alternative theopolitics of my own to present. . . . [My] purpose . . . is negative: to contribute to a dismantling of the myth of religious violence. To dismantle the myth would have multiple benefits. . . . It would free empirical studies of violence from the distorting categories of religious and secular. It would help us to see that the foundational possibilities for social orders, in the Islamic world and the West, are not limited to a stark choice between theocracy and secularism. It would help us to see past the stereotype of non-secular Others as religious fanatics, and it would question one of the justifications for war against those Others. It would help Americans to eliminate one of the main obstacles to having a serious conversation about the question "Why do they hate us?"—a conversation that would not overlook the history of U.S. dealings with the Middle East in favor of pinning the cause on religious fanaticism.

Bridging the threatening gap between us and them requires that we not only know the Other, but know ourselves. This . . . is intended as a contribution to that pursuit.

NOTES

1. "The specific political distinction to which political actions and motives can be reduced is that between friend and enemy"; Carl Schmitt, *The Concept of the Political* (New Brunswick, NJ: Rutgers University Press, 1976), 26.

2. One such book is Keith Ward's *Is Religion Dangerous?* (Grand Rapids, MI: Eerdmans, 2007). The introduction to the book, entitled "What Is Religion?" takes on the question of definition and shows how fraught it is. Ward takes one common definition of religion from the Shorter Oxford English Dictionary and shows how belief in Superman and the constitution of the Labour Party would count as religions. Ward remarks, "If you do

not know what 'religion' is, you can hardly decide whether it is dangerous or not." But Ward then changes the subject and leaves the question unexplored. In the first chapter, he writes, "At last, having discussed and then side-stepped the almost insuperable difficulties in saying what a religion is, I can get around to the question of whether religion is dangerous." The assumption is that there must be something out there, even if we have trouble defining it. The rest of the book is a defense of religion from the charge of violence.

3. Linda M. G. Zerilli, "Doing without Knowing: Feminism's Politics of the Ordinary," *Political Theory* 26, no. 4 (August 1998): 443, quoted in Elizabeth Shakman Hurd, *The Politics of Secularism in International Relations* (Princeton, NJ: Princeton University Press, 2008), 109.

4. The only one . . . who gives a definition of violence is Charles Selengut, who borrows John Hall's definition of violence as "'actions that inflict, threaten or cause injury' and such action[s] may be 'corporal, written or verbal'"; Charles Selengut, *Sacred Fury: Understanding Religious Violence* (Walnut Creek, CA: AltaMira, 2003), 9. Selengut thus expands the definition beyond physical injury.

5. Samuel Huntington, "If Not Civilizations, What?" *Foreign Affairs* 72 (November–December 1993): 192

DISCUSSION QUESTIONS

1. Evaluate James W. Jones's claim that "sacred values and ultimate concerns" encourage violence more than secular nationalistic and revolutionary ideals.

2. Analyze the evidence to support Sean McElwee's assertion that eliminating all religions would not reduce human levels of violence.

3. Detail the main areas of disagreement between Jones and McElwee on the relationship between religion and violence.

4. Summarize in plain language the meaning of William T. Cavanaugh's statement that "there is no transhistorical and transcultural essence of religion."

5. Describe what Cavanaugh says are the principle uses of the myth of religious violence for people in Western nation-states.

6. Explain how Cavanaugh would likely go about offering a rebuttal to Jones's claims about religion. Also explain how McElwee would likely critique Cavanaugh's assertions.

Debates about Terrorism

The previous section examined some disagreements about whether religious beliefs tend to increase terrorism and other forms of violence. This section looks more closely at terrorism as a political tactic, both when it is associated with religion and when it is not.

The first selection by Max Abrahms, "Why Terrorism Does Not Work," presents one of the most often cited articles in terrorism studies. Abrahms offers a careful empirical analysis of twenty-eight *strategic terrorist groups* that aimed to coerce one or more governments into policy changes. (Abrahms's analysis explicitly excludes what he calls *redemptive terrorist groups*, violence that aims to win specific human or material resources.) Abrahms's data demonstrate that strategic terrorists achieve their goals less than ten percent of the time. Abrahms also offers a theory that strategic terrorists commonly fail because they have "high correspondence"; their target countries usually mistake terrorist means—violence—for terrorist goals. Government leaders thus tend to believe they are in a "fight to the death" and are not inclined to listen to actual terrorist demands or agree to negotiations aimed at changing current policies.

Abrahms emphasizes terrorism's frequent failures, but a second selection maintains that terrorism has been highly effective over the last fifteen years in making Europe and the United States both less safe and less stable. David Rothkopf contends these increasingly perilous conditions were caused not by the acts of terrorists but rather by the West's hysterical and incoherent reactions. Rothkopf argues that Europe and the United States are foolishly wounding themselves more deeply than any terrorists have the capacity to do.

Scot Atran, in a third selection, offers a more pessimistic view of contemporary terrorism than the views of either Abrahms or Rothkopf. Atran says that terrorist organizations such as ISIS appeal to youth yearning to do something significant with their lives. Atran's research shows that one person usually joins and then other friends also join, in a pattern of peer-bonding especially common among young people. Opponents of terrorism misunderstand the thrilling call to action that terrorism can offer. Recruits to terrorism may have their deep-seated psychological needs fulfilled at levels unavailable through most other activities present in their societies. Atran warns that terrorism will not decrease as long as opponents ignore the genuine appeal and joy young recruits feel when they dedicate their lives to a grand purpose.

In a final selection, Maria J. Stephan and Shaazka Beyerle argue there are effective ways to reduce terrorism before it starts. Whereas Atran's suggestions for reducing terrorism in the third selection focus on culture and ideals, in this final selection, Stephan and Beyerle focus on the problem of corruption and on the effectiveness of nonviolent, grassroots movements. Far too much emphasis is given to seeking top-down, government-oriented solutions to terrorism, Stephan and Beyerle declare. Much more support is needed instead for citizen-led campaigns and movements that both increase levels of democracy and decrease terrorism.

Selections from "Why Terrorism Does Not Work"

BY MAX ABRAHMS

Max Abrahms teaches political science at Northeastern University, where he specializes in empirical studies of the consequences of terrorism, its motives, and the implications for counterterrorism strategy. Due to space limitations, notes have been omitted from this selection. Selections from "Why Terrorism Does Not Work." *International Security* 31, no. 2 (2006): 42–78. Used by permission.

Terrorist groups attack civilians to coerce their governments into making policy concessions, but does this strategy work? If target countries systematically resist rewarding terrorism, the international community is armed with a powerful message to deter groups from terrorizing civilians. The prevailing view within the field of political science, however, is that terrorism is an effective coercive strategy. The implications of this perspective are grim; as target countries are routinely coerced into making important strategic and ideological concessions to terrorists, their victories will reinforce the strategic logic for groups to attack civilians, spawning even more terrorist attacks.

This pessimistic outlook is unwarranted; there has been scant empirical research on whether terrorism is a winning coercive strategy, that is, whether groups tend to exact policy concessions from governments by attacking their civilian populations. . . .

. . . Within the past several years, numerous scholars have purported to show that terrorism is an effective coercive strategy, but their research invariably rests on game-theoretic models, single case studies, or a handful of well-known terrorist victories. To date, political scientists have neither analyzed the outcomes of a large number of terrorist campaigns nor attempted to specify the antecedent conditions for terrorism to work. In light of its policy relevance, terrorism's record in coercing policy change requires further empirical analysis.

[In] this study, [I] analyze the political plights of twenty-eight terrorist groups—the complete list of foreign terrorist organizations (FTOs) as designated by the U.S. Department of State since 2001. The data yield two unexpected findings. First, the groups accomplished their forty-two policy objectives only 7 percent of the time. Second, although the groups achieved certain types of policy objectives more than others, the key variable for terrorist success was a tactical one: target selection. Groups whose attacks on civilian targets outnumbered attacks on military targets systematically failed to achieve their policy objectives, regardless of their nature. These findings suggest that (1) terrorist groups rarely achieve their policy objectives, and (2) the poor success rate is inherent to the tactic of terrorism itself. Together, the data challenge the dominant scholarly opinion that terrorism is strategically rational behavior. The bulk of the article [by the U.S. Department of State] develops a theory to explain why terrorist groups are unable to achieve their policy objectives by targeting civilians.

. . .

Measuring Terrorism's Effectiveness

Terrorist campaigns come in two varieties: strategic terrorism aims to coerce a government into changing its policies; redemptive terrorism is intended solely to attain specific human or material resources such as prisoners or money. Because my focus is on terrorism's ability to compel policy change, terrorism in this study refers only to strategic terrorism campaigns. Terrorism's effectiveness can be measured along two dimensions: combat effectiveness describes the level of damage inflicted by the coercing power; strategic effectiveness refers to the extent to which the coercing power achieves its policy objectives. This study is confined to analyzing the notion that terrorism is strategically effective, not whether it succeeds on an operational or tactical level. Finally, because this study is concerned with terrorism's effect on the target country, intermediate objectives—namely, the ability of terrorist groups to gain international attention and support—are outside the scope of analysis.

This study analyzes the strategic effectiveness of the twenty-eight terrorist groups designated by the U.S. Department of State as foreign terrorist organizations since 2001. The only selection bias would come from the State Department. Using this list provides a check against selecting cases on the dependent variable, which would artificially inflate success rate because the most well-known policy outcomes involve terrorist victories (e.g., the U.S. withdrawal from southern Lebanon in 1984). Furthermore, because all of the terrorist groups have remained active since 2001, ample time has been allowed for each group to make progress on achieving its policy goals, thereby reducing the possibility of artificially deflating the success rate through too small a time frame. In fact, the terrorist groups have had significantly more time . . . to

accomplish their policy objectives: the groups, on average, have been active since 1978; the majority has practiced terrorism since the 1960s and 1970s; and only four were established after 1990.

For terrorist groups, policy outcomes are easier to assess than policy objectives. Instead of arbitrarily defining the objectives of the terrorist groups in this study, I define them as the terrorists do. In general, the stated objectives of terrorist groups are a stable and reliable indicator of their actual intentions. This assumption undergirds the widely accepted view within terrorism studies that groups use terrorism as a communication strategy to convey to target countries the costs of noncompliance. Because these groups seek political change and because their stated objectives represent their intentions, terrorism's effectiveness is measured by comparing their stated objectives to policy outcomes. A potential objection to this approach is that terrorists possess extreme policy goals relative to those of their supporters, and thus terrorist campaigns may be judged unsuccessful even when they compel policy changes of significance to their broader community. What distinguish terrorists from "moderates," however, are typically not their policy goals, but the belief that terrorism is the optimal means to achieve them. As Pape has observed, "It is not that terrorists pursue radical goals" relative to those of their supporters. Rather, it is that "terrorists are simply the members of their societies who are the most optimistic about the usefulness of violence for achieving goals that many, and often most, support." There are no broadly based data sets with coded information on the objectives of terrorist campaigns, but those ascribed to the terrorist groups in this study are all found in standard descriptions of them, such as in RAND's MIPT [National Memorial Institute for the Prevention of Terrorism] Terrorism Knowledge Base and the Federation of American Scientists' Directory of Terrorist Organizations (see Table 1).

To capture the range of policy outcomes, this study employs a four-tiered rating scale. A "Total success" [as listed in the table] denotes the full attainment of a terrorist group's policy objective.

Table 1. Terrorist Groups: Objectives, Targets, and Outcomes

Group	Objective	Type	Main Target	Outcome
Abu Nidal Organization	Destroy Israel	Maximalist	Civilian	No success
Abu Sayyaf Group	Establish Islamic state in Philippines	Maximalist	Civilian	No success
Al-Qaida	Expel the United States from Persian Gulf	Limited	Civilian	Limited success
Al-Qaida	Sever U.S.-Israel relations	Idiosyncratic	Civilian	No success
Al-Qaida	Sever U.S.-apostate relations	Idiosyncratic	Civilian	No success
Al-Qaida	Spare Muslims from "Crusader wars"	Idiosyncratic	Civilian	No success
Armed Islamic Group	Establish Islamic state in Algeria	Maximalist	Civilian	No success
United Forces of Colombia	Eliminate left-wing insurgents	Idiosyncratic	Civilian	No success
Aum Shinrikyo	Establish utopian society in Japan	Maximalist	Civilian	No success
People's Liberation Front	Establish Marxism in Turkey	Maximalist	Civilian	No success
People's Liberation Front	Sever U.S.-Turkish relations	Idiosyncratic	Civilian	No success
Egyptian Islamic Jihad	Establish Islamic state in Egypt	Maximalist	Civilian	No success
National Liberation Army	Establish Marxism in Colombia	Maximalist	Civilian	No success
Revolutionary Armed Forces of Colombia	Establish peasant rule in Colombia	Maximalist	Military	Limited success
Fatherland and Liberty	Establish Basque state	Limited	Civilian	No success
Hamas	Establish state in historic Palestine	Maximalist	Civilian	Limited success
Hamas	Destroy Israel	Maximalist	Civilian	No success
Harakat ul-Mujahidin	Rule Kashmir	Limited	Military	No success
Harakat ul-Mujahidin	Eliminate Indian insurgents	Idiosyncratic	Military	No success
Hezbollah (Lebanese)	Expel peacekeepers	Limited	Military	Total success
Hezbollah (Lebanese)	Expel Israel	Limited	Military	Total success
Hezbollah (Lebanese)	Destroy Israel	Maximalist	Military	No success
Islamic Movement of Uzbekistan	Establish Islamic state in Uzbekistan	Maximalist	Military	No success
Islamic Group	Establish Islamic state in Egypt	Maximalist	Civilian	No success
Islamic Jihad	Establish state in historic Palestine	Maximalist	Civilian	Limited success
Islamic Jihad	Destroy Israel	Maximalist	Civilian	No success
Kach	Transfer Palestinians from Israel	Idiosyncratic	Civilian	No success

Table 1. Terrorist Groups: Objectives, Targets, and Outcomes (*Continued*)

Group	Objective	Type	Main Target	Outcome
Mujahideen-e-Khalq	End clerical rule in Iran	Maximalist	Military	No success
Popular Front for the Liberation of Palestine (PFLP)	Destroy Israel	Maximalist	Civilian	No success
PFLP	Establish Marxist Palestine	Maximalist	Civilian	No success
PFLP-General Command	Destroy Israel	Maximalist	Military	No success
PFLP-General Command	Establish Marxist Palestine	Maximalist	Military	No success
Kurdistan Workers' Party	Establish Kurdish state in Middle East	Limited	Civilian	No success
Kurdistan Workers' Party	Establish communism in Turkey	Maximalist	Civilian	No success
Palestine Liberation Front	Destroy Israel	Maximalist	Civilian	No success
Real Irish Republican Army	Establish Irish unification	Limited	Military	No success
Revolutionary Nuclei	Establish Marxism in Greece	Maximalist	Military	No success
Revolutionary Nuclei	Sever U.S.-Greek relations	Idiosyncratic	Military	No success
Seventeen November	Establish Marxism in Greece	Maximalist	Civilian	No success
Seventeen November	Sever U.S.-Greek relations	Idiosyncratic	Civilian	No success
Shining Path	Establish communism in Peru	Maximalist	Civilian	No success
Tamil Tigers	Establish Tamil state	Limited	Military	Partial success

SOURCES: RAND, MIPT Terrorism Knowledge Base, http://www.tkb.org/Home.jsp; and Federation of American Scientists, "Liberation Movements, Terrorist Organizations, Substance Cartels, and Other Para-state Entities," http://www.fas.org/irp/world/para.

Conversely, "No success" describes a scenario in which a terrorist group does not make any perceptible progress on realizing its stated objective. Middling achievements are designated as either a "Partial success" or a "Limited success" in descending degrees of effectiveness. Several groups are counted more than once to reflect their multiple policy objectives. Hezbollah, for example, is credited with two policy successes: repelling the multinational peacekeepers and Israelis from southern Lebanon in 1984 and again in 2000. By contrast, Revolutionary Nuclei is tagged with two policy failures: its inability either to spark a communist revolution in Greece or to sever U.S.–Greek relations.

To construct a hard test for the argument that terrorism is an ineffective means of coercion, I afforded generous conditions to limit the number of policy failures. First, for analytic purposes both a "total success" and a "partial success" are counted as policy successes, while only completely unsuccessful outcomes ("no successes") are counted as failures. A "limited success" is counted as neither a success nor a failure, even though the terrorist group invariably faces criticism from its natural constituency that the means employed have been ineffective, or even counterproductive. Thus, a policy objective is deemed a success even if the terrorist group was only partially successful in accomplishing it, whereas an objective receives a failing grade only if the group has not made any noticeable progress toward achieving it. Second, an objective is judged successful even if the group accomplished it before 2001, the year the State Department assembled its official list of foreign terrorist organizations. Third, all policy successes are attributed to terrorism as the causal factor, regardless of whether important intervening variables, such as a peace process, may have contributed to the outcome. Fourth, terrorist groups are not charged with additional penalties for provoking responses from the target country that could be considered counterproductive to their policy goals. Fifth, the objectives of al-Qaida affiliates are limited to their nationalist struggles. Groups such as the Kashmiri Harakat ul-Mujahidin and the Egyptian Islamic Jihad are not evaluated on their

ability to sever U.S.–Israeli relations, for example, even though many of their supporters claim to support this goal.

Based on their policy platforms, the twenty-eight terrorist groups examined in this study have a combined forty-two policy objectives, a healthy sample of cases for analysis. Several well-known terrorist campaigns have accomplished their objectives. As frequently noted, Hezbollah successfully coerced the multinational peacekeepers and Israelis from southern Lebanon in 1984 and 2000, and the Tamil Tigers won control over the northern and eastern coastal areas of Sri Lanka from 1990 on. In the aggregate, however, the terrorist groups achieved their main policy objectives only three out of forty-two times—a 7 percent success rate. Within the coercion literature, this rate of success is considered extremely low. It is substantially lower, for example, than even the success rate of economic sanctions, which are widely regarded as only minimally effective. The most authoritative study on economic sanctions has found a success rate of 34 percent—nearly five times greater than the success rate of the terrorist groups examined in my study—while other studies have determined that economic sanctions accomplish their policy objectives at an even higher rate. Compared to even minimally effective methods of coercion, terrorism is thus a decidedly unprofitable coercive instrument.

. . .

High Correspondence of Terrorism

The theory posited here is that terrorist groups that target civilians are unable to coerce policy change because terrorism has extremely high correspondence. Countries believe that their civilian populations are attacked not because the terrorist group is protesting unfavorable external conditions such as territorial occupation or poverty. Rather, target countries infer from the short-term consequences of terrorism—the deaths of innocent citizens, mass fear, loss of confidence in the government to offer protection, economic contraction, and the inevitable erosion of civil liberties—the objectives of the terrorist group. In short, target countries view the negative consequences of terrorist attacks on their societies and political systems as evidence that the terrorists want them destroyed. Target countries are understandably skeptical that making concessions will placate terrorist groups believed to be motivated by these maximalist objectives. As a consequence, CCTGs ["civilian-centric terrorist groups"] are unable to coerce target countries into entering a political compromise, even when their stated goals are not maximalist. . . .

Conclusion

Thomas Schelling asserted more than a decade ago that terrorists frequently accomplish "intermediate means toward political objectives . . . but with a few exceptions it is hard to see that the attention and publicity have been of much value except as ends in themselves." This study corroborates that view; the twenty-eight groups of greatest significance to U.S. counterterrorism policy have achieved their forty-two policy objectives less than 10 percent of the time. As the political mediation literature would predict, target countries did not make concessions when terrorist groups had maximalist objectives. Yet even when groups expressed limited, ambiguous, or idiosyncratic policy objectives, they failed to win concessions by primarily attacking civilian targets. This suggests not only that terrorism is an ineffective instrument of coercion, but that its poor success rate is inherent to the tactic of terrorism itself.

Why are terrorist groups unable to coerce governments when they primarily attack civilian targets? Terrorism miscommunicates groups' objectives because of its extremely high correspondence. The responses of Russia to the September 1999 apartment bombings, the United States to the attacks of September 11, and Israel to Palestinian terrorism in the first intifada provide evidence that target countries infer the objectives of terrorist groups not from their stated goals, but from the short-term consequences of terrorist acts. Target countries view the deaths of their citizens and the resulting turmoil as proof that the perpetrators want to destroy their societies, their publics, or both. Countries are therefore reluctant to make concessions when their civilians are targeted irrespective of the perpetrators' policy demands.

"Our Reaction to Terrorism Is More Dangerous Than the Terrorists"

BY DAVID ROTHKOPF

David Rothkopf is the editor of *Foreign Policy* magazine and president of Garten Rothkoft, an international advisory firm specializing in transformational global trends. From *Foreign Policy*, November 25, 2015. Used by permission.

Donald Trump could not do more to aid the terrorists of the Islamic State were he to put on a suicide vest and detonate himself in the lobby of one of his apartment buildings. His demagoguery and hate-mongering in suggesting that we create a national database of Muslims—or promoting the sick fantasy that on 9/11 crowds of Muslims in New Jersey celebrated the destruction of the Twin Towers—is precisely the kind of reaction on which the extremists were counting to compound the impact of their depravity. It stokes the fears of Americans and alienates Islamic audiences worldwide. And having the leading candidate of one of America's two principal political parties promoting such ideas suggests that they are not his alone but representative of the view of a great cross-section of the American people. . . .

. . . Trump's actions are even more unsettling because they are symptomatic of a broader, deeper, and much more profound problem. Terrorism has, since 9/11, mushroomed into a greater global threat than it has ever been before—and it has been a problem in one form or another since the dawn of history. But as bad as terrorism is, our reactions to it have triggered a kind of worsening risk spiral that has made the world a much more dangerous place. Not only are we playing into the terrorists' hands, and thus giving them needed momentum, the countries of the world are reacting in such an uncoordinated and even conflicting fashion that new geopolitical fissures are emerging that are far more worrisome than any strike or campaign extremists could orchestrate.

In 2002, the year after 9/11, there were fewer than 1,000 deaths from terrorist attacks worldwide, according to the U.S. State Department. This past year, that number was more than 30,000. Al Qaeda delivered a shocking blow to the United States in 2001, but it was a small organization, incapable of repeating such an attack. Today, the terrorists of the Islamic State have changed the game, controlling territory in Iraq and Syria, recruiting fighters globally, and essentially offering the world's first open-source terrorist organization. Download a flag, embrace the name, and you are basically in. As open-source enterprises in other sectors have found, this is a great force multiplier. Suddenly, we are confronted with a "group" capable of brutality across many countries, and the threat posed by them and other terrorist groups that align with them or seek to rival them (see the . . . *New York Times* article on the competition between al Qaeda and the Islamic State) only seems to be growing.

The problem, however, has been compounded since 9/11 by the spasmodic, impulsive, ill-considered, and generally uncoordinated response of major powers and victims of extremism to terrorist attacks. The invasion of Iraq was the alpha error in this respect. It was the wrong mission against the wrong country for the wrong reasons that produced, not surprisingly, the wrong outcomes.

But since then we have seen a stunning lack of strategy, coordination, or even coherent thinking about how to deal with the threat. We have had the "Obama doctrine"; a "light footprint"; the employment of a surgical approach when force was needed; massive overreach on the surveillance front; rhetoric about restraint; confusion about red lines; tactical half-measures; and strategic incoherence. In the Middle East, we continue to see a wide variety of approaches linked to some variation on the "enemy of my enemy is my friend" doctrine and a kind of national hierarchy of hatreds

and fears. This is complicated by the proliferation of terrorist groups with conflicting agendas. So, in Syria, we have the real possibility that Bashar al-Assad's regime helped stoke the fires of the Islamic State through prisoner releases, etc., to justify its cause—which seemed to have worked to some degree as we now have the world's leading powers being more patient with the Syrian strongman if he will help fight the Islamic State. We might even see, after a political deal in Damascus (which will likely create an "Assad-lite" regime after a transition period and provide amnesty for the brutal dictator currently in power), an alliance between that regime and major powers and an al Qaeda spinoff, al-Nusra Front, to work to defeat the Islamic State.

Key to the anti-Islamic State alliance will be the Kurds, who themselves are locked in a struggle with another key player, Turkey. The Turks are, of course, the same key player that . . . shot down a Russian fighter jet. That a NATO nation could shoot down a Russian fighter plane and the story would be overshadowed by the hydra-headed threats of the current global security landscape says much about where we are. The Russians, of course, are ostensibly in Syria to fight extremists with us but are really there to defend Assad or whatever successor regime they may accede to. The Iranians are there doing likewise. The United States is not allied with these powers, as we regularly say, but if our primary immediate national security objective is degrading and ultimately defeating the Islamic State these days, the Russians and the Iranians are our most important allies. Even though the Iranians are themselves one of the world's most important state sponsors of terrorism and even though the Russians are actually benefitting from the chaos in Syria, because refugee flows from there to Europe are stimulating the rise of the European right, a group that is likely to weaken the EU as it gains power—which is in Moscow's interest.

The Europeans are all over the place on these issues. They are united in outrage at the Paris attacks and working together to stem related terrorist threats like those which emerged in Brussels. . . . But whereas the French are eager for action (except to the extent that it involves ground troops), their neighbors on the continent are not. European attitudes toward refugees are equally muddled. There is only one constant: Almost every response European leaders and opinion-shapers have had has exacerbated the problem. Hate speech empowers extremists. So, too, do anti-refugee politics that make ethnic tensions worse. So, paradoxically, do symbolic airstrikes without methodical follow-up on the ground. So, too, do apparent divisions among the nations of the world's leading military alliance about how to handle these situations or even about who the enemy is. (This last problem is worse still among America's allies in the Middle East.)

That is to say nothing of the conflicting views toward terrorism in places like Africa (see Mali or Boko Haram's continuing depraved run through Nigeria or the growing extremist threats in the Horn of Africa or the likely consequences of a further meltdown in Libya) or Asia, where China, India, Indonesia, and other nations face similar threats with differing approaches.

In my view, we have long overstated the threat posed by terrorists. This threat has not been strategic or existential. Creating an analogy between the "War on Terror" and past global conflicts (like the Cold War or World War II) was a great error. We have devoted too many resources to this issue, and the opportunity costs associated with our being distracted by it have been enormous. Further, overreaction is precisely the wrong response to terrorism. And it's exactly what terrorists want. As noted at the outset, it does the work of the terrorists *for* the terrorists. Focused, purposeful retaliation, sound intelligence and police work, national vigilance and a resolve not to let extremists change our way of life or control our airwaves, fears, or national debates are the essential elements of a wise reaction.

But such moderate reactions have not been the norm. We have had the worst possible combination of overreaction, misreaction, underreaction, and a lack of both international leadership and coordination. The result has been the vastly more complicated and dangerous landscape we face today. And whereas I believe, even in its current

state, the threat posed by terrorists is considerably less than much hysterical political rhetoric and understandable postattack emotion would suggest, I am now concerned that the compound effects of our reactions to terrorism are creating a genuinely perilous situation warranting the urgent attention of global leaders.

The problem stems not from the terrorists directly but from the conflicts and instability that are being left in the wake of our responses to their attacks. Invading Iraq was step one. Pulling out too quickly compounded it. Failure to address the issues of Sunni representation in that country compounded it and led to the rise of the Islamic State. Failure to address the problems in Syria when they were early enough to contain compounded it. Belated, uncoordinated halfway measures against the Islamic State were another problem. Failure to stand up to allies funding extremists compounded it. Conflicted policies in Afghanistan did too. Conflicting policies among allies on issues like Mohamed Morsi's government, the Muslim Brotherhood, the Iran nuclear deal, the future of the Assad regime, the situation in Libya, the situation in Yemen, inaction in the face of spreading threats in Africa, and a host of other related problems now have us in a grave situation. In the Middle East, Syria, Iraq, Yemen, and Libya are in chaos. Lebanon and Jordan are bending under the weight of the refugee burden. Refugee flows are posing a major political challenge in the EU. Nationalists and political opportunists are inflaming the situation and further weakening alliances with their rhetoric. There is very little alignment and very serious conflict among a wide-ranging group of powers that are allegedly in some areas working together. This list of collaborators at risk of coming to blows with one another includes the United States, Russia, Iran, Turkey, Saudi Arabia, the Gulf states, Israel, France, Iraq, and others.

I once referred to the risks associated with the destabilization of the region as echoing the problems in Europe prior to World War I when complexity and miscommunication led to a conflagration. "The Balkans on steroids" is what I called it. The thicket of interconnected problems has only grown more complex and thorny. The more we struggle with it, the worse the problems become for us.

This is the kind of problem that comes from a lack of leadership on the international stage. As the world's richest and most powerful nation and the historic leader of its largest alliances, the United States bears a special responsibility in this regard—but it is not alone. This is a moment when the world's leading powers need to work toward greater collaboration, set clearer priorities, and focus on the long-term issues (many economic and social in nature) associated with stabilizing the regions at risk from which these spreading problems are emerging.

It was very heart-warming in the wake of the Paris attacks to see so many people take to social media with new decorations for their Facebook and Twitter sites—tiny French flags were very popular. Setting aside for a moment the fact that similar displays did not crop up after the Beirut or Mali attacks, it is touching that people seem to care and want to show solidarity. The problem is that we have anything but solidarity among our leaders. And if we do not find our way to better coordination and a focus on effective collaboration and common goals soon, we are going to be inviting a further deterioration of the global situation of the type we have witnessed over the past decade-and-a-half. What is more, we will be inviting the kind of accidental conflict that comes from situations like these, situations in which everyone wants to take action but no one is leading.

Why ISIS Has the Potential to Be a World-Altering Revolution

BY SCOTT ATRAN

Scott Atran is the director of research in anthropology at the CNRS (The National Center for Scientific Research), École Normale Supérieure, and a senior research fellow at the University of Oxford. He is cofounder of Artis Research, and the author of *In Gods We Trust* (2002) and *Talking to the Enemy* (2010). From *Aeon*, December 15, 2015. This article was originally published by Aeon Media (http://www.aeon.co, twitter: @aeonmag). Used by permission.

As pundits and politicians stoked the . . . [2015] shootings in California into an existential threat; as French troops were deployed in Paris; as Belgian police locked down Brussels, and US and Russian planes intensified air attacks in Syria following yet another slaughter perpetrated in the name of the so-called Islamic State, it was easy to lose sight of a central fact. Amid the bullets, bombs and bluster, we are not only failing to stop the spread of radical Islam, but our efforts often appear to contribute to it.

What accounts for the failure of "The War on Terror" and associated efforts to counter the spread of violent extremism? The failure starts with reacting in anger and revenge, engendering more savagery without stopping to grasp the revolutionary character of radical Arab Sunni revivalism. This revival is a dynamic, countercultural movement of world-historic proportions spearheaded by ISIS (the Islamic State of Iraq and Syria, also known as ISIL, or the Islamic State of Iraq and the Levant). In less than two years, it has created a dominion over hundreds of thousands of square kilometres and millions of people.

What the United Nations community regards as senseless acts of horrific violence are to ISIS's acolytes part of an exalted campaign of purification through sacrificial killing and selfimmolation: *Know that Paradise lies under the shade of swords*, says a *hadith*, or saying of the Prophet; this one comes from the *Sahih al-Bukhari*, a collection of the Prophet's sayings considered second only to the Qu'ran in authenticity and is now a motto of ISIS fighters.

This is the purposeful plan of violence that Abu Bakr al-Baghdadi, the Islamic State's self-anointed Caliph, outlined in his call for "volcanoes of jihad": to create a globe-spanning jihadi archipelago that will eventually unite to destroy the present world and create a new-old world of universal justice and peace under the Prophet's banner. A key tactic in this strategy is to inspire sympathisers abroad to violence: do what you can, with whatever you have, wherever you are, whenever possible.

To understand the revolution, my research team has conducted dozens of structured interviews and behavioural experiments with youth in Paris, London and Barcelona, as well as with captured ISIS fighters in Iraq and members of Jabhat al-Nusra (Al-Qaeda's affiliate in Syria). We also focused on youth from distressed neighbourhoods previously associated with violence or jihadi support—for example, the Paris suburbs of Clichy-sous-Bois and Épinay-sur-Seine, the Moroccan neighbourhoods of Sidi Moumen in Casablanca and Jamaa Mezuak in Tetuán.

While many in the West dismiss radical Islam as simply nihilistic, our work suggests something far more menacing: a profoundly alluring mission to change and save the world.

In the West, the seriousness of this mission is denied. Olivier Roy, usually a deep and subtle thinker, wrote . . . in *Le Monde* that the Paris plotters represent most who flock to ISIS; they are marginal misfits largely ignorant of religion and geopolitics, and bereft of real historical grievances. They ride the wave of radical Islam as an outlet for their nihilism because it's the biggest and baddest countercultural movement around. And how else could one explain a mother who abandons her baby to die butchering innocents in San Bernadino [*sic*] who never did her harm?

But the worldwide ISIS revolution is hardly just a bandwagon for losers. Although attacked on all sides by internal and external foes, the Islamic State has not deteriorated to any appreciable degree, while rooting ever stronger in areas it controls and expanding its influence in deepening pockets throughout Eurasia and Africa. Despite recent White House reassurances, US intelligence tells us that ISIS is *not* being contained. Repeated claims that ISIS is being degraded and on the way to inevitable defeat ring hollow for almost anyone who has had direct experience in the field. Only Kurdish frontline combatants and some Iranian-led forces have managed to fight ISIS to a standstill on the ground, and only with significant French and US air support.

Despite our relentless propaganda campaign against the Islamic State as vicious, predatory and cruel—most of which might be right—there is little recognition of its genuine appeal, and even less of the joy it engenders. The mainly young people who volunteer to fight for it unto death feel a joy that comes from joining with comrades in a glorious cause, as well as a joy that comes from satiation of anger and the gratification of revenge (whose sweetness, says science, can *be* experienced by brain and body much like other forms of happiness).

But there is also a subliminal joy felt across the region for those who reject the Islamic State's murderous violence yet yearn for the revival of a Muslim Caliphate and the end to a nation-state order that the Great Powers invented and imposed. It is an order that has failed, and that the US, Russia and their respective allies are trying willy-nilly to resurrect, and it is an order that many in the region believe to be the root of their misery. What the ISIS revolution is *not*, is a simple desire to return to the ancient past. The idea that ISIS seeks a return to medieval times makes no more sense than the idea that the US Tea Party wants to return to 1776. "We are not sending people back to the time of the carrier pigeon," Abu Mousa, ISIS's press officer in Raqqa, has said. "On the contrary, we will benefit from development. But in a way that doesn't contradict the religion."

The Caliphate seeks a new order based on a culture of today. Unless we recognise these passions and aspirations, and deal with them using more than just military means, we will likely fan those passions and lose another generation to war and worse.

. . .

Still, the popular notion of a "clash of civilisations" between Islam and the West is woefully misleading. Violent extremism represents not the resurgence of traditional cultures, but their collapse, as young people unmoored from millennial traditions flail about in search of a social identity that gives personal significance and glory. This is the dark side of globalisation. Individuals radicalise to find a firm identity in a flattened world. In this new reality, vertical lines of communication between the generations are replaced by horizontal peer-to-peer attachments that can cut across the globe.

As I told the UN Security Council . . ., what inspires the most lethal assailants in the world today is not so much the Quran or religious teachings but rather a thrilling cause and a call to action that promises glory and esteem in the eyes of friends. Foreign volunteers for the Islamic State are often youth in transitional stages in their lives—immigrants, students, people between jobs and before finding their mates. Having left their homes, they seek new families of friends and fellow travellers to find purpose and significance.

France's Centre for the Prevention of Sectarian Drift Related to Islam estimates that 80 per cent come from non-religious families; West Point's Center for Combating Terrorism finds that their average age is 25. For the most part, they have no traditional religious education and are "born again" to religion through the jihad. About one in four, often the fiercest followers, are converts. Self-seekers who have found their way to jihad reach out through private gatherings or the [I]nternet. They might be people who feel uncomfortable with binge-drinking or casual sex, or have seen their parents humiliated by employers or the government, or their sisters insulted for wearing a headscarf. Most do not follow through to join the jihad, but some do. More than 80 per cent who join the Islamic State do so through peer-to-peer relationships, mostly with friends and sometimes family. Very few join in mosques or through recruitment by anonymous strangers.

. . .

The 9/11 attacks cost between $400,000 and $500,000 to execute, whereas the military and security response by the US and its allies is in the order of 10 million times that figure. On a strictly cost-benefit basis, this violent movement has been wildly successful, beyond even Bin Laden's original imagination, and is increasingly so. Herein

lies the full measure of jujitsu-style asymmetric warfare. After all, who could claim that we are better off than before, or that the overall danger is declining?

This alone should inspire a radical change in our counter-strategies. Yet, like the proverbial notion of insanity being the repetition of the same mistakes while expecting different results, our side continues to focus almost exclusively on security and military responses. Some of these responses have proven hopelessly ineffective from the outset, such as relying on the Iraqi, Afghan or Free Syrian armies.

By contrast, there is precious little attention to social and psychological needs. I don't mean to suggest that we solve things by offering potential jihadists better jobs. A still-unpublished report by the World Bank shows no reliable relationship between job production and violence reduction. If people are ready to sacrifice their lives, then it is not likely that offers of greater material advantages will stop them.

Instead, we must meet their psychological and aspirational needs. In just one example of how we fall short, the US State Department continues to send off-target tweets through negative mass messaging in its ineffectual "Think Again Turn Away" campaign. Compare this to ISIS, which can spend hundreds of hours trying to enlist single individuals. Through its social media, the sophisticated Islamic State learns how personal frustrations and grievances can fit into a universal theme of persecution against all Muslims, and then translates anger and unrealised aspiration into moral outrage. Some estimates have ISIS managing upwards of 70,000 Twitter and Facebook accounts, with hundreds of thousands of followers, and sending approximately 90,000 texts daily. ISIS also pays close attention to the pop songs, video clips, action movies and television shows that garner high ratings among youth, and uses them as templates to tailor their own messages.

By contrast, the US government has few operatives who personally engage with youth before they become a problem. The FBI is pressing to get out of the messy business of prevention and just stick to criminal investigation. "No one wants to own any of this," one group from the US National Counterterrorism Center told us. And public diplomacy efforts don't quite get that hackneyed appeals to "moderation" fall flat on restless and idealistic youths seeking adventure, glory and significance. As one imam and former Islamic State facilitator told us in Jordan:

> The young who came to us were not to be lectured at like witless children; they are for the most part understanding and compassionate, but misguided. We have to give them a better message, but a positive one to compete. Otherwise, they will be lost to Daesh.

Local grass-roots approaches have had better luck in pulling people away. The United Network of Young Peacebuilders has had remarkable results in convincing young Taliban in Pakistan that enemies can be friends, and then encouraging those so convinced to convince others. But this will not challenge the broad attraction of the Islamic State for young people from nearly 90 nations and every walk of life. The lessons of local successes must be shared with government, and ideas allowed to bubble up before they boil over. To date, no such conduit exists, and young people with good ideas have few institutional channels to develop them.

Even if good ideas find ways to emerge from youth and obtain institutional support for their development to application, they still need intellectual help to persuade the public to adopt them. But where are the intellectuals to do this? Among Muslim leadership I've interviewed around the world, I listen to PowerPoint presentations intoning on "dimensions of ideology, grievance, and group dynamics," notions that originate exclusively with Western "terrorism experts" and think tanks. When I ask: "What ideas come from your own people?," I'm told in moments of candour, as I was most recently by a Muslim leadership council in Singapore, that: "We don't have many new ideas and we can't agree on those we have."

And where among our own current or coming generation are the intellectuals who might influence the moral principles, motivations and actions of society towards a just and reasonable way through the morass? In academia, you'll find few willing to engage with power. They thus render themselves irrelevant and morally irresponsible by leaving the field of power entirely to those they censure. Accordingly, politicians pay them little heed, and the public couldn't care less, often with good reason. For example, in the immediate aftermath of the 9/11 attacks, many in my own field of anthropology principally occupied themselves with the critique of empire: is the US a classic empire or "empire light"? This was arguably a justifiable academic exercise, and perhaps a useful reflection in the long run, but hardly helpful in the context of a country moving fast to open-ended war, with all the agony and suffering that extended wars inevitably bring.

Responsible intellectual endeavour in the public sphere was once a vibrant part of our public life: not to promote "certain, clear, and strong" action, as Martin Heidegger wrote in support of Hitler, but to generate just and reasonable possibilities and pathways for consideration. Now this sphere is largely abandoned to the Manichean preachings of blogging pundits, radio talk-show hosts, product-pushing podcasters, and television evangelicals. These people rarely do what responsible intellectuals ought to do. "The intellectual," explained France's Raymond Aron 60 years ago, "must try never to forget the arguments of the adversary, or the uncertainty of the future, or the faults of one's own side, or the underlying fraternity of ordinary men everywhere."

Civilisations rise and fall on the vitality of their cultural ideals, not their material assets alone. History shows that most societies have sacred values for which their people would passionately fight, risking serious loss and even death rather than compromise. Our research suggests this is so for many who join ISIS, and for many Kurds who oppose them on the frontlines. But, so far, we find no comparable willingness among the majority of youth that we sample in Western democracies. With the defeat of fascism and communism, have their lives defaulted to the quest for comfort and safety? Is this enough to ensure the survival, much less triumph, of values we have come to take for granted, on which we believe our world is based? More than the threat from violent jihadis, this might be the key existential issue for open societies today.

How to Stop Extremism Before It Starts

BY MARIA J. STEPHAN AND SHAAZKA BEYERLE

Maria J. Stephan is a Senior Policy Fellow at the U.S. Institute of Peace and a Nonresident Senior Fellow at the Atlantic Council. Another selection co-authored by Stephan appears in part 5. Shaazka Beyerle is a Senior Advisor with the International Center on Nonviolent Conflict, and a Visiting Scholar at the School of Advanced International Studies, Johns Hopkins University. She is the author of *Curtailing Corruption: People Power for Accountability and Justice* (2014). From *Foreign Policy*, March 17, 2015. Used by permission.

In the global fight against violent extremism, a major element has been missing from the conversation that has focused on mostly top-down, official efforts: how ordinary citizens and communities are successfully challenging the acute corruption that drives young people and others into the folds of radicals.

Imagine growing up in a country where poverty is the norm, officials at every level demand a constant stream of bribes, the government is abusive and greedy and/or tied to organized crime, and rule of law leaves ordinary citizens in the dust while coddling cronies and those who can pay the price. No wonder young citizens rush into the ranks of extremist groups like the self-styled "Islamic State" in the Middle East, Boko Haram in Africa, or the *marabuntas* gangs in Central America.

Yet, in some of the world's most repressive places, millions of people have become protagonists of successful nonviolent campaigns that challenge corruption and impunity, improve accountability, and promote political, economic, and social change. A new qualitative study by one of the authors documents 16 such cases in Afghanistan, Bangladesh, Bosnia-Herzegovina, Brazil, Egypt, India, Indonesia, Italy, Kenya, Mexico, Philippines, Russia, South Korea, Turkey, and Uganda.

The link between corruption and violent extremism is starting to make its way into policy conversations and the popular consciousness, thanks to groundbreaking research such as work conducted by Sarah Chayes and by Louise Shelley. Chayes just published the book *Thieves of State: Why Corruption Threatens Global Security*, prompting an appearance on Comedy Central's *The Daily Show* with Jon Stewart. Shelley

outlines the connections between these scourges in her book *Dirty Entanglements: Corruption, Crime, and Terrorism....* [A] Transparency International-U.K. report on the international community's mission in Afghanistan concluded that anti-corruption and integrity-building measures must be included in future security, peace-building, and reconstruction efforts.

Grassroots efforts already are doing their part. They wield creative nonviolent tactics like civil disobedience, monitoring initiatives, petition drives, low-risk mass actions, digital dissent, street theater, reverse boycotts, youth clubs, and campaigns to refuse cooperation with bribery. The impact has disrupted venal practices, spurred political will, and provided a way out for those caught in systems of corruption. The pressure from below also has strengthened the position of office holders who are pursuing reform in the face of obstacles and intimidation from vested interests.

What does this look like on the ground? Operating in a context of pitched violent extremism, Integrity Watch Afghanistan developed a community-monitoring framework that—through listening, training, access to information, and the creation of Provincial Monitoring Boards—has empowered villagers to systematically scrutinize internationally and domestically funded projects and pressure implementers and officials, with the aim of curbing corruption and improving reconstruction and development. By the end of 2014, civic groups monitored approximately 900 projects in seven provinces. A study of the first 400 initiatives found that, in two-thirds of the cases, either problems were uncovered and rectified as a result of community pressure, none were found, or those responsible for the projects being monitored cooperated from the outset.

In Kenya, Muslims for Human Rights (MUHURI) has empowered slum communities in Mombasa to conduct social audits of development funds and projects, consisting of six steps from information gathering and capacity building to inspections and public hearings, in order to fight poverty and curb misuse of these resources. Within three years, comprehensive citizen-led initiatives were implemented in 10 areas, uncovering corruption and leading to concrete solutions carried out by the authorities. MUHURI activists had learned about grassroots strategies and tactics from veterans of the Right to Information Movement in India, which led to the passing of one of the best and most user-friendly Right to Information laws in the world.

Civic initiatives targeting corruption and impunity also can help build a culture of democracy and accountability in countries wrestling with transitions from authoritarian rule. Citizens experience democratic practices firsthand through tactics such as informal elections, surveys, reporting to other community members, and public forums with public or private figures in power. A publication of the International Budget Partnership referred to MUHURI's social audits as "exercises in participatory democracy that challenge the traditional 'rules of the game' in governance."

These results echo findings from the historical record of people power over the past 110 years. Not only have nonviolent resistance campaigns dramatically outperformed their violent counterparts in challenging authoritarian and autocratic regimes, where corruption is systemic and institutionalized, citizen movements also have contributed to democratic consolidation. Even in Syria and Iraq, the coalition building, mobilization skills, and local self-organization that drive people-power movements have also helped local communities both challenge and remain resilient against the so-called "Islamic State" militants.

External Support Options

Although people-power efforts targeting corruption and impunity are homegrown phenomena, the international community can support their efforts.

Doing so, however, requires a movement mindset. This means that governments and other international aid providers need to look beyond formal non-governmental organizations, and engage with civil society groups and other non-state players close to the grassroots, as well as informal civic groups and social movements. It also means providing modest funding for pilot efforts in anti-corruption civic mobilization, helping translate materials on strategic nonviolent action into local languages, and supporting opportunities for peers to learn from each other.

This support should go beyond financial backing, though, to include legal and technical assistance, as well as information not readily available to civic activists, such as information about how foreign aid and domestic revenues are being allocated. Such aid can be coordinated to help amplify voices of local anti-corruption and integrity leaders through support of their digital communication and information outlets.

Efforts to help local actors must also involve concerted action to counter growing global crackdowns against civil society around the world. This requires helping create new tools and platforms to help besieged activists connect with each other and the outside world. Support for regional civil society innovation "hubs" by the U.S. Agency for International Development (USAID), the Swedish International Development Agency (Sida), and other donors as part of President Obama's Stand with Civil Society Initiative is a step in the right direction. Perhaps most importantly, the international community must respect the wishes and judgments of those on the ground, as international attention is not always wanted or helpful.

It is clear that terrorism, violent insurgencies, and organized crime cannot be tackled unless policymakers understand the inextricable links to corruption. Citizen-led nonviolent campaigns and movements complement top-down measures and can add an essential component to the anti-corruption equation.

In stark contrast to violent coercion, people power confronts injustice and oppression constructively while engaging with both those in power and the public. And it can proactively address a critical driver of violent extremism around the world.

DISCUSSION QUESTIONS

1. Summarize the evidence that Max Abrahms presents to support his claim that strategic terrorism usually fails because it miscommunicates its primary goals.

2. Describe why Abrahms's results might be different if he examined cases of redemptive terrorism rather than only cases of strategic terrorism.

3. Review each of the ways that David Rothkopf believes that Europe and the United States have unnecessarily harmed themselves through their responses to terrorist attacks.

4. Evaluate the likely effectiveness of Rothkopf's policy suggestions aimed at lessening what he calls the "further deterioration of the global situation."

5. Summarize and assess the strength of each of the principle causes that Scott Atran claims tend to lead young people to join terrorist organizations.

6. Describe experiences you have had or have witnessed that support Atran's claim that young people are more likely than older adults to seek grand causes to give their lives a deeper meaning.

7. Assess the evidence and analysis that Maria J. Stephan and Shaazka Beyerle offer to support their view that corruption is a major cause of terrorism.

8. Contrast Atran's view on the causes of terrorism with the view presented by Stephan and Beyerle. Explain which view you believe offers the most accurate explanation.

NONVIOLENCE, FORGIVENESS, AND RESTORATION

In part 4, Maria J. Stephan and Shaazka Beyerle argue that nonviolent campaigns are among the most effective methods for combatting terrorism. The selections in part 5 expand this debate to examine the effect of nonviolence on all types of violence. The selections in section 1 focus on controversies associated with methods used in nonviolent campaigns, while selections in section 2 present disagreements about the specific nonviolent methods of forgiveness and restoration.

Debates about Nonviolent Action

The first selection is from the humor magazine *The Onion*. Although meant as satire, the article invokes many of the typical justifications that people give for using yet more violence to address problems associated with earlier violence. When this further violence fails, as *The Onion* makes clear, violence advocates frequently then argue that people or their governments simply have not yet been destructive enough. Ever harsher penalties or escalating wars are called for, many believe, as violence "cuts right to the heart of a problem" with an effectiveness lacking in nonviolent approaches.

A second selection by Simone Sebastian examines the connection between non-violence and violence to argue that nonviolence is often ineffective unless it provokes violence from its opponents. Nonviolence is "useless without violence," Sebastian proposes, and she reviews some events in the history of Martin Luther King Jr.'s civil rights campaigns to support her claim. Sebastian insists that contemporary campaigns such as the Black Lives Matter movement must provoke violent reactions if they wish to achieve their goals.

The third selection draws on the authors' pioneering study of 323 nonviolent campaigns between 1900 and 2006. In that earlier work, Erica Chenoweth and Maria J. Stephan discovered nonviolent campaigns were twice as successful as comparable violent campaigns, suggesting that in general, civil resistance is much more effective than violence. Chenoweth and Stephan here argue that (1) creating mass participation; (2) inducing defections from government and security forces; and (3) using many, diverse tactics encourages success.

Chenoweth and Stephan focus on the effectiveness of nonviolent campaigns in *intrastate conflicts*, conflicts mostly within the borders of a single nation-state. In a fourth selection, Maciej Bartkowski focuses on the use of nonviolence in *interstate conflicts*, conflicts between crossborder belligerents. Bartkowski is particularly interested in the efficacy of "nonviolent civilian defense" in crises where one nation seeks to annex, invade, or control another. Bartkowski argues that in contemporary "hybrid wars," organized nonviolent civil resistance will usually work better than the alternatives: surrender and armed resistance.

In their selections, both Bartkowski and Chenoweth and Stephan use the concept of "civil resistance" rather than nonviolence in part because they wish to emphasize that they understand nonviolence as a political tactic and not as moral or ethical choice.

In a final selection, Michael N. Nagler maintains that nonviolence is best adopted not as a tactic but rather as a "way of being" and as a power "to redirect human destiny to a higher goal."

These contesting perspectives on nonviolence are often described as a choice between (1) pragmatic or strategic nonviolence and (2) principled nonviolence. *Pragmatic and strategic nonviolence* are guided by judgments of what works, while *principled nonviolence* is guided by judgments of what is right and good. Bartkowski and Chenoweth and Stephan represent the pragmatic view as they evaluate nonviolent action as one among many possible types of political tactics. On the other hand, Nagler champions principled nonviolence by recommending nonviolence as a belief system with much broader implications than simply as a political tactic. Mohandas Gandhi developed this broader principled view of nonviolence in the first decades of the twentieth century as he refined his thinking about *satyagraha*. In his selection and through his Metta Center for Nonviolence, Nagler promotes Gandhi's vision as he calls for people to embrace principled nonviolence as a guiding philosophy for nonviolent living. (Additional positions on the debate between strategic and principled nonviolence will be found in part 7.)

Violence: Is it the Answer?

The Onion is a 2009 Peabody Award-winning satirical website that began as a print college humor newspaper in 1988, became a national magazine, and ended its print editions in 2013. From *The Onion,* January 27, 1999. Reprinted with permission of The Onion. Copyright © 2016, by Onion, Inc. www.theonion.com

Violence. The question of whether it ever really solves anything is, of course, nothing new. The value of violence has been fiercely debated, largely without resolution, since time immemorial.

But though violence has never gone entirely out of style, conventional wisdom over the last several decades has held that it is an unacceptable option. Ever since the anti-war and civil-rights movements of the Vietnam Era, the nation's cultural cognoscenti has regarded the human tendency toward violence as a cowardly, barbaric impulse, shunned by members of civilized society in favor of more diplomatic and compromise-based problem-solving techniques.

Yet, according to recent studies, all that has begun to change.

Increasingly, Americans are turning to violence—the use of brute, animal aggression against an opposing force—as a viable means of conflict resolution. From the inner city to the suburbs, from the boardroom to the bedroom, violence is making a stunning comeback. And, surveys indicate, more and more Americans are agreeing that it's about time.

"Whoever said that violence never solved anything obviously never met my wife Edith," says Nick Petrakis of Chicago. "For months, her constant nagging about my drinking, the bills, the drapes—you name it—drove me up the freaking wall. I tried marriage counseling, church, even so-called 'quality time,' but nothing worked. Then, one day, I finally hauled off and whaled her right in the solar plexus as hard as I could."

"And you know what?" he adds with a grin. "I haven't heard a peep out of her goddamn fat trap since."

The Petrakis case is far from unique, and it points to one of the main reasons behind violence's resurgent popularity: pragmatism.

"Sure, all of those 'talking it out' solutions look good on paper, but in real life, who has the time?" Harvard University sociology professor Dr. Hugh Brentley says. "Reasoned, calm conflict-mediation can exact a terrible toll on the patience of those involved. On the other hand, swift, violent action—such as the kind Alexander the Great employed in severing the fabled Gordian knot with one swipe of his sword—cuts right to the heart of a problem."

This direct, results-oriented approach is being put into practice every day across America. Children mercilessly beat one another on the playground, achieving instant social standing amongst their peers. In the political sphere, long-range bombing has proven an effective means of resolving marital-infidelity disputes. And the drug lords of the nation's blighted ghettos have long championed the merciless machine-gunning of competitors as an expedient solution to the seemingly insoluble dilemmas of urban poverty and racial discrimination.

Critics of violence say that such short-term approaches only leave other, greater problems in their wake. But as violence advocates are quick to point out, a great majority of these problems can easily be fixed with more violence. For example, the skyrocketing crime rate can be addressed through either the death penalty or vigilante justice, both of which are effective alternatives to expensive, complex social-reform programs that stress prevention over cure.

"We must also remember," psychologist and longtime violence advocate Jane Gelfand notes, "that emotional violence can, in many cases, be just as effective as actual bodily harm. Breaking a child psychologically, through generous, sustained helpings of verbal abuse, is a far more effective way of handling disobedience and misbehavior than a thousand hours of tedious positive reinforcement."

"Not that simple hitting or kicking should be ruled out, of course," Gelfand adds.

But whether hurling chairs at one another on daytime television or stabbing strangers to death in parking ramps for some quick cash, millions of Americans are giving violence a second look as a viable solution to the challenges with which life presents them. And, as savagery and brutality continue to capture the hearts and minds of the American people, one thing is certain: Violence, in all its forms, is no longer confined to the realm of escapist Hollywood dramas or video-game space-invader shoot-'em-ups. Whether we cower in fear behind the walls of gated communities or actively prowl the alleyways looking for rape victims, violence is a major part of our shared American experience, and it isn't going away any time soon.

Violence, it would appear, is something we can all rely on.

Don't Criticize Black Lives Matter for Provoking Violence. The Civil Rights Movement Did, Too

BY SIMONE SEBASTIAN

Simone Sebastian is a deputy America editor for *The Washington Post*. From *The Washington Post*, October 1, 2015.

Black Lives Matter [BLM] protests have produced one spectacle after another. Peaceful demonstrations in Baltimore and Ferguson, Mo., were followed by riots in which police and activists clashed. Many Americans, weaned on tales of how 20th-century civil rights leaders used nonviolent resistance, criticize today's advocates for "extreme" tactics and accuse them of inciting violence. Even Martin Luther King Jr.'s niece, Alveda King, called BLM's methods inappropriate. Mike Huckabee said the civil rights leader would be "appalled" by BLM's strategy: To address racial injustice, "you don't do it by magnifying the problems," he said.

But magnifying the problems was King's key strategy, and he received the same admonishments. Protesters who marched in the streets of America's most staunchly racist cities and towns were attacked by police dogs, their clothing was tattered by high-pressure fire hoses, and their lives were taken by police officers' bullets. Alarmed by what they saw, eight liberal, white clergymen wrote a public statement in 1963, calling King's movement foolish and counterproductive. They sympathized with his cause but said his actions were too aggressive, too disruptive and drove people to violent uprising. The clergymen urged black Americans to reject King's leadership and adopt peaceful means to achieve racial equality. King's "nonviolent" movement, they said, was anything but.

King's response, written while he was detained in Alabama, was the famous "Letter From Birmingham Jail." He wrote that, in fighting racial injustice, the goal of his demonstrations was "so to dramatize the issue that it can no longer be ignored." In other words, violence was not something that simply happened to activists; they invited it. Violence was critical to the success of the 1960s civil rights movement, as it has been to every step of racial progress in U.S. history.

As much as BLM's opponents and supporters (who insist that "this ain't yo mama's civil rights movement") differentiate it from the 1960s effort, these two historical moments have a lot in common. Both have been opposed by more than half of Americans, both have needed violent confrontations to attract national media attention, and both have been criticized for their combative tactics. Whether in the 1960s or the 2010s, the aggressive disruption of American race relations has caused the same anger and fear—from Northerners and Southerners, from blacks and whites, from liberal "allies" and racist adversaries.

Today, King is remembered for "I have a dream" and "the content of their character." For our purposes, he's about nonviolence, turning the other cheek and loving thy enemy. In contemporary textbooks and collective memory, his was a non-confrontational, even passive approach.

But the civil rights movement wasn't seen as nonviolent in its day—and for good reason. The most jarring evidence of this came just a month after King's Birmingham jail letter. In May 1963, movement organizers assembled black children, some still in pigtails, to march through the streets of Birmingham and confront Bull Connor's violent police force. It was a controversial tactic within the movement, but organizers must have known that images of jailed, beaten and cowering children would affect hearts, force a response from officials and move the movement toward its goals.

"They couldn't have been ignorant of the terrible response," says King biographer and New York University historian David Levering Lewis. "King and his inner circle appreciated the probable certainty of violence on the part of the establishment to trigger responses that they wanted, in terms of legislation and policies." The children called it "D-Day."

Connor didn't disappoint. He attacked the marchers with German shepherds and baton-wielding policemen. Connor's army funneled hundreds of children and teenagers into overcrowded jail cells. Still, the kids returned to the streets the next day. And the day after that. Malcolm X, whom history treats as the movement's violent alter ego, criticized King for the event, saying that "real men don't put their children on the firing line." King, on the other hand, called it "one of the wisest moves we made."

The Children's Crusade changed the way the movement was covered by the press. Where the crushing effects of segregated schools hadn't won hearts, where brutal, state-sanctioned beatings of hymn-singing black men and women hadn't gained sympathy, the nation couldn't ignore the images of children recoiling from the raised batons of sneering police officers. Only the most distressing type of violence worked.

This was King's strategy. "Freedom is never voluntarily given by the oppressor; it must be demanded by the oppressed," he said—an aggressive and confrontational stance that Americans rejected at the time and have forgotten today. Most people, including Northerners, opposed King's March on Washington, fearing that it was a call to uprising. A Gallup poll conducted in May 1963, the same month as the Children's Crusade, found that 46 percent of Americans held an unfavorable view of King. The only public figure more disliked in the poll was Soviet leader Nikita Khrushchev. By 1966, more than two-thirds of Americans had an unfavorable view of the civil rights leader.

Black Lives Matter doesn't fare much better: In a September PBS-Marist poll, 59 percent of white Americans said BLM is a distraction and, in response to a separate question, 41 percent said it advocates violence (16 percent said they were unsure whether it does).

King, likewise, faced editorials admonishing him for provoking riots and isolating those sympathetic to his cause with his "excessive" demonstrations. Progressive white Americans, who distinguished themselves from the "bigots and hatemongers" in the South, turned against King when he came into their de facto segregated neighborhoods to protest racist housing practices—in much the same way Bernie Sanders supporters slammed the "extreme" tactics of activists who took the presidential candidate's stage in August to demand that he address systemic racism.

Even black Americans criticized King's strategy. In response to a demonstration that turned violent in Memphis in 1968, a black man penned a derisive letter to King, blaming him for the death of a 16-year-old boy who was shot by a police officer in the chaos that followed the protest. "I know that you think that you are helping all of us Negroes," the man wrote, adding: "After knowing the honest truth about this and many other deaths caused by your calm riots, we as a body had rather not have anything else to do with you or your so called righteous riots or better, righteous murders."

Similarly, many have held today's movement responsible for the burned buildings, broken windows and police and civilian deaths that followed protests during the past year [2015]. Yet history shows that this violence is the inevitable consequence of challenging the racial status quo.

Public opinion of King turned 180 degrees in just two decades. In 1986, he was given a national holiday, and a year later, more than three-quarters of white Americans had a favorable view of him, according to Gallup. As Oakland University political science professor Sheldon Appleton has noted, our collective ignorance is largely to blame. Just 30 years after the March on Washington, 57 percent of white Americans admitted knowing little or nothing about the event. By that point, it was easiest simply to believe that racial justice had been achieved peacefully and that the civil rights movement had solved our racial problems.

No wonder so many today dismiss the need for another civil rights movement and contrast BLM's aggression and violence with the earlier movement. "It's whitewashing not just King the person, but also of what the movement was challenging and how vicious the opposition was," says historian Jeanne Theoharis, who notes that Rosa Parks has received similar treatment. "We've made them comfortable to us. They make us feel good about our past."

Certainly, nonviolence was a central theme in King's rhetoric—and a kind of spiritual philosophy. The preacher was heavily influenced by Mohandas Gandhi, and he called nonviolence the only moral means for fighting oppression. But he learned that, as a tactic, nonviolence was useless without violence.

That lesson came in Albany, Ga., where police chief Laurie Pritchett ordered his officers to arrest civil rights protesters peacefully, without bully clubs or fire hoses. As a result, Albany's streets remained placid; the town produced no disturbing images to generate national attention and pressure its officials. After seven months of demonstrations, starting in late 1961, Albany remained as segregated as it was when activists arrived. "This is when he [King] became convinced that he . . . had to find a gut segregationist who would think nothing of clubbing black people on the head," Gene Roberts, who covered the civil rights movement for the New York Times, recalled in a recorded interview by the Newseum.

That's when the movement moved to Alabama and confronted Bull Connor.

It's rare that social progress comes without force—typically violent force. Gay and transgender Americans fought police and rioted in New York and San Francisco to overthrow homophobic policies. Violent labor riots helped end unsafe work conditions. Slavery in the United States ended only after the deadliest war in the nation's history.

We remember, even celebrate, the by-any-means-necessary grit of the people who ultimately made American lives better in these historic moments. But when it comes to the American fight for racial equality, we bury the truth about the tactics that are necessary for progress. We've convinced ourselves that racism can be eradicated passively, without aggression or violence. "As America progressed, violence was always part of it," says St. Louis University historian Stefan Bradley, who studies black youth activism. "No other movement in history has ever been held to these standards."

Black Americans have peacefully protested police brutality for decades. It was a regular subject of hip-hop lyrics during the 1980s. Nonviolent protests followed numerous deaths of unarmed black people in the 1990s and 2000s: Amadou Diallo in 1999, Sean Bell in 2006, Oscar Grant in 2009. But no substantive changes in police operations resulted.

King, we've convinced ourselves, is proof that any lingering racism can be eliminated without tumult. Yet the civil rights movement was one of the most violent moments in American history. As the Rev. Jesse Jackson recalls, the tactics of the 1960s demonstrators "worked very well because the violent forces against us weren't able to justify attacking us." While the activists' nonviolent response magnified the brutality, the aggressive reaction of today's protesters has proved effective as well. "The police overreaction, the tear gas—that's what made Ferguson," Jackson says.

Black Lives Matter has more in common with the civil rights movement than we'd like to acknowledge. It fights the same injustices and encounters the same resistance. The truth is, if you oppose Black Lives Matter's tactics, you would have abhorred King's.

Drop Your Weapons: When and Why Civil Resistance Works

BY ERICA CHENOWETH AND MARIA J. STEPHAN

Erica Chenoweth and Maria J. Stephan are coauthors of *Why Civil Resistance Works: The Strategic Logic of Nonviolent Conflict* (2011). Chenoweth is a professor and associate dean for research in international studies at the University of Denver. Stephan is a Senior Policy Fellow at the U.S. Institute of Peace and a Nonresident Senior Fellow at the Atlantic Council. Another selection from Stephan appears in part 4. Selections from "Drop Your Weapons: When and Why Civil Resistance Works." *Foreign Affairs,* July/August, 2014. Used by permission.

Over the past three years, the world has witnessed a surge of nonviolent resistance movements. Pictures of huge demonstrations in public squares have become a staple of international news broadcasts, and *Time* named "the protester" as its Person of the Year for 2011. These days, it seems that at any given moment, thousands of people are mobilizing for change somewhere in the world.

But these movements have varied widely in terms of their duration, their success, their ability to remain nonviolent, and their cost in terms of human life. Building on years of intermittent protests and strikes, Tunisians toppled Zine el-Abidine Ben Ali, the dictator who had ruled their country for 23 years, after a sustained period of 28 days of protests beginning in December 2010.

Between 300 and 320 Tunisians civilians died in the upheaval, all of them killed by police or security forces. Weeks later, Egyptians ended Hosni Mubarak's three-decade reign after a decade of lower-level opposition and civil resistance culminated in 18 days of nonviolent mass demonstrations—but Mubarak's security forces killed around 900 people in the process. In Libya, scattered protests against Muammar al-Qaddafi that began in February 2011 quickly became an armed rebellion. NATO soon intervened militarily, and within nine months, Qaddafi was dead and his regime demolished, but between 10,000 and 30,000 Libyans, according to various estimates, had lost their lives. In Syria, Bashar al-Assad brutally cracked down on mostly nonviolent demonstrations against his rule between March and August 2011, killing thousands and setting in motion a civil war that has since resulted in over 150,000 deaths and the displacement of around nine million people. Most recently, in February [2014], Ukrainians ousted President Viktor Yanukovych after three months of mass civil resistance and occasionally violent protests. Around 100 Ukrainian protesters died during the clashes between demonstrators and riot police—fewer than in most of the confrontations of the Arab Spring in 2011. But Russia's response to Yanukovych's overthrow—seizing the Ukrainian territory of Crimea and attempting to destabilize the eastern parts of Ukraine—has created the most dangerous and unpredictable security situation Europe has seen in decades.

The basic trajectory of these recent movements—each successive one seemingly more violent and more geopolitically charged—has encouraged skepticism about the prospects for civil resistance in the twenty-first century. Such doubts are understandable but misplaced. A longer view is required to see the real potential of nonviolent resistance, which is evident in a historical data set that we assembled of 323 campaigns that spanned the twentieth century—from Mahatma Gandhi's Indian independence movement against British colonialism, which began in earnest in 1919, to the protests that removed Thai Prime Minister

Thaksin Shinawatra from power in 2006. This global data set covers all known nonviolent and violent campaigns (each featuring at least 1,000 observed participants) for self-determination, the removal of an incumbent leader, or the expulsion of a foreign military occupation from 1900 to 2006. The data set was assembled using thousands of source materials on protest and civil disobedience, expert reports and surveys, and existing records on violent insurgencies.

Between 1900 and 2006, campaigns of nonviolent resistance against authoritarian regimes were twice as likely to succeed as violent movements. Nonviolent resistance also increased the chances that the overthrow of a dictatorship would lead to peace and democratic rule. This was true even in highly authoritarian and repressive countries, where one might expect nonviolent resistance to fail. Contrary to conventional wisdom, no social, economic, or political structures have systematically prevented nonviolent campaigns from emerging or succeeding. From strikes and protests to sit-ins and boycotts, civil resistance remains the best strategy for social and political change in the face of oppression. Movements that opt for violence often unleash terrible destruction and bloodshed, in both the short and the long term, usually without realizing the goals they set out to achieve. Even though tumult and fear persist today from Cairo to Kiev, there are still many reasons to be cautiously optimistic about the promise of civil resistance in the years to come.

In the United States and Europe, policymakers often seem at a loss when confronted with the questions of whether to support civilians resisting authoritarian regimes using nonviolent protest and, if so, what form that support should take. Liberal interventionists cited a "responsibility to protect" civilians to justify NATO's intervention in Libya and have also invoked that argument in advocating for similar action in Syria. But the promise of civil resistance suggests an alternative: a "responsibility to assist" nonviolent activists and civic groups well before confrontations between civilians and authoritarian regimes devolve into violent conflicts.

Power to the People

Civil resistance does not succeed because it melts the hearts of dictators and secret police. It succeeds because it is more likely than armed struggle to attract a larger and more diverse base of participants and impose unsustainable costs on a regime. No single civil resistance campaign is the same, but the ones that work all have three things in common: they enjoy mass participation, they produce regime defections, and they employ flexible tactics.

Historically, the larger and more diverse the campaign, the more likely it was to succeed. Large campaigns have a greater chance of seriously disrupting the status quo, raising the costs of government repression, and provoking defections among a regime's pillars of support. When large numbers of people engage in acts of civil disobedience and disruption, shifting between concentrated methods such as protests and dispersed methods such as consumer boycotts and strikes, even the most brutal opponent has difficulty cracking down and sustaining the repression indefinitely. Mohammad Reza Pahlavi, Iran's last shah, had little difficulty neutralizing the Islamist and Marxist-inspired guerilla groups that challenged his rule in the 1960s and early 1970s. But when large numbers of oil workers, bazaar merchants, and students engaged in acts of collective nonviolent resistance, including work stoppages, boycotts, and protests, the regime's repressive apparatus became overstretched and the economy tanked. From there, it didn't take long for the shah to flee the country.

Broad-based support for a resistance movement can also weaken the loyalty of economic elites, religious authorities, and members of the state media who support the regime. When such figures defect to the opposition, they can sometimes force the regime to surrender to the oppositions demands, which is what happened with the Philippines' People Power movement of 1983–86. Broad movements also enjoy a tactical advantage: diverse, nonviolent campaigns that include women, professionals, religious figures, and civil servants—as opposed to violent ones comprised of mostly young, able-bodied men trained to become militants—reduce the risk of violent crackdowns, since security forces are often reluctant to use violence against crowds

that might include their neighbors or relatives. And even when governments have chosen to violently repress resistance movements, in all the cases under review, nonviolent campaigns still succeeded in achieving their goals almost half the time, whereas only 20 percent of violent movements achieved their goals, because the vast majority were unable to produce the mass support or defections necessary to win. In cases in which the security forces remain loyal to the regime, defections among economic elites can play a critical role. In South Africa, boycotts against white businesses and international divestments from South African businesses were decisive in ending the apartheid regime.

But civil resistance requires more than just mass participation and defections; it also requires planning and coordinated tactics. Successful nonviolent campaigns are rarely spontaneous, and the seemingly rapid collapse of the Ben Ali and Mubarak regimes shouldn't fool observers: both revolutions were rooted in labor and opposition movements going back nearly a decade. Indeed, between 1900 and 2006, the average nonviolent campaign lasted close to three years. As Robert Helvey, a retired U.S. Army colonel who organized civil resistance workshops in Myanmar (also called Burma), the Palestinian territories, and Serbia in the 1990s and the early years of this century, told activists during his workshops: if they wanted their campaign to succeed in one year, they should plan as if the struggle would last for two.

During the 1980s in the United States, Helvey worked closely with the scholar Gene Sharp, who has identified 198 different tactics that nonviolent resistance movements employ. These include various methods of protest, persuasion, noncooperation, and what Sharp calls "nonviolent intervention"—all of which have worked in various contexts. Tech-savvy scholars, such as Patrick Meier and Mary Joyce, have updated Sharp's list to include tactics linked to new technologies, such as using social media to report repressive actions in real time and even using small drones to monitor police movements.

Even campaigns that possess the holy trinity of features—mass participation, regime defections, and flexible tactics—don't always succeed. Much depends on whether state authorities can outmaneuver the protesters and sow division in their ranks, perhaps even provoking nonviolent resisters to abandon their protests and strikes, lose their discipline and unity, and take up arms in response to repression. But even when nonviolent campaigns fail, all is not lost: from 1900 to 2006, countries that experienced failed nonviolent movements were still about four times as likely to ultimately transition to democracy as countries where resistance movements resorted to violence at the outset. Nonviolent civic mobilization relies on flexibility and coalition building—the very things that are needed for democratization.

Of course, nonviolent revolutionaries are not necessarily equipped to govern during a political transition. In Egypt, for example, the young secular activists who filled Tahrir Square in January and February of 2011 have failed to organize effective political parties or interest groups. Nonviolent mass uprisings cannot always resolve systemic governance problems, such as co-opted institutions, entrenched corruption, and a lack of power sharing between a regime's military or security forces and the civilian bureaucracy.

But revolutionary campaigns can still maximize their chances of achieving more representative government—of bringing the successes of the street into the halls of power—if they develop so-called parallel institutions during the course of their struggles. Poland offers one of the best examples. In 1980, after some 16,000 workers launched a strike at the Gdansk shipyard, Polish labor groups, which had already been fomenting resistance to the Soviet-backed communist regime in Poland for a decade, formed Solidarity, a trade union that morphed into a civil resistance movement and gradually eroded the communist authority's grip on the country. Solidarity published underground dissident newspapers, organized demonstrations and radical theater performances in churches, and resisted years of repression, including the imposition of martial law in 1981. Eventually, ten million Poles joined the group, which operated as a kind of shadow government, facilitating its ability to step into a leadership role as communism crumbled. In 1988, Solidarity organized a series of strikes that led to direct negotiations with the regime, which resulted in semi-free

elections in 1989. When Poland emerged from communist rule a year later, it did so with a new set of electoral rules and practices, many of them shepherded by Solidarity through a series of negotiations, which allowed for a much more durable and confident turn toward democracy. Although problems remained, Polish civil society was fully capable of holding its new leaders to account—including Solidarity's Lech Walesa, who was elected president in 1990. . . .

You Say You Want A Revolution

Comparing these cases brings out a few key points. First, nonviolent campaigns attracted far more diverse participation than armed ones, which increased the chances of defections among security forces and other regime elites. There is, in fact, safety in numbers, especially when protesters represent a cross section of society. Second, the nonviolent campaigns that succeeded used a variety of tactics. In Syria, on the other hand, nonviolent activists tended to rely solely on demonstrations and occupations, which are among the riskiest methods of civil resistance. Attempted strikes, boycotts, and other forms of mass noncooperation were weak, localized, and lacked support.

Third, although the protests of the Arab Spring inspired one another and were united by a similar, iconic slogan that was first chanted in Tunisia—"The people want the fall of the regime!"—they were hardly all the same. In fact, the different outcomes in each country underscore why nonviolent groups must resist the temptation to replicate a mass demonstration in another country without a broader strategy of their own, especially when that mass demonstration represents the endgame of a much longer nonviolent campaign. Fourth, in addition to killing more unarmed civilians and undermining participation, armed resistance makes rebel groups dangerously dependent on outside support. In both Libya and Syria, that total reliance made the rebels more vulnerable to accusations that they were agents of foreign enemies. Moreover, international support for armed groups is usually conditional and fickle, subjecting rebel groups to the whims of their sponsors (as Washington's reluctance to follow through on its pledges of significant help for the Syrian rebels shows).

During last year's [2013] UN General Assembly meeting, U.S. President Barack Obama spoke to a roundtable about the essential role that civil society has played in nearly every major social and political transformation of the last half century, from the civil rights movement in the United States, to the fight against communism in Eastern Europe, to the antiapartheid struggle in South Africa. The right of peaceful assembly and association, Obama said, is "not a Western value; this is a universal right." But the space for this right is shrinking in many parts of the world. Countries are passing laws to stifle civil society, restrict nongovernmental organizations' access to foreign funding, crack down on communications technology, and, in more extreme cases, arrest and harass journalists and activists. Obama called on governments to embrace civil society groups as partners and, in a slightly edgier appeal, pressed governments and nongovernmental organizations to come up with more innovative and effective ways to support groups and activists fighting against injustice and oppression.

But that raises the question of which forms of external assistance to nonviolent civic groups work and which ones don't. The idea of "do no harm" remains an anchoring principle for how outside governments and institutions should promote democracy and aid civil society groups in other countries. International support to such movements can take many forms, such as monitoring trials of political prisoners, engaging in solidarity movements to support the right of peaceful assembly, providing alternative channels of news and information, targeting warnings to security officials who might be tempted to use lethal force against nonviolent protesters, and supporting general capacity building for civic groups and independent media. But local actors are in the best position to determine which type of support is appropriate and if it is worth the associated risks.

Strengthening civil society is not only a precondition for sustained democratic development. It can also protect civilians from the worst excesses of violent repression. Although regimes may not refrain from using violence against peaceful protesters, history suggests that helping civic groups maintain nonviolent discipline—a practice that often requires coordination, preparation, and training—can ultimately minimize civilian casualties. In addition to staving off armed rebellion, sticking to civil resistance can insulate protesters from the most extreme forms of state violence by raising the costs of repression (although as Tunisia and Egypt proved, hundreds of protesters could still pay with their lives). Nonviolent movements are not as reliant on outside support as armed ones are, but the international community can help ensure that civil society groups maintain the space they need to exercise their basic rights of free speech and assembly while avoiding the temptation to turn to arms to pursue their goals.

Policymakers should prioritize a "responsibility to assist" nonviolent activists and civic groups, rather than only seeking to protect civilians through military force, as in NATO's Libya intervention. Of course, civil resistance campaigns are and must remain homegrown movements. But in recent years, the international community has done much to undermine civil resistance by quickly and enthusiastically supporting armed actors when they arrive on the scene. Syria's tragedy is a case in point. Although regime repression, supported by Iran and Russia, undoubtedly helped turn a principally nonviolent uprising into a civil war, external actors could have done more to aid civil resistance and prolong the original nonviolent uprising. They could have helped encourage, coordinate, and exploit for political gain regime defections (including from key Alawite elites); demanded that Assad allow foreign journalists to remain in the country; accelerated direct financial support to grass-roots nonviolent networks and local councils; and provided more information to Syrian activists about what it takes to remain nonviolent under highly repressive conditions. Instead, the international community provided political recognition and sanctuary to armed actors, supplied both nonlethal and lethal aid to them, and helped militarize the conflict, undermining the momentum of the nonviolent movement. There was no silver bullet for effectively aiding the nonviolent

Syrian opposition. But speed and coordination on the part of external actors, particularly early on in the revolution, were lacking.

Syria highlights the moral and strategic imperative of developing more flexible, nimble ways to support nonviolent resistance movements. The local champions of people power will continue to chart their own future. But outside actors have an important role to play in assuring that civil resistance has a fighting chance.

Countering Hybrid War: Civil Resistance as a National Defence Strategy

BY MACIEJ BARTKOWSKI

Maciej Bartkowski is Senior Director for Education & Research at International Center on Nonviolent Conflict. He edited and contributed to *Rediscovering Nonviolent History: Civil Resistance in Liberation Struggles and Nation-Making* (2013). From *openDemocracy*, May 12, 2015. Used by permission.

Since the annexation of Crimea and the start of conflict in eastern Ukraine, the Russian form of hybrid war that spearheaded these events has raised significant concerns among eastern European states about an effective response to non-traditional warfare. Russia's hybrid war—a term meaning a mixture of conventional and irregular warfare—has presented a vexing problem to conventional armed defense. It also demonstrates the need to determine whether a national strategy of nonviolent civilian defence can be a viable option for the current and potential victims of hybrid war to fight back non-militarily.

The meeting between former Russian and US defence and intelligence officials in March [2015] gave us a glimpse into the Kremlin's thinking about hybrid war. Instead of sending troops without insignia across the border with the Baltic states, Moscow would use at first non-military means to entice local, mainly Russian but sometimes non-Russian populations (like the Polish-speaking minority in Lithuania) toward Russia. This would hardly constitute a rationale for deployment of tanks and warplanes and would put a defending military in a dilemma of whether or not to shoot at unarmed civilians. As the commander of the US army in Europe, Lt-Gen Frederick "Ben" Hodges observed . . .: Russians "don't want a clear attack, they want a situation where all 28 [NATO member countries] won't say there's a clear attack." If the alliance decided to go heavy-handed against mobilized and seemingly peaceful minorities it would turn itself into an aggressor, offer Putin a propaganda coup for more interference and rally Russian society even closer around the Kremlin's belligerent policies.

Despite facing such unconventional threats, the western response has been predicated on a show of military force, while nonviolent strategies have largely been absent from defence plans. The most recent Operation Dragoon Ride publicity stunt saw hundreds of US soldiers and their armed vehicles meandering through the roads of central Europe in a public display of force. Meanwhile, countries such as Poland have beefed up their armouries while civilians have volunteered to join shooters' clubs and paramilitary groups to prepare for potential armed resistance.

Thinking Beyond the "Fight or Capitulate" Dichotomy

The choice society has in facing foreign aggression seems rather simple: fight with arms or surrender. That sentiment was reflected in the 2014 Gallup survey conducted in more than 60 countries that asked: "Would you fight for your country?" Globally, 60 percent were willing to fight or, as it was interpreted, "take up arms," while 27 percent would not. By default, "fight" was understood as armed struggle while its opposite—not to fight—as a capitulation.

A recent opinion poll in Poland, however, showed a far more nuanced gamut of responses. ... [T]he survey asked Poles what they would do if their state faced armed invasion by another country. Tellingly, 37 percent of respondents—the equivalent of almost 12 million Polish adults if applied to the nation's population—said they would resist foreign aggression "not by fighting with arms, but by engaging in other, non-military activities." Only 27 percent declared it would take up arms. The remaining would emigrate, were undecided or would surrender.

Many more Poles—a population that could very well find itself in Russia's crosshairs—are ready to engage in nonviolent resistance than in armed struggle to defend their country. While at first blush, Gallup's global survey suggests the default is armed struggle, responses by Poles indicate that when given more choices, nonviolent resistance has more support than is often recognized.

That point is not lost on Russia and China. My study published by the Krieger School of Johns Hopkins University in March 2015 on countering hybrid war with nonviolent civilian defense shows that these countries are preoccupied equally with shielding themselves against nonviolent resistance, while at the same time using civilian mobilization to propel their hybrid war machines. The new Russian military doctrine released at the end of 2014 identifies social movements and civilian-led demonstrations as a major weapon in territorial conflicts. This strategy is no doubt the result of Russia's lessons from the so-called colour revolutions, the Arab Spring and the Ukrainian Euromaidan.

Nonviolent Resistance as Part of a Nation's Defence Strategy?

Ironically, authoritarian states seem to give more credit to people power than their democratic counterparts. Only one tiny democratic state— recognizing both the historical contribution of this type of warfare to its pro-democratic and pro-independence struggle in the 1980s and beginning of the 1990s, as well as the costs and risks of armed defence against a militarily stronger adversary— has explicitly integrated strategies of nonviolent resistance into its territorial defence. ... [T]he Lithuanian Ministry of Defence published a manual that asks Lithuanian citizens to engage in civil resistance in case of invasion and occupation. It offers specific examples of how civilians can wage nonviolent actions against a foreign adversary while referring to Gene Sharp's 198 methods of nonviolent resistance. The manual acknowledges that "Civilian-based defense or nonviolent civil resistance is another way for citizens to resist aggression. ... This method is especially important for threats of hybrid war."

Lithuanians recognized that nonviolent civilian defence could turn a whole nation into a resistant society as it strengthens its cohesion, solidarity and self-organization—essential ingredients in a struggle against a polarizing hybrid war. Nationwide, nonviolent civilian defence turns the whole nation into a fighting society that is disciplined to wage a long-term, all-encompassing and targeted noncooperation effort with the aggressor, including its allies at home and abroad to disrupt their control and undermine their legitimacy in each area of social, political, economic and cultural life.

Seemingly weak, occupied populations have in fact been able to exercise direct and indirect leverage over the occupiers when they engaged in nonviolent resistance. The experience of the past anti-colonial and anti-occupation struggles suggests that civil resisters were most effective when they were able to look beyond their domestic struggle and extend their immediate battlefield outside the borders to mobilize external actors, including adversaries' international allies, as well as drive a wedge between the aggressor's government and its own society.

As a result, organized collective actions of millions of ordinary people were able to erode the loyalty of the adversary's allies often more effectively than arms. During the occupation of the Ruhr after World War I, German citizens were so effective in nonviolent outreach to the occupying French troops that Paris was gravely concerned about their loyalties and readiness to continue implementing occupation orders. This and other civil resistance actions forced the French government to call up reservists, which increased the cost of occupation, deepened the budget deficit and raised resentment among the French public.

Civil resistance has also undermined oppressors' domestic constituencies, as it did during the Indian independence struggle when Gandhi effectively reached out to the British media and the public to put pressure on the British government. Similarly, during World War II, civil resistance by the Norwegian teachers and trade unions against the pro-Nazi Quisling regime, the Danes' collective nonviolent actions against the Nazi occupation, the first Palestinian nonviolent intifada against Israeli occupation and the East Timorese nonviolent pro-independence struggle against the Suharto regime were all credited with protecting civilians, and reducing civilian deaths particularly in comparison with violent resistance. Nonviolent resistance also increased the economic, political and social costs on the violent adversary, often forcing it to offer tangible concessions that were hardly likely to have been extracted through direct violent challenge.

The Untapped Potential of Nonviolent Defence

At its core, nonviolent civilian defence is about engaging the greatest number of people with the least amount of risk for civilians and greatest number of disruptions for the adversary, including its key domestic and international supporters.

Historically, nonviolent resistance has worked far better than its armed alternative. Civil resistance has been determined to be twice as effective against a violent adversary than armed struggle, able to mobilize campaigns that are 11 times larger than average armed resistance ones, likely to reduce civilian deaths and tenfold more likely to bring about a democratic outcome compared to a victory though arms.

The untapped powers of nonviolent resistance offer a serious alternative against the threat of contemporary hybrid wars. Furthermore, as shown in the Polish survey results, pursuing this form of waging conflict might match people's own instincts in the face of external aggression. When it comes to mobilizing the masses, enhancing internal solidarity and unity, limiting overall human costs, maximizing strategic effectiveness of disruptions to a foreign adversary and increasing chances for post-conflict stability, democracies would do well to take note of the potential that nonviolent civilian defence holds for their defensive capabilities to counter protracted hybrid wars.

This is particularly relevant to smaller nations and their populations vulnerable to external threats from authoritarian states who are equally afraid of people power and eager to manipulate it to their benefit.

Satyagraha: A New Term for an Eternal Principle

BY MICHAEL N. NAGLER

Michael Nagler was a cofounder of the Peace and Conflict Studies program at the University of California, Berkley, and is a past president of the Peace and Justice Studies Association. Nagler's book *The Search for a Nonviolent Future: A Promise of Peace for Ourselves, Our Families, and Our World* has influenced many peace studies researchers and activists. Nagler is the founder of the Metta Center for Nonviolence. Due to space limitations, notes have been omitted from this selection. Selections from *The Nonviolence Handbook: A Guide for Practical Action.* Copyright © 2014 by Michael N. Nagler, Berrett-Koehler Publishers, Inc., San Francisco, CA. All rights reserved. www.bkconnection.com

Reading "history" might give you the impression that life unfolds in an endless series of competitions, conflicts, and wars. But as far back as 1909, Gandhi pointed out that history as we have practiced it is "a record of every interruption of the even working of the force of love or the soul.... Soul-force, being natural, is not noted in history." Note that Gandhi does not use the word *nonviolence* here, which had not yet become current (as a translation of *ahimsa*), and he had rejected the misleading term "passive resistance." Around this period he had to invent another term, *satyagraha* (pronounced sat-YAH-gra-ha), which literally means "clinging to truth." Satyagraha is sometimes used to mean nonviolence in general, as in this quote, but sometimes it means nonviolence in the form of active, resistant struggle.

By coining the term *satyagraha,* based on the Sanskrit word *sat,* which means "truth" or "reality" (as well as "the good"), Gandhi made it quite clear that he saw nonviolence as the positive reality of which violence is the shadow or negation. Consequently, nonviolence was bound to prevail in the long run: "The world rests upon the bedrock of *satya* or truth. *Asatya,* meaning untruth, also means nonexistent, and *satya* or truth also means that which is. If untruth does not so much as exist, its victory is out of the question. And truth being that which is, can never be destroyed. This is the doctrine of satyagraha in a nutshell."

Though *satyagraha* literally means "clinging to truth," it is often translated, not inappropriately, as "soul force." We all have that force within us, and under the right circumstances it can come forth from anyone, with amazing results. This can best be seen in what's called a *nonviolent moment,* when the "unstoppable force" of one party's nonviolence confronts the apparently immoveable commitment to violence of another. This moment will always lead to success, sometimes evidently and immediately, sometimes further down the road.

For instance, in 1963 in Birmingham, Alabama, black marchers, inspired by the intention to "win our freedom, and as we do it . . . set our white brothers free," in the words of one of their leaders, found themselves unexpectedly blocked by a line of police and firemen with dogs and hoses. The marchers knelt to pray. After a while they became "spiritually intoxicated," as David Dellinger recounts. They got up off their knees as though someone had given a signal and steadily marched toward the police and firemen. Once they got within earshot, some of them said, "We're not turning back. We haven't done anything wrong. All we want is our freedom. How do you feel doing these things?" Even though the police commissioner, a notorious segregationist, repeatedly shouted, "Turn on the hoses!" the firemen found their hands frozen. The marchers walked steadily on, passing right through the lines of the police and firemen. Some of these men were seen to be crying.

Gandhi, who had seen this working time and again, gave a beautiful explanation of how this transformation takes place: "What satyagraha does in these cases is not to suppress reason but to free it from inertia and to establish its sovereignty over prejudice, hatred, and other baser passions. In other words, if one may paradoxically put it, it does not enslave, it compels reason to be free." What he calls "reason" here is better described as the innate awareness that we are all connected and that nonviolence is "the law of our species." As we've noted, this is an awareness latent in everyone, a natural human state, however temporarily obscured it may be by the fog of hatred. In principle, we should be able to awaken this awareness in virtually anyone, given enough time and knowhow. Once awake, such awareness automatically takes precedence over the "baser passions."

That human beings have the potential to be nonviolent—and to respond to nonviolence when it's offered—implies a much higher image of the human being than we are presented with in the mass media and throughout our present culture, but because of that very culture, we can't expect our nonviolent potential to manifest by itself. To bring it to fruition we must first try to understand it better and get into the habit of using it creatively in our relationships, our institutions, and our culture. Then, to use it in situations of intense conflict such as Birmingham, there are two basic ingredients that make the nonviolent magic work:

1. We approach our situation with right intention. We are not and do not need to be against the well-being of any person.
2. We employ right means. Wrong means such as violence can never, in the long run, bring about right ends.

The source of our empowerment and strength in satyagraha lies in our having right intention and using right means. If we operate from anger or envy or ignorance, then no matter how good the cause, we are not approaching it correctly.

Note that the Birmingham marchers asked, "How do you feel doing this?" In other words, they credited the opponent with some moral awareness and thereby helped to awaken that awareness—for the opponent's own benefit.

Likewise, obviously, if we give in to violence, we are not employing right means.

Five Basic Training Practices for Nonviolent Living

The temptation to shame someone who's behaving badly—that is, to try to make them ashamed of themselves rather than ashamed of what they're doing—can be very strong. Giving dignity to someone like that, acknowledging that they have a point of view, does not come naturally. But the attitude can be cultivated. Here are some elements of a nonviolent training program by which we can empower ourselves as individuals and cultivate right intention.

1. *Avoid the major networks and media outlets.* Whether we realize it or not (because it has grown up gradually), mass media today are saturated with violence and with the low image of humanity violence implies. Innumerable studies have shown that this violent imagery gets into our minds, even if we consciously disapprove, and makes us markedly more violent and aggressive. Normalizing the media would require a major campaign. Fortunately, there are alternative media today through which we can get news and entertainment. . . . Through them we are less likely to see the world as a violent place and ourselves as helpless to change it. We can safely reduce our exposure to the commercial mass media, beholden to corporate and power-structure interests—even to zero.

2. *Learn about nonviolence.* To fill the space left when we avoid such media, nothing is better than a greater appreciation and knowledge of nonviolence, which, as we have seen, is no mere technique but embodies in itself a worldview, an entire culture. Simply learning to spot the nonviolence happening around us is quite helpful. Formal learning, such as reading books like this . . ., adds another dimension. And a final potent means of gaining nonviolent culture is to practice it mindfully.

3. *Take up a spiritual practice* if you do not already have one. Meditation, which need not be connected with a particular religion, is extremely helpful for the nonviolent—or for anyone. Meditation is a great humanizer because it puts us in touch with the deeper reaches of our own humanity, which is simultaneously that of others. We all need some form of self-discipline, whether religiously sanctioned or not, and many nonviolent actors today have gotten access to their inner resources and vision through meditation, prayer, or some other spiritual practice.

4. *Be more personal with others.* Throughout your daily interactions, give people your undivided attention. Take the trouble to chat with the toll collector (if there's not a long line of cars behind you); call someone up instead of texting—or better yet, go have tea with them. Use technology to connect with people rather than to distance yourself from them. These seemingly small habits can change the texture of our lives, helping us to develop compassion and see the humanity in others while, of course, helping them as well.

5. *Find a project and get active.* What is your unique contribution? Where does the world need you most? What project do you see as doable and critical to making an essential change in our present system? Quite a few studies have shown that those who are active are more optimistic and vice versa. We influence ourselves very much by what we do, perhaps as much or more than we influence ourselves by how we articulate why we're doing it.

These steps help to prepare us for nonviolent living. Even without step 5 they would make a difference in the world, because how we live affects the world around us even if we do nothing else.

What Have We Learned?

Nonviolence is an innate capacity of human nature. It is not a moral commandment; still less is it a philosophical abstraction. Nonviolence, at least the kind I've presented here, is an energy that operates in and on all living beings. It can be understood, predicted, and controlled like many other forces in nature. Probably the most important thing we need to know about nonviolence is that it's not the *absence* of anything as much as it is a *positive force*. It is the force of love, though at times it may not feel that way. The U.S. Civil Rights movement, King explained, did not cause outbursts of anger but "expressed anger under discipline for maximum effect." This discipline of conserving our anger is not an act of repression. When we do it correctly, it enables our anger to be converted into a creative power. Nonviolence is the power released by the conversion of a negative drive.

That transformation of negative or disruptive energies within the human being is not only a growth process for the individual; it can have an astounding effect on opponents—an effect that threats and weapons cannot match. During the successful Philippines People Power Revolution of 1986—which is only one example among thousands we could cite—soldiers defied direct orders from their superiors and refused to fire on peaceful protesters. In many cases, they were actually seen to break down in tears and defect.

Observing this effect, Kenneth Boulding, a founder of modern peace research, coined the term "integrative power," which he compared to "threat power" and "exchange power." Integrative power is the power released when we make a commitment to bear witness to the truth of our interconnectedness, even when our opponent is doing violence to that truth, and perhaps to our persons. The opponent sees himself as radically separate from us, whereas we can see the unity he has lost sight of and can thereby help him to see it as well. The result, Boulding points out, is that both parties end up closer. When we control the divisive drives within us for this purpose, then "control" does not mean "repress." Gandhi was quite familiar with this dynamic: "I have learnt through bitter experience the one supreme lesson to conserve my anger, and as heat conserved is transmuted into energy, even so our anger controlled can be transmuted into a power that can move the world."

King adds some clarification to that transmuting process in his above-quoted (and worth repeating) statement that the Civil Rights activists controlled anger and *released it under discipline* for maximum effect. Seen in this light, it becomes intriguingly clear that the power of nonviolence is latent within us, waiting to be released, if we check the tendency to act from a place of anger or fear. If we define nonviolence as the force released by the conversion of a negative drive, such as fear or anger that would tear people apart if expressed in its raw forms, the converse is that those negative forces and their expression are known as violence.

A Way of Being

So nonviolence is not a moral or philosophical abstraction. It also is not just a set of tactics, a mere method. People fighting for their freedom have brought about impressive changes simply by not taking up weapons. As a Yemeni protester said to a friend of mine in 2012, "They can't defeat us because we've left our guns at home!" But deeper and more lasting changes happen when we leave our *hatred* at home.

Once we have mastered this trick—and I hope . . . [I have] provided some insight into how to do this—we can see the violence in our world today in a more optimistic and more challenging light. All this anger, whether roused by the mass media, by the gross inequalities in our economy, or whatever, is raw material for nonviolence! To express it in its raw form would be a waste.

Many people think of nonviolence as a tactic to be adopted when they have no better choice, because any violence from them would meet with fierce repression, or because they just plain don't have the necessary weapons, and they often reserve the right to go back to violence if they do not meet with success. Whatever may be the merits of this approach—and it is any day better and can require more courage than violence—I hope I've made it clear that we can go much further when we hold nonviolence as a principle, a way of being in the world.

In this approach, nonviolence is not really the recourse of the weak but actually calls upon an uncommon kind of strength; it is not a refraining from something but the engaging of a positive force. The more we are able to act—and be—without hatred, the more we are able to resist what someone is *doing* without wishing them any harm, the more we are able to "liquidate antagonism but not the antagonists themselves," in Gandhi's words, the more available this power or force becomes. In a way that we don't yet understand, this attitude and worldview of interconnectedness unlocks energies that lead to deeper and more permanent change.

To say that nonviolence is not merely a strategy does not mean that no strategy is necessary. As we have seen, this is far from true. But there's a remarkable feature of nonviolence that cannot be claimed by militarism or violence: that carrying out the principle is *also* effective strategy. Unlike violence, where we bank on the hopeless idea that wrong means can bring about a right end, in nonviolence we do not have to choose between the right thing and the most effective thing to do. In the long run, they're the same. If you pass up an opportunity to humiliate someone, for example, simply because you believe on principle that everyone is entitled to respect, it gives you a nearly infallible strategy to bring them closer. As Nobel Peace Prize winner Adolfo Perez Esquivel put it, "Nonviolent action implants, by anticipation within the very process of change itself, the values to which it will ultimately lead. Hence it does not sow peace by means of war. It does not attempt to build up by tearing down."

A Movement Oversweeping the World

In 1939, Gandhi wrote, "My optimism rests on my belief in the infinite possibilities of the individual to develop nonviolence. The more you develop it in your own being, the more infectious it becomes till it overwhelms your surroundings and by and by might oversweep the world." In the years since Gandhi penned those words, though they have been violent years, the world has also begun to see just such an awakening. In fact, it has been estimated that more than half the world now lives in a society that has been significantly affected by a nonviolent movement.

The modern history of nonviolence has been aided by several qualitative changes that are potentially of immense help in "oversweeping the world." First, we are learning that every culture has local ways of responding creatively to conflict, and that these approaches can be mobilized in the context of a protracted nonviolent struggle. For instance, indigenous people, who play a critical role in environmental struggles, are beginning to organize and network among themselves.

Second, we now know that nonviolence can be carried out without a single charismatic leader if there is no such person on hand, which is most of the time. However, movements can be aided materially by the intervention of peace teams or the help of a skilled outsider. Moreover—and this may be the most important development of all—people are learning as never before how to teach others what they've gained from the successes and failures of their own movements. For example, the Center for Advanced Nonviolent Actions and Strategies has sent veterans of the successful Otpor rebellion that overthrew President Slobodan Milosevic in 2000 to Egypt and other places facing similar struggles.

Third, the majority of the movements that have been nonviolent, in one way or another, in the years since Gandhi and King—and they are many—have been almost exclusively obstructive, like the cascade of insurrections called the "color revolutions" in Eastern Europe and the Arab Spring that followed. A few have been almost exclusively constructive; the largest and most dramatic example of such a movement being the MST, or Landless Worker Movement, in Brazil, which has given land and livelihood to tens of thousands of families and created communities in the process—but has not found a creative way to deal with resistance from landowners. With few exceptions—such as the First Intifada in Palestine, which ran from 1987 to 1993—we have not seen a sustained campaign that, like the Indian freedom struggle, could operate in both modes and had a way to decide strategically when to be obstructive and when to be constructive.

Nonetheless, there is growing awareness of this possibility, and when *that* kind of movement happens once more, building on a progression from personal empowerment to constructive program, to satyagraha when needed (and it probably will be), we may well start to see the full power of nonviolence to change our world.

Finally, modern science has dramatically shifted from an emphasis on rational materialism (and the separateness and meaninglessness that such a view entails) to a more robust picture of human nature and the world that is surprisingly consistent with timeless wisdom traditions. This picture of innate empathy and cooperation, confirmed by both wisdom and science, paves the way for a cultural story in which nonviolence would be as much at home as violence is at home—however we may consider it an unwelcome guest—today.

"Those who are attracted to nonviolence," Gandhi wrote, "should join the experiment," and it has become clearer with each passing year that nothing less than the survival of life on earth could be at stake. I hope that the glimpse into the history and potential of nonviolence that I've offered here, brief as it is, serves to show that although it will call for work and sacrifice, we can use this power to redirect human destiny to a higher goal. This is the most compelling challenge of our time.

DISCUSSION QUESTIONS

1. Review the serious reasons that *The Onion* article provides embedded its satire that explain why many people support the use of violence.

2. Summarize the principle similarities that Simone Sebastian claims exist between Martin Luther King Jr.'s historic civil rights campaigns and the contemporary Black Lives Matter movement.

3. Erica Chenoweth and Maria J. Stephan argue mass participation, regime defections, and flexible tactics are necessary for successful nonviolent campaigns. Explain which of these three is likely the most important and which is likely the least important.

4. Review why Chenoweth and Stephan maintain that strengthening civil society is essential across the world today. (See also Stephan and Shaazka Beyerle's selection in part 4, section 2, for further discussion of the importance of civil societies.)

5. Explain the advantages that Maciej Bartkowski maintains nonviolent civilian defense has over the alternatives of surrender and armed resistance.

6. Describe the benefits that Michael N. Nagler believes can result from adopting nonviolence as a way of life.

7. Adopt a principled nonviolent perspective to expose the main weaknesses of pragmatic nonviolent campaigns. Next, adopt a pragmatic nonviolent perspective to expose the main weaknesses of principled nonviolent campaigns.

8. Justify the perspective on principled or on pragmatic nonviolence you would adopt if you were leading a nonviolent campaign.

Debates about Forgiveness, Reconciliation, and Restoration

Individuals, groups, and countries sometimes harm and kill innocent people. Victims afterward have at least three choices on how to react. They can seek retribution from and punishment of the perpetrators. Or, they can aim instead for forgiveness and reconciliation. Or, finally, they can choose a path of restorative justice. There is much disagreement about which choice is best.

Retribution and punishment, the first of these three approaches to justice is the most common choice of victims in many regions of the world. Justifications for this approach are offered in several books of the Old Testament (e.g. Deuteronomy, Exodus, and Leviticus), although the doctrine is even older and more widespread than the Abrahamic religions. The King James Bible (Deuteronomy 19:21) explains, "And thine eye shall not pity; but life shall go for life, eye for eye, tooth for tooth, hand for hand, foot for foot." Retributive punishment, it is thought, should be proportionate to the crime.

In the first selection, Andrew Moss describes retributive and proportionate punishment as a search for "just deserts." Moss maintains that contemporary retributivists tend to justify their view in three ways: (1) By appeals to what is "fair," (2) by considering punishments as messages sent to all citizens, and (3) by trusting intuitive feelings of what offenders deserve. Moss maintains that each of these justifications is flawed and that, therefore, systems of retributive justice are also flawed.

Moss offers restorative justice as a superior form of justice. Restorative justice and many other alternative, non-retributive forms of justice draw inspiration from the work of the Truth and Reconciliation Commission (TRC) established in South Africa in 1995 after the peaceful ending of apartheid, a system of white supremacy that for decades oppressed and often violently harmed a black majority population. In the second selection, Desmond Tutu reviews some of the work that the TRC completed in its attempts to heal the emotional wounds of apartheid and so prepare South Africa to become a more equitable society.

The successes and failures of the TRC have been much studied by advocates for approaches to justice based on *forgiveness and reconciliation*. This approach accepts Tutu's claim that victims should strive to accept the common humanity of those who have harmed them, even if complete forgiveness is beyond their reach. Even incomplete forgiveness is often difficult to achieve, however, so many people doubt that justice based on work like that associated with the TRC and related initiatives can succeed in modern societies. In the third selection, Ted Wachtel argues that asking victims to forgive perpetrators is often not only impossible but also often not necessary. Wachtel maintains that *restorative justice* approaches like those described by Moss in the first selection help victims and their families most while also reducing rates of re-offending.

A final selection, by Molly Rowan Leach, explores differences between retributive and restorative justice systems and argues for the superiority of a restorative approach in the case of six young boys who broke into a dangerous chemical plant.

Responding to Retributivists: A Restorative Justice Rejoinder to the Big Three Desert Theories

BY ANDREW MOSS

Andrew Moss is a 2014 graduate of the University of New Brunswick Faculty of Law. Due to space limitations, notes have been omitted from this selection. Selections from "Responding to Retributivists: A Restorative Justice Rejoinder to the Big Three Desert Theories." *Contemporary Justice Review* 16.2 (2013): 214–27.

Introduction

Attack retributivists. This is the strategy that must be employed if restorative justice advocates are to establish that restorative justice provides the best framework for responding to convicted offenders. Restorative justice theorists have provided superior models, yet retributivism continues to enjoy prominence in scholarship and practice. When promoting restorative justice, advocates must not only offer and defend models. They must engage retributivists in the same manner retributivists engage them: with direct critique. Prominent retributivists like von Hirsch and Ashworth have spilled considerable ink trying to persuade readers against restorative justice, but their own models have not been subjected to comparable criticism from a restorative justice perspective. The flaws in prominent retributive theories of legal punishment must be exposed.

The critique of retributivism is nuanced. Not all elements of retributive theories are problematic. Where they fail is in their attempt to justify imprisoning convicted offenders. There are three prominent retributive theories that attempt to justify imprisonment: Fair Play theory, Moral Communication theory, and Intuitive Desert theory. "Fair Play" retributivists seek to imprison offenders in order to re-balance the distribution of benefits and burdens that was upset by the criminal offense. "Moral Communication" retributivists seek to imprison offenders as a means of communicating society's condemnation of criminality. "Intuitive Desert" retributivists seek to imprison offenders because it is a deserved response to wrongdoing (the supporting evidence is our intuitive reactions to criminality). These retributive models are in direct competition with restorative justice models. They provide alternative answers to the question "how should we respond to convicted offenders?" So, it is important for restorative justice advocates to demonstrate the failings of retributivist models. . . .

Fair Play theory

According to Fair Play theory, legal punishment of criminal offenders is justified because the offenders gained an unfair advantage over law-abiding citizens (Cottingham, 1979). In his influential article, "Persons and Punishment," Herbert Morris (1968) explains that the criminal law provides rules that prohibit citizens from interfering with others and acting violently towards them. These rules benefit all citizens by securing valued ends such as life, bodily security, and property. Citizens can obtain this mutual benefit only if they assume the burden of restraining behaviors that interfere or risk interfering with others in proscribed ways. When criminals break the law they refuse this burden and take advantage of lawful citizens. Criminals owe something to these citizens because they took an advantage that does not rightfully belong to them. Justice requires that this balance be restored. Morris argues that punishing criminals (or pardoning them) restores the equilibrium of benefits and burdens by exacting the criminals' debt to the other citizens.

Dagger (1993) explains that when a thief steals goods from a store, merely returning the goods does not achieve balance because the lawbreaker has yet to restore the balance between him and other law-abiding citizens. The thief gained not only whatever he stole, but also the double advantage of not obeying the law while enjoying the advantages of the rule of law provided by law-abiding citizens. Fair play insists that punishing the offenders to take away the advantage gained by their unfairness is a proper response and that there is no entirely suitable substitute for punishment. . . .

The problem with Dagger's argument is that imposing hard treatment, such as imprisonment, is a counter-productive way to accomplish his aim of re-balancing the distribution of benefits and burdens in society. First, incarcerating convicted offenders actually burdens the victims, because it is they and the other law-abiding citizens who must pay the significant expenses of the offenders' imprisonment. Second, incarcerating offenders will often prevent them from being able to access employment. This is a problem because then they will not be able to earn the necessary monies to pay compensation to their victims for damaged property, pain and suffering. Third, secondary victims of the crime and other residents of the political community who have been taken advantage of will suffer these same problems.

A better response to convicted offenders would require them to make amends for their wrongdoing. Amends are achieved when offenders make reparations for the criminal wrong they committed and their resulting harms. This subsumes both moral and material repairs as the overall aim is to restore victims to their previously enjoyed level of well-being. This can hardly be accomplished when an offender is incapacitated in prison.

Restorative justice dispositions, on the other hand, can provide offenders with a number of avenues for compensating victims for harm to their property such as earning money, returning or replacing property, or performing direct services or repairs. Victims can also secure compensation for pain and suffering related to injuries or time lost without property.

Restorative justice processes may also provide a method for offenders to help ease the psychological harms that their victims suffered. Encounter processes allow victims to meet with their offenders and seek out answers to the questions that plague them. It is reported that encountering their offenders can provide considerable healing for victims and release them from fears and compulsions (Cayley, 1998). This should not be surprising as there is evidence that forgiving can result in psychological healing (Garvey, 2003). Restorative justice encounters may also work in a manner similar to exposure therapy. In traditional exposure therapy, patients are forced to confront what they fear so that they will realize their fear is exaggerated or unjustified (Oltmanns, Emery, & Taylor, 2006). In a restorative justice encounter, the victim is exposed to the offender and forced to see her/him as s/he truly is. This may rid the victim of any nightmarish caricaturing of the offender that might be producing anxiety. Victims even report that meeting the offender is the most satisfying part of the entire criminal justice process, even more so than receiving restitution (Van Ness & Strong, 2006).

Criminal offenders should also attempt to repair the moral damage they caused. Wrongdoing damages normative relationships, which also need to be restored. The paradigmatic way of compensating for a moral wrong is apology. The verbal apology should generally include: acknowledgment of wrongdoing, recognition of moral responsibility, expression of guilt and remorse and repudiation of behavior. To properly repudiate the wrongdoing, the offender must also commit to reform. Many scholars accept this conception of apology (O'Hara & Yarn, 2002). . . .

Moral Communication Theory

The second retributive theory proposes that the central focus of our response to convicted offenders ought to be moral communication. There are a number of reasons why this would be beneficial. . . .

von Hirsch (2009) attempts to justify a system of legal punishment by referencing the need to achieve the important goals of moral communication. He argues that the state ought to express disapprobation of criminal conduct and offenders. von Hirsch also argues for an institution of legal punishment that provides a disincentive against engaging in crime. So, he proposes a hybrid theory: an institution in which punishments express condemnation and deter potential offenders. Criminal sanctions, unlike taxes, can convey disapproval and censure. von Hirsch argues that we should use hard treatment as a vehicle through which to express our censure. The reason for expressing this disapproval through hard treatment (as opposed to merely censuring) has to do with minimizing predatory behavior. The threat of hard treatment provides an additional reason against offending for those tempted to disobey the law.

The primary basis for deciding the severity of sentences is the principle of proportionality which requires the severity of the penalties to be proportionate to the gravity of the offender's criminal conduct. Since punishment embodies blame, the severity of punishments in a system must be arrayed according to the gravity of the offences. von Hirsch states that any other order would be unfair because offenders would be censured more or less than the blameworthiness of their conduct warrants. He argues that although we cannot discover exactly what quantum of punishment is appropriate for a given type of offense based on intuition, we must ensure ordinal proportionality: persons convicted of similar crimes should receive similar punishments. The anchoring of this scale should be lower rather than higher, so that the penalties do not "drown out" the moral message and become a system of bare threats. von Hirsch's theory is problematic because meting out hard treatment is not the most effective way to express condemnation or the most effective way to prevent crime. Ultimately, his theory embodies the worst of both worlds.

The conventional criminal justice system of trial and imprisonment that von Hirsch endorses is not an effective tool for moral communication. Most criminal trials involve no more than a guilty plea followed by a sentence handed down by a sole professional judge. When trials are contested, defendants need not testify and may remain passive while others argue the case. Defendants must attend certain phases of trial but cannot be considered to be actively engaged in any sort of moral dialogue. The defendant can easily neutralize the criticism of her/his behavior because s/he never engages with those sitting in judgment. Without meeting the victim, the offender may not learn the full extent of the negative consequences of her/his criminal act or recognize the true character of her/his wrongdoing. The offender is not required to apologize or repudiate the offense. In most cases, offenders plead to a lesser charge, in which case, the formal judgment does not even represent the offense alleged. The criminal offense is not even named properly (Weigand, 2006). . . .

Restorative processes can also provide a proper forum for calling the offender to account for her/his actions. The dialogical nature of restorative encounters ensures that offenders are treated as responsible agents who must account for their behavior. Unlike in conventional criminal justice processes, offenders who admit guilt must apologize and answer questions from those they have harmed. This process prevents offenders from denying responsibility, denying the wrongfulness of the act, or denying the authority behind the condemnation. Offenders cannot get away with the standard excuses that allow criminals to commit crime without troubling their conscience. Standard excuses include: "I did not mean to do it," "I did not really hurt anybody," "They had it coming to them," etc. (Agnew, 1994). . . .

Intuitive Desert Theory

Proponents of the third retributive account, the "Intuitive Desert" theory of punishment, claim that criminal offenders deserve to be punished (censure and hard treatment) for their wrongdoing. The justification for hard treatment is independent from its ability to secure other aims like fair play, censure, or crime prevention. On this view, hard treatment is justified because it is itself deserved. The rationale for this view is found in our intuitive reactions to particular crimes and the response that strikes us as merited. Proponents of this theory argue that there is an intuitive connection between crime and punishment (von Hirsch, Ashworth, & Roberts[,2009]). Boonin [2008] explains that this type of retributivism is made using an argument from particular cases. Proponents focus on our intuitive reactions to instances of criminality and then argue that retribution best explains these moral judgments. Proponents then typically appeal to our reactions to horrendous atrocities and attempt to generalize from such cases in order to justify a general institution of punishment.

In his important essay "The Moral Worth of Retribution," Moore (1987) attempts to justify a retributive institution of punishment by showing that it best accounts for a number of particular moral judgments that we believe to be true. He claims that most people react to atrocious crimes with an intuitive judgment that punishment is warranted. . . .

So, if the reader is confronted with examples of brutal crimes about which s/he intuitively judges that punishment is appropriate, s/he should be willing to go all the way and demand that justice be done for all other less serious crimes as well. Boonin explains that intuitive desert retributivists use these extreme cases where many people agree that punishment is morally permissible to establish a general principle that all wrongdoers should be punished.

Admittedly, Moore is probably correct that some readers will feel an intuitive urge to punish such an offender. However, it is far from clear how this establishes that we should set up a system of retributive punishment. When setting up a response to convicted offenders, there are a number of valuable aims we may want to accomplish, and Moore has not shown that retribution is more important than the rest. Moore tries to make his point by setting up a false dichotomy.

He presents the reader with the choice between inflicting pain on an offender and doing nothing. It may be true that some would choose to punish the offender rather than doing nothing. However, restorative justice models do not respond by doing nothing. . . .

So, Moore is probably right in concluding that society favors retributive justice over no justice (retributive punishment can take away the offenders' unfair advantage). In the real world, however, people are in favor of a response that requires offenders to make amends and reform, especially when such an approach requires fewer resources and reduces crime. . . .

Conclusion

The prominent three desert theories fail in their attempt to justify a system of legal punishment in which convicted offenders are subjected to incarceration. An acceptable response to convicted offenders requires them to suffer certain burdens, but these burdens are not justified on the basis of retributive theory. Dagger argues that hard treatment is necessary to restore the equilibrium of benefits and burdens, but restorative justice processes can better accomplish the aim of corrective justice. von Hirsch argues that hard treatment is necessary to communicate condemnation and prevent criminal behavior, yet restorative justice processes more effectively communicate censure, and proportionate incarceration does not effectively prevent crime. Moore argues that our intuitive responses to criminality signify the moral acceptability of an institution of legal punishment. The central defect with Moore's argument is that people do not in fact judge retributive responses to be more appropriate than restorative ones.

REFERENCES

Agnew, R. (1994). The techniques of neutralization and violence. *Criminology, 32*, 555–579.

Boonin, D. (2008). *The problem of punishment.* Cambridge: Cambridge University Press.

Cayley, D. (1998). *The expanding prison: The crisis in crime and punishment and the search for alternatives*. Toronto, ON: House of Anansi Press.

Cottingham, J. (1979). Varieties of retribution. *Philosophical Quarterly, 29*, 238–246.

Dagger, R. (1993). Playing fair with punishment. *Ethics, 103*, 473–488.

Garvey, S. (2003). Restorative justice, punishment, and atonement. *Utah Law Review, 1*, 303–317.

Moore, M. (1987). The moral worth of retribution. In F. Schoeman (Ed.), *Responsibility, character, and the emotions: New essays in moral psychology* (pp. 179–219). Cambridge: Cambridge University Press.

Morris, H. (1968). Persons and punishment. *The Monist, 52*, 475–501.

O'Hara, E., & Yarn, D. (2002). On apology and consilience. *Washington Law Review, 77*, 1121–1192.

Oltmanns, T., Emery, R., & Taylor, S. (2006). *Abnormal psychology* (2nd ed.). Toronto, ON: Pearson Education.

Van Ness, D., & Strong, K. (2006). *Restoring justice* (3rd ed.). Cincinnati, OH: Anderson.

von Hirsch, A. (2009). Proportionate sentences: A desert perspective. In A. von Hirsch, A. Ashworth, & J. K. Roberts (Eds.), *Principled sentencing: Readings on theory and policy* (3rd ed.) (pp. 115–125). Portland, OR: Hart.

von Hirsch, A., Ashworth, A., & Roberts, J. (2009). *Principled sentencing: Readings on theory and policy*. Portland, OR: Hart.

Weigand, T. (2006). Why have a trial when you can have a bargain? In A. Duff, L. Farmer, S. Marshall, & V. Tadros (Eds.), *The trial on trial, volume two: Judgment and calling to account* (pp. 207–222). Oxford: Hart.

Selections from *No Future Without Forgiveness*

BY DESMOND TUTU

Desmond Tutu, an Episcopal priest, was a leader of the South African antiapartheid movement, for which he was awarded the 1984 Nobel Peace Prize. He headed South Africa's Truth and Reconciliation Commission, and his books on the necessity and power of forgiveness have been widely read across the world. Excerpts from NO FUTURE WITHOUT FORGIVENESS by Desmond Tutu, copyright © 1999 by Desmond Tutu. Used by permission of Doubleday, an imprint of the Knopf Doubleday Publishing Group, a division of Penguin Random House LLC. All rights reserved.

In relations between individuals, if you ask another person for forgiveness you may be spurned; the one you have injured may refuse to forgive you. The risk is even greater if you are the injured party, wanting to offer forgiveness. The culprit may be arrogant, obdurate, or blind; not ready or willing to apologize or to ask for forgiveness. He or she thus cannot appropriate the forgiveness that is offered. Such rejection can jeopardize the whole enterprise. Our leaders were ready in South Africa to say they were willing to walk the path of confession, forgiveness, and reconciliation with all the hazards that lay along the way. And it seems their gamble might be paying off, since our land has not been overwhelmed by the catastrophe that had seemed so inevitable.

It is crucial, when a relationship has been damaged or when a potential relationship has been made impossible, that the perpetrator should acknowledge the truth and be ready and willing to apologize. It helps the process of forgiveness and reconciliation immensely. It is never easy. We all know just how difficult it is for most of us to admit that we have been wrong. It is perhaps the most difficult thing in the world—in almost every language the most difficult words are, "I am sorry." Thus it is not at all surprising that those accused of horrendous deeds and the communities they come from, for whom they believed they were committing these atrocities, almost always try to find ways out of even admitting that they were indeed capable of such deeds.

They adopt the denial mode, asserting that such-and-such has not happened. When the evidence is incontrovertible they take refuge in feigned ignorance. The Germans claimed they had not known what the Nazis were up to. White South Africans have also tried to find refuge in claims of ignorance. The former apartheid cabinet member Leon Wessels was closer to the mark when he said that they had not wanted to know, for there were those who tried to alert them. For those with eyes to see there were accounts of people dying mysteriously in detention. For those with ears to hear there was much that was disquieting and even chilling. But, like the three monkeys, they chose neither to hear, nor see, nor speak of evil. When some did own up, they passed the blame to others, "We were carrying out orders," refusing to acknowledge that as morally responsible individuals each person has to take responsibility for carrying out unconscionable orders.

We do not usually rush to expose our vulnerability and our sinfulness. But if the process of forgiveness and healing is to succeed, ultimately acknowledgment by the culprit is indispensable—not completely so but nearly so. Acknowledgment of the truth and of having wronged someone is important in getting to the root of the breach. If a husband and wife have quarreled without the wrongdoer acknowledging his or her fault by confessing, so exposing the cause of the rift; if a husband in this situation comes home with a bunch of flowers and the couple pretend all is in order, then they will be in for a rude shock. They have not dealt with their immediate past adequately. They have glossed over their differences, for they have failed to stare truth in the face for fear of a possible bruising confrontation. They will have done what the prophet calls healing the hurt lightly by crying, "Peace, peace where there is no peace."[1] They will have only papered over the cracks and not worked out why they fell out in the first place. All that will happen is that, despite the beautiful flowers, the hurt will fester. One day there will be an awful eruption and they will realize that they had tried to obtain reconciliation on the cheap. True reconciliation is not cheap. It cost God the death of His only begotten Son.

Forgiving and being reconciled are not about pretending that things are other than they are. It is not patting one another on the back and turning a blind eye to the wrong. True reconciliation exposes the awfulness, the abuse, the pain, the degradation, the truth. It could even sometimes make things worse. It is a risky undertaking but in the end it is worthwhile, because in the end dealing with the real situation helps to bring real healing. Spurious reconciliation can bring only spurious healing.

If the wrongdoer has come to the point of realizing his wrong, then one hopes there will be remorse, or at least some contrition or sorrow. This should lead him to confess the wrong he has done and ask for forgiveness. It obviously requires a fair measure of humility, especially when the victim is someone in a group that one's community had despised, as was often the case in South Africa when the perpetrators were government agents.

The victim, we hope, would be moved to respond to an apology by forgiving the culprit. As I have already tried to show, we were constantly amazed in the commission at the extraordinary magnanimity that so many of the victims exhibited. Of course there were those who said they would not forgive. That demonstrated for me the important point that forgiveness could not be taken for granted; it was neither cheap nor easy. As it happens, these were the exceptions. Far more frequently what we encountered was deeply moving and humbling.

In forgiving, people are not being asked to forget. On the contrary, it is important to remember, so that we should not let such atrocities happen again. Forgiveness does not mean condoning what has been done. It means taking what happened seriously and not minimizing it; drawing out the sting in the memory that threatens to poison our entire existence. It involves trying to understand the perpetrators and so have empathy, to try to stand in their shoes and appreciate the sort of pressures and influences that might have conditioned them.

Forgiveness is not being sentimental. The study of forgiveness has, become a growth industry. Whereas previously it was something often dismissed pejoratively as spiritual and religious, now because of developments such as the Truth and Reconciliation Commission in South Africa it is gaining attention as an academic discipline studied by psychologists, philosophers, physicians, and theologians. In the

United States there is an International Forgiveness Institute attached to the University of Wisconsin, and the John Templeton Foundation, with others, has started a multimillion-dollar Campaign for Forgiveness Research. Forgiving has even been found to be good for your health.

Forgiving means abandoning your right to pay back the perpetrator in his own coin, but it is a loss that liberates the victim. In the commission we heard people speak of a sense of relief after forgiving. A[n] . . . issue of the journal *Spirituality and Health* had on its front cover a picture of three U.S. ex-servicemen standing in front of the Vietnam Memorial in Washington, D.C. One asks, "Have you forgiven those who held you prisoner of war?" "I will never forgive them," replies the other. His mate says: "Then it seems they still have you in prison, don't they?"[2]

Does the victim depend on the culprit's contrition and confession as the precondition for being able to forgive? There is no question that, of course, such a confession is a very great help to the one who wants to forgive, but it is not absolutely indispensable. Jesus did not wait until those who were nailing him to the cross had asked for forgiveness. He was ready, as they drove in the nails, to pray to his Father to forgive them and he even provided an excuse for what they were doing. If the victim could forgive only when the culprit confessed, then the victim would be locked into the culprit's whim, locked into victimhood, whatever her own attitude or intention. That would be palpably unjust.

I have used the following analogy to try to explain the need for a perpetrator to confess. Imagine you are sitting in a dank, stuffy, dark room. This is because the curtains are drawn and the windows have been shut. Outside the light is shining and a fresh breeze is blowing. If you want the light to stream into that room and the fresh air to flow in, you will have to open the window and draw the curtains apart; then that light which has always been available will come in and air will enter the room to freshen it up. So it is with forgiveness. The victim may be ready to forgive and make the gift of her forgiveness available, but it is up to the wrongdoer to appropriate the gift—to open the window and draw the curtains aside. He does this by acknowledging the wrong he has done, so letting the light and fresh air of forgiveness enter his being.

In the act of forgiveness we are declaring our faith in the future of a relationship and in the capacity of the wrongdoer to make a new beginning on a course that will be different from the one that caused us the wrong. We are saying here is a chance to make a new beginning. It is an act of faith that the wrongdoer can change. According to Jesus,[3] we should be ready to do this not just once, not just seven times, but seventy times seven, without limit—provided, it seems Jesus says, your brother or sister who has wronged you is ready to come and confess the wrong they have committed yet again.

That is difficult, but because we are not infallible, because we will hurt especially the ones we love by some wrong, we will always need a process of forgiveness and reconciliation to deal with those unfortunate yet all too human breaches in relationships. They are an inescapable characteristic of the human condition.

Once the wrongdoer has confessed and the victim has forgiven, it does not mean that is the end of the process. Most frequently, the wrong has affected the victim in tangible, material ways. Apartheid provided the whites with enormous benefits and privileges, leaving its victims deprived and exploited. If someone steals my pen and then asks me to forgive him, unless he returns my pen the sincerity of his contrition and confession will be considered to be nil. Confession, forgiveness, and reparation, wherever feasible, form part of a continuum.

In South Africa the whole process of reconciliation has been placed in very considerable jeopardy by the enormous disparities between the rich, mainly the whites, and the poor, mainly the blacks. The huge gap between the haves and the have-nots, which was largely created and maintained by racism and apartheid, poses the greatest threat to reconciliation and stability in our country. The rich provided the class from which the perpetrators and the beneficiaries of apartheid came and the poor produced the bulk of the victims. That is why I have exhorted whites to support transformation taking place in the lot of blacks.

For unless houses replace the hovels and shacks in which most blacks live, unless blacks gain access to clean water, electricity, affordable health care, decent education, good jobs, and a safe environment—things which the vast majority of whites have taken for granted for so long—we can just as well kiss reconciliation goodbye.

Reconciliation is liable to be a long-drawn-out process with ups and downs, not something accomplished overnight and certainly not by a commission, however effective. The Truth and Reconciliation Commission has only been able to make a contribution. Reconciliation is going to have to be the concern of every South African. It has to be a national project to which all earnestly strive to make their particular contribution—by learning the language and culture of others; by being willing to make amends; by refusing to deal in stereotypes by making racial or other jokes that ridicule a particular group; by contributing to a culture of respect for human rights, and seeking to enhance tolerance—with zero tolerance for intolerance; by working for a more inclusive society where most, if not all, can feel they belong—that they are insiders and not aliens and strangers on the outside, relegated to the edges of society.

NOTES

1. Jeremiah 6:14 and 8:11.

2. Vol. 2, No.1 (New York, Trinity Church: Spirituality & Health Publishing).

3. Matthew 18:22.

Restorative Justice Is Not Forgiveness

TED WACHTEL

Ted Wachtel is President and Founder of the International Institute for Restorative Practices Graduate School. From *Huffington Post*, January 30, 2013. Used by permission.

Restorative justice has been receiving a lot of attention lately, due to Paul Tullis's January 4 *New York Times* Magazine article, "Can Forgiveness Play a Role in Criminal Justice?"

This story about a restorative justice conference following the murder of a young woman by her boyfriend was also covered on the January 5 episode of the *Today Show*, "Parents who forgave their daughter's killer: It 'frees us.'"

Both the *Times* and the *Today* stories do their audience a disservice by dwelling on forgiveness as the apparent reason for restorative justice. Forgiveness is neither an expectation nor a goal of restorative justice. Forgiveness may be a by-product, but the notion that a crime victim should forgive an offender imposes unrealistic and potentially hurtful demands on a crime victim.

Sujatha Baliga, the woman who facilitated the restorative justice conference covered by the *NY Times* and *Today*, shared her feelings about this issue on her Facebook page: "A little bummed that the [Today show] headline conflates restorative justice and forgiveness (restorative justice never requires forgiveness, although it does show up fairly often in restorative dialogues . . .)."

Terry O'Connell, the former Australian police officer who pioneered restorative justice conferences, saw them as "an opportunity to achieve a shared understanding of how everyone been affected by an incident." This benefits the 90-plus percent of victims, offenders, family and friends who reported "satisfaction" and "a sense of fairness" to researchers in many varied locales in restorative conferences for a wide range of criminal offenses.

In *Facing the Demons*, the award-winning Australian documentary, Terry O'Connell convened a restorative conference four-and-a-half years after the bungled armed robbery that took the life of 19-year-old Michael Marslew. After the conference, all the participants experienced some benefit that had eluded them for all those years. Michael's mother, Joan, recovered all of her fond memories of her son's life, obscured by the haunting image of his bloodied face in the morgue, on the night she identified his body. As for forgiveness, she explained simply, "If you could give me back my son, I could forgive you anything."

From seemingly minor crimes to the most severe, victims and their loved ones feel angry, hurt, betrayed or frightened by offenders. The restorative justice process gives them an opportunity to express those feelings directly to offenders, to ask questions such as "Why me?," to get an apology and to help determine restitution—outcomes that our court system cannot provide.

According to Dr. Caroline M. Angel, "The most striking thing was that conferences reduced symptoms of post-traumatic stress disorder." A lecturer in criminology at the University of Pennsylvania, Angel studied the impact of restorative justice on post-traumatic stress symptoms in victims of robbery and burglary and concluded that, "What you have here is a one-time program that's effective in producing benefits for the majority of people." So instead of focusing on the not-always attainable and sometimes detrimental expectation of forgiveness, we should recognize that restorative justice reliably helps victims, and those who love them, to cope with the trauma of crime.

There is also evidence that restorative justice may reduce re-offending. "Restorative Justice: The Evidence," published in the UK by the Jerry Lee Center of Criminology at the University of Pennsylvania, concluded that restorative justice conferences were as, or more effective than traditional methods of criminal justice for reducing crime with respect to nearly every group of offender studied.

A later research report, "Does restorative justice affect reconviction?" published by the University of Sheffield, UK, shows that face-to-face restorative justice conferences not only reduce crime but also cost less than traditional justice processes.

Offenders, victims and their supporters all benefit from the free exchange of emotion that happens in a restorative justice conference. The conference process provides a way for all participants to discover their common humanity and move forward. Although forgiveness sometimes happens, none of these benefits of restorative justice are predicated on the victim forgiving the offender.

Six Boys, One Cop, and the Road to Restorative Justice

BY MOLLY ROWAN LEACH

Molly Rowan Leach is Restorative Justice Fellow to The Peace Alliance and host of the web/telecast dialogue series, *Restorative Justice on the Rise*. From *openDemocracy*, August 21, 2013. Used by permission.

It's a warm summer night in Longmont, Colorado, a vibrant midsized city in the Rocky Mountains. On a dare, six young men aged between ten and thirteen years plan to break into a giant chemical processing plant. High levels of alcohol and testosterone, peer pressure and a moonless night propel the group towards the locked gates of the factory, and they break in.

Across town at the Police Department, Officer Greg Ruprecht is about to embark on night patrol. A former Army Captain and top of his class at the Police Academy, Ruprecht believes his job is to arrest everyone who commits a crime and throw away the key. Justice means punishment: an eye for an eye, no questions asked. You do something bad and you get what you deserve. There's a clear line to walk. But what occurred at the chemical plant that night changed him forever by awakening a very different sensibility: instead of an instrument of vengeance, justice requires that we work to restore all those who have been injured by a crime.

The police transponder went off not long after he arrived in the industrial area of the town. "Six suspects breaking and entering at BioChem Industries, 644 Southwest Way, over." "Roger, patrol 33 in vicinity and responding" he replied. As with any emergency, in the time between receiving the call and arriving at the scene, Ruprecht imagined what was happening, and tried to prepare himself mentally to avoid underestimating any of the circumstances. It was known in town that the plant had highly toxic chemicals inside, and he assumed he'd be dealing with seasoned thieves who would be armed.

Carefully emerging from his car, the scene was quiet except for the tall grasses in the field to the left of the plant that provided a possible route of escape. Given the moonless night he had to switch on his searchlight to back up his suspicion that the suspects might be hiding in the grass. He carefully pulled his gun, just in case. Bingo. The spotlight beam illuminated the bobbing heads that were running for their lives. But these were not the heads of adults. Kids, he thought—these are just kids. He called out for them to halt. Almost out of earshot but just enough to look back, two stopped, while the rest stumbled on, hesitated, and then realized the seriousness of what was happening.

Once he was next to the group, Ruprecht found he was dealing with six boys. It shocked him. Not only had these kids committed a felony with their break-in, but they had endangered their own lives and the lives of others because of the chemicals that were housed in the plant. He took them to the police station and kept them there, ready for processing into the US criminal justice system.

This is a system with a national recidivism rate of between sixty and seventy per cent, dominated by a growing, for-profit prison industry with giant companies like the GEO Group and Correctional Corporations of America that rake in billions of dollars a year. It's an industry that is built on incarceration and punishment instead of rehabilitation, with one in every ten young black males in the USA currently in prison. People with mental illness are thrown away, into a system that is glaringly unfit to treat and care for them. Children are subject to zero-tolerance policies and get wrapped up in the lethal web of the US prison-industrial complex. Corporate interests push for even higher rates of incarceration because their bottom line improves with every prison bed they fill.

These are dark times for justice in America, and they offend the moral core of many US citizens.

Still, what difference would six boys make? Six more to process; six more lives to waste.

Except that this is not what happened. As Ruprecht was about to leave his shift the day after the arrests, his phone rang and the call almost knocked him off his chair. The case he'd handled the previous night was being re-directed, into a process that's called "restorative justice"—an easy way out for offenders in his mind, some sort of hippie gathering where everyone would hug.

Later that week the process got started. Ruprecht and the boys joined a small group of professionals from the Longmont Community Justice Partnership. Along with representatives from the boys' families and from the chemical plant, they talked about what had happened and how to make things right. They discussed accountability, and how nothing would stay permanently on their records if the boys kept their word, so crucially, they would not become permanently considered as "high risk" in the criminal justice system. Separate meetings between all the members of the group prepared them for a larger "circle process" that got everyone involved.

The boys each got an opportunity to sit with the consequences of their choices, to discuss the ways they would do things differently in the future, and to share anything from their home or personal lives that might have influenced their decision to break into the plant that night. Held in a safe environment that did not undercut the importance of accountability, each boy heard the plant representatives speak, and began to understand that their acts had real consequences. Apologies were made. The restorative justice process gave the boys one clear message: their actions were the problem, not themselves as human beings. They rolled up their sleeves and took part in creating their own contracts for restitution in the form of one hundred hours of sweat equity in the same plant the group broke into, plus alcohol awareness classes and an agreement to write a story about what they'd learned for the local newspaper. Then they signed the contracts and got to work.

Officer Ruprecht continued to feel skeptical about this process, but something was definitely changing. He saw how much money had already been saved by choosing to go down this route instead of jailing the boys and sending them into a lengthy and expensive judicial process. He realized that restorative justice had more teeth than conventional punishment because it imposes real, face-to-face accountability among offenders for their actions, and makes them listen directly to the victims of their crimes. He realized that six young lives might be saved from years of cycling in and out of the prison system. He learned that the human brain doesn't develop fully until the age of twenty-two or thereabouts, so punishment and fear-inciting prison regimes have an even bigger impact on the development of young people. He remembered his own children, and recognized that more than anything else, they and others deserve the chance to make mistakes and pick themselves back up again, sure in the knowledge of their own inherent worth and value.

So he decided to stay engaged in the process. He took on other cases and found that the usual suspects weren't recycling through the police department any more. Recidivism dropped to ten per cent, and surveys showed high rates of satisfaction with the process among everyone involved.

In fact Ruprecht is now a Police Ambassador for Restorative Justice, one of the first of a growing number of law enforcement officials and corrections officers in the USA who believe in, and are enacting, the systemic changes that are saving lives and not just Dollars in the American justice sector.

The role of justice, as portrayed by Lady Justice's scales, is to bring back balance, to make things right again. Punishment and the warehousing of human beings in prisons destroys vast amounts of human potential. By contrast, restorative justice meets the needs of everyone involved in the most humane ways possible—those who commit crimes, and those who suffer from them. In so doing, it brings humanity back into the justice system. It converts a limited worldview based around isolation and individualism into a much more positive vision that is rooted in honesty, accountability, and the visible connection of causes with effects. And it works in concrete terms by cutting recidivism and costs. Most important of all, it nurtures new relationships and a strong sense of human unity. In this sense, the root power of restorative justice is love expressed in action.

DISCUSSION QUESTIONS

1. Explain which you believe is the most valid of the three justifications for retributive justice that Andre Moss describes. Also explain which justification you believe is the least valid.
2. Analyze both the logic and the accuracy of Desmond Tutu's claim that forgiveness benefits victims who forgive perpetrators.
3. Explain why you agree, or disagree, with Tutu's claim that forgiveness can work for victims of national violence as well as for victims of interpersonal violence.
4. Conduct some research to determine what contemporary analysts believe were the main successes and the main failings of South Africa's Truth and Reconciliation Commission (TRC).
5. Adopt Ted Wachtel's perspective to discuss weaknesses in Tutu's claims for the necessity of forgiveness.
6. Using evidence from the case study provided by Molly Rowan Leach as well as from your own experience, explain why the use of restorative justice remains rare in the country that you know best.
7. Summarize what you believe are the main strengths of justice based 1) on retribution, 2) on forgiveness, and 3) on restoration.
8. Explain which systems of justice—retribution, forgiveness, or restoration—you would prefer to face if you were the victim of a crime. Also explain your choice if you were the perpetrator of a crime.

CLIMATE CHANGE AND ENVIRONMENTAL JUSTICE

Part 6 presents debates associated with twenty-first-century climate change. It accepts the scientific consensus and the position of contemporary military planners that weather patterns will change significantly and often cataclysmically in the decades ahead. Temperatures and ocean heights will rise, old agriculturally friendly ecosystems will disappear and new ecosystems appear. Researchers in peace studies accept that these changes will occur but disagree about what effects extreme climate change will likely have on levels of local and global peace.

Section 1 offers debates about the causal relationship between climate change and violence. Selections there show that although some researchers believe that climate change is likely to substantially increase levels of violence, other researchers argue the opposite, that climate disasters tend to decrease violence.

Section 2 looks more broadly at how people and societies should react in the face of massive global environmental changes. One author argues against traditional environmental campaigns and calls for new, more radical environmental justice campaigns. Another author promotes a peace ecology perspective that emphasizes interconnections and mutual dependencies both of people and ecosystems. A final selection calls for a radical overturning of many social and economic arrangements that have guided modern societies for hundreds of years.

Debates about the Effects
of Climate Change

Debates about the likely future consequences of *climate change* are among the most important now occurring within peace studies. Many thinkers predict that twenty-first-century climate change will increase levels of violence in most if not all regions of the world. The United Nations Security Council supported this belief in a 2007 report that concluded that climate change will likely lead to more frequent border disputes, swelling migrations, struggles over energy and resource shortages, and increasing humanitarian crises (see Bamidele 2013). Nonetheless, there are probably just as many analysts who argue that there are no necessary links between Earth's climate and its rates of conflict and peace. Both perspectives sometimes build their arguments from examinations of large archives of historical data.

This debate is introduced with a selection from Bill McKibben's widely read book, *Eaarth: Making a Life on a Tough New Planet*. McKibben summarizes the claims of experts who fear that a warming Earth will lead to failing governments, mass migrations, and increasingly frequent wars. A second selection, by Solomon M. Hsiang, Marshall Burke, and Edward Miguel, which first appeared in the prestigious journal *Science*, analyzes 60 studies as it attempts to quantify just how much climate change has impacted past rates of violence. The authors conclude that both warmer temperatures and more extreme variations in rainfall have increased rates of conflict throughout history in all major regions of the world. The authors maintain that temperature and violence increase proportionately: the greater the rise in temperature, the greater will be the rise in violence. They further suggest that the accelerated pace of climate change Earth now faces makes it unlikely that humans will change sufficiently to stop future spikes in violence.

A third and final selection directly disputes this conclusion. In his aptly titled article, "Don't Blame the Weather!," Rune T. Slettebak reviews how hundreds of natural disasters affected rates of interstate violence in regions across the world over the past 60 years. He looked specifically at how climate-related natural disasters such as storms, floods, and droughts impacted rates of civil wars. Slettebak's data demonstrate a clear relationship between natural disasters and human war and violence, but this relationship is opposite to what Hsiang, Burke, and Miguel predict. Slettebak found that counties that suffer from climate-related natural disasters have a lower-than-expected incidence of civil war. He thus concludes that climate-related natural disasters tend to reduce the rate of violence in the modern world. Slettebak also offers several hypotheses that could account for why natural catastrophes have this positive effect.

REFERENCES

Bamidele, Oluwaseun. "Climate Change, War, and Global Struggle." *Peace Review* 25, no. 4 (October 2013): 510–17.

Selections from *Eaarth: Making a Life on a Tough New Planet*

BY BILL MCKIBBEN

Bill McKibben has written several books, including *The End of Nature* (1989), one of the first mass-market books to call attention to the threat of climate change. McKibben is a leader of the environmental advocacy group 350.org. He won the Gandhi Peace Award in 2013. Due to space limitations, notes have been omitted from this selection. Excerpt: Pages 82–85 from the book: EAARTH: Making A Life On a Tough New Planet by Bill McKibben. Copyright © 2010 by Bill McKibben, Used by permission of Henry Holt and Company, LLC. All rights reserved.

So one can hope for unexpected breakthroughs. But one can also fear novel kinds of trouble. On the new world we've built, conflict seems at least as likely as cooperation. In 2006, British home secretary John Reid publicly fingered global warming as a driving force behind the genocide in Darfur, arguing that environmental changes "make the emergence of violent conflict more rather than less likely. The blunt truth is that the lack of water and agricultural land is a significant contributory factor to the tragic conflict we see unfolding in Darfur. We should see this as a warning sign." When *Time Magazine*'s Alex Perry traveled to the region the following year, he reported that "the roots of the conflict may have more to do with ecology than ethnicity." The few pockets of good land had always been prized; as rainfall has decreased for the last five decades and the Sahara advanced, smothering grazing land with sand, "the competition is intensifying." In Darfur, "there are too many people in a hot, poor, shrinking land, and it's not hard to start a fight in a place like that." Eight years of drought have also accelerated fighting in Somalia, while crop failures have made the misery in Zimbabwe ever worse. Many of the refugees who fled the expanding Sahara settled on the borders of massive Lake Chad, only to see its waters shrink by 90 percent since 1973. In Syria, 160 villages were abandoned after a 2008 drought, and elsewhere in the Middle East the International Institute for Sustainable Development predicts that even modest global warming will lower the volume of the Euphrates River by 30 percent and will shrink the Dead Sea by 80 percent. (A follow-up study in the summer of 2008 predicted that the "ancient 'Fertile Crescent' will disappear this century.") A one-meter rise in sea level would obliterate at least a fifth of the Nile delta. Meanwhile, increased evaporation and new upstream demand seem set to reduce the river's flow by 70 percent. It's a region, said one observer in 2009, whose "death warrant may already have been signed." In Kashmir, Indian Pakistani troops have long faced off over the Siachen Glacier, at nineteen thousand feet the highest war zone on earth. But now the glacier is melting fast, leaving "not much left to fight over," in the words of the journalist Priyanka Bhardwaj, except of course the millions of Pakistanis who will be affected by a "severe water crisis" when it disappears. Here's former British foreign secretary Margaret Beckett, speaking during the first ever debate on climate change and armed conflict at the UN Security Council. "What makes wars start?" she asked. "Fights over water. Changing patterns of rainfall. Fights over food production, land use. There are few greater potential threats to our economies too . . . but also to peace and security itself."

She's not alone in that assessment. Four major studies in the last two years from centrist organizations in the United States and Europe have concluded that "a warmer planet could find itself more often at war." Each report "predicted starkly similar problems: gunfire over land and natural resources as once-bountiful soil turns to desert and coastlines slip below the sea." The experts also expected violent storms to topple weak governments—which makes a certain amount of sense to those of us who watched George W. Bush begin his descent in the polls after he bumbled the response to Katrina. "Billions of people would have to move" if temperatures rise four or five degrees, the British economist Nicholas Stern predicted recently. The directors of climate research for the Center for Strategic and International Studies in Washington predicted recently that as "climate migration" increased the number of "weak and failing states," terrorism would likely grow. By midcentury, according to some recent models, as many as 700 million of the world's billion people will be climate change refugees.

What would such mass migration look like? Consider Bangladesh: melting glaciers upstream, rising seas downstream, dengue spreading in the cities. It's the most densely populated large nation on earth, and already "climate refugees" are on the move, after floods drowned crops in recent years. Some pile into the slums ringing Dhaka; about half a million arrive each year, 70 percent of them for environmental reasons. Already neighboring India is worried they won't stop there; "if one-third of Bangladesh is flooded, India can soak in some refugees, but not all," the former commander of the country's air force warned recently. Worried enough, in fact, that India has spent the last five years quietly building a 2,500-mile-long wall, modeled on the West Bank barrier between the Palestinians and Israelis, portions of which will be electrified. This may work for a while, but as one military historian put it, "People will pay no attention to borders. They will swamp borders. They will trample over them in desperation." But even if they make it to India, they may find their troubles following close behind. The closest big Indian city is Calcutta, where a new report found rising seas pushing saltwater up to its borders; mangrove trees, normally found a hundred kilometers downstream along the Ganges, were beginning to colonize the city's riverbanks. "We have already spotted more saline water fish in the river," one official reported.

The U.S. military—besides worrying about sixty-three of its own coastal facilities that are in danger of flooding as sea level rises—has begun planning for a future where "climate change will require mass mobilizations of the military to cope with humanitarian disasters," in the words of one researcher. The Defense Department has to ask "if our forces are adequate enough to respond to several more Katrinas," said retired U.S. Army general Paul Kern. We used to worry about having to fight two wars at once—now the military worries about "a string of bad events, of landslides, tornadoes, and hurricanes." In August 2009, the Defense Department reported that "recent war games and intelligence studies" could "destabilize entire regions." The scenarios "get real complicated real quickly," one deputy assistant secretary of defense explained. The most lurid account of all came from a Pentagon-sponsored report forecasting possible scenarios a decade or two away, when the pressures of climate change have become "irresistible—history shows that whenever humans have faced a choice between starving or raiding, they raid. Imagine Eastern European countries, struggling to feed their populations, invading Russia—which is weakened by a population that is already in decline—for access to its minerals and energy supplies. Or picture Japan eyeing nearby Russian oil and gas reserves to power desalination plants and energy-intensive farming. Envision nuclear-armed Pakistan, India, and China skirmishing at their borders over refugees, access to shared rivers, and arable land." Here's the bottom line from that Pentagon report, a picture of a new planet that, at least as far as conflict goes, resembles nothing so much as the old one: "Wars over resources were the norm until about three centuries ago. When such conflicts broke out, 25% of a population's adult males usually died. As abrupt climate change hits home, warfare may again come to define human life."

Quantifying the Influence of Climate on Human Conflict

BY SOLOMON M. HSIANG, MARSHALL BURKE, AND EDWARD MIGUEL

Solomon M. Hsiang is the Chancellor's Associate Professor of Public Policy at the University of California, Berkeley; Marshall Burke is in the Department of Earth System Science at Stanford University; and Edward Miguel is the Oxfam Professor in Environmental and Resource Economics at the University of California, Berkeley. Due to space limitations, notes and data sets have been omitted from this selection. From *Science*, 341, no. 6151 (September 13, 2013). Used by permission.

Abstract

A rapidly growing body of research examines whether human conflict can be affected by climatic changes. Drawing from archaeology, criminology, economics, geography, history, political science, and psychology, we assemble and analyze the 60 most rigorous quantitative studies and document, for the first time, a striking convergence of results. We find strong causal evidence linking climatic events to human conflict across a range of spatial and temporal scales and across all major regions of the world. The magnitude of climate's influence is substantial: for each one standard deviation (1σ) change in climate toward warmer temperatures or more extreme rainfall, median estimates indicate that the frequency of interpersonal violence rises 4% and the frequency of intergroup conflict rises 14%. Because locations throughout the inhabited world are expected to warm 2σ to 4σ by 2050, amplified rates of human conflict could represent a large and critical impact of anthropogenic climate change.

Human behavior is complex, and despite the existence of institutions designed to promote peace, interactions between individuals and groups sometimes lead to conflict. When such conflict becomes violent, it can have dramatic consequences on human well-being. Mortality from war and interpersonal violence amounts to 0.5 to 1 million deaths annually, with nonlethal impacts, including injury and lost economic opportunities, affecting millions more. Because the stakes are so high, understanding the causes of human conflict has been a major project in the social sciences.

Researchers working across multiple disciplines including archaeology, criminology, economics, geography, history, political science, and psychology have long debated the extent to which climatic changes are responsible for causing conflict, violence, or political instability. Numerous pathways linking the climate to these outcomes have been proposed. For example, climatic changes may alter the supply of a resource and cause disagreement over its allocation, or climatic conditions may shape the relative appeal of using violence or cooperation to achieve some preconceived objective. Qualitative researchers have a well-developed history of studying these issues dating back, at least, to the start of the 20th century. Yet, in recent years, growing recognition that the climate is changing, coupled with improvements in data quality and computing, has prompted an explosion of quantitative analyses seeking to test these theories and quantify the strength of these previously proposed linkages. Thus far, this work has remained scattered across multiple disciplines and has been difficult to synthesize given the disparate methodologies, data, and interests of the various research teams.

Here, we assemble the first comprehensive synthesis of this rapidly growing quantitative literature. We adopt a broad definition of "conflict," using the term to encompass a range of outcomes from individual-level violence and aggression to country-level political instability and civil war. We then collect all available candidate studies and, guided by previous criticisms that not all correlations imply causation, focus on only those quantitative studies that can reliably infer causal associations between climate variables and conflict outcomes. The studies we examine exploit either experimental or natural-experimental variation in climate; the latter term refers to variation in climate over time that is plausibly independent of other variables that also affect conflict. To meet this standard, studies must account for unobservable confounding factors across populations, as well as for unobservable time-trending factors that could be correlated with both climate and conflict. In many cases, we obtained data from studies that did not meet this criterion and reanalyzed it with a common statistical model that did meet the criterion. . . . The importance of this rigorous approach is highlighted by an example in which our standardized analysis generated findings consistent with other studies but at odds with the original conclusions of the study in question.

In total, we obtained 60 primary studies that either met this criterion or were reanalyzed with a method that met this criterion (Table 1). Collectively, these studies analyze 45 different conflict data sets published across 26 different journals and represent the work of more than 190 researchers from around the world. Our evaluation summarizes the recent explosion of research on this topic, with 78% of studies released since 2009 and the median study released in 2011. We collected findings across a wide range of conflict outcomes, time periods spanning 10,000 B.C.E. to the present day, and all major regions of the world.

Although various conflict outcomes differ in important ways, we find that the behavior of these outcomes relative to the climate system is markedly similar. Put most simply, we find that large deviations from normal precipitation and mild temperatures systematically increase the risk of many types of conflict, often substantially, and that this relationship appears to hold over a variety of temporal and spatial scales. Our meta-analysis of studies that examine populations in the post-1950 era suggests that these relationships continue to be highly important in the modern world, although there are notable differences in the magnitude of the relationship when different variables are considered: The standardized effect of temperature is generally larger than the standardized effect of rainfall, and the effect on intergroup violence (e.g., civil war) is larger than the effect on interpersonal violence (e.g., assault). We conclude that there is substantially more agreement and generality in the findings of this burgeoning literature than has been recognized previously. Given the large potential changes in precipitation and temperature regimes projected for the coming decades, our findings have important implications for the social impact of anthropogenic climate change in both low- and high-income countries.

Implications for Future Climatic Changes

These large climatological changes, combined with the quantitatively large effect of climate on conflict—particularly intergroup conflict—suggest that amplified rates of human conflict could represent a large and critical impact of anthropogenic climate change.

Two reasons are often given as to why climate change might not have a substantive impact on human conflict: Future climate change will occur gradually and will, thus, allow societies to adapt, and the modern world today is less susceptible to climate variation than it has been in the past. However, if slower-moving climate shocks have smaller effects, or if the world has become less climate-sensitive, it is unfortunately not obvious in the data. Gradual climatic changes appear to adversely affect conflict outcomes, and the majority of the studies we review use a sample period that extends into the 21st century (recall Fig. 1). Furthermore, some studies explicitly examine whether populations inhabiting hotter climates exhibit less conflict when hot events occur but find little evidence that these areas are more adapted. We also note that many of the modern linkages

Table 1 Primary quantitative studies testing for a relationship between climate and conflict, violence, or political instability. "Stat. test" is Y if the analysis uses formal statistical methods to quantify the influence of climate variables and uses hypothesis testing procedures (Y, yes; N, no). "Large effect" is Y if the point estimate for the effect size is considered substantial by the authors or is greater in magnitude than 10% of the mean risk level for a 1σ change in climate variables. "Reject β = 0" is Y if the study rejects an effect size of zero at the 95% confidence level. "Reject β = 10%" is Y if the study is able to reject the hypothesis that the effect size is larger than 10% of the mean risk level for a 1σ change in climate variables.–, not applicable. SSA, sub-Saharan Africa; PDSI; Palmer Drought Severity Index; ENSO, El Niño–Southern Oscillation; NAO, North Atlantic Oscillation; N. Hem., Northern Hemisphere.

Study	Sample period	Sample region	Time unit	Spatial unit	Independent variable	Dependent variable	Stat. test	Large effect	Reject β = 0	Reject β = 10
Interpersonal conflict (15)										
Anderson et al. 2000	1950–1997	USA	Annual	Country	Temp	Violent crime	Y	Y	Y	–
Auliciems et al.1995	1992	Australia	Week	Municipality	Temp	Domestic violence	Y	Y	Y	–
Blakeslee et al. 2013	1971–2000	India	Annual	Municipality	Rain	Violent and property crime	Y	Y	Y	–
Card et al.2011	1995–2006	USA	Day	Municipality	Temp	Domestic violence	Y	Y	Y	–
Cohn et al. 1997	1987–1988	USA	Hours	Municipality	Temp	Violent crime	Y	Y	Y	–
Jacob et al.2007	1995–2001	USA	Week	Municipality	Temp	Violent and property crime	Y	Y	Y	–
Kenrick et al. 1986	1985	USA	Day	Site	Temp	Hostility	Y	Y	Y	–
Larrick et al.2011	1952–2009	USA	Day	Site	Temp	Violent retaliation	Y	Y	Y	–
Mares 2013	1990–2009	USA	Month	Municipality	Temp	Violent crime	Y	Y	Y	–
Miguel 2005	1992–2002	Tanzania	Annual	Municipality	Rain	Murder	Y	Y	N	N
Mehlum et al. 2006	1835–1861	Germany	Annual	Province	Rain	Violent and property crime	Y	Y	Y	–
Ranson 2012	1960–2009	USA	Month	County	Temp	Personal violence	Y	Y	Y	–
Rotton et al. 2000	1994–1995	USA	Hours	Municipality	Temp	Violent crime	Y	Y	Y	–
Sekhri et al.2013	2002–2007	India	Annual	Municipality	Rain	Murder and domestic violence	Y	Y	Y	–
Vrij et al. 1994	1993	Netherlands	Hours	Site	Temp	Police use of force	Y	Y	Y	–
Intergroup conflict (30)										
Almer et al. 2012	1985–2008	SSA	Annual	Country	Rain/temp	Civil conflict	Y	Y	N	N
Anderson et al. 2013	1100–1800	Europe	Decade	Municipality	Temp	Minority expulsion	Y	Y	Y	–
Bai et al. 2010	220–1839	China	Decade	Country	Rain	Transboundary	Y	Y	Y	–

Study	Sample period	Sample region	Time unit	Spatial unit	Independent variable	Dependent variable	Stat. test	Large effect	Reject $\beta = 0$	Reject $\beta = 10$
Bergholt et al. 2012	1980–2007	Global	Annual	Country	Flood/storm	Civil conflict	Y	N	N	Y
Bohlken et al. 2011	1982–1995	India	Annual	Province	Rain	Intergroup	Y	Y	N	
Buhaug 2010	1979–2002	SSA	Annual	Country	Temp	Civil conflict	Y	N	N	N
Burke 2012	1963–2001	Global	Annual	Country	Rain/temp	Political instability	Y	Y	N**	N
Burke et al. 2009	1981–2002	SSA	Annual	Country	Temp	Civil conflict	Y	Y	Y	–
Cervellati et al. 2011	1960–2005	Global	Annual	Country	Drought	Civil conflict	Y	Y	Y	–
Chaney 2011	641–1438	Egypt	Annual	Country	Nile floods	Political Instability	Y	Y	Y	–
Couttenier et al. 2011	1957–2005	SSA	Annual	Country	PDSI	Civil conflict	Y	Y	Y	–
Dell et al. 2012	1950–2003	Global	Annual	Country	Temp	Political instability and civil conflict	Y	Y	Y	–
Fjelde et al. 2012	1990–2008	SSA	Annual	Province	Rain	Intergroup	Y	Y	N**	N
Harari et al. 2013	1960–2010	SSA	Annual	Pixel (1°)	Drought	Civil conflict	Y	Y	Y	–
Hendrixet al. 2012	1991–2007	SSA	Annual	Country	Rain	Intergroup	Y	Y	Y	–
Hidalgo et al. 2010	1988–2004	Brazil	Annual	Municipality	Rain	Intergroup	Y	Y	Y	–
Hsiang et al. 2011	1950–2004	Global	Annual	World	ENSO	Civil conflict	Y	Y	Y	–
Jia 2012	1470–1900	China	Annual	Province	Drought/flood	Peasant rebellion	Y	Y	Y	–
Kung et al. 2012	1651–1910	China	Annual	County	Rain	Peasant rebellion	Y	Y	Y	–
Lee et al. 2013	1400–1999	Europe	Decade	Region	NAO	Violent conflict	Y	Y	Y	–
Levy et al. 2005	1975–2002	Global	Annual	Pixel (2.5°)	Rain	Civil conflict	Y	Y	N**	N
Maystadt et al. 2013	1997–2009	Somalia	Month	Province	Temp	Civil conflict	Y	Y	Y	–
Miguel et al. 2004	1979–1999	SSA	Annual	Country	Rain	Civil war	Y	Y	Y	–
O'Laughlin et al. 2012	1990–2009	E. Africa	Month	Pixel (1°)	Rain/temp	Civil/intergroup	Y	Y	Y	–
Salehyan et al. 2012	1979–2006	Global	Annual	Country	PDSI	Civil/intergroup	Y	Y	Y	–
Sarsons 2011	1970–1995	India	Annual	Municipality	Rain	Intergroup	Y	Y	Y	–
Theisen et al. 2011	1960–2004	Africa	Annual	Pixel (0.5°)	Rain	Civil conflict	Y	N	N	N
Theisen 2012	1989–2004	Kenya	Annual	Pixel (0.25°)	Rain/temp	Civil/intergroup	Y	Y	N**	N
Tol et al. 2009	1500–1900	Europe	Decade	Region	Rain/temp	Transboundary	Y	Y	Y	–
Zhang et al. 2007	1400–1900	N. Hem.	Century	Region	Temp	Instability	Y	Y	Y	–

Continued

Table 1 *Continued*

Study	Sample period	Sample region	Time unit	Spatial unit	Independent variable	Dependent variable	Stat. test	Large effect	Reject β = 0	Reject β = 10
Institutional breakdown and population collapse (15)										
Brückner et al. 2011#	1980–2004	SSA	Annual	Country	Rain	Inst. change	Y	Y	Y	–
Buckley et al. 2010‖‖	1030–2008	Cambodia	Decade	Country	Drought	Collapse	N	–	–	–
Büntgen et al. 2011‖‖	400 BCE–2000	Europe	Decade	Region	Rain/temp	Instability	N	–	–	–
Burke et al. 2010‡#	1963–2007	Global	Annual	Country	Rain/temp	Inst. change	Y	Y	Y	–
Cullen et al. 2000‖‖	4000 BCE–0	Syria	Century	Country	Drought	Collapse	N	–	–	
D'Anjou et al 2012	550 BCE–1950	Norway	Century	Municipality	Temp	Collapse	Y	Y	Y	–
Ortloff et al. 1993‖‖	500–2000	Peru	Century	Century	Drought	Collapse	N	–	–	
Haug et al. 2003‖‖	0–1900	Mexico	Century	Century	Drought	Collapse	N	–	–	
Kelly et al. 2013	10050 BCE–1950	USA	Century	State	Temp/rain	Collapse	Y	Y	Y	–
Kennett et al. 2012	40 BCE–2006	Belize	Decade	Country	Rain	Collapse	N	–	–	
Kuper et al. 2006	8000–2000 BCE	N. Africa	Millennia	Region	Rain	Collapse	N	–	–	
Patterson et al. 2010	200 BCE–1700	Iceland	Decade	Country	Temp	Collapse	N	–	–	
Stahle et al. 1998	1200–2000	USA	Multiyear	Municipality	PDSI	Collapse	N	–	–	
Yancheva et al. 2007‖‖	2100 BCE–1700	China	Century	Country	Raw/temp	Collapse	N	–	–	
Zhang et al. 2006	1000–1911	China	Decade	Country	Temp	Civil conflict and Collapse	Y	Y	Y	—
					Number of studies (60 total):		50	47	37	1
					Fraction of those using statistical tests:		100%	94%	74%	2%

Table is presented here without with the footnotes provided in the original publication.

between high-temperature anomalies and inter-group conflict have been characterized in Africa or the global tropics and subtropics, regions with hot climates where we would expect populations to be best adapted to high temperatures. Neverthe-less, it is always possible that future populations will adapt in previously unobserved ways, but it is impossible to know if and to what extent these adaptations will make conflict more or less likely.

Studies of nonconflict outcomes do indicate that, in some situations, historical adaptation to climate is observable, albeit costly, whereas in other cases there is limited evidence that any adaptation is occurring. To our knowledge, no study has char-acterized the scale or scope for adaptation to cli-mate in terms of conflict outcomes, and we believe this is an important area for future research. Given the quantitatively large effect of climate on con-flict, future adaptations will need to be dramatic if they are to offset the potentially large amplifica-tion of conflict.

Although there is marked convergence of quantitative findings across disciplines, many open questions remain. Existing research has suc-cessfully established a causal relationship between climate and conflict but is unable to fully explain the mechanisms. This fact motivates our proposed research agenda and urges caution when applying statistical estimates to future warming scenarios. Importantly, however, it does not imply that we lack evidence of a causal association. The studies

in this analysis were selected for their ability to provide reliable causal inferences and they con-sistently point toward the existence of at least one causal pathway. To place the state of this research in perspective, it is worth recalling that statisti-cal analyses identified the smoking of tobacco as a proximate cause of lung cancer by the 1930s, although the research community was unable to provide a detailed account of the mechanisms explaining the linkage until many decades later. So although future research will be critical in pinpointing why climate affects human conflict, disregarding the potential effect of anthropogenic climate change on human conflict in the interim is, in our view, a dangerously misguided interpre-tation of the available evidence.

Numerous competing theories have been pro-posed to explain the linkages between the climate and human conflict, but none have been convinc-ingly rejected, and all appear to be consistent with at least some existing results. It seems likely that climatic changes influence conflict through mul-tiple pathways that may differ between contexts, and innovative research to identify these mechanisms is a top research priority. Achieving this research objec-tive holds great promise, as the policies and institu-tions necessary for conflict resolution can be built only if we understand why conflicts arise. The suc-cess of such institutions will be increasingly impor-tant in the coming decades, as changes in climatic conditions amplify the risk of human conflicts.

Selections from "Don't Blame the Weather! Climate-Related Natural Disasters and Civil Conflict"

BY RUNE T. SLETTEBAK

Rune T. Slettebak is an associate researcher at the Centre for the Study of Civil War, Peace Research Institute Oslo (PRIO), one of the world's oldest and best-known institutions focused on peace promotion. Selections from "Don't Blame the Weather! Climate-Related Natural Disasters and Civil Conflict." *Journal of Peace Research* 49, no. 1 (January 1, 2012): 163–76. Used by permission.

The academic, policy, and popular discussions that surround the issue of climate change predict changing weather patterns to increase natural

disasters. Hurricane Katrina, which hit the city of New Orleans in 2005, has given much impe-tus to this discussion. Tropical cyclones, floods, heat waves (even cold spells), and droughts are apparently likely to be more destructive and carry higher consequences for humans in the future because rising temperatures (global warming) is expected to increase the frequency and intensity of these events (van Aalst, 2006; IPCC [International Panel on Climate Change], 2007a, b). Many even expect these disasters to increase the risk of violent conflict, which would create double burdens to states and societies trying to cope and adjust to climate change. In this article, I investigate whether there is a systematic tendency that climate-related natural disasters cause civil conflict to arise, or reignite, within the same or the following year.

In order to assess whether natural disasters have any real effect on the risk of armed conflict, an existing, well-tested model should be used as a starting point. Only if natural disasters can add explanatory power to such a model might one be able to be confident in the proposition that disasters also increase the risk of armed conflict. I will use one candidate for such a model, developed by Fearon & Laitin (2003), to test how disasters affect the risk of civil war onset, when controlling for the most important other relevant factors. Dixon (2009) finds that the model used by Fearon & Laitin (2003) has fared very well, as the academic community has achieved some level of consensus on the role of all the variables they found to be significant. Hence, the scope of this study is limited to violent security issues (Goldstone, 2001), which may possibly be a consequence of the non-violent security challenges brought about by natural disasters. By studying how climate-related natural disasters have affected the likelihood of civil war in the past, this article aims to increase knowledge about to what extent future disasters, possibly exacerbated by the effects of climate change, can be expected to affect the likelihood of outbreaks of civil war. Thereby, this study may also contribute to informing governments about response strategies for managing the potential double impacts of natural disasters. . . .

Why Do Disasters Matter for Conflict?

The debate on security implications of climate change has contributed to increasing the attention to how environmental factors may affect the risk of armed conflict. Environmental shocks generate insecurity, frustration, scarcity of important resources, and weakened enforcement of law and order, which are frequently suggested to increase the likelihood of outbreaks of armed violence (Brancati, 2007; Burke et al., 2009; Homer-Dixon, 1999; Miguel, Satyanath & Sergenti, 2004; Nel & Righarts, 2008). While no one debates that severe environmental shocks cause suffering and destruction, there is no consensus on how humans should be expected to respond to these challenges. On the contrary, sociological research on post-disaster behavior has reached the opposite conclusion of the popular perception, finding that the likelihood of anti-social behavior tends to drop during and after disasters. . . .

Natural disasters will, almost by definition, overstrain governments' capacities in affected areas for a certain amount of time. However, it is not straightforward that this should increase the opportunities for insurgency. First, the insurgents may be set back by the disaster as well. Second, a time when potential insurgents and their families are busy trying to survive and recover from a disaster may not be the best period to attempt to instigate a rebellion. Also, if disasters contribute to reducing grievances and group differences, the foundation for an insurgency may be severely undermined.

A more serious objection against disaster sociology can be derived from the argument of how disaster victims are unified by their common experiences. Even if this is generally true, it begs the question of who become victims. Disasters generally do not select their victims at random— the poorest and most vulnerable are most likely to be affected. These groups usually live in the least disaster-resistant habitations, in the most exposed areas, and are generally less able to secure the resources needed for quick and effective recovery (Wisner et al., 2004). If disaster damages follow ethnic or social divides, this may be suspected to increase the likelihood of conflict, while damage—and aid efforts—across such divides may reduce it. . . .

One of the first cross-national quantitative studies aimed at investigating the relation between natural disasters and the risk of violent conflict was conducted by Drury & Olson (1998). They find a positive relation between disaster severity and the level of political unrest, using a sample of the 12 countries that experienced one or more disasters that killed at least 1,500 persons[1] between 1966 and 1980. Country-years from two years before the first disaster until seven years after the last are included in the analysis. They find a positive association between disaster severity and the risk of post-disaster conflict and present six cases where severe natural disasters have been followed by conflict. Although pathbreaking at its time, the study suffers from a sample that is limited both in time and in the number of countries included. The model also lacks important controls. The findings are highly interesting, but would benefit from a revisit with an improved and expanded model that incorporates a broader sample and sufficient control variables. This study proceeds in this spirit. . . .

The most extensive cross-national analysis focusing specifically on natural disasters to date was undertaken by Nel & Righarts (2008). Using a sample of 183 political units covering the period

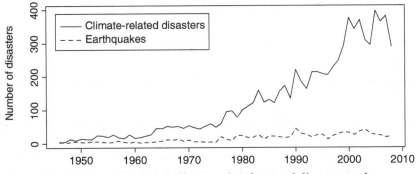

Figure 6.1   Number of recorded climate-related natural disasters and earthquakes, 1946–2008.
Source: CRED (2007).

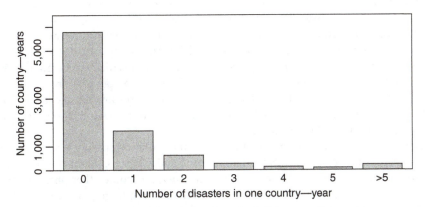

Figure 6.2   Number of climate-related natural disasters per country-year, 1946–2008.
Source: CRED (2007).

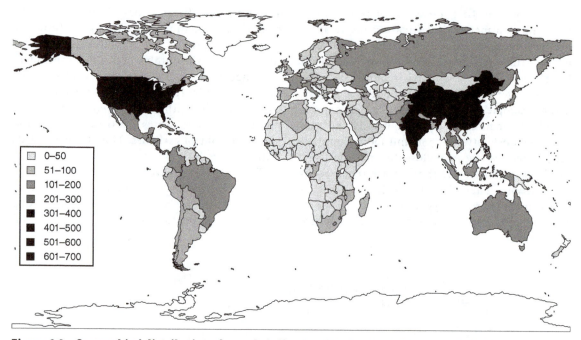

Figure 6.3 Geographical distribution of recorded climate-related natural disasters, 1946–2008.

1950–2000, they find a positive relationship between natural disasters and the risk of armed conflict. They test measures for geological disasters and climate-related disasters and a measure combining all natural disasters on dependent variables of minor violent civil conflict onset (less than 1,000 killed), major conflict onset (more than 1,000 killed), and a variable including both these. Their findings indicate that disasters increase the risk of conflict onset in the same year and following year. Climate-related disasters are found to follow this pattern, except that they do not appear significantly related to minor conflict.

The indicator for disasters used by Nel & Righarts is the number of disasters per capita for each country-year. Although this approach has some merit as a proxy for the share of a population that may be affected by disasters, I am skeptical for two main reasons. First, it reduces the weight of disasters that affect large populations. A disaster does not get diluted by hitting a large population—if anything, it becomes more severe. Second, this approach is used instead of including population

size as a control variable in the model. Large populations are, *ceteris paribus*, more likely to experience both natural disasters and armed conflict. Not including population size in the models may therefore cause the effect of disasters on conflict risk to become confounded with the effect of population size.[2]

The increased risk of disasters is mainly due to the fact that large populations hold more potential victims of natural hazards. This makes natural hazards turn into disasters more often, and the death toll is likely to be higher. With regard to conflict, a large population size is among the few factors that appear robustly related to an increased risk of civil war (Dixon, 2009; Hegre & Sam-banis, 2006). . . .

If population size is not included in a regression model aiming to explain the occurrence of armed conflict, and some other phenomenon that occurs more often in large populations is included in the model, this phenomenon is likely to capture some of the explanatory power of population size. . . . I argued that, *ceteris paribus*, large populations experience more natural disasters and more armed conflict. This means that without population size in the model, the effect disasters have on conflict risk is likely to be overestimated. . . .

Discussion and Conclusion

I set out to test whether natural disasters can add explanatory power to an established model of civil conflict. The results indicate that they can, but that their effect on conflict is the opposite of popular perception. To the extent that climate-related natural disasters affect the risk of conflict, they contribute to reducing it. This holds for a measure of climate-related natural disasters in general, as well as drought in particular. While this finding contradicts recent debate, it is consistent with a large amount of research, in particular research carried out in the 1950s and 1960s, on the relation between disasters and the risk of anti-social behavior.

An important weakness of these studies is the lack of variation in important factors such as political system, economic level, and cultural conditions. Despite this, Fritz (1996: 15) argues that disaster victims have a striking similarity in behavior across space, time, and culture. The results presented in this article support his argument; the effect of climate-related natural disasters appears robust and cross-nationally valid. An important question is the dependence of specification: while the binary measure is robust, other specifications such as a pure count of disasters, checks for a curvilinear effect, and various ordinal measures were tested but performed more poorly. The main difference is between those who experience disasters and those who do not: the number of disasters that occur within a country-year appears less important. This finding also underscores the importance of being cautious about assuming that adversity will automatically translate into increased levels of conflict– a perception that appears frequent among a number of vocal actors in the debate around the political consequences of climate change.

One explanation of the interaction effect between population size and natural disasters may be that the unifying effect described among others by Fritz (1996) may reduce the willingness to join insurgent organizations. Another possible effect relates to Goldstone's (2001: 46) suggestion that disasters provide an opportunity for governments to display both their competence and incompetence. The negative effect of disasters on conflict risk may be read as that governments tend to improve their popularity—the population in affected areas (and perhaps other areas as well) may be left with a more positive impression of the government than they had before the disaster. This should in itself contribute to reducing the pool of potential recruits for insurgent organizations. A third, less optimistic alternative is that disasters simply overstrain societies and would-be insurgents to such an extent that they contribute to limiting rather than expanding the window of opportunity for insurgents.

For further research, investigating the mechanisms connecting disasters to reduced conflict risk could possibly provide interesting avenues towards reducing conflict in general. While the country-year-level analytical approach holds merit in studying aggregate country-level effects, such as the absence or presence of civil war or natural disasters within a country, it appears less suited to capturing specific causal effects between them. Both are commonly limited to specific geographic areas, which means that future studies aimed at investigating in greater detail the relation between natural disasters and conflict risk are likely to benefit from geographically disaggregated designs.

One cannot read into these results that climate change is not dangerous. Even if climate-related natural disasters do not appear to increase the risk of armed conflict, people are still likely to suffer. However, adversity and suffering do not necessarily translate into severe violence. Citizens as well as investors and developers in poor countries seem to have scant reason to fear that climate change-driven disasters will cause armed unrest, even though climate-related natural disasters may cause increasing rates of death and destruction in years to come. Also, while this is the main trend, it is not unlikely that there will be exceptions, that a single disaster incident may be followed by an outbreak of armed conflict. These, like most other armed conflict onsets, should be expected in poor countries with low level of development and weak, inefficient regimes. Despite climate change, economic and political variables remain the most important predictors of conflict. Rather than overemphasizing conflict as a result of climate change, I would recommend keeping the focus on societal development, including building resilience against adverse effects of climate change. While this promises the possibility of alleviating the danger of climate change, it can also lead to strengthened societies in the face of natural disaster and civil war.

Replication Data

The dataset, codebook and do-files for the empirical analysis in this article can be found at http://www.prio.no/jpr/datasets. All analysis was done using Stata 11.1.

NOTES

1. These countries are Bangladesh, China, Guatemala, Honduras, India, Iran, Nicaragua, Nigeria, Pakistan, Peru, the Philippines, and Turkey.

2. The number of people affected by disaster could be used as a control variable, but the high share of apparently non-randomly distributed missing information on the variable provided by EM-DAT (CRED, 2007) would diminish and potentially bias the sample.

REFERENCES

Brancati, Dawn (2007) Political aftershocks: The impact of earthquakes on intrastate conflict. *Journal of Conflict Resolution* 51(5): 715–743.

Burke, Marshall B; Edward Miguel, Shanker Satyanath, John A Dykema & David B Lobell (2009) Warming increases the risk of civil war in Africa. *Proceedings of the National Academy of Sciences* 106: 20670–20674.

CRED (2007) *EM-DAT: The OFDA/CRED International Disaster Database*. Brussels: Universite´ Catholique de Louvain.

Dixon, Jeffrey (2009) What causes civil wars? Integrating quantitative research findings. *International Studies Review* 11(4): 707–735.

Drury, Cooper A & Richard Stuart Olson (1998) Disasters and political unrest: An empirical investigation. *Journal of Contingencies and Crisis Management* 6(3): 153–161.

Fearon, James D & David D Laitin (2003) Ethnicity, insurgency, and civil war. *American Political Science Review* 97(1): 75–90.

Fritz, Charles E (1996) Disasters and mental health: Therapeutic principles drawn from disaster studies. *Historical and Comparative Disaster Series 10*. University of Delaware Disaster Research Center (http://dspace.udel.edu:8080/dspace/handle/19716/1325, accessed 24 May 2010).

Goldstone, Jack A (2001) Demography, environment, and security. In: Myron Weiner & Sharon Stanton Russel (eds) *Demography and National Security*. New York: Berghahn, 38–61.

Hegre, Håvard & Nicholas Sambanis (2006) Sensitivity analysis of empirical results on civil war onset. *Journal of Conflict Resolution* 50(4): 508–535.

Homer-Dixon, Thomas (1999) *Environment, Scarcity, and Violence*. Princeton, NJ: Princeton University Press.

IPCC (2007a) *Climate Change 2007: Impacts, adaptation and vulnerability. Contribution of working group 2 to the Fourth Assessment Report of the Intergovernmental Panel on Climate Change*. OF Canziani, ML Parry, JP Palutikof, PJ van der Linden & CE Hanson (eds). Cambridge: Cambridge University Press.

IPCC (2007b) *Climate Change 2007: The physical science basis. Contribution of working group 1 to the Fourth Assessment Report of the Intergovernmental Panel on Climate Change*. S Solomon, D Qin, M Manning, Z Chen, M Marquis, KB Averyt, M Tignor & HL Miller (eds). Cambridge: Cambridge University Press.

Miguel, Edward; Shanker Satyanath & Ernest Sergenti (2004) Economic shocks and civil conflict: An instrumental variables approach. *Journal of Political Economy* 112(4): 725–753.

Nel, Philip & Marjolein Righarts (2008) Natural disasters and the risk of violent civil conflict. *International Studies Quarterly* 52(1): 159–185.

van Aalst, Maarten K (2006) The impacts of climate change on the risk of natural disasters. *Disasters* 30(1): 5–18.

Wisner, Ben; Piers Blaikie, Terry Cannon & Ian Davis (2004) *At Risk: Natural Hazards, People's Vulnerability and Disasters.* 2nd edn. London: Routledge.

DISCUSSION QUESTIONS

1. Explain which of the many possible problems that Bill McKibben describes seems to you most likely to influence world events in the twenty-first century.

2. Summarize the evidence presented by Hsiang, Burke, and Miguel that offers the most convincing case that climate change will increase future levels of violence.

3. Describe how Rune T. Slettebak's results could be used to support policies that discourage further vigorous efforts *to reduce* anthropogenic climate change. Also describe how Slettebak himself instead uses his results to argue that efforts to reduce anthropogenic climate change should continue.

4. Explain which you believe is likely to prove to be the most accurate of the three possible explanations Slettebak offers to account for his results: (1) the unifying effect of disasters, (2) the opportunity for government displays, or (3) the overstraining of would-be insurgents.

5. Hsiang, Burke, and Miguel examine human groups across thousands of years, whereas Slettebak focuses on societies over only the last 60 years. Explore how these differences in data sets might account for their conflicting findings.

6. Compose a position statement with evidence to support your own view on whether climate change is likely to increase, to reduce, or to have little effect on rates of violence in the twenty-first century.

Debates about Environmental Justice

Selections in section 1 debate whether climate change will increase levels of violence across the world. Selections in this section explore a related question: How should people respond to the climate crisis transforming ecosystems across the world? In the first selection, Wen Stephenson draws on interviews with American activists to argue that a radical, bottom-up movement for climate justice is needed to replace traditional environmental movements that have long been dominated by reformists comfortable with the corporate status quo. The climate justice movement that Stephenson mentions seeks to minimize the suffering that climate change inflicts on poor people more than on the rich. (The "Tim" that Stephenson describes is Tim DeChristopher, an American climate activist and cofounder of the environmental group Peaceful Uprising.)

A second selection by Randall Amster recommends peace ecology as a useful perspective for dealing with Earth's climate crises. In this excerpt from his book *Peace Ecology*, Amster uses an extended case study of the human use of water resources to advance the broader argument that environmental problems transcend political borders and so require cooperative transnational solutions. Humans are innately interdependent both with other humans and with the Earth, Amster argues; therefore, solutions built on control of others and of natural sources will not work as well as solutions built on an ecological perspective that cultivates "a sense of shared destiny and mutual necessity." Amster believes a peace ecology perspective is capable of guiding societies toward a long-term sustainability.

In a final selection, Maria Mies maintains that only revolutionary changes can produce societies capable of thriving in the decades ahead. Mies argues for the adoption of a *subsistence perspective* to create new economies that will replace the current drive for ever-increasing industrialized, capitalist development. The new societies Mies seeks would be non-exploitative, non-patriarchal, and self-sustaining; they would likely begin by eliminating the unequal division of labor that Mies says has for too long encouraged man's domination of women, along with man's domination of nature. Mies offers multiple examples of contemporary movements mostly in the global south where a subsistence perspective is already guiding successes in what she believes is necessary revolutionary work.

What We're Fighting for Now Is Each Other: Dispatches from the Front Lines of Climate Justice

BY WEN STEPHENSON

Stephenson is a former editor at *The Atlantic* and at the *Boston Globe*. He helped launch the grassroots climate-action network *350 Massachusetts*. From *What We're Fighting for Now Is Each Other: Dispatches from the Front Lines of Climate Justice*, Boston: Beacon Press, 2015; pages ix–x; xii–xv; 199–201; 205–206. Used by permission.

Preface

This is really happening.

The Arctic and the glaciers are melting. The oceans are rising and acidifying. The corals are bleaching, the great forests dying and burning. The storms and floods, the droughts and heat waves, are intensifying. The farms and savannahs are parched and drying. Nations are disappearing. People are dying. Mass extinction is unfolding. And all of it sooner and faster than science predicted. The window in which to prevent the worst scenarios is closing before our eyes.

And the fossil-fuel industry—which holds the fate of humanity in its carbon reserves—is doubling down, economically and politically, on all this destruction. We face an unprecedented situation—a radical situation. It demands a radical response. A serious response.

This is . . . about waking up. It's about waking up, individually and collectively, to the climate catastrophe that is upon us—truly waking up to it, intellectually, morally, and spiritually, as the most fundamental and urgent threat humanity has ever faced. And it's about some of the remarkable, wide-awake people I have come to know and at times worked alongside—those I think of as new American radicals—in the struggle to build a stronger movement for climate justice in this country, still the most powerful, morally accountable, and indispensable nation on Earth. A movement that's less like environmentalism and more like the human-rights and social-justice struggles of the nineteenth and twentieth centuries. A movement for human solidarity.

Of course, . . . [I] must begin by acknowledging the science and the sheer lateness of the hour—the fact that, if we intend to address the climate catastrophe in a serious way our chance for any smooth, gradual transition has passed. We must acknowledge the fact that without immediate action at all levels to radically reduce greenhouse emissions and decarbonize our economies—requiring a society-wide mobilization and a thus-far unseen degree of global cooperation, leading to the effective end of the fossil-fuel industry as we know it—the kind of livable and just future we all want is simply inconceivable.

The international community has committed to keeping the global temperature from rising more than two degrees Celsius (3.6 Fahrenheit) above the preindustrial average—the level, we're told, at which catastrophic warming can still be avoided (we've already raised it almost one degree Celsius, with still more "baked in," perhaps half a degree, within the coming decades). But there's good reason to believe that even a rise of two degrees will set in motion "disastrous consequences" beyond humanity's control—as former top NASA climatologist James Hansen, now at Columbia University's Earth Institute, and seventeen coauthors concluded in a December 2013 study. Catastrophic warming, by any humane definition, is virtually certain—indeed, already happening. Because even in the very near term, what's "catastrophic" depends on where you live, and how poor you are, and more often than not the color of your skin. If you're one of the billions of people who live in the poorest and most vulnerable places on the planet, from Bangladesh to the Sahel to Louisiana, even one degree can mean catastrophe.

The question now is not whether we're going to "stop global warming" or "solve the climate crisis"; it is whether humanity will act quickly and decisively enough to salvage civilization itself—in any form worth salvaging. Whether any kind of stable, humane, and just future—any kind of just society—is still possible.

We know that if the governments of the world actually wanted to address this situation, in a serious way, they could. Indeed, a select few, such as Denmark and Germany, have begun to do so. (Denmark already produces nearly half of its electricity from renewables, and Germany close to 40 percent; both are moving aggressively toward the goal of 100 percent renewable energy by 2050.) Stanford's Mark Jacobson published an influential 2009 report outlining a path to 100 percent renewable energy globally and in 2014 created state-by-state roadmaps for the United States to be fully powered by renewables by mid-century. The IPCC [International Panel on Climate Change], the IEA [International Energy Agency], and many others are telling us that it is likely still possible, technically and economically, to hold warming to the two-degree limit—but *only* if the world takes the necessary action *now*.

The point, these experts want us to understand, is that the barriers are not technological or financial—they're political. And in the United States, without which there can be no effective global action, this is largely the result of a successful decades-long effort by the fossil-fuel industry and those who do its bidding (as shown by scholars like Harvard's Naomi Oreskes and Drexel University's Robert Brulle, as well as the public record of lobbying and campaign funding) to sow confusion, doubt, and opposition—obstructing any policies that might slow the warming, or their profits, and buy us time.

Let's be clear about what the preceding statement really means: given what we know and have known for decades about climate change, to deny the science, deceive the public, and willfully obstruct any serious response to the climate catastrophe is to allow entire countries and cultures to disappear. It is to rob people, starting with the poorest and most vulnerable on the planet, of their land, their homes, their livelihoods, even their lives—and their children's lives, and their children's children's lives. For profit. And for political power.

There's a word for this: these are *crimes*. They are crimes against the earth, and they are crimes against humanity.

Where does this leave us? What is the proper response? *Remain calm*, we're told. *No "scare*

tactics" or "hysterics," please. Cooler heads will prevail. Enjoy the Earth Day festivities.

I'm sorry, the cooler heads have not prevailed. It's been a quarter-century since the alarm was sounded. The cooler heads have failed.

If you want sweet, cool-headed reason, try this: masses of people—most of them young, a generation with little or nothing to lose—physically, nonviolently disrupting the fossil-fuel industry and the institutions that support it and abet it. Getting in the way of business as usual. Forcing the issue. Finally acting as though we accept what the science is telling us—and as though we actually care about our fellow human beings.

Isn't that a bit extreme?

Really? Extreme? Business as usual is extreme. Just ask a climate scientist. The building is burning. The innocents—the poor, the oppressed, the children, your *own* children—are inside. And the American petro state—which, under the "all of the above" energy policies of Barack Obama, has overtaken Saudi Arabia as the largest producer of oil and gas on the planet—is spraying fuel, not water, on the flames. That's more than extreme. It's homicidal. It's psychopathic. It's fucking insane.

This is hard. Coming to terms with the climate catastrophe is hard. It's frightening. It's infuriating. It's heartbreaking. A friend of mine, a young woman . . ., says that it's like walking around with a knife in your chest.

And so I ask again, in the face of this situation—in the face of despair—how does one respond?

Rather than retreat into various forms of denial and fatalism and cynicism, many of us, and especially a young generation of activists, have reached the conclusion that something more than merely "environmentalism," and virtuous green consumerism, is called for. That the only thing offering any chance of averting an apocalyptic future—and of getting through what's already coming with our humanity intact—is the kind of radically transformative social and political movement that has altered the course of history in the past. A movement like those that have made possible what was previously unthinkable, from abolition to civil rights.

On September 21, 2014, some three hundred thousand people converged on the streets of Manhattan for the historic People's Climate March, demanding serious climate action from world leaders meeting at the United Nations two days later, a summit convened by UN Secretary General Ban Ki-moon to prod those leaders toward a global agreement at Paris in December 2015. I was there that day with my wife and our two children, along with many of my friends and colleagues in the grassroots climate movement—and it was thrilling, as we were joined by hundreds of thousands of people in New York and in cities around the world, the single largest day of climate demonstrations ever.

One of the slogans for the march was, "To change everything, we need everyone." And I couldn't agree more. That's what this . . . is about. But here's what would really change everything: first acknowledging that the mainstream, Washington-focused environmental movement—and the mainstream, Big Green "climate movement" that grew out of it—has failed. That we've already lost the "climate fight," if that means "solving the climate crisis" and saving some semblance of the world we know. That it was lost before it began—because we started so late. That it's time now to fight like there's nothing left to lose but our humanity.

And yet where does the courage and commitment and sacrifice required for that kind of fight—for the kind of radical movement we need—actually come from?

What I have found, in the stories of those profiled here, and many others, is that the climate struggle, like so many struggles of the past, is essentially a *spiritual* struggle—it forces us to confront the deepest, most difficult questions about ourselves. The climate catastrophe is so fundamental that it strikes to the root of who we are: it's a radical situation, and it requires a radical response. But not radical, necessarily, in the conventional sense of ideology. Rather, it confronts us with a kind of radical necessity—a moral necessity. It requires us to wake up—to face the facts, to find out who we really are—and to act. In some cases, to lay everything on the line: our relationships,

our reputations, our careers, our bodies, maybe even our lives.

Historically, you could say that transformative movements arise from such an awakening—an awakening that you might call spiritual. But whatever you name it, this kind of awakening transforms individuals—and, sometimes, it transforms the world. To suggest that the kind of awakening I'm describing here might lead to such a transformation may seem fanciful. But it's our only hope.

"The mainstream climate movement has absolutely nothing to stand on when it comes to efficacy," Tim told me. "Nothing. They've had billions of dollars poured into these NGOs [nongovernmental organizations] for decades, and they haven't done shit. I think being in the environmental movement for a long time should be considered a liability. It should be like someone who stands up and says, 'I've been in Congress for thirty years.' You know, you better have a good excuse."

I knew he was trying to be provocative—he admitted as much. In fact, he told me later that he came to regret aspects of his Oregon speech, for which he took a fair amount of heat. "I meant what I was saying to be taken *seriously*, but not *literally*," Tim told me. "Expanding what's possible to be discussed and considered, creating that space, can be healthy for the movement." In other words, sometimes you have to go to the edge, as he once said, and push.

Nevertheless, I pushed back. I understood the frustration and the anger toward the mainstream environmental movement, especially the Big Green NGOs and their failure to confront the true dimensions of the catastrophe. I felt it, and I'd talked with others, like Ken Ward, who felt it even more—who'd lived it. But I was skeptical of such a wholesale indictment—much less the notion that we should, or could, somehow replace the organizations, large or small, that formed the movement's infrastructure and that had the resources and the scale to meet the magnitude and urgency of the political challenge we faced. After all, those people are working hard, devoting their lives, to keep fossil fuels in the ground, still our overriding moral imperative if we're going to salvage any hope of climate justice, social justice, in the future. And in the near term, that means not only pushing from the outside. It often means working within the current political system, the only system we've got.

"But the kind of change you're talking about—anything feasible within the current political system—really won't do us any good," Tim shot back. "You're talking about going off the cliff at forty miles per hour instead of sixty."

"So, yes," he said, "the most urgent thing is keeping fossil fuels in the ground. The question is how to do that. We need a different kind of movement, a movement that's about taking power and changing power structures on a fundamental level. And I'm saying the climate movement is not equipped for that kind of struggle. The climate movement that has grown out of the environmental movement—primarily driven by comfortable people, rich people, white people—is about keeping things more or less the same. That's no longer the challenge that we have. On a really fundamental level it's about retaking power, and challenging those at the top—and the movement that we have has proven to be completely ineffective at that, and unwilling to take that challenge on."

The only places Tim saw that kind of movement being built, he said, were in the kinds of groups making up the Climate Justice Alliance, or Indigenous movements like Idle No More and the Moccasins on the Ground gatherings, the people on reservations in South Dakota fighting the "black snake," Keystone XL; or those groups in Appalachia fighting mountaintop removal.

"I don't think it's a coincidence," he said, "that it's the groups from impoverished and oppressed areas or oppressed constituencies that are building the kind of movement we need. I think it's because they've experienced part of the challenge that lies ahead for all of us—when there's plenty of reasons for hopelessness, they've chosen to fight back."

If our primary challenge now, in addition to the urgency of keeping carbon in the ground, is "how to maintain our humanity" in the face of inevitable hardship and scarcity then it becomes all the more important, Tim is saying, that our movement have social justice at its core—and

the willingness to confront power. "Looking only at the physical impacts, the food shortages, droughts, floods, mass migrations—that's really bad," Tim said. "But if you look at how our current power structure would deal with that—we have a power structure in our society, without a doubt, that is willing to scapegoat classes of people, pitting people against one another. And that's where things get really, really ugly."

"The determining factor in whether this crisis turns us toward one another or pits us against one another—whether it uplifts our humanity or kills our humanity—is how we go into it, and what kind of power is rising as we go into it. Whether it's corporate power or a people power, a community power."

Holding onto our humanity in the face of what's coming, Tim said, will be "a never-ending challenge." He quoted Alice Paul, one of the great leaders in the movement for women's suffrage, who famously said, "When you put your hand to the plow, you can't put it down until you get to the end of the row." Now, Tim said, "we're in a position where there's no end to the row. We need an endless movement and a constant revolution."

What are we fighting for? What are any of us who care about climate justice really fighting for? What does "climate justice" mean in the face of the inhuman and dehumanizing maw of the world-devouring carbon-industrial machine—of which we ourselves are a part? What does it mean in the face of the science—which keeps telling us, in its bloodless language, just how late the hour really is?

It seems that movements often reach a critical juncture at which unity—the need to come together around common principles and a common struggle, and a common understanding of what that struggle is about—becomes all important. Or if not unity—which may in fact be impossible for any movement big enough and broad enough to be powerful—then at least something like solidarity. So I ask again: At this late hour, what are we fighting for?

Trust me, I know full well that any talk of a "transformative," "radical" movement for climate justice, or any kind of deep political transformation, sounds hopelessly naïve. I get it. I know.

I know the country, and the political culture, in which I live and work.

And yet—here I am anyway. Because I also know that abolishing slavery sounded hopeless and naïve in 1857, when Frederick Douglass spoke of struggle. I know that throwing off the British Raj sounded hopeless and naïve in 1915, when Gandhi returned to India. I know that ending Jim Crow sounded hopeless and naïve in 1955, when Rosa Parks stayed in her seat on that bus in Montgomery. I know that ending apartheid sounded hopeless and naïve in 1962, when Nelson Mandela went to prison in South Africa.

For that matter, even stopping the Keystone XL pipeline sounded hopeless and naïve in 2011—before thousands of people started getting arrested and literally laying their bodies on the line, with tens of thousands more pledging to do so, in order to stop it. And before a president of the United States started listening. Yes, the southern leg got built. And yes, the whole thing is just one pipeline—one very big, very dangerous, very symbolic and political pipeline. And yes, Montgomery, Alabama, was just one Southern city. And that bus was just one city bus.

And so history says never quit, never give up. But science—we keep coming back to the science. And the science keeps telling us just how late it is. And it's true—we have to be honest, with ourselves and with others. After all, what good is a movement if it can't even be honest about the situation it faces? We have to ask ourselves, in all honesty, given the facts we now face, what it is that we're really fighting for.

Peace Ecology: Deep Solutions in an Age of Water Scarcity and War

BY RANDALL AMSTER

Randall Amster is the director of the Program on Justice and Peace at Georgetown University. He has written several books on anarchism and peacebuilding and was a cofounder of the New Clear Vision website, "a blog filled with (generally) CLEAR intentions and a (positive) VISION for the future." From *Peace Ecology*, New York: Routledge, 2016; 154–160. Used by permission.

Mark Twain once purportedly said that "whiskey's for drinking—water's for fighting." While the evidence for attributing this to Twain is shaky at best, the quote is nonetheless frequently invoked as a foregone conclusion: people will fight over water because it is scarce, essential, and invaluable for the growth and development of human societies. In reality, "water wars" are exceedingly rare, with the overwhelming majority of the world's 263 shared river basins being subject to treaties, agreements, and other mechanisms for allocating their flow. Still, there is a deeper concern reflected in Twain's apocryphal quote, namely that while water wars between nations may be rare, modern water utilization on the whole often reflects a collective war that humankind is waging on the environment. All too often, what are coded as "shared waters" and "peaceful resolutions" to human–human conflicts still involve deep incursions against the natural flow of surface waters, including channelizing rivers to fix national boundaries, altering the saline and sediment levels, and damming rivers for hydroelectric plants. Such outcomes are part of a larger orientation that comes to equate peace with control—especially control of nature.

As human cultures expand, water is emerging as the central resource in local and global politics alike. Pressures to privatize and commodify water are continually being brought to bear, often under the guise of development schemes that are portrayed as linking growth with security. To ensure that water flows even in places where it is highly problematic—from Abu Dhabi to Phoenix—massive delivery infrastructures are contemplated, including energy-intensive desalination plants and circuitous concrete canals transporting water hundreds of miles across deserts. Science fiction scenarios abound, as plans are conceived to capture clouds, drag icebergs, and create mountains and lakes for delivering water supplies to thirsty nations. One of the first high-tech regional water projects, which would serve as a template for similar projects worldwide, was the Tennessee Valley Authority (TVA) developed in the 1930s, comprised of a series of elaborate dams and hydropower generating stations. When World War II broke out, the project was reoriented toward wartime production, doubling its power generation and producing a majority of the phosphorous used by the U.S. military for bullets, bombs, and chemical weapons, as well as aluminum for aircraft. The "most significant contribution to the war" was created at a TVA-powered laboratory: the fissionable uranium-235 that was used to fuel the Manhattan Project that developed the world's first nuclear weapon (Ward 2003, 85).

The TVA example is stark for its specific militarism, yet it reveals something deeper about how we tend to view water. Oftentimes the choice for transnational actors appears to be one of engaging in either water wars or joint development projects—in essence, either militarism or capitalism; a World War and/or the World Bank. If we are inclined to associate the latter with peace, then it obviously becomes preferable to the alternative, and yet deeper questions about the meaning of water remain unresolved. Water is inherently fluid, unpredictable, prone to extremes of either floods or droughts, both transient and in situ, primeval in its simplicity and purity (cf. Postel 2010). Water reshapes images beneath its surface and accurately reflects those above it; it is "an active agent, changing all it touches . . . creating new courses and possibilities yet to be appreciated by humans" (Blatter, Ingram, and Doughman 2001, 3). As we co-evolve with all of the essential resources in our midst, we must also apprehend "the limitations of instrumental rationality in capturing the meanings of water and shortcomings of modern science in improving our understanding of its treatment in society" (Blatter, Ingram, and Doughman 2001, 3).

Increasingly, we come to recognize that no peace between nations is possible without reconciling underlying water issues. It has been surmised that the failure to attain peace in the Middle East between Israel and its Arabic neighbors has been due in part to the concomitant failure to achieve a mutually cognizable agreement over the Jordan River and underground aquifers in the region, yielding a climate of "mistrust, fears of dependency, and perceived threats to national sovereignty (Blatter, Ingram, and Levesque 2001, 38)." In the case of India and Pakistan, where border clashes and war-like tensions have persisted for decades, a treaty governing the Indus River basin was signed in 1960, following a World Bank proposal to divide the waters between the two countries. While the agreement may have helped forestall violent interstate conflict, it also led to "an all-out effort to build a monumental array of dams and canals"—leading one of the Pakistani (formerly Indian) engineers on the project to observe: "This was like a war. These were huge works. . . . Everybody was after us. They said we had sold the rivers, that we were traitors to our country" (Ward 2003, 93).

What we learn from these examples is that water is more than a mere resource, and that both fighting over it and dividing its spoils are equally problematic resolutions to looming global water issues. . . . [B]oth the hardware and software of conflict must be addressed, requiring a simultaneous emphasis on peacemaking at both the human–human and human–environment interfaces. As Vandana Shiva (2002, 66–67) documents, efforts to privatize water and dam rivers often result in the displacement of peoples and the despoliation of the environment—as well as an ensuing "centralization of power over water" that conjures a double meaning for the concept of "hydropower." While it may be the case that "the world is more conscious than ever of the unbreakable nexus between water and life" (Hiscock 2012, 58). this realization—coupled with depletion of freshwater sources and a rising contingent of global competitors for resources—has led many to speculate that the wars of the 21st century will be fought primarily over water, not oil or other valuable resources. On the other hand, more promisingly, a spate of literature has emerged in recent years suggesting that water can be a powerful basis for transborder cooperation, collaboration, conservation—and peace.

* * *

There are myriad lessons to be gleaned from the field of hydro-politics, which we may take as the "systematic study of conflict and cooperation between states over water resources that transcend international borders" (quoted in Dinar 2009, 111). Chief among these lessons are that water highlights our innate interdependence with one another and the environment alike, and likewise that water directly connects the economic and ecological spheres of human life. As with other environmental components, "water bodies respect no political borders" (Dinar 2009, 111), thus engendering a wider perspective that is particularly useful in light of global scarcity and the essential nature of the resource. While studies of water in relation to violent conflict have reached varied conclusions . . ., there is an emerging consensus that scarcity in the context of renewability coupled with the "critical need" for water can provide the impetus for cooperation—yielding "peaceful and successful conflict management schemes" even among "states with recent militarized conflicts" (Dinar, Dinar, and Kurukulasuriya 2011, 810, 830).

If we take to heart the premise that scarcity and essentiality can promote cooperation, then the prospects for water to spur transborder peace initiatives are indeed promising. Nearly half of the earth's land mass abuts river basins shared by more than one nation, and more than three-quarters of the available fresh water flows through an international river basin—reminding us in stark geographical terms that "a river is without a nationality" (Ward 2003, 188). It is becoming increasingly clear that lasting peace is possible, from the Middle East to the American Southwest, "only if water is taken into account" (Ward 2003, 195). Highlighting these themes, the United Nations declared 2013 as the "International Year of Water Cooperation" and the years from 2005–2015 as the "Water for Life Decade"—optimistically citing the operative notion that "history has often shown that the vital nature of freshwater is a powerful incentive for cooperation and dialogue, compelling stakeholders to reconcile even the most divergent views. Water more often unites than divides people and societies." In order to reach this ambitious horizon, we must strive to "build bridges between various meanings and understandings" and

to enhance "the legitimacy of noninstrumental uses of water" (Blatter, Ingram, and Levesque 2001, 52). In short, we must recognize water as boundless—as life.

If we are thus seeking the robust peace contemplated by the peace ecology perspective, then we will need to do more than sign treaties that allocate every drop of water among competing users. Control and peace are often dichotomous, at least in the context of transnational security issues and a complex geopolitical landscape where looming resource wars and ongoing processes of economic colonization continue to dominate the discourse. Physical borders between nations are increasingly militarized in the post-9/11 era, even as the barriers to so-called "free trade" and footloose capital are simultaneously relaxed. This has the effect of diminishing the potential for genuine exchange among peoples and communities on opposite sides of national borders, interrupting the natural processes of ecosystems that do not abide the largely artificial lines on maps. It also serves to exacerbate tensions among nations, leading to the creation of permanent war economies whose explicit "national security" focus is the procurement and control of dwindling resources—down to even the essentials of food, water, and energy. The zero-sum logic of scarcity and competition is palpable, and has become a central norm of international relations, even as its workings are becoming little more than a self-fulfilling downward spiral in which vast resources are expended in the attempt to secure more of them.

Any exploration of processes confronting these eventualities is potentially revolutionary in its full dimensions. The set of interrelated themes brought together under the rubric of peace ecology remain grounded in the notion that the crises of scarcity and conflict are also opportunities for mutually beneficial engagement born of necessity yet aimed at longer-term sustainability. The cultivation of a sense of shared destiny and mutual necessity can bring even ardent transnational adversaries to the negotiating table, since, as Alexander Carius (2006, 11) reminds us, "environmental problems ignore political borders." This emerging holistic perspective suggests that peoples and nations have the potential to find ways of managing ecological concerns that not only work to avoid conflicts but that can also serve to promote peaceful relations among human communities and with the environment itself.

REFERENCES

Blatter, Joachim, Helen Ingram, and Pamela M. Doughman. 2001. "Emerging Approaches to Comprehend Changing Global Contexts." In *Reflections on Water: New Approaches to Transboundary Conflicts and Cooperation*, edited by Joachim Blatter and Helen Ingram, 3–29. Cambridge, MA: The MIT Press.

Blatter, Joachim, Helen Ingram, and Suzanne Lorton Levesque. 2001. "Expanding Perspectives on Transboundary Water." In *Reflections on Water: New Approaches to Transboundary Conflicts and Cooperation*, edited by Joachim Blatter and Helen Ingram, 31–53. Cambridge, MA: The MIT Press.

Carius, Alexander. 2006. "Environmental Peacebuilding: Environmental Cooperation as an Instrument of Crisis Prevention and Peacebuilding: Conditions for Success and Constraints." Report commissioned by the German Federal Ministry for Economic Cooperation and Development. https://www.adelphi.de/en/system/files/mediathek/bilder/us_503_-_carius_environmental_peacemaking_06-07-02.pdf.

Dinar, Shlomi. 2009. "Scarcity and Cooperation Along International Rivers." *Global Environmental Politics* 9 (1): 109–135.

Dinar, Shlomi, Ariel Dinar, and Pradeep Kurukulasuriya. 2011. "Scarcity and Cooperation Along International Rivers: An Empirical Assessment of Bilateral Treaties." *International Studies Quarterly* 55: 809–833.

Hiscock, Geoff. 2012. *Earth Wars: The Battle for Global Resources*. Hoboken, NJ: Wiley.

Klare, Michael T. 2002. *Resource Wars: The New Landscape of Global Conflict*. New York: Owl Books.

Postel, Sandra. 2010. "Water: Adapting to a New Normal." In *The Post Carbon Reader: Managing the 21st Century's Sustainability Crisis*, edited by Richard Heinberg and Daniel Lerch. Healdsburg, CA: Watershed Media.

Shiva, Vandana. 2002. *Water Wars: Privatization, Pollution, and Profit*. Cambridge, MA: South End Press.

Ward, Diane Raines. 2003. *Water Wars: Drought, Flood, Folly, and the Politics of Thirst*. New York: Riverhead Books.

The Need for a New Vision: the Subsistence Perspective

BY MARIA MIES

Maria Mies is a professor of sociology at the Cologne University of Applied Sciences and the author of several books examining connections between women, patriarchy, and capitalism. From *Ecofeminism*, 2nd Ed. Edited by Maria Mies and Vandana Shiva. New York: Zed Books, 2014; 297–299, 318–324. Used by permission.

The Earth Summit in Rio de Janeiro (UNCED, June 1992) again made clear that solutions to the present worldwide ecological, economic and social problems cannot be expected from the ruling elites of the North or the South. As Vandana Shiva points out . . ., a new vision—a new life for present and future generations, and for our fellow creatures on earth—in which praxis and theory are respected and preserved can be found only in the survival struggles of grassroots movements. The men and women who actively participate in such movements radically reject the industrialized countries' prevailing model of capitalist-patriarchal development. They do not want to be developed according to this blueprint, but rather want to preserve their subsistence base intact, under their own control.

This quest for a new vision, however, is to be found not only among people in the South, who cannot ever expect to reap the fruits of "development"; the search for an ecologically sound, non-exploitative, just, non-patriarchal, self-sustaining society can also be found among some groups in the North. Here, too, this search for a new perspective involves not only middle-class people, disenchanted and despairing about the end-result of the modernization process, but even by some at the bottom of the social pyramid.

We have called this new vision the *subsistence perspective*, or the *survival perspective*.

This concept was first developed to analyse the hidden, unpaid or poorly paid work of housewives, subsistence peasants and small producers in the so-called informal sector, particularly in the South, as the underpinning and foundation of capitalist patriarchy's model of unlimited growth of goods and money. Subsistence work as life-producing and life-preserving work in all these production relations was and is a necessary precondition for survival; and the bulk of this work is done by women.[1]

With increasing ecological destruction in recent decades, however, it becomes obvious that this subsistence—or life production—was and is not only a kind of hidden underground of the capitalist market economy, it can also show the way out of the many impasses of this destructive system called industrial society, market economy or capitalist patriarchy.

This has become particularly clear since the alternative to capitalist industrialism, which the socialist version of catching-up development had provided, collapsed in Eastern Europe and what was the USSR. The socialist alternative had been a guiding star for many countries in the South. But it is now evident that the path of development pursued in these ex-socialist countries can no longer be seen as a blueprint for a better society. In their efforts to emulate the capitalist model of industrial society these systems caused greater environmental destruction than have their capitalist counterparts; their relationship to nature was based on the same exploitative principles as in the West. Furthermore, as Kurz points out, they were based on the same economic model of alienated, generalized

commodity production first developed by capitalism[2] which, as we have shown elsewhere,[3] is based on the colonization of women, nature and other peoples. It is due to this inherent colonialism that this model of commodity-producing society is neither sustainable nor generalizable worldwide.

Kurz does not identify the inherent need for colonies in the capitalist or socialist versions of commodity-producing systems; rather he sees the reason for the breakdown of erstwhile "Actually Existing Socialism" (AES) in the dilemma of generalized commodity production as such. Before trying to delineate the contours of a subsistence perspective as an alternative to generalized commodity production it may be useful to look again at the contradictions of this strange economic system which is now propagated as the only possible way of satisfying human needs.

The Schizophrenia of Commodity-producing Societies

The logic of commodity-producing systems consists in the principle of surplus value production and the impetus for permanent growth. This logic is / was the same in both capitalist and AES-states, differing only in so far as in capitalist societies the surplus is accumulated privately and in the AES-countries it was accumulated by the state. In both systems people are in principle *subjects,* both as producers and as consumers. As producers they exchange their labour power for a wage (money); as consumers they exchange this money for commodities to satisfy their needs. In both systems there is a fundamental contradiction between production and consumption, because the sphere of production of commodities is principally separated from that of consumption by the sphere of circulation or the market.

But also the individuals, the economic subjects, are dichotomized into producers and consumers with contradictory interests. "As producer the commodity-subject or exchange subject is not interested in the use-value of his products, irrespective of whether he is 'worker' or 'capitalist', capitalist manager or production-director in a 'real' socialist unit. They do not produce for their own consumption but for an anonymous market. The objective of the whole enterprise is not the sensuous, direct satisfaction of needs but the transformation of work into money (wages, profit)."[4]

For the producer his own products are de-sensualized, have become abstract "work-amalgams [gallerts] . . . because they are nothing but potential money."[5] It makes no difference to them whether they produce Sachertortes or neutron bombs, writes Kurz. But as consumer, the same person has a quite opposite interest in the sensuous, concrete use-value of the things bought ". . . as individuals who eat, drink, need a house, wear clothes, people have to be sensuous. . . ."[6]

It is this contradiction between production and consumption, between exchange and use-values, which is ultimately responsible for the destruction of nature in industrial, commodity-producing society. The exclusive concern of people as producers is maximizing the money output of their production and they will therefore continue to produce poisonous substances, nuclear power, weapons, more and more cars. But as consumers they want clean air, unpolluted food, and a safe place for their waste, far away from their home.

As long as production and consumption are structured in this contradictory way, inherent in generalized commodity production, no solution of the various economic, ecological and political/ethical/spiritual crises can be expected.

In summarizing the main features of the subsistence perspective which has informed and inspired the initiatives described . . ., as well as many ecological and feminist grassroots movements referred to . . . [here], we can see that these struggles for survival are a practical critique not only of an aggressive, exploitative, ecologically destructive technology, but of commodity-producing, growth-oriented capitalist, or socialist industrial systems. Although none of these movements, initiatives, communities have spelt out a full-fledged explicit new utopia for an ecologically sound, feminist, non-colonial, non-exploitative society there is enough evidence in their practice and theory to show that their concept of a "good society" differs from the classical Marxian utopia. While Marx and his followers saw capitalism as the "'midwife" of the "material base" upon which a socialist society could be built, these movements and initiatives demonstrate their rejection of the

universal supermarket as a model of a better society, even if it was equally accessible to all. Neither do they accept Engels' statement that what is good for the ruling class should be good for everybody.[7] These women's and men's concept of what constitutes a "good life," of "freedom" is different, as is their concept of economics, politics and culture. Their utopia may not yet be spelt out explicitly but its components are already being tested in everyday practice, it is a potentially *concrete utopia*. What are the main characteristics of this subsistence perspective?

1. The aim of *economic activity* is not to produce an ever-growing mountain of commodities and money (wages or profit) for an anonymous market but the creation and re-creation of *life*, that means, the satisfaction of fundamental human needs mainly by the production of use-values not by the purchase of commodities. Self-provisioning, self-sufficiency particularly in food and other basic needs; regionality; and decentralization from a state bureaucracy are the main economic principles. The local and regional resources are used but not exploited; the market plays a subordinate role.

2. These economic activities are based on new *relationships*: a) to *nature*: nature is respected in her richness and diversity, both for her own sake and as a precondition for the survival of all creatures on this planet. Hence, nature is not exploited for the sake of profit, instead, wherever possible, the damage done to nature by capitalism is being healed. Human interaction with nature is based on respect, cooperation and reciprocity. Man's domination over nature—the principle that has guided Northern society since the Renaissance—is replaced by the recognition that humans are part of nature, that nature has her own subjectivity.

   b) *Among people.* As man's domination over nature is related to man's domination over women and other human beings[8] a different, non-exploitative relationship to nature cannot be established without a change in human relationships, particularly between *women and men.* This means not only a change in the various *divisions of labour* (sexual division; manual/mental and urban/rural labour, and so on) but mainly the substitution of money or commodity relationships by such principles as reciprocity, mutuality, solidarity, reliability, sharing and caring, respect for the individual and responsibility for the "whole." The need for *subsistence security* is satisfied not by trust in one's bank account or a social welfare state, but by trust in the reliability of one's community. A subsistence perspective can be realized only within such a network of reliable, stable human relations, it cannot be based on the atomized, self-centred individuality of the market economy.

3. A subsistence perspective is based on and promotes participatory or grassroots' democracy—not only in so far as political decisions per se are concerned, but also with regard to all economic, social and technological decisions. Divisions between politics and economics, or public and private spheres are largely abolished. The personal is the political. Not only the parliament but also everyday life and life-style are battlefields of politics. Political responsibility and action is no longer expected solely from elected representatives but assumed by all in a communal and practical way.

4. A subsistence perspective necessarily requires a multidimensional or synergic problem-solving approach. It is based on the recognition that not only the different dominance systems and problems are interconnected, but also that they cannot be solved in isolation or by a mere technological fix. Thus social problems (patriarchal relations, inequality alienation, poverty) must be solved together with ecological problems. This interconnectedness of all life on earth, of problems and solutions is one of the main insights of ecofeminism.[9]

5. A subsistence perspective demands a new paradigm of science, technology and knowledge. Instead of the prevailing instrumentalist, reductionist science and technology—based on dualistic dichotomies which have constituted and maintain man's domination over nature,

women and other people—ecologically sound, feminist, subsistence science and technology will be developed in participatory action with the people. Such a grass-roots, women and people-based knowledge and science will lead to a re-evaluation of older survival wisdom and traditions and also utilize modern knowledge in such a way that people maintain control over their technology and survival base. Social relations are not external to technology but rather incorporated in the artefacts as such. Such science and technology will therefore not reinforce unequal social relationships but will be such as to make possible greater social justice.

6. A subsistence perspective leads to a reintegration of culture and work, of work as both burden and pleasure. It does not promise bread without sweat nor imply a life of toil and tears. On the contrary, the main aim is happiness and a fulfilled life. Culture is wider than specialized activity exclusive to a professional elite—it imbues everyday life.

   This also necessitates a reintegration of spirit and matter, a rejection of both mechanical materialism and of airy spirituality. This perspective cannot be realized within a dualistic worldview.

7. A subsistence perspective resists all efforts to further privatize, and/or commercialize the commons: water, air, waste, soil, resources. Instead it fosters common responsibility for these gifts of nature and demands their preservation and regeneration.

8. Most of the characteristics in the foregoing would also be appropriate to the conception of an ecofeminist society. In particular, the practical and theoretical insistence on the interconnectedness of all life, on a concept of politics that puts everyday practice and experiential ethics, the consistency of means and ends, in the forefront. And yet, the two examples previously documented are not feminist projects in the narrow sense in which this term is often understood, namely, all-women initiatives in which men have no role to play. In fact, the initiators of these projects were men. In the ecofeminist

movement there are many examples of women-only projects and initiatives. But the question is: can we conceive of a perspective for a better future society by concentrating only on women, or by building all-women islands within a capitalist-patriarchal ocean? As ecofeminists emphasize overcoming established dualisms and false dichotomies, as they want to put the interdependence of all life at the centre of a new ethic and politics,[10] it would be quite inconsistent to exclude men from this network of responsibility for the creation and continuation of life. Ecofeminism does not mean, as some argue, that women will clean up the ecological mess which capitalist-patriarchal men have caused; women will not eternally be the *Trutnmerfrauen* (the women who clear up the ruins after the patriarchal wars). Therefore, a subsistence perspective necessarily means men begin to share, *in practice,* the responsibility for the creation and preservation of life on this planet. Therefore, men must start a movement to redefine their identity. They must give up their involvement in destructive commodity production for the sake of accumulation and begin to share women's work for the preservation of life. In practical terms this means they have to share unpaid subsistence work: in the household, with children, with the old and sick, in ecological work to heal the earth, in new forms of subsistence production.

In this respect it is essential that the old sexist division of labour criticized by the feminists in the 1970s—that is, men become the theoreticians of the subsistence perspective while women do the practical work—is abolished. This division between mental and manual labour is contrary to the principles of a subsistence perspective. The two examples documented . . . are significant in this respect, in so far as they demonstrate that men have begun to see the importance of the need to overcome this dichotomy.

9. Moreover, if the dichotomy between life-producing and preserving and commodity-producing activities is abolished, if men acquire caring and nurturing qualities which have so far been considered women's domain, and if, in an economy based on self-reliance, mutuality, self-provisioning, not women alone but men too are involved in subsistence production they will have neither time nor the inclination to pursue their destructive war games. A subsistence perspective will be the most significant contribution to the de-militarization of men and society. Only a society based on a subsistence perspective can afford to live in peace with nature, and uphold peace between nations, generations and men and women, because it does not base its concept of a good life on the exploitation and domination of nature and other people.

Finally, it must be pointed out that we are not the first to spell out a subsistence perspective as a vision for a better society Wherever women and men have envisaged a society in which all—women and men, old and young, all races and cultures—could share the "good life," where social justice, equality, human dignity, beauty and joy in life were not just Utopian dreams never to be realized (except for a small elite or postponed to an after-life), there has been close to what we call a subsistence perspective. Kamla Bhasin, an Indian feminist who tried to spell out what "sustainable development" could mean for all women in the world lists a number of principles of sustainability similar to the features of a subsistence perspective.[11] It is clear to her, as it is to many women and men who are not blind to the reality that we live in a limited world, that sustainability is not compatible with the existing profit- and growth-oriented development paradigm. And this means that the standard of living of the North's affluent societies cannot be generalized. This was already clear to Mahatma Gandhi 60 years ago, who, when asked by a British journalist whether he would like India to have the same standard of living as Britain, replied: "To have its standard of living a tiny country like Britain had to exploit half the globe. How many globes will India need to exploit to have the same standard of living?"[12] From an ecological and feminist perspective, moreover, even if there were more globes to be exploited, it is not even desirable that this development paradigm and standard of living was generalized, because it has failed to fulfil its promises of happiness, freedom, dignity and peace, even for those who have profited from it.

NOTES

1. Mies, Maria, et al, *Women: the Last Colony,* Zed Books, London, 1988; Mies, M. *Patriarchy and Accumulation on a World Scale: Women in the International Division of Labour,* Zed Books, London, 1991.

2. Kurz, R. *Der Kollaps der Modernisierung,* Vom Zusammenbruch des Kasernen Sozialismus zur Krise der Weltökonomie. Eichborn Verlag, Frankfurt, 1991.

3. Mies, et al, (1988) op. cit.

4. Kurz, op. cit. p. 101.

5. Ibid.

6. Ibid. p. 102.

7. Engels, Friedrich, "Origin of the Family, Private Property and the State" in: Marx / Engels *Selected Works,* Vol 3, Progress Publishers, Moscow 1976.

8. Bookchin, Murray, *Toward an Ecological Society.* Black Rose Books, Montreal, Buffalo, 1986. Mies, 1991, op. cit. Ackelsberg, Martha and Irene Diamond, "Is Ecofeminism a New Phase of Anarchism?" Paper presented at Eighth Berkshire Conference on the History of Women, Douglass College, New Brunswick, New Jersey, 8–10 June, 1990.

9. Ackelsberg, Martha and Irene Diamond, "Is Ecofeminism a New Phase of Anarchism?" Paper presented at Eighth Berkshire Conference on the History of Women, Douglass College, New Brunswick, New Jersey, 8–10 June, 1990.

10. Diamond, Irene and Gloria Feman-Orenstein, *Reweaving the World: The Emergence of Ecofeminism.* Sierra Club Books, San Francisco, 1990.

11. Bhasin, Kamla, "Environment, Daily life and Health: Women's Strategies for Our Common Future." Speech at Fifth International Congress on Women's Health. Copenhagen, 25 August 1992.

12. Quoted by Kamla Bhasin, op. cit. p. ll.

DISCUSSION QUESTIONS

1. Summarize the evidence that Wen Stephenson offers to support the claim that a radical transformative climate justice movement is necessary to "salvage civilization itself—in any form worth salvaging."

2. Explain the benefits and also possible problems with Stephenson's depiction of climate change as, at root, a moral and spiritual struggle.

3. Evaluate the accuracy of Randall Amster's claim that the long human history of shared waters provides support for the utility of a peace ecology perspective.

4. Explore the implications for nation-state policies if it is true, as Amster contends, that in dealing with the environment, "control and peace are often dichotomous."

5. Describe the principle ways that modern life would be different if most people were more concerned with the needs of Earth than with the needs of their particular country.

6. Explain why you agree, or disagree, with Maria Mies's suggestion that capitalist societies encourage sexism and patriarchy.

7. Support, or refute, Mies's argument that the subsistence perspective is the best means for creating women-and-children friendly, ecologically sustainable, peaceful societies.

PART 7

VISIONS AND PERSONAL PEACE

Many of the earlier selections offered more or less explicit policy recommendations including, for example, calls for revolutionary changes like those made by Maria Mies in part 6. Selections in this final portion of the book present additional contending visions for how best to build an enduring peace across the world. Authors in section 1 describe different ideas for creating a sustainably peaceful world. Selections in section 2 continue this debate by focusing on the specific, vexing question of whether people should seek first to cultivate peace within themselves before moving on to projects aimed at bringing peace to others.

Debates about Peace Visions

The first selection, "Price of Peace: Abundance for All," presents the vision of BigPictureSmallWorld, an educational and advocacy group. This group argues that there are ample resources and know-how already available to meet the basic economic, educational, and health care needs of everyone on Earth. BigPictureSmallWorld offers eleven strategies to create a sustainable global peace at the cost of about one-fourth of what countries now spend for war and war preparations.

Anthropologist Douglas P. Fry offers a different vision in the second selection. Fry argues that world peace requires the creation of a global peace system. Fry maintains that crucial elements of this system are already emerging but that three elements in particular need to be further nourished. These elements are (1) cultural beliefs that peace is possible; (2) economic, political, and social interdependence among nations; and (3) a broadened sense of personal identity.

The third selection offers a different vision of how best to create a global peace. Here Kent Shifferd, Patrick Hiller, and David Swanson write on behalf of World Beyond War, an international campaign that emphasizes the need to replace the existing "war system." World Beyond War's vision calls for a mass, global movement of educators to share the news that "war is a failed social institution." World Beyond War also encourages nonviolent action campaigns to confront and disrupt the current war system.

In a final selection, John Arquilla points toward the development of a unifying, global consciousness like that which Pierre Teilhard de Chardin envisioned almost 100 years ago. Teilhard believed evolution was carrying humans toward a "noosphere" of shared, mutual awareness. Arquilla argues that Internet connectivity is today forging an actual noosphere that could, with effort, yield a peaceful world built on a shared conscience and ethics.

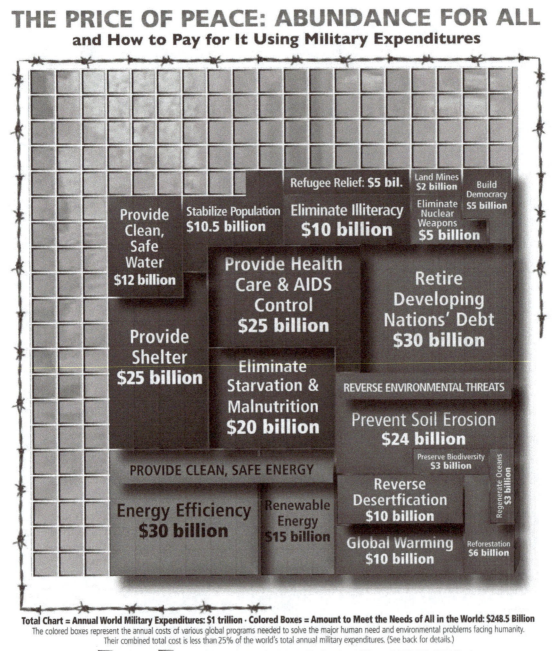

THE PRICE OF PEACE: ABUNDANCE FOR ALL
and How to Pay for It Using Military Expenditures

Refugee Relief: $5 bil.

Land Mines $2 billion

Build Democracy $5 billion

Provide Clean, Safe Water $12 billion

Stabilize Population $10.5 billion

Eliminate Illiteracy $10 billion

Eliminate Nuclear Weapons $5 billion

Provide Health Care & AIDS Control $25 billion

Retire Developing Nations' Debt $30 billion

Provide Shelter $25 billion

Eliminate Starvation & Malnutrition $20 billion

REVERSE ENVIRONMENTAL THREATS

Prevent Soil Erosion $24 billion

Preserve Biodiversity $3 billion

Regenerate Oceans $3 billion

PROVIDE CLEAN, SAFE ENERGY

Energy Efficiency $30 billion

Renewable Energy $15 billion

Reverse Desertification $10 billion

Global Warming $10 billion

Reforestation $6 billion

Total Chart = Annual World Military Expenditures: $1 trillion · Colored Boxes = Amount to Meet the Needs of All in the World: $248.5 Billion
The colored boxes represent the annual costs of various global programs needed to solve the major human need and environmental problems facing humanity. Their combined total cost is less than 25% of the world's total annual military expenditures. (See back for details.)

☐ = $1 billion   ▣ = Amount that was needed to eradicate Smallpox from the world (accomplished 1978): $300 million

Figure 7.1   Total Chart = Annual World Military Expenditures: $1 trillion, Boxes = Amount to Meet the Needs of All in the World: $248.5 Billion.
The shaded boxes represent the annual costs of various global programs needed to solve the major human need and environmental problems facing humanity. Their combined total cost is less than 25% of the world's total annual military expenditures.

Price of Peace: Abundance for All

BY BIGPICTURESMALLWORLD

Medard Gabel created BigPictureSmallWorld, where he continues to serve as CEO. Gabel was a long-time associate of Buckminster Fuller, with whom he co-created the World Game (also known as the World Peace Game). He has worked as a consultant for over 400 organizations throughout the world. From BigPictureSmallWorld. Online at: <http://www.bigpicturesmallworld.com/war-peace/PriceofPeace.pdf >. Used by permission.

This chart and explanatory text document that the basic human needs of everyone in the world can be met with existing technology, resources, and financial capacities—that what we need to solve the major systemic problems confronting humanity is both available and affordable. Clearly, to deal with a problem as complex and large as, for example, the global energy situation, with just a small part of a single graph and its explanatory text is incomplete, at best. The following explanations of the chart's various components are not intended as complete or detailed plans, but rather as very broad brush-stroke strategic themes intended to give the overall direction, scope and strategy. The book, *Seven Billion Billionaires*, goes into more detail. For information on the book's availability, and more details and references on the . . . strategies, see www.BigPictureSmallWorld.com

Strategy 1. Food for All: Eliminate Starvation and Malnourishment—$20 billion per year for ten years, allocated for: a) *Global Hunger Relief Agency* ($5 billion) spent on international grain reserve and emergency famine relief; b) *Global Fertilizer Agency* ($5 billion) for increasing the amount of indigenous fertilizer used in developing world; c) *Increased Irrigation* ($2 billion); d) *School Lunch Programs* ($500 million) for school lunch programs in developing countries; e) *Regenerative Food Systems Education and Training* ($7.5 billion) for vastly expanding in-country extension services that teach/demonstrate sustainable agriculture, use of local fertilizer sources, pest and soil management techniques, post harvest preservation, and for providing clear market incentives for increased local production; f) $1 billion for *Local Food Systems* promotion. Educational resources of Strategy 5 coupled with this strategy. Closely linked with #'s 2, 3, 5, 6, 7, 8, 11.

Cost: 50% of what US spends on weight loss per year; 17% of what the US spends on the health care costs of obesity; 8.5% of the rich world's annual subsidies to their richest farmers.

Strategy 2. Provide Clean and Abundant Water for All—$12 billion/year for ten years, allocated for: a) *Clean Water Infrastructure* ($10 billion) spent on making available materials, tools, and training needed to build and maintain needed wells, water and sewage pipes, sanitation facilities, and water purifying systems; b) *Water Use Efficiency* ($2 billion) for increasing water use efficiency in agriculture. Closely related to #'s 1, 3, 4, 5, 6, 7, 11.

Cost: 6% of what the world spends on illegal drugs per year; 34% of what is spent worldwide on bottled water.

Strategy 3. Provide Health Care For All—$25 billion/year for ten years, allocated for: a) Providing primary health care ($12 billion) through *Community Health Workers* to all areas in the world that do not have access to health care; *Special Child Health Care*: ($2.5 billion) for: (1) immunizing 1 billion children in developing world against measles, tuberculosis, diphtheria, whooping cough, polio and tetanus, thereby preventing the death of 6–7 million children/year; (2) providing *oral rehydration* therapy for children with severe diarrhea; and (3) providing *Vitamin A* to children who lack it in their diet, thereby preventing blindness in 250,000 children/year; b) *Iodine Deficiency Program*: $40 million/year for iodine addition to table salt to eliminate iodine deficiency, thereby reducing the 566 million people who suffer from goiter and not adding to the 3 million who suffer from overt cretinism; c) *AIDS Prevention and Control Program*: $9 billion/year allocated as follows: (1) $4 billion for a global AIDS prevention education program;

(2) $4 billion for providing multiple drug therapy to AIDS patients in the developing world; (3) $1 billion for research and development for an AIDS vaccine or cure; d) *Prevent and Control Malaria:* $3 billion/year for bed nets and other malaria prevention and treatment efforts, with $1 billion spent on R & D for an effective malaria vaccine; e) *Diabetes Initiative:* $1 billion for education and mass screenings. Closely linked with #'s 1, 2, 4, 5, 7, 11.

Cost: 19% of what US spends on alcohol and tobacco per year; less than what the U.S. and Japan spend on golf each year.

Strategy 4. Shelter for All: Eliminate Inadequate Housing and Homelessness—$21 billion/year for ten years, allocated for *Self-Help Housing* that makes available materials, tools and techniques to people without adequate housing ($20 billion/year) and the *Housing Tenure Initiative* that works to protect people from unfair evictions and secures property rights for them. Closely linked with #'s 1, 2, 3, 5, 6, 11.

Cost: Amount US spends on hunting and fishing every 8 months.

Strategy 5. Education for All: Eliminate Illiteracy—$10 billion/year for ten years, allocated for: a) *Television Literacy Campaign for* satellite network, solar-powered television sets, satellite receivers in villages without adequate schools; appropriate educational programming ($2 billion/year); textbooks, teaching aids, in-service teacher training and supervision ($3 billion/year); $140 million/year for training 1 million new teachers in Africa; b) *Internet Access for All* for global wireless Internet access via communications satellites, land-based technology where appropriate ($4 billion/year); $1 billion/year for the preparation of Internet materials for use in developing countries. Closely related to #'s 1, 2, 3, 4, 6, 7, 10, 11.

Cost: 12.5% of the cost of Guff War 1, or 2.8% of the 2003 tax cut given to the richest U.S. citizens; 14 months of what the U.S. spends on video games.

Strategy 6. Provide Clean, Safe Energy for All—$45 billion/year for ten years allocated for a) *Increasing Energy Efficiency* ($30 billion) for raising fleet mileage to 50 m.p.g.; doubling appliance, industrial processes, household energy,

materials use efficiency and phase out of coal power plants; b) *Sustainable Energy Systems* ($15 billion) for sustainable energy assessment, fossil and nuclear subsidy eradication, hydrogen fuel incentives, a global energy extension service, sustainable energy microfinance, and sustainable energy R & D. Closely linked with #'s 1, 2, 3, 4, 7, 10, 11.

Cost: 13% of what U.S. teenagers spend/year; 22% of annual subsidies given to corporations in U.S.

Strategy 7. Stabilize Population—$10.5 billion/year for ten years, allocated for making birth control universally available. Closely linked with #'s 1, 2, 3, 4, 5.

Cost: 0.08% of the worlds annual military expenditures.

Strategy 8. Credit for All: Debt Management—$30 billion/year for ten years, allocated for a) *Debt Retirement* ($25 billion/year) for $500 billion or more of current debt discounted to 50% face value to retire all debt of the poorest developing countries; b) *Debt for Nature Swap* to whereby debt is forgiven for preserving nature; c) *Credit for Humanity* ($5 billion) for expanding by an order of magnitude the amount micro-loans available in the developing world. Closely linked with #'s 1, 2, 3, 4, 6, 7, 10, 11.

Cost: 9% of what the US pays in interest on its national debt; 6.7% of what the world spends on advertising.

Strategy 9. Secure World for All: Eliminating Nuclear Weapons—$15 billion/year for ten years, allocated for: a) *Dismantling/Eliminating Nuclear Weapon Programs* ($5 billion/year) wherein all the world's nuclear weapons are dismantled and the bombs' plutonium and enriched uranium is processed in nuclear reactors that produce power and render the radioactive materials into non-weapons grade material; b) *Refugee Relief* ($5 billion); c) *Landmine Eradication* ($2 billion); d) *Global PeaceKeepers'* Force ($3 billion). Closely linked with #'s 1, 10.

Cost: 55% of what the US spends on preparing for nuclear war; 53% of what is spent each year on private "security"—private guards, weapons detectors, video surveillance, etc.

Strategy 10. Building Democracy and Diversity— $5 billion/year for ten years, allocated for: a) *International Democratic Election Fund* to finance voter education and multi-party elections in countries making the transition to democracy; b) *Global Polling and Referendum Program* to ascertain what people from all over the world think and feel about key global issues; c) *Global Problem Solving Simulation Tool* to enable anyone with Internet access to propose, develop and test strategies for solving real-world problems; d) *Global Arts Program;* and e) *Global Spiritual Heritage Program.* Closely linked with #'s 1, 2, 3, 4, 5, 6, 7, 8, 9, 11.

Cost: 13.5% of what the world spends on hair care; 29% of what Europe and the U.S. spend on pet food.

Strategy 11. Reversing Environmental Threats— $32 billion/year for ten years, allocated for: a) *Reversing Global Warming* ($10 billion) spent on removing fossil energy subsidies, taxing carbon emissions (and other measures—see above #6); b) *Planting Trees Initiative* ($6 billion); c) *Preserving Cropland/Reversing Desertification* ($10 billion) $5 billion spent on converting vulnerable lands; $5 billion on conserving topsoil and reversing desertification; d) *Preserve Biodiversity* ($3 billion for 30 years) to inventory entire flora and fauna of Earth and to determine the genetic code of every species of life that inhabits the planet; e) *Regenerating the Oceans* ($3 billion). Closely linked to #'s 1, 2, 3, 6.

Cost: $3 billion less than the annual cost of US farmland loss; half the amount of price subsidies given to U.S. and E.U. farmers.

Major References: UNDP, *Human Development Reports;* UNEP, *GEO Yearbooks,* UNICEF, *State of the World's Children;* UNESCO, *Education for All;* ITU, World Information Reports; WHO, *World Health Reports;* FAO, *State of World Food Insecurity,* The World Bank, *World Development Reports; World Development Indicators; World Economic Outlook;* CIESIN, *Atlas of Poverty;* World Resources Institute, *World Resources;* World Watch Institute, *Vital Signs; State of the World;* Medard Gabel *Ho-Ping: Food for Everyone; Energy, Earth and Everyone.*

Selections from "Cooperation for Survival: Creating a Global Peace System"

BY DOUGLAS P. FRY

In *War, Peace, and Human Nature: The Convergence of Evolutionary and Cultural Views*, edited by Douglas P. Fry, 543–58. New York: Oxford University Press, 2013. Douglas P. Fry chairs the Department of Anthropology at the University of Alabama at Birmingham. He is the author and editor of several books that explore the biological and cultural bases of peace, conflict, and violence. WAR, PEACE, AND HUMAN NATURE: THE CONVERGENCE OF EVOLUTIONARY AND CULTURAL VIEWS by Douglas P. Fry (2013) 3200w from pp. 543-558. By permission of Oxford University Press, USA.

[W]e will consider some of the processes that appear to be important for the creation of security through peace systems. Topics of consideration will include the importance of having a visionary goal of peace, having an awareness of existing interdependence (and the deliberate augmentation of interdependence) to promote multilateral cooperation, and expanding the social identity to encompass all the members of the larger socio-political community.

The Importance of Vision

The importance of developing an alternative vision is overlooked in many discussions of peace and security. A common assumption is that a dramatic social transformation away from war is not possible. Such an attitude easily becomes a self-fulfilling prophecy. The point of this section is rather simple, yet critically important: having a vision of a new socio-political system without war is the first step toward bringing change to a flawed existing system (Hand, 2010).

A widespread cultural belief that warfare stems ultimately from a warlike human nature contributes to the self-fulfilling prophecy that war is just "in the nature of the beast." A main message of this . . . is that such fatalism is simply wrong, and that in fact game theory, ethology, archaeology, nomadic forager studies, primatology, as well as lines of evidence in various other fields reveal a more hopeful assessment of human nature that balances the obvious capacity to make war with the potential to make peace. Similarly, Hand (2010, p. 46) points out "to argue that we cannot end war because we are the passive victims of culture, or that ending war is an impractical goal to embrace because doing so would take centuries, are simply not legitimate arguments." Instead, we need to begin with a vision that it could be done and work to achieve the goal.

Prior to the development of their peace system, the ancestral tribes of the Iroquois confederacy lived in constant fear of attack from each other. The evidence documents how they constructed elaborate stockades around their villages. Archaeological excavations near Elbridge, New York, for instance, show how early Onondagas had dug trenches and built a 15-foot high double or triple wall around their village (Dennis, 1993, p. 54). The development of a new social and political system, the confederacy, which also is sometimes called the Iroquois Great League of Peace, brought an end to the fear of endemic raiding. In the epic myths of the Iroquois, the visions and teaching of one man, Deganawidah the prophet, were critical in transforming a war system into a peace system. In the epic tale, Deganawidah and his followers created a Great Tree of Peace . . ., whose spreading roots symbolized how peace and law could eventually extend to all humanity. Dennis (1993, pp. 94–95) explains:

> Deganawidah and the chiefs then uprooted a great and lofty pine, exposed a chasm, and discarded their weapons of war. A swift current of water swept them away, they replanted the tree, and they proclaimed "Thus we bury all weapons of war out of sight, and establish the 'Great Peace.' Hostilities shall not be seen nor heard of any more among you, but 'Peace' shall be preserved among the Confederated Nations."

Deganawidah saw things the way they could be if neighboring peoples viewed each other as kinfolks, expanded their identity beyond the single village or tribe, and addressed conflicts through council meetings rather than through bloodshed. According to legend, Deganawidah spoke of a new way of thinking, a new mindset with peace at its core, changes that would abolish war and create the Iroquois Great League of Peace. The prophet also transferred his vision of peace to future generations who could continue to extend the peace system by ritually transforming enemies from outside the confederacy into kins-people.

Jean Monnet and the birth of the European Union provide another illustration of the importance of having a vision. Monnet was "A man of vision rather than a man of power." (Harryvan interview in Smith, 2011). Former German Chancellor Konrad Adenauer expressed that Monnet has been sent by God, because he provided the leaders with a visionary insight and a plan for how to avoid the next war in Europe (Harryvan interview in Smith, 2011). Part of Monnet's perception was to realize that the centuries of warfare in Europe—in his own lifetime World Wars I and II—fundamentally stemmed from a nation-state system, and therefore to abolish warfare in Europe, a new order with centralized, supranational institutions must be set up. Like Deganawidah, Monnet was a prophet with a clear image of how to create a lasting peace, and like Deganawidah, Monnet realized the need to unify different groups, not just formulate agreements and treaties among them. The key was to create a higher level of governance, a new common identity, and a new unity of purpose. EU Commissioner Jose Manuel Barroso (2006) recalls how President Kennedy once praised Monnet: "In just 20 years, Jean Monnet did more to unite Europe than a thousand years of conquerors. Monnet's vision transformed a whole continent and forged an entirely new form of political governance."

Interdependence

The EU also provides a modern-day example of how interdependence can purposefully be augmented as part of a deliberate plan to create a new level of governance. It is sometimes forgotten that a major impetus behind the multistage process of European integration was to eliminate the threat of war in the region (Reid, 2004; Staab, 2008, p. 144; Wilson, 2000, p. 15;). "Amid the misery and ruin left behind by the twentieth century's two lethal world wars, a group of Europeans set out to create a lasting peace on the continent and a shared economy. They did not aim low. Their dream was to produce, once and for all, an end to war on the continent, and an end to poverty" (Reid, 2004, p. 25).

In Zurich in 1946, Winston Churchill proposed that a pan-European peace could be forged through the creation of strong trade relations. He called for the creation of the United States of Europe (Elliott, 2005, p. 20; Hill, 2010). The name did not stick, but a number of leaders such as French Foreign Minister Robert Schuman and Germany's Chancellor Konrad Adenauer adopted Churchill's and Monnet's dream of Europe as an interdependent union that would once and for all put an end to war (Reid, 2004; Smith, 2011). . . .

The approach these founding fathers took was to visualize and move toward a level of sovereignty above the level of the nation-state by increasing the interdependence among the national economies so as to make Europe progressively more and more economically integrated (Fry, 2009; Reid, 2004). They began in the early 1950s by placing coal and steel—critical resources in times of peace and war—under supranational control. This was the beginning of a series of cooperative steps toward unification that continues to this day (Staab, 2008). The architects of European integration envisioned that the augmentation of economic interdependence and unity would spill over into the social and political realms. Indeed, this is what has happened, and the significant outcome has been peace and security on the European continent. The EU is a deliberately created peace system. Reid (2004, p. 193) comments, "The EU, after all, is a cooperative community that has been an historic success at its main goals, preventing another war in Europe and giving European nations new stature on the world stage."

Using supranational institutions and the deliberate promotion of interdependence to create peace is a remarkable achievement. War between EU members has become unthinkable (Bertens, 1994; Hill, 2010; Smith, 2011). Wilson (2000, p. 16) point out that "In the EU, the emphasis has been put on the means to reduce political divergence between the nation-state governments in order to bring peace and tolerance." This shift in thinking represents a huge change from the first half of the twentieth century when World War I and World War II ravaged Europe.

Expanding the "Us": Creating Overarching Social and Political Identity

Charles Darwin (1998, pp. 126–127) understood the process of social aggregation that I like to call "Expanding the Us to include the Them" when he reflected, "As man advances in civilization, and small tribes are united into larger communities, the simplest reason would tell each individual that he ought to extend his social instincts and sympathies to all the other members of the same nation, though personally unknown to him. This point being once reached, there is only an artificial barrier to prevent his sympathies extending to the men of all nations and races." The ten tribes of the Upper Xingu River basin, the Iroquois, the Aborigine bands of the Western Desert, and other such cases unequivocally demonstrate that clusters of neighboring societies can Expand the Us and get along peacefully as members of a larger peace system (Fry, 2009, 2012; Miklikowska & Fry, 2010).

Anthropological and psychological research suggests that there are many ways to Expand the Us to develop higher-level social identity. First, cross-cutting ties can be created among groups, for example, through exchange relationships, intermarriage, cross-group friendships, and participation in common rituals and ceremonies (Rubin, Pruitt, & Kin, 1994; M. Sherif, Harvey, White, Hood, & C. Sherif, 1961; Deutsch & Coleman, 2012). Members of each Xingu tribe form trade relationships with members of other groups, a practice that helps to Expand the Us identification across all the ten tribes (Gregor, 1990). The role that intermarriage can play in "Expanding the Us" is reflected as a Xingu man gestured, so as to mark from head-to-toe the midline of his body, and said, "This side . . . Mehinaku. That side is

Waurá" (Gregor & Robarchek, 1996, p. 173). Second, working together on superordinate goals can contribute to a higher-level social identity (Sherif et al., 1961). Psychological studies demonstrate that engaging in cooperative activities among groups can enhance trust, friendship, positive relations, and a common identity (Aronson, Blaney, Sikes, & Snapp, 1978; Deutsch, 2006a, 2006b; Sherif et al., 1961). Some additional methods that may also facilitate Expanding the Us include empathy training, socialization for caring for people beyond one's own immediate group, and the teaching of nonviolent conflict resolution strategies (Deutsch, 2006a, 2006b; Miklikowska & Fry, 2010; Staub, 1996).

Returning to the EU, a new higher level European identity is gradually emerging, not to replace national identities, but rather as an additional level of social identity (Hill, 2010). Signs of the emerging European identity include the issuance of EU passports, the Euro as a common currency (now adopted by most member countries), EU car license plates, the opening of borders to the free movement of people, democratic elections for EU Parliamentarians, an EU flag, and so forth (Fry, 2009; Reid, 2004; Wilson, 2000;). In short, the continuing trend is toward the development of a new pan-European identity that parallels how the Western Dessert Aborigines, the Upper Xingu peoples, and the Iroquois developed an additional social identity as members of an overarching peaceful social system.

Conclusion

With by far the largest military on the planet, some US politicians still seem to think that safety and security can be achieved through the barrel of a gun. But such thinking does not take into consideration the current realities of global interdependence. Competitive military-based strategies are no longer effective in an interdependent world facing common challenges such as the urgent need to halt global warming (Fry, 2006, 2007). No nation on its own can successfully deal with the threat of climate change; international cooperation is mandatory in this "sink or swim together" world.

International cooperation is possible. One example that proves this point is the successful protection of the Earth's ozone layer. In the late 1980s, the countries of the world negotiated and implemented the Montreal Protocol on Substances that Deplete the Ozone Layer and subsequently have worked together to phase out ozone destructive chemicals such as CFCs worldwide (Ostrow, 1990; United Nations Environmental Program, 2000). Since the elimination of global CFCs and other ozone-depleting substances, the Earth's protective ozone layer has been mending. Through multilateral international cooperation among virtually all countries on the planet, "the world quickly, indeed almost painlessly, headed off a major man-made threat" (Sachs, 2008, p. 113). International cooperation, even at the global level, is possible. In a similar fashion, the peoples and nations of this interdependent planet now need to effectively address climate change and other common threats to human survival. . . .

The fact that people in different places and times have created and maintained nonwarring peace systems proves that alternatives to the current-day war system are possible. Ethnographic examples of peace systems including the EU can stimulate our imagination and provide insight for how to create a global peace system. There are several take-home messages in this chapter. First, creating an overarching level of governance can contribute substantially to peace within the constituent social units. This principle is well-established (e.g., Dennis, 1993; Ferguson, 1984; Fry, 2006, 2007; Nadel, 1947; Smith, 2011). Second, there must be the vision followed by concrete steps to transform the inspiration into a new reality. Third, understanding that interdependence exists (and can be augmented further) is critically important. Interdependence can provide the rationale for why cooperation and new supranational institutions of governance are necessary to address common threats such as global warming and climate change. Safety and security in an interdependent world require joint action among all the parties. This principle of interdependence clearly applied in the creation of the EU and continues to maintain other peace systems as well (Fry, 2009, 2012; Fry, Bonta, & Baszarkiewicz, 2009). The concerted cooperative effort to save the Earth's common ozone layer via the Montreal Protocol also illustrates that an understanding of interdependence can lead to cooperation (Fry, 2006; Rubin, Pruitt, & Kim, 1994; Sherif et al., 1961). The success of the Montreal Protocol shows that the nations of the world are capable of working effectively together when they realize that their fates are interlinked and that it is in their common interests to cooperate. Finally, as we think about our social identities, we must Expand the Us to include a common identity of humanity as a whole. The Iroquois turned enemies into kin, created unifying rituals and ceremonies, and created myths and symbolism to reinforce the values of peace. They Expanded the Us. The EU seems headed in the same direction within Europe. It may take some time but adding one more level of social identity to include all human beings on a shared planet is both possible and necessary for the long term safety, security, and survival of the species as a whole.

Human survival requires that nation-states give up the institution of war and replace it with a cooperatively-functioning global peace system— for the well-being and security of all people everywhere. Constructing a peace system for the entire planet involves many synergistic elements, including the transformative vision that a new peace-based global system is possible, the creation of new effective political institutions at a supranational level, the understanding that interdependence and common challenges require cooperation, an expanded perception of social identity along the lines that Darwin (1998) envisioned, and finally, the development of values, symbolism, expressive culture, and ceremonies that reinforce peace (Fry, 2012). The Great Peace of the Iroquois illustrates how peace is an active process that must be created and re-created. Could a global peace system really be created? I suspect that the Xinganos, Iroquois, and founders of the EU would say "yes" for they have already created their own peace systems. German philosopher Arthur Schopenhauer (1788–1860) is credited with saying: "All truth passes through three stages. First, it is ridiculed. Second, it is violently opposed. Third, it is accepted as being self-evident."

REFERENCES

Aronson, E., Blaney, N., Stephan, C., Sikes, J., & Snapp, M. (1978). *The jigsaw classroom.* Beverly Hills: Sage.

Barroso, J.M. (2006). *Jean Monnet.* Time.com. Retrieved from http://content.time.com/time/magazine/article/0,9171,1552584,00.html. Accessed June 4, 2017.

Bertens, J.-W. (1994). The European movement: Dreams and realities. Paper presented at the seminar *The EC after 1992: The United States of Europe?* Maastricht, The Netherlands, January.

Darwin, C. (1998). *The descent of man.* New York: Prometheus Books. (Originally published in 1871).

Dennis, Matthew (1993). *Cultivating a landscape of peace.* Ithaca: Cornell University Press.

Deutsch, M. (2006a). Cooperation and competition. In M. Deutsch, P. Coleman, & E. Marcus (Eds.), *The handbook book of conflict resolution* (pp. 23–42). San Francisco: Jossey-Bass.

Deutsch, M. (2006b). Justice and conflict. In M. Deutsch, P. Coleman, & E. Marcus (Eds.), *The handbook of conflict resolution* (pp. 43–68). San Francisco: Jossey-Bass.

Deutsch, M., & Coleman, P. (2012). Psychological components of sustainable peace: An introduction. In M. Deutsch & P. Coleman (Eds.), *The psychological components of sustainable peace* (pp. 1–14). New York: Springer.

Elliott, M (2005). The decline and fall of Rome. *Time,* European Edition. 165 (24) 20–21.

Ferguson, R. Brian (1984). Introduction: Studying war. In R. B. Ferguson (Ed.), *Warfare, culture, and environment* (pp. 1–81). Orlando: Academic Press.

Fry, D. P. (2006). *The human potential for peace: An anthropological challenge to assumptions about war and violence.* New York: Oxford University Press.

Fry, D. P. (2007). *Beyond war: The human potential for peace.* New York: Oxford University Press.

Fry, D. P. (2009). Anthropological insights for creating non-warring social systems. *Journal of aggression, conflict and peace research, 1*(2), 4–15.

Fry, D. P. (2012). Life without war. *Science, 336,* 879–884.

Fry, D. P., Bonta, B. D., & Baszarkiewicz, K. (2009). Learning from extant cultures of peace. In J. De Rivera (Ed.), *Handbook on building cultures of peace* (pp. 11–26). New York: Springer.

Gregor, T. (1990). Uneasy peace: Intertribal relations in Brazil's Upper Xingu. In J. Haas (Ed.), *The Anthropology of War* (pp. 105–124). Cambridge: Cambridge University Press.

Gregor, T. & Robarchek, C. A. (1996). Two paths to peace: Semai and Mehinaku on violence. In T. Gregor (Ed.), *A natural history of peace* (pp. 159–188). Nashville: Vanderbilt University Press.

Hand, J. (2010). To abolish war. *Journal of Aggression, Conflict, and Peace Research,* 2, 44–56.

Hill, S. (2010). *Europe's promise: Why the European way is the best hope in an insecure age.* Berkeley: University of California Press.

Miklikowska, M. & Fry, D. P. (2010). Values for peace. *Beliefs and Values,* 2, 124–137.

Nadel, S. F. (1947). *The Nuba.* London: Oxford University Press.

Ostrow, M. (1990). *Race to save the planet: Now or never* (episode 10). Annenberg, PBS series.

Reid, T. R. (2004). *The United States of Europe: The new superpower and the end of American supremacy.* New York: Penguin.

Rubin, J., Pruitt, D., & Kim, S. (1994). *Social conflict: Escalation, stalemate, and settlement.* New York: McGraw-Hill.

Sachs, J. (2008). *Common wealth: Economics for a crowded planet.* New York: Penguin Press.

Sherif, M., Harvey, O., White, B., Hood, W., & Sherif, C. (1961). *Intergroup conflict and cooperation: The Robbers Cave experiment.* Norman: University of Oklahoma Press.

Smith, Donald C. (2011). *Jean Monnet: The father of Europe* [documentary film]. Retrieved from http://www.law.du.edu/index.php/jean-monnet-father-of-europe/documentary. Accessed August 28, 2011.

Staab, A. (2008). *The European Union explained: Institutions, actors, global impact.* Bloomington: Indiana University Press.

Staub, E. (1996). The psychological and cultural roots of group violence and creation of caring societies and peaceful group relations. In T. Gregor (Ed.), *A natural history of peace* (pp. 29–155). Nashville: Vanderbilt University Press.

United Nations Environmental Program (2000). *The Montreal Protocol on Substances that Deplete the Ozone Layer.* Retrieved from http://www.unep.org/ozone/pdfs/montreal-protocol2000.pdf.

Wilson, T (2000). Building, imagining, and experiencing Europe: Institutions and identities in the European Union. In I. Bellier & T. Wilson (Eds.), *An anthropology of the European Union* (pp. 1–27). Oxford: Berg.

Selections from *A Global Security System: An Alternative to War*

BY KENT SHIFFERD, PATRICK HILLER, AND DAVID SWANSON

Kent Shifferd, Patrick Hiller, and David Swanson are researchers and writers associated with World Beyond War, a movement aimed at building an international campaign of education, lobbying, and nonviolent direct action to end war. Another selection from David Swanson appears in part 2. Selections from *A Global Security System: An Alternative to War,* 64-71. Charlottesville VA: World Beyond War, 2015. Used by permission.

Accelerating the Transition to a Global Alternative Security System

World Beyond War intends to accelerate the movement toward ending war and establishing a peace system in two ways: massive education, and nonviolent action to dismantle the war machine.

If we want war to end, we are going to have to work to end it. Even if you think war is lessening—by no means an uncontroversial claim—it won't continue doing so without work. And as long as there is any war, there is a significant danger of widespread war. Wars are notoriously hard to control once begun. With nuclear weapons in the world (and with nuclear plants as potential targets), any war-making carries a risk of apocalypse. War-making and war preparations are destroying our natural environment and diverting resources from a possible rescue effort that would preserve a habitable climate. As a matter of survival, war and preparations for war must be completely abolished, and abolished quickly, by replacing the war system with a peace system.

To accomplish this, we will need a peace movement that differs from past movements that have been against each successive war or against each offensive weapon. We cannot fail to oppose wars, but we must also oppose the entire institution and work toward replacing it.

World Beyond War intends to work globally. While begun in the United States, World Beyond War has worked to include individuals and organizations from around the globe in its decision making. Thousands of people in 90 countries have thus far signed the pledge on the WorldBeyondWar.org website to work for the elimination of all war.

War does not have a single source, but it does have a largest one. Ending war-making by the United States and its allies would go a very long way toward ending war globally. For those living in the United States, at least, one key place to start ending war is within the U.S. government. This can be worked on together with people affected by US wars and those living near U.S. military bases around the world, which is a fairly large percentage of the people on earth.

Ending U.S. militarism wouldn't eliminate war globally, but it would eliminate the pressure that is driving several other nations to increase their military spending. It would deprive NATO of its leading advocate for and greatest participant in wars. It would cut off the largest supply of weapons to Western Asia (a.k.a. the Middle East) and other regions. It would remove the major barrier to reconciliation and reunification of Korea. It would

create U.S. willingness to support arms treaties, join the International Criminal Court, and allow the United Nations to move in the direction of its stated purpose of eliminating war. It would create a world free of nations threatening first-use of nukes, and a world in which nuclear disarmament might proceed more rapidly. Gone would be the last major nation using cluster bombs or refusing to ban landmines. If the United States kicked the war habit, war itself would suffer a major and possibly fatal set-back.

A focus on U.S. war preparations cannot work as well without similar efforts everywhere. Numerous nations are investing, and even increasing their investments, in war. All militarism must be opposed. And victories for a peace system tend to spread by example. When the British Parliament opposed attacking Syria in 2013 it helped block that U.S. proposal. When 31 nations committed in Havana, Cuba, in January 2014 to never making use of war, those voices were heard in other nations of the world.

Global solidarity in educational efforts constitutes an important part of the education itself. Student and cultural exchanges between the West and nations on the Pentagon's likely target list (Syria, Iran, North Korea, China, Russia, etc.) will go a long way toward building resistance toward those potential future wars. Similar exchanges between nations investing in war and nations that have ceased to do so, or which do so at a greatly reduced scale, can be of great value as well.

Building a global movement for stronger and more democratic global structures of peace will also require educational efforts that do not stop at national borders.

Educating the Many and the Decision and Opinion Makers

Using a bi-level approach and working with other citizen based organizations, World Beyond War will launch a world-wide campaign to educate the masses of people that war is a failed social institution that can be abolished to the great benefit of all. Books, print media articles, speaker's bureaus, radio and television appearances, electronic media, conferences, etc., will be employed to spread the word about the myths and institutions that perpetuate war. The aim is to create a planetary consciousness and a demand for a just peace without undermining in any way the benefits of unique cultures and political systems.

World Beyond War has begun and will continue to support and promote good work in this direction by other organizations, including many organizations that have signed the pledge at WorldBeyondWar.org. Already distant connections have been made among organizations in various parts of the world that have proved mutually beneficial. World Beyond War will combine its own initiatives with this sort of assistance for others' in an effort to create greater cooperation and greater coherence around the idea of a movement to end all war. The result of educational efforts favored by World Beyond War will be a world in which talk of a "good war" will sound no more possible than a "benevolent rape" or "philanthropic slavery" or "virtuous child abuse."

World Beyond War seeks to create a moral movement against an institution that should be viewed as tantamount to mass-murder, even when that mass-murder is accompanied by flags or music or assertions of authority and promotion of irrational fear. World Beyond War advocates against the practice of opposing a particular war on the grounds that it isn't being run well or isn't as proper as some other war. World Beyond War seeks to strengthen its moral argument by taking the focus of peace activism partially away from the harm wars do to the aggressors, in order to fully acknowledge and appreciate the suffering of all.

In the film *The Ultimate Wish: Ending the Nuclear Age* [italics added] we see a survivor of Nagasaki meeting a survivor of Auschwitz. It is hard in watching them meeting and speaking together to remember or care which nation committed which horror. A peace culture will see all war with that same clarity. War is an abomination not because of who commits it but because of what it is.

World Beyond War intends to make war abolition the sort of cause that slavery abolition was and to hold up resisters, conscientious objectors, peace advocates, diplomats, whistleblowers, journalists, and activists as our heroes—in fact, to develop alternative avenues for heroism and glory, including nonviolent activism, and including serving as peace workers and human shields in places of conflict.

World Beyond War [WBW] will not promote the idea that "peace is patriotic," but rather that thinking in terms of world citizenship is helpful in the cause of peace. WBW will work to remove nationalism, xenophobia, racism, religious bigotry, and exceptionalism from popular thinking.

Central projects in World Beyond War's early efforts will be the provision of useful information through the WorldBeyondWar.org website, and the collection of a large number of individual and organizational signatures on the pledge posted there. The website is constantly being updated with maps, charts, graphics, arguments, talking points, and videos to help people make the case, to themselves and others, that wars can/should/must be abolished.…

World Beyond War is collecting signatures on this statement on paper at events and adding them to the website, as well as inviting people to add their names online. If a large number of those who would be willing to sign this statement can be reached and asked to do so, that fact will potentially be persuasive news to others. The same goes for the inclusion of signatures by well-known figures. The collection of signatures is a tool for advocacy in another way as well; those signers who choose to join a World Beyond War email list can later be contacted to help advance a project initiated in their part of the world.

Expanding the reach of the Pledge Statement, signers are asked to make use of WBW tools to contact others, share information online, write letters to editors, lobby governments and other bodies, and organize small gatherings. Resources to facilitate all kinds of outreach are provided at WorldBeyondWar.org.

Beyond its central projects, WBW will be participating in and promoting useful projects begun by other groups and testing out new specific initiatives of its own.

One area that WBW hopes to work on is the creation of truth and reconciliation commissions, and greater appreciation of their work. Lobbying for the establishment of an International Truth and Reconciliation Commission or Court is a possible area of focus as well.

Other areas in which World Beyond War may put some effort, beyond its central project of advancing the idea of ending all war, include: disarmament; conversion to peaceful industries; asking new nations to join and current Parties to abide by the Kellogg-Briand Pact; lobbying for reforms of the United Nations; lobbying governments and other bodies for various initiatives, including a Global Marshall Plan or parts thereof; and countering recruitment efforts while strengthening the rights of conscientious objectors.

Nonviolent Direct Action Campaigns

World Beyond War believes that little is more important than advancing common understanding of nonviolence as an alternative form of conflict to violence, and ending the habit of thinking that one can ever be faced with only the choices of engaging in violence or doing nothing.

In addition to its education campaign, World Beyond War will work with other organizations to launch nonviolent, Gandhian-style protests and nonviolent direct action campaigns against the war machine in order to disrupt it and to demonstrate the strength of the popular desire to end war. The goal of this campaign will be to compel the political decision makers and those who make money from the killing machine to come to the table for talks on ending war and replacing it with a more effective alternative security system.

This nonviolent effort will benefit from the education campaign, but will also in its turn serve an educational purpose. Huge public campaigns/movements have a way of bringing people's attention to questions they have not been focused on.

Partial steps toward replacing the war system will be pursued, but they will be understood as and discussed as just that: partial steps on the way toward creating a peace system. Such steps may include banning weaponized drones or closing particular bases or eliminating nuclear weapons or closing the School of the Americas, defunding military advertising campaigns, restoring war powers to the legislative branch, cutting off weapons sales to dictatorships, etc.

Finding the strength in numbers to do these things is part of the purpose of the collection of signatures on the simple Pledge Statement. World Beyond War hopes to facilitate the forming of a broader coalition suited to the task. This will mean bringing together all those sectors that rightfully ought to be opposing the military industrial complex: moralists, ethicists, preachers of morality and ethics, religious community, doctors, psychologists, and protectors of human health, economists, labor unions, workers, civil libertarians, advocates for democratic reforms, journalists, historians, promoters of transparency in public decision-making, internationalists, those hoping to travel and be liked abroad, environmentalists, and proponents of everything worthwhile on which war dollars could be spent instead: education, housing, arts, science, etc. That's a pretty big group.

Many activist organizations want to stay focused in their niches. Many are reluctant to risk being called unpatriotic. Some are tied up in profits from military contracts. World Beyond War will work around these barriers. This will involve asking civil libertarians to view war as the root cause of the symptoms they treat, and asking environmentalists to view war as at least one of the major root problems—and its elimination as a possible solution.

Green energy has far greater potential to handle our energy needs (and wants) than is commonly supposed, because the massive transfer of money that would be possible with the abolition of war isn't usually considered. Human needs across the board can be better met than we usually imagine, because we don't usually consider withdrawing $2 trillion a year globally from the world's deadliest criminal enterprise.

Toward these ends, WBW will be working to organize a bigger coalition ready and trained to engage in nonviolent direct action, creatively, generously, and fearlessly.

Conclusion

War is always a choice and it is always a bad choice. It is a choice that always leads to more war. It is not mandated in our genes or our human nature. It is not the only possible response to conflicts. Nonviolent action and resistance is a better choice because it defuses and helps resolve conflict. But the choice for nonviolence must not wait until conflict erupts. It must be built into society: built into institutions for conflict forecasting, mediation, adjudication, and peacekeeping. It must be built into education in the form of knowledge, perceptions, beliefs and values—in short, a culture of peace. Societies consciously prepare far in advance for the war response and so perpetuate insecurity.

Some powerful groups benefit from war and violence. The vast majority of humans, however, will gain a lot from a world without war. The movement will work on strategies for outreach to a wide variety of constituencies globally.

Such constituencies might include people in many parts of the world, key organizers, well-known leaders, peace groups, peace and justice groups, environmental groups, human rights groups, activist coalitions, lawyers, philosophers/moralists/ethicists, doctors, psychologists, religious groups, economists, labor unions, diplomats, towns and cities and states or provinces or regions, nations, international organizations, the United Nations, civil liberties groups, media reform groups, business groups and leaders, billionaires, teachers groups, student groups, education reform groups, government reform groups, journalists, historians, women's groups, senior citizens, immigrant and refugee rights groups, libertarians, socialists, liberals, Democrats, Republicans, conservatives, veterans, student- and cultural-exchange groups, sister-cities groups, sports enthusiasts, and advocates for investment in children and health care and in human needs of every sort, as well as those working to oppose contributors to militarism in their societies, such as xenophobia, racism, machismo, extreme materialism, all forms of violence, lack of community, and war profiteering.

For peace to prevail, we must prepare equally far in advance for the better choice. If you want peace, prepare for peace.

Forget that this task of planet-saving is not possible in the time required. Don't be put off by people who know what is not possible. Do what needs to be done, and check to see if it was impossible only after you are done.

Paul Hawken (Environmentalist, Author)

Be inspired:

- In less than two years, thousands of people from 135 countries have signed World Beyond War's pledge for peace.
- Demilitarization is underway. Costa Rica and more than 20 other countries have disbanded their militaries altogether.
- European nations, which had fought each other for over a thousand years, including the horrendous world wars of the twentieth century, now work collaboratively in the European union.
- Former advocates of nuclear weapons, including former U.S. senators and secretaries of state and numerous retired, high-ranking military officers, have publicly rejected nuclear weapons and called for their abolition.
- There is a massive, worldwide movement to end the carbon economy and hence the wars over oil.
- Many thoughtful people and organizations around the world are calling for an end to the counter-productive "war on terror."
- At least one million organizations in the world are actively working toward peace, social justice, and environmental protection.
- Thirty-one Latin American and Caribbean nations created a zone of peace on January 29, 2014.
- In the last 100 years, we humans have created for the first time in history institutions and movements to control international violence: the UN, the World Court, the International Criminal Court; and treaties such as the Kellogg-Briand Pact, the Treaty to Ban Landmines, the Treaty to Ban Child Soldiers, and many others.
- A peace revolution is already underway.

Noosphere and Noopolitik: Our Transcendental Destination

BY JOHN ARQUILLA

John Arquilla, a former analyst for the RAND Corporation, is now a professor of defense analysis at the Naval Postgraduate School. Arquilla's research explores the power of networked military organizations and the effectiveness of cyber-attacks in reducing potentially violent conflicts. From *Building Peace: A Forum for Peace & Security in the 21st Century,* September 2014. Used by permission.

In 1922, not long after the end of the "war to end all wars" and at the beginning of what has since proved one of the bloodiest centuries in recorded history, the French scientist and theologian Pierre Teilhard de Chardin envisioned everyone's being able to communicate with everyone, swiftly and efficiently. This vision was not the Internet but what he called a global "realm of the mind." It would, he maintained, provide a profound impetus to peace. Contrary to Thomas Hobbes's notion of a world driven by "the war of all against all," Teilhard's notion was of a global consciousness. What he termed the *noosphere*—a neologism whose root is the Greek *noos*, meaning mind—was, in his view, the next step in the evolution of mankind toward an ethical paradigm more concerned with pursuing what is right than with the power politics of might.

Sadly, two global wars and countless insurgencies have been waged since then. Social revolutions and modern networked terrorism have become commonplace. Nation-states have proliferated, many of them—like South Sudan—born failing. It is ironic that the United Nations, which has seen its membership grow nearly four-fold since its founding in 1945, has been able to do so little to contain or reverse the course of conflict and suffering, especially in those places where the innocent and helpless are the most preyed upon.

Cause for concern is no less when it comes to the fundamental peace paradigm of our time— that the spread of democracy will contribute to global amity. This concept was in fact first articulated by Immanuel Kant in his 1795 essay "Perpetual Peace." The past decade of American-led efforts to pursue a Kantian democracy agenda by force of arms, however, has for the most part simply brought fresh miseries—to Iraq, Afghanistan, Libya, and beyond. Perhaps the problem is not with democratization per se, but that US foreign policy has become far too militarized—a byproduct of the realpolitik-oriented belief that the dissolution of the Soviet Union left America alone in a position of global leadership. The costly, mixed military results of Washington's wars since 9/11 may thus reflect an over-reliance on force—and its corollary, continuing policy blindness toward the great opportunity to test Teilhard's intriguing hypothesis about connectivity and amity.

It is now fifteen years since David Ronfeldt and I advanced the argument that the Internet and World Wide Web were not only realizing Teilhard's dream of a *noosphere*, but that their rise heralded the emergence of *noopolitik*, a mode of statecraft driven by the attractiveness of ethical values that form the core of our common humanity. This is something much more than soft power, which is all about persuasiveness, and which can be used for good or ill. *Noopolitik* is about acknowledging what is right and just, as a basis for negotiated settlements to conflict, peaceful interactions, and the protection of human dignity.

Unfortunately, this idea remains "on the shelf," not only in the United States, but also in most halls of power in all too many nation-states. The sword is not yet sheathed. Some glimmerings of *noopolitik* can be seen in nineteenth-century antislavery movements as well as in early civil society efforts to curb colonial abuses of indigenous peoples. The telegraph, what Tom Standage has called the Victorian Internet, helped these movements back then. Today, the global consciousness that technology has wrought has the opportunity to go even further, creating a global conscience as well. That this has not yet happened is testament to the persistent pull of realpolitik. This is sadly so, given the poor results—at massive material and human cost—of power politics in our time.

Clearly, Teilhard's moment has come. The *noosphere* is here. *Noopolitik* looms, if we but see it, and humankind's transcendental destination is within reach. In today's world, we are constantly reminded of the darker aspects of increased connectivity: more intrusive intelligence gathering, aggressive cyberwarfare, and cyberterrorism. What we don't think about enough is the role that "cyber" can play in fostering peace by forging global interconnections—this was Teilhard's dream. What if we, too, could imagine the Internet serving as a vehicle for cooperation, the sharing of hopeful stories; the communications link between moderate citizens creating positive social change; and as a voice for democratic action? Many peacebuilding organizations are already doing this; for example, Soliya's online platform for improving understanding between American and Middle Eastern students. If movements of this sort can thrive and multiply, then perhaps Teilhard's vision of a peaceful *noosphere* will be realized.

DISCUSSION QUESTIONS

1. Explain which one of "The Price of Peace's" eleven strategies you believe would best increase levels of peace across the world.

2. Describe the major obstacles thwarting efforts to shift portions of military expenditures toward implementation of strategies like those that "The Price of Peace" advocates.

3. Assess how well the already increasing economic, political, and social interdependence among nations might by itself produce Douglas P. Fry's other goals of transforming ethnocentric cultural beliefs and broadening people's sense of personal identity.

4. Review how much of your own social identity presently does, or does not, exemplify what Douglas P. Fry describes as a state of "Expanding the Us."

5. Evaluate how well World Beyond War's campaign does, or does not, illustrate Fry's call for the development of an alternative vision of peace and security.

6. Use your own knowledge and the best evidence that John Arquilla provides to support the claim that something like a noosphere is, or is not, now emerging.

7. Draw on the various ideas presented in these four selections to create your own vision for a more peaceful future.

Debates about Personal Peace, Prefigurative Politics, and Pedagogy

The first section in part 5 introduced the debate between promoters of pragmatic and of principled nonviolence, roughly a debate between those who view nonviolence as a political tactic and those who view it as a moral way of life. The current section broadens this debate by presenting contending views on whether individuals should first aim to transform themselves before attempting to transform the world.

In the first selection, clinical psychologist Christina Michaelson offers wholehearted support for the belief that people should first develop inner peace before trying to bring peace to others. Michaelson describes some practices that can help develop personal peace, then argues that people who possess inner peace can best "give peace" because they have peace to give.

In a second selection, Cynthia Boas argues that many people are misled by a fundamental ambiguity associated with the term "nonviolence." Practices called pragmatic or strategic nonviolence are then thought not to count as real nonviolence at all. Boas argues that this is a mistake and that a "commitment to a spiritual philosophy" is not the best grounds on which to build practical, political, nonviolent movements. Boas maintains that most nonviolent movements have been rooted in diverse secular and spiritual beliefs. Changing hearts and transforming individuals may be a worthwhile ultimate goal, Boas says, but it is not commonly the best place to start.

Mark Engler and Paul Engler offer yet another view on the debate about inner and outer peace work in the third selection. Engler and Engler contrast strategic and prefigurative politics. *Strategic politics* are associated with the pragmatic and strategic nonviolence positions discussed in part 5, a perspective like that which Boas in the second section also supports. Strategic politics engage with and sometimes directly fight against the economic, political, and social system as it is. *Prefigurative politics*, on the other hand, aim to nourish new economic, political, and social systems. Those who adopt a prefigurative politics may not transform their individual selves quite as much as Michaelson calls for in her selection, but adopters of prefigurative politics do change themselves by working closely with others in like-minded groups and organizations. Similarly to those who adopt nonviolence as a way of life, adopters of prefigurative politics thus aim "to be the change they wish to see." Engler and Engler argue for approaches that balance the strengths of strategic and prefigurative politics in effective projects for social change.

In a final, fourth selection, Tony Jenkins proposes it is a mistake to think of inner and outer peace as working in separate spheres. Jenkins describes an approach that builds "a bridge between the false divides of the inner and the outer, the principled and the strategic, and helps the peacebuilder to see, imagine and construct the whole." The usual distinctions between private individuals and social structures are obstacles that need to be overcome, Jenkins argues. He also rejects the belief that knowledge of how to build peace can be divided among separate academic fields. Building a culture of peace instead requires a radical reorientation of how people understand both the individual self and society and also how they conceive of the very nature of knowledge itself. Jenkins maintains that merely shifting the emphasis from the inner to the outer, or vice versa, will not transform the current culture and structures of violence.

Cultivating Inner Peace

BY CHRISTINA MICHAELSON

Christina Michaelson is a clinical psychologist who teaches psychology at Le Moyne College. From Rachel MacNair (ed.), *Working for Peace: A Handbook of Practical Psychology and Other Tools*, pp. 16–23. Atascadero, CA: Impact Publishers, 2006. Used by permission.

Peace. It does not mean to be in a place where there is no noise, trouble, or hard work. It means to be in the midst of those things and still be calm in your heart.

—Unknown

Peace activists invest tremendous amounts of time, talent, energy, and resources into changing the world. You work for peace between individuals, among groups, and between nations, but are you at peace? Do you experience inner peace? Within each of us are the seeds of peace, love, and compassion and also the seeds of violence, anger, and hate. We can choose which seeds we will nurture and cultivate. When we choose to cultivate peace within ourselves, we can transform ourselves and the world.

While your focus on peace work is on change in the external world, you probably spend much less time on developing peace in your inner world—such as practicing methods to create peacefulness in your thoughts and emotions. Perhaps that's because you feel that inner peace isn't really important to your peace work or that you don't have time to devote to developing inner peace. Yet inner peace is a vitally important component in peacemaking because you cannot give what you do not have. If you're to bring peace to others, then you first must manifest peace in your own life.[1] Your peace work in the World should begin with cultivating an inner state of peacefulness, and then you truly can offer peace to others. Mahatma Gandhi said, "Be the change you want to see in the world." If you want to see peace in the world, then you must "be" peace in the world.

What Is Inner Peace?

Inner peace is a subjective experience for each person. The experiences of peace change over time and circumstances and therefore can be described in many different ways. In general, inner peace is a calm and tranquil state of mind. Author Don Miguel Ruiz offered the following description, "The voice in your head is like a wild horse taking you wherever it wants to go. . . . When the voice in your head finally stops talking, you experience inner peace."[2]

Inner peace is transformational. It can make deep changes in you and in how you relate to the world. The path to inner peace is to quiet and focus your thoughts and patterns of thinking. This, in turn, can have profound effects on other areas of your functioning. Your thoughts, emotions, physical functioning, and behavior are interrelated, and changes in one area affect the other areas in continuous feedback.[3] Therefore, as you induce inner peace and calm your thoughts, you also will feel more tranquil emotionally and physically, and your behavior can become more peaceful.

Why Should You Care about Inner Peace?
Inner peace can help you to be more effective in your work.
One day, when my son was 12 years old, he told me that he didn't want to go to another protest against the war in Iraq. When I asked him why, he responded, "Because the protestors are too angry about what they're fighting for. They're angry for peace—it's ironic."

It's very easy to get angry about the causes for peacemaking or to feel depressed, frustrated, or afraid. However, these feelings, if left unchecked, can interfere with accomplishing your goals. Your anger can distract others from hearing your message. Instead, they just remember the anger. For example, the public may remember the arrests for disorderly conduct at a human rights demonstration, while the real issues of concern get lost in the media coverage of the arrests.

Feeling depressed and hopeless about the hard work of peacemaking can make you less motivated to work for peace and can even leave you immobilized. Strong, unregulated emotions can impair your ability to express yourself clearly and appropriately and to think and respond "on your feet" in difficult circumstances. Yelling at legislators surely lets them know that you feel deeply about the issues, but it usually is not effective for engaging them in a dialog.

Inner peace can help. Practicing inner peace can help you manage strong emotions, and thus you can more effectively keep your message of peace

clear and strong, without feeling overwhelmed by negative emotions.

I used to work as a psychotherapist with adults who were sexually abused as children, and I often became very angry listening to my clients' stories of victimization. However, my outrage was not helpful to them. Instead, it distracted me from my purpose of being truly present for my clients and focused on their recoveries from their pasts. I needed to find a way to manage my strong negative feelings, and practicing strategies to induce inner peace was a very effective way of accomplishing this. Outside of therapy sessions, as I focused on clearing and calming my thoughts, my emotions also quieted. No longer distracted by intense thoughts and emotions, I was able to develop new insights and understanding. Inner peace truly allowed me to become more useful to my clients.

Perhaps the most important reason to cultivate inner peace in your peace work is that you model peacemaking to others. By inducing inner peace, you can interact with others in a more peaceful manner. In turn, this can improve your relationships, enhance the outcome of your interactions, and model peacefulness to others. By your personal example, you demonstrate that while you remain strongly focused on the purpose of your peacemaking, you can effect change peacefully.
Inner peace can keep you healthier.
Peace work can be stressful, and stress can make you sick. There's a large body of research that shows a link between stress and many diseases, including everyday illnesses such as colds and headaches and more serious health problems such as heart disease and diabetes.[4] For health reasons, it's wise to engage in stress management techniques. Practicing inner peace can be an important method in your efforts to care for your health. Inner peace calms your mind, body, and emotions, and this can help you recover from the effects of stress.

With continued practice, as you change your patterns of thinking you may respond to stressors in a different way. Thus, inner peace even can help you prevent stress responses from occurring. In practicing inner peace, you are increasing your potential for good health.

How Do You Cultivate Inner Peace?

There are many paths to inner peace. You can try any or all of the methods I describe and add some of your own. I recommend practicing and developing a repertoire of inner peace practices so that you have a choice of coping strategies ready whenever needed.

Meditation.

Throughout history, people in cultures around the world have used meditation to experience inner peace. Meditation practices are numerous, but all have in common calming the mind while remaining alert and training the mind in focused attention. Most meditative techniques also include focusing mental attention on breathing, and this contributes to both training the mind and calming the body. In addition to being a method for inducing inner peace, meditation has positive effects on many areas of psychological and physical functioning, including memory, anxiety, stress management, happiness, and heart disease.[5] Meditation also was found to increase activity in parts of the brain that create positive emotions and to improve the functioning of the immune system.[6] This supports the use of meditation to help keep you happy and healthy and to manage the effects of stress.

If you're interested in meditating, I recommend taking a class in your community or self-study with books and Internet resources. Here, I briefly outline several types of meditation:

- *One-pointed awareness meditation.* This meditation trains your mind by having you focus on the inhalation and exhalation of each breath and away from all other distracting thoughts. As the mind wanders, you gently guide it back to the point of awareness, which is the focus on the breath. Alternatively, instead of focusing on the breath, you can focus your attention on a mantra, which is a word or sound repeated silently or aloud, or on your mind's image of a word or object.
- *Mindfulness meditation.* This type of meditation involves becoming an observer of your thoughts and emotions. In a nonjudgmental manner, you watch your thoughts and emotions as they rise and fall—like watching the water in a river flow by. This helps you develop an awareness of your experiences in the present moment. With practice, mindful awareness can be extended out of meditation time and into all experiences in your life. Mindfulness then becomes a way of being more present and aware in the world.
- *Guided meditation.* This meditation begins with inducing calmness through deep breathing and a focus on the breath. Then you are directed through relaxation exercises or to think about a beautiful place in nature, such as the woods or another relaxing location, to deepen your sense of tranquility. Guided meditations are available on tapes, on CDs, on the Internet, and written out in meditation books.
- *Reflective meditation.* After inducing calmness, reflective meditations allow you to focus on a question or concern. When distractions in thinking occur, you keep guiding your thoughts back to the question. When distracting thoughts and emotions are minimized, you can more easily develop insights and new ways of thinking about your areas of concern. With reflective meditation, you can directly address issues of peace by contemplating questions related to your peace work, such as, "How can I be more effective in expressing my views?" "How can I mobilize others to speak out for this cause?" or "How can I better understand the other person's perspective?"
- *Lovingkindness meditation.* This is a traditional Buddhist meditation for increasing peace. Lovingkindness is a state of mind of deep compassion for yourself and all others. This meditation begins with inducing mental and physical calming through focused attention on the breath. Next, you generate loving acceptance of yourself and wishes for your happiness and freedom from suffering. Then you systematically apply these principles to all others—beginning with those you love, then those you feel neutral about or have never met, on to those with whom you have conflicts or who are your enemies—and finish with sending lovingkindness to all types of beings in the world.

Nature.

Spending quiet time in nature helps many people experience inner peace. You can climb a mountain, walk the beach, or just sit in your own backyard. You can find peace by appreciating the glory of nature, from the delicate beauty of a flower to the magnificence of the ocean. What's important is that you allow your mind to become quiet and calm so that you can transcend the stressors of your life.

Prayer.

For centuries, religious traditions have emphasized the importance of inner peace. It's regarded as a highly valued spiritual goal and as a way to connect with God and bring peace to others. If it's consistent with your religious and spiritual beliefs, then engaging in prayer is a method that can help you develop inner peace. Also, becoming part of the community at your house of worship can connect you with like-minded others and support you in your spiritual peace practices.

Inner Peace in Action

There are many practices for inducing inner peace, and what's most important is that you discover the ones that are helpful to you. Inner peace is its own reward, because it relieves stress and brings calmness and tranquility to your psychological, emotional, and physical functioning. It also allows you to make your behavior more peaceful and to model peacemaking to others.

Even just a few deep breaths can help you decrease stress and become clearer in your thinking. A prayer or short focus on the breath can be done quickly and quietly anywhere, without others even knowing. This can allow you to induce a more tranquil inner state so that you can choose to interact with others in a more peaceful manner.

It's relatively easy to be peaceful in pleasant circumstances, but what about experiencing and expressing peacefulness in the midst of the difficult challenges of peace work? The seeds of inner peace are within everyone, but to access this, you often need to become quiet and removed from the noise of the world. With practice, you can carry your inner peace into the world and even remain peaceful in the midst of stress and chaos.

A survey of peace workers found that the most rewarding as well as the most stressful aspects of peace work were the interactions with the community of fellow activists.[7] Your relationships with the peace workers in your organization can be a good place to practice inner peace and observe its effects.

Let's use the example that you are angry with another peace activist because you feel she's not doing her fair share of the work. Holding a grudge against her, you find yourself disagreeing with her at meetings and arguing with her. You recognize that you don't have a peaceful relationship with her. Because of that awareness, you now can choose to change that relationship. The first step is to become peaceful, to induce a state of inner peace by quieting and focusing your thoughts. This can allow you to access your inner compassion and understanding while thinking of your colleague, and your view of her can change. Now you see her struggles and realize that her strengths are not being utilized by your organization. She has difficulties interfacing with other community groups, while her stronger skills lie in making plans for others behind the scenes. You have shifted your thinking about this person, and now you also can change your behavior toward her. You no longer see her as shirking her responsibilities, and you no longer find yourself arguing with her. You may even be able to help your group assign work to her that more effectively uses her strengths. You have worked on developing inner peace and changing your mind, and this is very important peace work. When peace starts with peace workers and peace organizations, you more effectively can bring peace to the world. With inner peace, you can give peace because you have peace.

Some may think that if you become too peaceful and calm, you cannot be effective for peace. Thich Nhat Hanh, a Zen Buddhist monk from Vietnam, teaches that practicing peace is not a sign of weakness but, rather, an act of courage.[8] Inner peace doesn't produce apathy or passivity in your desire to change the world. Instead, inner peace allows you to work from a position of strength to express peace to others. From this strength, you cultivate the seeds of inner peace and then you can grow peace in the world.

REFERENCES

1. Leyden-Rubenstein, L. (2001). *Peace on earth begins with inner peace. Annals of the American Psychotherapy Association,* November/December, 24.
2. Ruiz, D. M. (2004). *The voice of knowledge: A practical guide to inner peace.* San Rafael, CA: Amber-Allen Publishing, Inc., p. 100.
3. Greenberger, D., & Padesky, C. A. (1995). *Mind over mood: Change how you feel by changing the way you think.* New York: The Guilford Press.
4. Sapolsky, R. M. (1994). *Why zebras don't get ulcers: A guide to stress, stress-related diseases, and coping.* New York: W. H. Freeman and Company.
5. Shapiro, S. L., & Walsh, R. (2003). An analysis of recent meditation research and suggestions for future directions. *The Humanistic Psychologist, 31,* 86–114.
6. Davidson, R. J., Kabat-Zinn, J., Schumacher, J., Rosenkranz, M., Muller, D., Santorelli, S. E, et al. (2003). Alterations in brain and immune function produced by mindfulness meditation. *Psychosomatic Medicine, 65,* 564–570.
7. Gomes, M. E. (1992). The rewards and stresses of social change: A qualitative study of peace activists. *Journal of Humanistic Psychology, 32,* 138–146.
8. Hanh, T. N. (2003). *Creating true peace.* New York: Free Press.

SUGGESTED READINGS

Borysenko, J. (2001). *Inner peace for busy people: 52 simple strategies for transforming your life.* Carlsbad, CA: Hay House, Inc.
Includes strategies for taking care of yourself, changing your relationship to time, managing your mind, developing compassion, and creating a purpose in your life.

Chopra, D. (2005). *Peace is the way.* New York: Harmony Books.
Insights into how violence has developed and been maintained in the world. Includes strategies for changing cultural belief systems and practices for being a peacemaker.

Kornfield, J. (2004). *Meditation for beginners.* Boulder, CO: Sounds True, Inc.
Provides excellent descriptions of different types of meditation. Includes a CD of guided meditations.

Weiss, B. L. (2003). *Eliminating stress, finding inner peace.* Carlsbad, CA: Hay House, Inc.
Good information about the relationship between stress and disease. Includes a CD of guided meditations.

Must We Change Our Hearts before Throwing off Our Chains?

BY CYNTHIA BOAZ

Cynthia Boaz teaches political science at Sonoma State University. Boaz is also a contributing writer and adviser to Truthout.org and associate editor of *Peace and Change Journal.* From *Waging Nonviolence,* July 9, 2012. Used by permission.

In an article called "How to Sustain a Revolution" that appeared on *Truthout* several months ago, Stephanie Van Hook made an eloquent case for personal transformation in the context of nonviolent struggle. The essence of her argument was that acting nonviolently is not enough to sustain a people-powered revolution, and that a person must have nonviolent intentions and the willingness and ability to engage in an internal discipline of personal nonviolence if the struggle is to be truly won. On this point, I don't have any serious disagreement. . . .

However, in describing what she sees as a key challenge to nonviolent success in the ongoing people power struggles around the world, Van Hook writes:

> Those who profess a commitment to what is called strategic nonviolence know how to start a revolution, that is, in the same way that one would have to fight if one is the weaker party: you do what your opponent is trying to prevent you from doing, you cast all or most of the blame on them, and you draw upon the sympathies of the masses—the "reference public"—to express your power. In this approach it's acceptable to use threat, humiliation, and coercion to get what you want, and you often accept short-term and short-lived "success" as your goal. Nonviolence in this approach is simply refraining from physical violence while one's inner frustrations and pains continue to grow, or are left wholly unresolved. After lighting the match of revolution, a person using nonviolence by this definition can walk away from the responsibility to carrying it forward for the long run. So a people left their guns at home this round? Where will it get them when they decide to take them back out because a limited vision of nonviolence did not bring about the deep changes needed?

Although I believe it was unintentional, Van Hook's characterization of adherents of "strategic nonviolence" seems to be guilty of the same sort of stereotyping with which she takes issue. I know hundreds of scholars, activists and journalists who study and engage in this form of struggle, and have yet to meet one who has "professed a commitment to strategic nonviolence." Such an assertion does not make sense because nonviolent strategy is not an article of faith or a belief system. More concerning, though, is the implication that those engaging in strategic nonviolent action are not just unprincipled, but also undisciplined and lacking in a basic sense of social or civic responsibility.

One part of the problem is in the mislabeling of the phenomenon. By calling it "strategic nonviolence" instead of "strategic nonviolent action" or "nonviolent strategy," she implies that the phenomenon is fairly classified as a category of nonviolence, but this isn't accurate. Nonviolence implies commitment to a philosophy that eschews violence in all forms and that adheres to some key principles. By calling it "strategic nonviolence," which is juxtaposed conceptually against "principled nonviolence," the field of study with which Van Hook identifies, the suggestion is that the commitment to nonviolence has been made for non-principled reasons. But according to Van Hook's principled outlook, a person who engages in nonviolent action for reasons other than commitment to principle is suspect because they are not embracing or practicing "true" nonviolence. No wonder there is tension—the person practicing principled nonviolence sees the person practicing "strategic nonviolence" as a pretender.

The other problem with this terminology is that it implies that the phenomenon being discussed is actually attempting to be what is understood by adherents of principled nonviolence as nonviolence. Recall that nonviolence embodies an entire philosophy and set of principles regarding the ethics of eschewing violence. Nonviolent strategy—defined as organized, collective action in pursuit of a clear and achievable objective, carried out with nonviolent weapons—does not, on the other hand, require the practitioner to adopt a philosophy in order to utilize it. In fact, to me, this is a great appeal of nonviolent strategy: its inclusiveness. Anyone can practice it. There is no spiritual or philosophical litmus test. And since unity is a criterion for success in nonviolent struggle, inclusiveness is a very helpful means to achieving that end. And moreover, contrary to principled critics of "strategic nonviolence," I would argue, the unwillingness to adopt a philosophy of principled nonviolence from the outset does not necessarily make the subsequent action an inferior form of nonviolence. I suppose this is where Van Hook and I really part ways. She wants nonviolent action to be engaged in with full intention and consciousness of the power of nonviolence, while I believe that the use of nonviolent tools produces an appreciation for the power of the phenomenon and probably does more to convert skeptics than any other mechanism. In other words, I believe that commitment to the principle can evolve from the action, which itself is a result of the strategy.

On the other hand, by demanding a commitment to a spiritual philosophy as a prerequisite for joining the struggle, there is a danger of being perceived as (or of actually being) exclusionary. Such a requirement suggests that in order for the practice of nonviolence to be effective, the activist must hold a set of spiritual beliefs about, say, the unity of all life or the imperative to turn the other cheek. But there have been many successful nonviolent struggles waged by people who either held religious or spiritual beliefs different than those commonly found amongst practitioners of principled nonviolence, or who held spiritual beliefs very different from others in the movement, so that there was no unity over fundamental belief systems. The unity came from the commitment to nonviolent action as the most effective set of means to address the injustice. Would these movements have been formed and the struggles been waged if there had been a spiritual litmus test in place before action was taken? I doubt it.

Nonviolent action, when done well, can achieve results. When people come to see its efficacy and power through its use, they may develop more appreciation for the principles called for in Van Hook's treatise. But whether activists get to the principle prior to action or through it does not matter. One need not necessarily be fully converted to the philosophy of nonviolence before being willing to try a new means of waging struggle. Willingness to take such a risk is the essence of courage—the most important personal quality in the nonviolent activist.

My second major concern about Van Hook's article can be summed up by a look at her closing paragraph, where she states, "It is time we moved away from cruelty and alienation, and refused to give it a place in our toolkits of revolution . . . [E]very small victory in becoming kinder is fuel for the fire for the long-term struggle for freedom. It is much harder than strategic nonviolence."

Again, this is a cogent argument, and I absolutely endorse the notion that our evolution as a species depends on cultivating more empathy and compassion for others. But, in the process, Van Hook conflates emphasis on strategy with unharnessed anger. Earlier in the article, she references Occupy protesters who seem to be engaging in nothing but venting their anger publicly. I am not sure, why, however, she associates that phenomenon with "strategic nonviolence." The assumption seems to be based on a caricature of nonviolent strategy.

In reality, it is quite rare that overt anger and an emphasis on strategy are seen together in the context of a struggle. As a strategist, I would strongly discourage activists from the kinds of behavior with which Van Hook takes issue. Such behavior alienates people, the death knell for a nascent movement. Additionally, it is hard to be constructive as an activist if your energy is focused only on obstruction. By starting with the questionable assumption that strategy and anger are interchangeable, it is not at all surprising that Van Hook comes to the conclusion that emphasis on strategy is not enough to sustain a revolution.

Ironically, I would use the same quote from Martin Luther King Jr. cited by Van Hook—"We harnessed our anger and released it under discipline for maximum effect"—but would interpret it a little differently. To me, King is arguing here for the strategic effectiveness of disciplining anger, even while recognizing anger as an inevitable consequence of injustice. He is not, in my view, arguing against anger as such. Gandhi himself was not above the occasional use of sarcasm—a form of speech often considered to be verbal aggression by adherents of principled nonviolence.

Once again, Van Hook essentially creates a straw man by opposing principle and strategy against one another, and then adds insult to injury by stating that the former is "harder" than the latter. The truth is that I'm not sure it always *is* harder. Deeply ingrained behaviors, standard operating procedures and habits can be incredibly hard to break, even after a person's heart has been transformed. Every person who has felt the sting of their conscience after backsliding on a personal commitment understands this.

Even the most principled of history's nonviolent advocates did not lead flawless movements filled with activists whose hearts were always in the right place, and none were able to transform all of the individuals around them. Which is not to say personal commitment to nonviolence should not be an objective or that Van Hook is wrong to argue for changing our hearts in the end. I'm just not so sure we must always start there.

Van Hook's version of nonviolence is very personal in that it addresses transformation at the level of the individual human being, in a very existential sense. But the target for transformation in the people-power struggles around the world is, in most cases, the state or some other trans- or subnational political entity. Such entities, for whom repression is status quo, will not likely be persuaded against using violence simply because they have been exposed to and saturated with the moral righteousness of principled nonviolence by earnest and loving activists. Such an approach assumes that violence is a force unto itself. But here, I throw in my lot with Hannah Arendt, who argued that violence is merely instrumental—a means to an end. And if violence is only a means (not a belief or an ideology or a force), then those who use it can be persuaded away from it when its use as a mechanism for social or political change is neutralized. When violence no longer has the ability to command fear or respect, it is no longer an effective tool. And bringing about this state of things is the ultimate objective of nonviolent strategy. Thus, ironically, I think

Van Hook's article actually represents a case for both more principle and more strategy, and—with a corrected understanding of strategic nonviolent action—makes the point that these two things are not distinct phenomena at all. . . .

At a presentation last month to international activists and journalists during the Fletcher Summer Institute for the Advanced Study of Nonviolent Conflict, U.S. civil rights veteran and Korean War resister Reverend James Lawson told the group about how strategy and planning were the keys to success in the Nashville sit-in campaign, which he helped lead. "I'm all for redemption and transformation of people," he said. "I'm all for the enemy taking a different vision of himself and of his world. But I insist that while that is an important element, it is not the critical element of nonviolence."

The critical element of nonviolent power, argued Lawson, is that it puts "a new agenda on the table." In other words, the exercise of nonviolent power is its own best advocate. As it succeeds, it reduces the perceived efficacy of violence and offers empowering alternatives to the status quo—both at the level of society and in the lives of individuals taking part.

Should We Fight the System or Be the Change?

BY MARK ENGLER AND PAUL ENGLER

Mark Engler is a senior analyst with *Foreign Policy In Focus,* an editorial board member at *Dissent,* and a contributing editor at *Yes! Magazine.* Paul Engler is founding director of the Center for the Working Poor, in Los Angeles. Enlger and Engler are coauthors of *This Is an Uprising: How Nonviolent Revolt Is Shaping the Twenty-First Century* (2016). From *openDemocracy,* June 25, 2014. Used by permission.

It is an old question in social movements: Should we fight the system or "be the change we wish to see"? Should we push for transformation within existing institutions, or should we model in our own lives a different set of political relationships that might someday form the basis of a new society?

Over the past 50 years—and arguably going back much further—social movements in the United States have incorporated elements of each

approach, sometimes in harmonious ways and other times with significant tension between different groups of activists.

In the recent past, a clash between "strategic" and "prefigurative" politics could be seen in the Occupy movement. While some participants pushed for concrete political reforms—greater regulation of Wall Street, bans on corporate money in politics, a tax on millionaires, or elimination of debt for students and underwater homeowners—other occupiers focused on the encampments themselves. They saw the liberated spaces in Zuccotti Park and beyond—with their open general assemblies and communities of mutual support—as the movement's most important contribution to social change. These spaces, they believed, had the power [to] foreshadow, or "prefigure," a more radical and participatory democracy.

Once an obscure term, prefigurative politics is increasingly gaining currency, with many contemporary anarchists embracing as a core tenet the idea that, as a slogan from the Industrial Workers of the World put it, we must "build the new world in the shell of the old." Because of this, it is useful to understand its history and dynamics. While prefigurative politics has much to offer social movements, it also contains pitfalls. If the project of building alternative community totally eclipses attempts to communicate with the wider public and win broad support, it risks becoming a very limiting type of self-isolation.

For those who wish to both live their values and impact the world as it now exists, the question is: How can we use the desire to "be the change" in the service of strategic action?

Naming the Conflict

Coined by political theorist Carl Boggs and popularized by sociologist Wini Breines, the term "prefigurative politics" emerged out of analysis of New Left movements in the United States. Rejecting both the Leninist cadre organization of the Old Left and conventional political parties, members of the New Left attempted to create activist communities that embodied the concept of participatory democracy, an idea famously championed in the 1962 Port Huron Statement of the Students for a Democratic Society, or SDS. In a 1980 essay, Breines argues that the central imperative of prefigurative politics was to "create and sustain within the live practice of the movement, relationships and political forms that 'prefigured' and embodied the desired society." Instead of waiting for revolution in the future, the New Left sought to experience it in the present through the movements it created.

Current discussion of prefigurative politics has been rooted in the experience of U.S. movements in the 1960s. However, the tension between waging campaigns to produce instrumental gains within the existing political system, on the one hand, and creating alternative institutions and communities that more immediately put radical values into practice, on the other, has existed for centuries. Unfortunately, there is no universal agreement on the vocabulary used to describe this split. Various academic and political traditions discuss the two differing approaches using overlapping concepts including "cultural revolution," "dual power," and theories of "collective identity." Max Weber distinguished between the "ethic of ultimate ends" (which roots action in heartfelt and principled conviction) and an "ethic of responsibility" (which more pragmatically considers how action impacts the world). Most controversially, some scholars have discussed aspects of prefigurative action as forms of "lifestyle politics."

Used as an umbrella category, the term prefigurative politics is useful in highlighting a divide that has appeared in countless social movements throughout the world. In the 1800s, Marx debated utopian socialists about the need for revolutionary strategy that went beyond the formation of communes and model societies. Throughout his life, Gandhi wavered back and forth between leading campaigns of civil disobedience to exact concessions from state powers and advocating for a distinctive vision of self-reliant village life, through which he believed Indians could experience true independence and communal unity. (Gandhi's successors split on this issue, with Jawaharlal Nehru pursing the strategic control of state power and Vinoba Bhave taking up the prefigurative "constructive program.") Advocates of strategic nonviolence, who push for the calculated use of unarmed uprising, have counter-posed their efforts against long-standing lineages of "principled nonviolence"—represented by religious organizations that espouse a lifestyle of pacifism (such as the Mennonites) or groups that undertake symbolic acts of "bearing moral witness" (such as the Catholic Workers). . . .

The Power of the Beloved Community

The 1960s counter-culture—with its flower children, free love and LSD trips into new dimensions of consciousness—is easy to parody. To the extent that it interacted with political movements, it was profoundly disconnected from any practical sense of how to leverage change. In *Berkeley in the Sixties*, Jack Weinberg, a prominent anti-war organizer and New Left "politico" described a 1966 meeting where counter-cultural activists were promoting a new type of event. "They wanted to have the first be-in," Weinberg explains. "One fellow in particular, trying to get us really excited about the plan . . . said, 'We're going to have so much music—and so much love, and so much energy—that we are going to stop the war in Vietnam!'"

Yet prefigurative impulses did not merely produce the flights of utopian fantasy seen at the counter-cultural fringes. This approach to politics also made some tremendously positive contributions to social movements. The drive to live out a vibrant and participatory democracy gave the New Left much of its vitality, and it produced groups of dedicated activists willing to make great sacrifices for the cause of social justice.

As one example, within the Student Nonviolent Coordinating Committee, or SNCC, participants spoke of the desire to create the "beloved community"—a society that rejected bigotry and prejudice in all forms and instead embraced peace and brotherliness. This new world would be based on an "understanding, redeeming goodwill for all," as Martin Luther King (an allied promoter of the concept) described it.

This was not merely an external goal; rather, SNCC militants saw themselves as creating the beloved community within their organization—an interracial group which, in the words of one historian, "based itself on radical egalitarianism, mutual respect and unconditional support for every person's unique gifts and contributions. Meetings lasted until everyone had their say, in the belief that every voice counted." The strong ties fostered by this prefigurative community encouraged participants to undertake bold and dangerous acts of civil disobedience—such as SNCC's famous sit-ins at lunch counters in the segregated South. In this case, the aspiration to a beloved community both facilitated strategic action and had a significant impact on mainstream politics.

The same pattern existed within the Clamshell Alliance, Abalone Alliance, and other radical anti-nuclear movements of the 1970s, which historian Barbara Epstein chronicles in her 1991 book, *Political Protest and Cultural Revolution*. Drawing from a lineage of Quaker nonviolence, these groups established an influential organizing tradition for direct action in the United States. They pioneered many of the techniques—such as affinity groups, spokes councils, and general assemblies—that became fixtures in the global justice movement of the late 1990s and early 2000s, and which were also important to Occupy Wall Street. In their time, the antinuclear groups combined consensus decision-making, feminist consciousness, close interpersonal bonds, and a commitment to strategic nonviolence to create defining protests. Epstein writes, "What was new about the Clamshell and the Abalone was that for each organization, at its moment of greatest mass participation, the opportunity to act out a vision and build community was at least as important as the immediate objective of stopping nuclear power."

The Strategic Tension

Wini Breines defends prefigurative politics as the lifeblood of the 1960s New Left and argues that, despite its failures to produce lasting organization, this movement represented a "brave and significant experiment" with lasting implications. At the same time, she distinguishes prefigurative action from a different type of politics—strategic politics—that are "committed to building organization in order to achieve power so that structural changes in the political, economic and social orders might be achieved." Breines further notes, "The unresolved tension, between the spontaneous grassroots social movement committed to participatory democracy, and the intention (necessitating organization) of achieving power or radical structural change in the United States, was a structuring theme" of the New Left.

Tension between prefigurative and strategic politics persists today for a simple reason: Although they are not always mutually exclusive, the two approaches have very distinct emphases and present sometimes contradictory notions of how activists should behave at any a given time.

Where strategic politics favors the creation of organizations that can marshal collective resources and gain influence in conventional politics, prefigurative groups lean toward the creation of liberated public spaces, community centers and alternative institutions—such as squats, co-ops and radical bookstores. Both strategic and prefigurative strategies may involve direct action or civil disobedience. However, they approach such protest differently.

Strategic practitioners tend to be very concerned with media strategy and how their demonstrations will be perceived by the wider public; they design their actions to sway public opinion. In contrast, prefigurative activists are often indifferent, or even antagonistic, to the attitudes of the media and of mainstream society. They tend to emphasize the expressive qualities of protest—how actions express the values and beliefs of participants, rather than how they might impact a target.

Strategic politics seeks to build pragmatic coalitions as a way of more effectively pushing forward demands around a given issue. During the course of a campaign, grassroots activists might reach out to more established unions, non-profit organizations or politicians in order to make common cause. Prefigurative politics, however, is far more wary of joining forces with those coming from outside the distinctive culture a movement has created, especially if prospective allies are part of hierarchical organizations or have ties with established political parties.

Countercultural clothing and distinctive appearance—whether it involves long hair, piercings, punk stylings, thrift-store clothing, *keffiyehs* or any number of other variations—helps prefigurative communities create a sense of group cohesion. It reinforces the idea of an alternative culture that rejects conventional norms. Yet strategic politics looks at the issue of personal appearance very

differently. Saul Alinsky, in his book *Rules for Radicals*, takes the strategic position when he argues, "If the real radical finds that having long hair sets up psychological barriers to communication and organization, he cuts his hair." Some of the politicos of the New Left did just that in 1968, when Senator Eugene McCarthy entered the Democratic presidential primary as an anti-war challenger to Lyndon Johnson. Opting to "Get Clean for Gene," they shaved beards, cut hair and sometimes donned suits in order to help the campaign reach out to middle-of-the-road voters.

Taking Stock of Prefiguration

For those who wish to integrate strategic and prefigurative approaches to social change, the task is to appreciate the strengths of prefigurative communities while avoiding their weaknesses.

The impulse to "be the change we wish to see" has a strong moral appeal, and the strengths of prefigurative action are significant. Alternative communities developed "within the shell of the old" create spaces that can support radicals who chose to live outside the norms of workaday society and to make deep commitments to a cause. When they do take part in wider campaigns to change the political and economic system, these individuals can serve as a dedicated core of participants for a movement. In the case of Occupy, those most invested in prefigurative community were the people who kept the encampments running. Even if they were not those most involved in planning strategic demonstrations that brought in new allies and drew larger crowds; they played a pivotal role.

Another strength of prefigurative politics is that it is attentive to the social and emotional needs of participants. It provides processes for individuals' voices to be heard and creates networks of mutual support to sustain people in the here and now. Strategic politics often downplays these considerations, putting aside care for activists in order to focus on winning instrumental goals that will result in future improvements for society. Groups that incorporate prefigurative elements in their organizing, and thus have a greater focus on group process, have often been superior at intensive consciousness-raising, as well as at addressing issues such as sexism and racism within movements themselves.

But what works well for small groups can sometimes become a liability when a movement tries to scale up and gain mass support. Jo Freeman's landmark essay, "The Tyranny of Structurelessness," makes this point in the context of the women's liberation movement of the 1960s and 1970s. Freeman argued that a prefigurative rejection of formal leadership and rigid organizational structure served second-wave feminists well early on when the movement "defined its main goal, and its main method, as consciousness-raising." However, she contends, when the movement aspired to go beyond meetings that raised awareness of common oppression and began to undertake broader political activity, the same anti-organizational predisposition became limiting. The consequence of structurelessness, Freeman argues, was a tendency for the movement to generate "much motion and few results."

Perhaps the greatest danger inherent in prefigurative groups is a tendency toward self-isolation. Writer, organizer and Occupy activist Jonathan Matthew Smucker describes what he calls the "political identity paradox," a contradiction that afflicts groups based on a strong sense of alternative community. "Any serious social movement needs a correspondingly serious group identity that encourages a core of members to contribute an exceptional level of commitment, sacrifice and heroics over the course of prolonged struggle," Smucker writes. "Strong group identity, however, is a double-edged sword. The stronger the identity and cohesion of the group, the more likely people are to become alienated from other groups, and from society. This is the political identity paradox."

Those focused on prefiguring a new society in their movements—and preoccupied with meeting the needs of an alternative community—can become cut off from the goal of building bridges to other constituencies and winning public support. Instead of looking for ways to effectively communicate their vision to the outside world, they are prone to adopt slogans and tactics that appeal to hardcore activists but alienate the majority. Moreover, they grow ever more averse to entering into popular coalitions. (The extreme fear of "co-optation" among some Occupiers was indicative of this tendency.) All these things become self-defeating. As Smucker writes, "Isolated groups are hard-pressed to achieve political goals."

Smucker cites the notorious 1969 implosion of SDS as an extreme example of the political identity paradox left unchecked. In that instance, "Key leaders had become encapsulated in their oppositional identity and grown more and more out of touch." Those most intensely invested in SDS at the national level lost interest in building chapters of students that were just beginning to be radicalized—and they became entirely disenchanted with the mainstream American public. Given what was happening in Vietnam, they grew convinced that they needed to "bring the war home," in the words of one 1969 slogan. As a result, Smucker writes, "Some of the most committed would-be leaders of that generation came to see more value in holing up with a few comrades to make bombs than in organizing masses of students to take coordinated action."

The self-destructive isolation of the Weathermen is a far cry from SNCC's beloved community. Yet the fact that both are examples of prefigurative politics shows that the approach is not something that can simply be embraced or rejected wholesale by social movements. Rather, all movements operate on a spectrum in which different public activities and internal processes have both strategic and prefigurative dimensions. The challenge for those who wish to produce social change is to balance the competing impulses of the two approaches in creative and effective ways—so that we might experience the power of a community that is committed to living in radical solidarity, as well as the joy of transforming the world around us.

Transformative Peace Pedagogy: Fostering an Inclusive, Holistic Approach to Peace Studies

BY TONY JENKINS

Tony Jenkins is the Co-Director of the Peace Education Center at Teachers College, Columbia University. He also serves as Global Coordinator of the International Institute on Peace Education (IIPE) and Program Coordinator of the Global Campaign for Peace Education (GCPE). From 2010 to 2014, Tony served as the Vice President for Academic Affairs at the National Peace Academy. Adapted from *Factis Pax*, 10, no. 1 (2016): 1-7. Used by permission.

One of the key conclusions of a 2014 conference on "Reconstructing Peace Studies,"[1] was that *how we teach* is as important as *what we teach*. Faculty participating in the conference agreed they had minimal knowledge or preparation in the methods and pedagogies of peace education seen as essential to pursuing the transformative outcomes of peace studies programs. Transformative peace pedagogy, as a preferred approach and philosophy of teaching and learning in peace studies, fosters the development of a self-reflective praxis and nurtures a holistic, inclusive relationship between the inner (personal) and outer (political, action oriented) dimensions of peacebuilding. This praxis is the basis for both internal consideration and social and political action.

The social purposes of peace studies are oriented toward the transformation of a culture of violence. Johan Galtung (1969) observed, "Violence is present when human beings are being influenced so that their actual somatic and mental realizations are below their potential realizations." Accordingly, a culture of violence may be understood as a dynamic system of reciprocally reinforcing physical, psychological and structural influences working together to impede human potential (as well as the potential of other living things). One aspect of peace studies is to develop awareness of these influences, understand their causes and conditions, and identify interrelationships. However, peace studies is equally, if not more so concerned with developing knowledge, skills and capacities essential for resisting and transforming these influences and establishing new, preferred conditions as the foundations for a culture of peace.

The transformative work of peacebuilding is rooted in two fundamental dimensions: the psychological (inner) and the structural (outer). The Constitution of UNESCO famously captures what is implied in the psychological task where it states, "since wars begin in the minds of men, it is in the minds of men that the defenses of peace must be constructed." The structural dimensions, interdependent with the psychological, are more outward looking, involving transformation of social and cultural constructions imbedded in political, institutional and ecological relationships.

The relationship(s) between these inner and outer dimensions is a subject of much rhetorical debate. Most peace scholars and practitioners support the position that the inner work is foundational to—or at the very least enhances—the ability to effectively engage in the outer work. However, under conditions of extreme violence and oppression there is little luxury afforded to focus on personal and spiritual development. In such contexts resistance and engagement in forms of strategic nonviolent action are the entry points to transformation. In addition to disrupting injustice, structural transformation also requires envisioning and modeling of preferred alternatives. This is the constructive work pursued by Gandhi, and in some instances the more socially isolated prefigurative politics described by Engler & Engler (2014).

From a transformative pedagogical perspective, the inner, strategic and constructive are equally valid entry points into the transformative work. The point at which an agent enters is largely contingent upon context, experience and worldview. The path taken is one that helps give meaning to the violence or conflict that is or has been experienced. While there may be contextually relevant points of entry, a transformative pedagogical approach to the teaching of peace studies would emphasize developing capacities of holistic, inclusive, critical and reflective thinking. Such capacities are the basis for both personal growth and socially transformative action.

In the context of transformative learning, transformation indicates a reorientation of worldview that leads to a new rendering of the world and one's place within it. There are many worldview obstacles that peace studies seeks to redress (militarism, gender, development and economics, racism . . .), and these violent worldviews are reproduced and codified into social institutions and human arrangements. The pedagogical approach of peace studies, however, should not be to simply replace these violent ideologies with more peaceful ones. Such an approach is indoctrination. The learner in such an arrangement is treated as an object onto or into which knowledge and ideas are imparted; not permitting the learner to critically and ethically grapple with concepts under consideration. Transformative peace pedagogy is the antithesis of indoctrination. It is an ethical, elicitive and learner-centered approach to worldview transformation that honors the dignity and subjectivity of the learner. Fostering ethical, inter and intra-subjective relationships with concepts, knowledge, knowledge creation, and other persons is the hallmark of transformative learning. This is consistent with Betty Reardon's articulation of pedagogy as the "determinant of human relationships in the educational process. It is itself the medium of communication between teacher and learner, and that aspect of the educational process which most affects what learners receive from their teachers" (Reardon, 1993). From this perspective, transformative pedagogy requires establishing ethical relationships in and through all dimensions of teaching and learning.

Peace is a moral and ethical pursuit. Inquiry into the definition of peace, the conditions of peace, and the processes through which those conditions are pursued is a process of moral interpretation. Values and ethics form the core inquiry for assessment of ethical action. Developing the skills and capacities to interpret and negotiate values and morality in social and political contexts forms the foundation of many peacemaking and peacebuilding skills.

Knowledge construction itself is a moral and ethically reflective, transformative and formative process. Transformative learning theory is thus concerned with the modes and processes of facilitating worldview transformation and shifts of perception. The processes through which such learning is pursued are dialectical, requiring internal and external dialogue between existing knowledge and perceptions and fresh considerations towards the development of potential new phenomenological dispositions. Construed dialogically, it is an ethical, learner-centered, non-indoctrinating process. Theorist Jack Mezirow (1991) describes transformative pedagogy as having a constructivist phenomenological orientation based on the assumption that "meaning exists within ourselves rather than in external forms such as books and that the personal meanings that we attribute to our experience are acquired and validated through human interaction and communication" (Mezirow, 1991, p. xiv).

Implied in this social constructionist theory of knowledge creation is the necessity for dialogical encounters with diverse perspectives toward the possibility of identifying and agreeing upon a shared moral or ethical position. Betty Reardon suggests "were it [the reflective learning] to be left at the inward without the communal sharing, it might become meditative rather than ruminative, remaining personal, not becoming a social learning process, preparatory to the public political discourse for change" (Reardon & Snauwaert, 2015, p. 8). This rationale can be extended to another premise, that the pursuit of peace knowledge should be transdisciplinary in nature. Peace researcher Kenneth Boulding (1956) proposed the need for a unified or transdisciplinary approach to knowledge and theory construction that he named eiconics. His rationale was premised on his observation of an interconnected global web of violence that he believed could only be transformed through knowledge sharing across the disciplines. He proposed the approach as an ethical imperative in pursuit of knowledge creation for the common good. Betty Reardon (2000) identifies "peace knowledge" as an umbrella term, encompassing the more discrete realms of peace research, peace studies, peace education and peace action. Each of these realms characterizes a particular study or approach to the pursuit of peace of various academic disciplines, yet they all share the common purpose of knowledge development for a culture of peace. Academically, these realms are studied in a reductionist fashion, orienting such studies as false dichotomies. The academic obstacles to transdisciplinary knowledge generation need to be addressed by peace studies as a unique form of structural violence (Jenkins, 2008; Galtung, 1969).

It follows from the preceding premises, therefore, that the methods of research, analysis and interpretation called for in pursuing the socially transformative purposes of peace knowledge should be multiple in scope and not limited to one theory of knowledge or science. Johan Galtung argued that peace studies should "be concerned with both nomothetic, universalizing and ideographic, singularizing methodologies" (Galtung, 2002, p. 16). The rationale for this holistic methodology is rooted in the applied nature of peace studies and the place peace studies finds itself situated within the cosmology of time. Galtung observes that "Peace studies can be conveniently and usefully divided into: past-oriented, *empirical*, what worked and what did not; present-oriented, *critical*, evaluating present policies; future-oriented, *constructive*, elaborating future policies" (p. 16). Each of these approaches has a unique scientific basis and accompanying limitations. Empiricism is useful in learning from fact and past observations, but it is not useful in guiding the unobserved future. The critical approach is moral/ethical, scientifically interpreting present conditions through a values lens. The constructive is the most future oriented, relating "theories to values to construct a transcendence from reality into potential reality ..." (p. 17). Elise Boulding (1988) emphasized this constructive, futures orientation in her research. She was resolute in her call for nurturing social imagination, which she described as "the capacity to visualize the present in fresh ways and to visualize the not-yet in positive ways, in order to release society from the paralysis induced by technological dependency and the fear of nuclear war" (1988, p. 116). Without imaginative/interpretive processes new possibilities, theories and testable hypotheses would never be pursued.

The arguments and premises presented here attempt to provide a philosophical and pedagogical framework and rationale for a more inclusive and transformative approach to teaching and learning in peace studies. Ultimately, personal and social transformation—a range of which is sought through peace studies—is a radical endeavor. Transformation requires a complete reorientation of self and society; as such transformation is not achieved by simply exchanging old parts with new. Transformation, as outlined here, is pursued through critical, reflective inquiry and requires an inclusive-holistic understanding of the relationship of knowledge, learning and action. This orientation may seem to extend a superhuman standard to the expected learning outcomes of a student of peace studies: to be rooted in a Meta consciousness while simultaneously engaged in the micro details of peacebuilding work. To be in all places at once means one is never fully present in the moment. A more human goal is the development of a reflective, critical and transformative praxis. Such a praxis establishes a bridge between the false divides of the inner and the outer, the principled and the strategic, and helps the peacebuilder to see, imagine and construct the whole.

NOTE

1. Co-hosted by the Baker Institute for Peace and Conflict Studies at Juniata College and the Peace and Justice Studies Association.

REFERENCES

Boulding, E. (1988). *Building a global civic culture: Education for an interdependent world*. New York, NY: Syracuse University Press.

Boulding, K. (1956). *The image: Knowledge in life and society*. Ann Arbor, MI: University of Michigan Press.

Engler & Engler (2014). Should we fight the system or be the change? *Waging Nonviolence*. Retrieved from: http://wagingnonviolence.org/feature/fight-system-change

Galtung, J. (1969). Violence, Peace, and Peace Research. *Journal of Peace Research, 6* (3):167–191.

Galtung, J. (2002). The epistemology and methodology of peace studies. *Tromsø Papers No. 1.* Tromsø, Norway: University of Tromsø and Transcend.

Jenkins, T. (2008). A Peace education response to modernism: Reclaiming the social and pedagogical purposes of academia. In Lin, J., Brantmeier, E., & Bruhn, C. (Eds.). *Transforming education for peace.* Charlotte, NC: Information Age Publishing.

Mezirow, J. (1991). *Transformative dimensions of adult learning.* San Francisco, CA: Jossey-Bass.

Reardon, B. (1993). Pedagogy as Purpose: Peace Education in the Context of Violence. In Cremin, P. (Ed.), *Education for Peace* (pp. 101-113). Ireland: Educational Studies Association of Ireland and Irish Peace Institute.

Reardon, B. (2000). Peace education: A review and projection. In Moon, B., Brown, S.& Peretz, M.B. (Eds.), *Routledge international companion to education* (pp. 397-423). New York, NY: Routledge.

Reardon, B. and Snauwaert, D.T. (2015). *Betty A. Reardon: A Pioneer in Education for Peace and Human Rights.* New York, NY: Springer.

DISCUSSION QUESTIONS

1. Summarize and evaluate the evidence that Christina Michaelson offers to support the claim that people should first cultivate inner peace before promoting peace for others.

2. Explain why people with high levels of inner peace are, or are not, the most effective workers for peace.

3. Assess the correctness of Cynthia Boas's claim that effective nonviolent action does not require a commitment to nonviolence as a way of life.

4. Evaluate the major strengths and weaknesses of prefigurative politics and offer a judgement on their general worth.

5. Explain what Tony Jenkins means when he claims that a transformative peace pedagogy bridges the "false divide" between the inner and outer.

6. Support, or critique, Jenkins's argument that building a culture of peace requires a radical new understanding of how people conceive of the relationship between the self and society.

Figures and tables are indicated by "f" and "t" following the page numbers.